THE MEN WILL TALK TO ME

Síobhra Aiken is an Irish Research Council Postgraduate Scholar at the Centre for Irish Studies, NUI Galway, focusing on literary narratives of the Irish Civil War. She was formerly a Fulbright Scholar and is the great-granddaughter of Frank Aiken. **Fearghal Mac Bhloscaidh** is the author of *Fenians and Ribbonmen* (2011) and *The Irish Revolution: Tyrone 1912–23* (2014). He teaches in Coláiste Feirste and at St Mary's University College, Belfast. **Liam Ó Duibhir** is the author of *The Donegal Awakening: Donegal and the War of Independence* (2010). **Diarmuid Ó Tuama** is a former Principal of the first Gaelscoil in the north, Bunscoil Phobal Feirste, and author of *Cogadh na gCarad (Ó Chonradh go Saorstát)* (2013).

THE MEN WILL TALK TO ME

ERNIE O'MALLEY'S INTERVIEWS WITH THE NORTHERN DIVISIONS

Síobhra Aiken, Fearghal Mac Bhloscaidh, Liam Ó Duibhir, Diarmuid Ó Tuama

MERRION PRESS

First published in 2018 by
Merrion Press
An imprint of Irish Academic Press
10 George's Street
Newbridge
Co. Kildare
Ireland
www.merrionpress.ie

9781785371646 (Paper)
9781785371653 (Kindle)
9781785371660 (Epub)
9781785371677 (PDF)

British Library Cataloguing in Publication Data
An entry can be found on request

Library of Congress Cataloging in Publication Data
An entry can be found on request

Interior design by www.jminfotechindia.com
Typeset in Minion Pro 11/14 pt

Cover design by www.phoenix-graphicdesign.com

Cover front: Sinn Féin prisoners from County Fermanagh being escorted to Belfast Prison under armed guard in May 1922. (*Belfast Telegraph*)

Cover back: Ernie O'Malley, New York, 1933. (Helen Hooker)

CONTENTS

Map vii

Acknowledgements viii

Abbreviations ix

Editors' Note xi

Preface by Cormac K. H. O'Malley xiii

Chronology of the War of Independence and Civil War in the North xvii

Introduction by Fearghal Mac Bhloscaidh 1

1st Northern Division (Donegal and Derry City) 21

- Peadar O'Donnell 21
- Joe Sweeney 28

2nd Northern Division (Tyrone and Derry) 46

- Dr Patrick McCartan 46
- Charlie Daly 53

3rd Northern Division (North Down and Antrim) 85

- Seamus Woods 85
- Roger McCorley 96
- Tom McNally 105
- Jack 'Seán' Leonard 112

4th Northern Division (Louth, Armagh, Monaghan and South Down) 127

- Michael O'Hanlon 127

Michael Donnelly 147
John McCoy 154
Michael Murney 181
Patrick McLogan 188
Frank Aiken 196

Short Biographical Sketches of Individuals Referenced in Endnotes 236

The Ernie O'Malley Interviews: Methodology, Chronology, Interviewees by Eve Morrison 244

Image Credits 249

Index 250

ACKNOWLEDGEMENTS

This collection could not have been conceived, written, nor completed without the help, support, and joint efforts of many. We owe a heartfelt thanks to Cormac O'Malley, who vigorously encouraged us to pursue this initiative. We also are grateful to the staff at the UCD Archives, Ó Fiaich Library, the National Library of Ireland, the National Archives of Ireland, and the *Belfast Telegraph* for their research assistance and kind permission to reproduce images.

We would like to thank the many individuals who assisted in transcribing these interviews, particularly Frank Aiken Jnr (Prionsias Mac Aogáin) who first attempted to transcribe O'Malley's interviews, and to his son, Frank, who assisted in the typing. We also would like to thank Dr Eoin Magennis for his early involvement in the project and invaluable insights. Many thanks also to Patrick J. Mahoney for his continued encouragement.

We greatly appreciate the help and support from family members of the interviewees. Thanks to Dr Rory O'Hanlon for his insights and to Kevin Murphy for kindly sharing his knowledge of Michael Donnelly. Many thanks also to Dónal Casey, Len Costello, the McCoy family, the Leonard family, and the Donnelly family.

We are also indebted to Eve Morrison, Jimmy McDermott, Dónal McAnallen, Kieran Glennon, and Trish Lamhe for their insights and encouragement. Last but not least, we are incredibly grateful to the staff of Merrion Press, in particular to Conor Graham and Fiona Dunne, whose professionalism and guidance are most appreciated.

Síobhra Aiken
Ardee, Co. Louth
April 2018

THE NORTHERN DIVISIONS

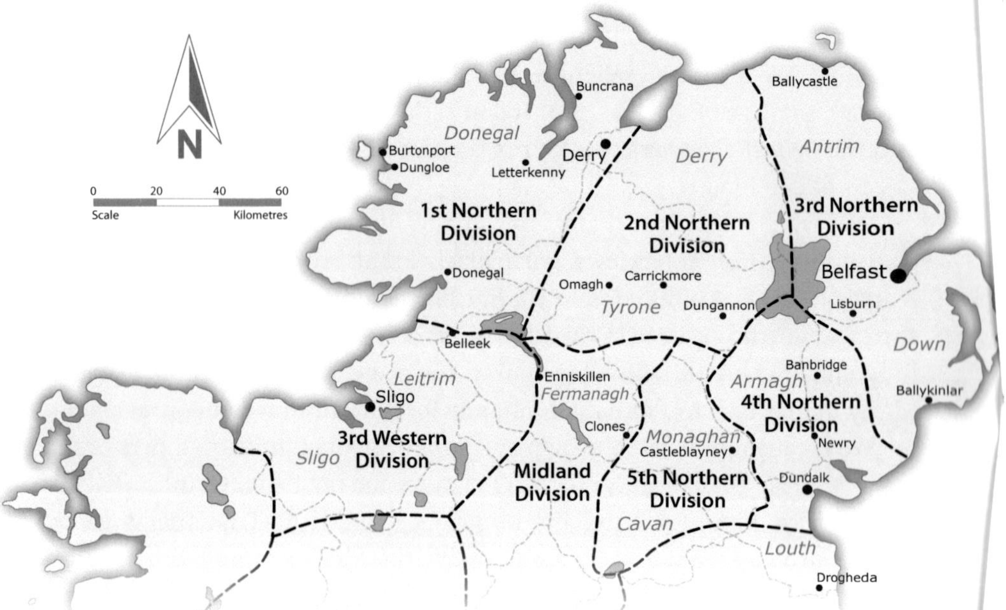

ABBREVIATIONS

AOH	Ancient Order of Hibernians
APL	Anti-Partition League of Ireland
ASU	Active Service Unit
Auxies	Auxiliary Division of RIC
BMH	Bureau of Military History
CAB	Cabinet Records, TNA
CBS	Crime Branch Special
CI	County Inspector, RIC
CO	Colonial Office, TNA
CÓFLA	Cardinal Ó Fiaich Archive, Armagh
DI	District Inspector
DIB	Dictionary of Irish Biography
EOM	Ernie O'Malley
GAA	Gaelic Athletic Association
GHQ	General Headquarters
GOIA	Government of Ireland Act
GOC	General Officer Commanding
GPO	General Post Office
HA	Home Affairs, PRONI
HC	Head Constable
ICA	Irish Citizen Army
IMA	Irish Military Archive
IPP	Irish Parliamentary Party
IRA	Irish Republican Army
IRB	Irish Republican Brotherhood
ITGWU	Irish Transport and General Workers' Union
IVF	Irish Volunteer Force

JMcG	Joseph McGarrity papers
KC	King's Counsel
MHA	Ministry of Home Affairs
MP	Member of Parliament
NAI	National Archives of Ireland
ND	Northern Division
NLI	National Library of Ireland
O/C	Officer Commanding
PR	Proportional Representation
PRONI	Public Records Office, Belfast
RIC	Royal Irish Constabulary
TD	Teachta Dála
TNA	National Archives, London
Treaty	Anglo-Irish Treaty
Truce	12 July 1921 ceasefire
UCDA	University College Dublin, Archives
UIL	United Ireland League
USC	Ulster Special Constabulary
UVF	Ulster Volunteer Force
V/C	Vice Commandant
WD	Western Division
WS	Witness Statement to BMH

EDITORS' NOTE

Where at all possible the commentary and terminology in this collection reflects that employed in the interviews. The six counties or 'the North' is employed instead of Northern Ireland and 'the Tan War' as opposed to the War of Independence or Anglo-Irish War. The perceptive reader may well notice that the British deployed very few Black and Tans or Auxiliaries in Ulster, but much of the area similarly did not gain independence.

As a result, the terminology employed by those who challenged British imperialism in Ireland has been adhered to throughout. Similarly, the equation between religious affiliation and ideology has been avoided. Catholic and Protestant are employed in statistical and specifically religious terms, but the commentary utilises the terms nationalist and unionist wherever possible, with capitalisation denoting specific affiliation to the (Ulster) Unionist Party or Irish Nationalist or Irish Party.

Those very familiar with the O'Malley notebooks will also note that several northern interviews have not been included, most notably some of the expansive and richly detailed material from John McCoy and an interview with Thomas McShea from Bundoran, who was sentenced to death (commuted) for his involvement in an attempted escape from Derry Gaol in December 1921 in which two RIC guards died from chloroform asphyxiation. In both cases, the details of the interviews are largely replicated in the men's Bureau of Military History Witness statements, the former a near *ver batim* copy, the latter a far more extensive account, running to thirty pages, which provides greater detail than the O'Malley interview. In addition, a short early interview with Frank Aiken (P17b/91 pp. 55–6), or moreover, notes taken by O'Malley concerning Aiken's role in the negotiation of the Collins–de Valera pact, has been omitted due to its fragmented nature.

The editors have also decided to omit two short ancillary interviews with Joseph and John Sheeran of Ballyshannon which O'Malley carried out shortly after the McShea interview. The rationale for this decision reflects the earlier point regarding McShea's testimony. Both brothers briefly told O'Malley how they operated as drivers, one of a hijacked Red Cross ambulance, in the IRA ambush on Belleek Barracks in September 1920. The substantive details are contained in McShea's witness statement as is an acknowledgement of Sheeran's poor treatment by British soldiers and subsequent imprisonment.

PREFACE
INTRODUCING THE ERNIE O'MALLEY NORTHERN DIVISION MILITARY INTERVIEWS

CORMAC K. H. O'MALLEY

Though born in Castlebar, Co. Mayo, in 1897, Ernie O'Malley moved to Dublin with his family in 1906 and attended the Christian Brothers secondary school and University College Dublin medical school there. After the 1916 Rising, he joined the Irish Volunteers in North Dublin while pursuing his medical studies, but in March 1918 he left home and went 'on the run'. He rose through the ranks of the Volunteers and later the Irish Republican Army, and by the time of the Truce in July 1921, as the end of the War of Independence, or Tan War, was known, he was a commandant-general commanding the Second Southern Division covering parts of three counties and with over 13,000 men under him.

O'Malley was suspicious of a compromise being made during the peace negotiations resulting in the Anglo-Irish Treaty of December 1921 and reacted strongly against the Treaty when it was announced. As a split developed in the senior ranks of the IRA in early 1922, in March he was appointed director of the organisation for the anti-Treaty Republicans who then took over the Four Courts in April. When the Four Courts garrison surrendered in June, he managed to escape. He was then appointed acting assistant chief of staff and officer commanding the Northern and Eastern Commands, or half of Ireland. In early November, he was captured in a dramatic shoot-out and was severely wounded. Ironically, his wounds saved his life as otherwise he would have been court-martialled and executed. While in Mountjoy Gaol in 1923, O'Malley was elected as a TD and in October, despite his continuing poor health, he went on a forty-one-day hunger strike. Notwithstanding, he survived – a matter of mind over body!

Having been released from prison in July 1924, and still in poor health, O'Malley went abroad to the south of Europe to aid his recovery. He later returned to his medical studies in 1926, but in 1928 headed for the USA. While there he began to write his much-acclaimed autobiographical memoir, *On Another Man's Wound*, published in 1936 after he returned to Dublin. He had spent seven years writing this book, which he meant to be more of a general story of the Irish struggle than of his own activities. It was deemed to be a literary success and added to his reputation among many of his former comrades.

O'Malley's memoir on the Civil War was not ready for publication in 1936 as it required more work. Over the next twenty years, he sought to become more familiar with the Civil War period to amend his earlier draft.

In the course of his interviews, O'Malley collected a vast amount of local lore around Ireland. He wrote a series of articles for the *Kerryman*, but withdrew them. Instead, he used the articles for a series of lectures on Radio Éireann in 1953. Subsequently, the lectures were published in an expanded series called 'IRA Raids' in the *Sunday Press* in 1955–6. In the meantime, he used the interviews to add to his own Civil War memoir, *The Singing Flame*, published posthumously in 1978, and to write a biographical memoir of a local Longford Republican organiser, Sean Connolly, entitled *Rising Out: Sean Connolly of Longford, 1890–1921*, also published posthumously, in 2007.

Given his overall knowledge of the period, based on his own Tan War and Civil War activities, he usually commanded a high regard from his informants. He felt that his former comrades would talk to him and tell him the truth.

In his rewrite of an interview he often labelled sections such as Tan War, Truce, Civil War, RIC, IRB, round-ups, gaols, treatment of prisoners, tunnels, escapes, hunger-strikes, boycotts, priests, spies, training, Sinn Féin courts, swap of arms, and the like. The tone is conversational, allowing the narrative to unfold. He wrote down the names of people and places phonetically rather than accurately and so the interviews are replete with misspellings. The interviews are fresh and frank, and many of their stories may have never been told, even to their children, as these men did not speak openly about those times. Family members have said they could hear the voices of their relatives speaking through the O'Malley interviews because O'Malley had been able to capture their intonations and phrasing.

This present volume reveals fourteen O'Malley interviews that cover activities in far-flung corners of the Northern counties during the War of Independence and the Civil War. Ten of these men rejected the Treaty, however this collection also includes four interviews from pro-Treaty veterans. Only four of these men made statements to the Bureau of Military History.

In transcribing O'Malley's series of interviews, some modest changes have been made to help the reader better understand the interview. To enable reference to O'Malley's pagination, his pages are given in bold brackets, such as **[48R]**, the R or L representing the right or left side of his original page. Unclear words have been put in italics indicating a best attempt to decipher them. The sequence of some interviews has been changed better to reflect the historical chronology, but the original pagination has been retained and referenced. Some interviews had two men speaking at the same time, and their names have been identified. Abbreviations have been standardised and many of them have been expanded to refer to the full word, such as Battalion or Brigade for Bn and Bde. Extensive endnotes provide a better understanding of the people, places, and incidents involved, and some are repeated in a subsequent chapter to allow each chapter to have its own integrity. The text has been revised to include the correct spelling of names and places, but the original spellings have been included in the endnotes at their first appearance in each interview. O'Malley's own comments or questions are given in parentheses, a method he used during his rewriting process. Editorial comments or supplements have been added in square brackets. Some new headings and subheadings with dates have also been added.

Each interview has been reproduced here almost completely. O'Malley left many blank spaces where he was missing information, and these are represented by ellipses in the text, so sometimes these sentences do not make complete sense. The style of local phrasing used in the interviews has been retained, some of which is no longer in common usage and may sound strange to the modern reader. In many instances O'Malley included names and facts in a seemingly random manner, and their relevance to the discussion can be difficult to ascertain. However, to maintain the veracity of O'Malley's original text, these additions have been left unedited.

The editors of this volume have relied on the integrity of O'Malley's general knowledge of the facts of this period and his ability to question and ascertain the 'truth', but clearly the details related here to O'Malley reflect only the perceptions of the individual informants rather than the absolute historical truth, and the reader must appreciate this important aspect.

O'Malley interviewed some of these men several times, and thus the same incident may be told more than once by the same person. The duplications have been included, as they illustrate clearly how the memory of one person about the same incident may differ at different times – especially if another person is present. O'Malley made many comments in these interviews, and some of them were quite critical. O'Malley's on-the-ground knowledge of the North was limited in the sense that he had only visited Donegal, Monaghan, and Tyrone during the War of Independence and made only one visit to the North during the Civil War.

For those not familiar with military organisational structures such as the IRA during this period, the largest military unit was a division (five in the North), which consisted of several brigades, each of which had several battalions, which in turn were composed of several companies at the local level. There were usually staff functions at the division, brigade, and battalion levels, and usually only officers at the company level.

CHRONOLOGY OF THE WAR OF INDEPENDENCE AND CIVIL WAR IN THE NORTH

1916

23 April	Tyrone – on Easter Sunday, Denis McCullough and Patrick McCartan demobilise Irish Volunteers from Belfast and Tyrone at Coalisland.

1917

25 October	Dublin, the Sinn Féin Ard Fheis – Éamon de Valera is elected president of Sinn Féin and the Irish Volunteers.

1918

2 February	South Armagh by-election – Patrick Donnelly wins for the IPP with 2,324 votes against 1,305 for the Sinn Féin candidate and IRB leader in neighbouring Tyrone, Dr Patrick McCartan.
3 April	East Tyrone by-election – T. J. Harbison wins for the IPP with 1,802 votes (against 1,222 for Sinn Féin's Seán Milroy).
14 December	General Election – Sinn Féin wins a mandate for the republic with seventy-three out of 105 Irish seats. In Ulster, Sinn Féin wins ten seats while the IPP wins six as a result of the Logue Pact. Ulster Unionists win twenty-three seats.

1919

21 January	Dublin – the inaugural session of Dáil Éireann takes place in the Mansion House.
12 December	Donegal – a lightly armed party under Joe Sweeny ambushes four RIC at Dungloe, wounding one.

1920

January	Municipal elections – nationalists control Derry City and labour win twelve seats in Belfast.
April	The IRA launches attacks on tax offices and unoccupied police barracks across Ulster.

12–13 May	Armagh – IRA attacks Newtownhamilton Barracks.
June	Nationalists win control of Tyrone and Fermanagh County Councils, as well as Rural District Councils in South Armagh and South Down.
2 June	Down – IRA ASU from Belfast attacks Crossgar Barracks; RIC Constables Fitzpatrick and Carey are wounded.
6 June	Armagh, Cullyhanna sports event – RIC sergeant Tim Holland and civilian Peter McCreesh are killed.
7 June	Tyrone – East Tyrone Brigade attacks Cookstown Barracks. Volunteer Patrick Loughran is killed.
13–25 June	Derry City – concerted violence rages in the city.
17 July	Cork – the IRA shoots Colonel G. F. Smyth.
21 July	Belfast – the shipyard expulsions begin on the day of Smyth's funeral.
6 August	Dublin – Belfastman Seán MacEntee TD, petitions the Dáil to start the Belfast Boycott.
22 August	Antrim – an IRA ASU of Cork and Belfast Volunteers shoots DI Oswald Swanzy in Lisburn. The Catholic population is expelled from the town.
26 August	Tyrone – Donegal IRA raids Drumquin Barracks. RIC Munnelly is killed.
26 September	Belfast – CI Harrison's police murder gang kills IRA volunteer Seán Gaynor and two civilians, Andrew Trodden and John McFadden.
2 October	Donegal – Frank Aiken and Ernie O'Malley lead a rather disappointing raid at Moville.
23 November	Tyrone – Charlie Daly leads an ambush of the RIC near Ballygawley; three RIC are wounded.
12 December	Newry/South Armagh – three IRA volunteers from Newry: William Canning, Peter Shields, and John Francis O'Hare are killed at the Egyptian Arch Ambush, which formed part of the unsuccessful attack on Camlough RIC Barracks.

1921

11 Januaary	Donegal, the Meenbanad Ambush – a column under Sweeney and O'Donnell attacks a trainload of 150 British soldiers between Derry and Burtonport.

26 January	Belfast – ASU kills two members of the Auxiliaries at Roddy's Hotel.
11 March	Belfast – ASU kills three Tans on Victoria Street.
1 April	Derry City – Peadar O'Donnell's column kills two RIC men, Michael Kenny and John Higgins.
6 April	Tyrone – after an attack on the USC at Dromore, three IRA volunteers are killed in reprisal.
17 April	Louth, South Armagh – IRA attacks troops protecting a local unionist at Plaster, Co. Louth.
20 April	Donegal – IRA ASU carries out the first failed attack on Glenties RIC Barracks.
23 April	Belfast – ASU kills two Auxiliaries in Donegall Place. During curfew the following night, the RIC murder gang kills Patrick Duffin and Daniel Duffin.
7 May	Belfast – ASU attacks and wounds DI Ferris in Cavendish Street.
8 May	Cavan – Volunteer Seán Mc McCartney is killed when Auxiliaries and the British Army attack a newly established flying column of Belfast IRA at Lappinduff, near Cootehill.
16–17 May	Tyrone – East Tyrone Brigade ambushes RIC at Altmore; DI Sloyne killed, then DI Walshe wounded in Dungannon.
18 May	Rock, Tyrone – USC carries out the reprisal killing of James Hayden.
21 May	Donegal – Flying column carries out a second failed attack on Glenties Barracks.
24 May	Ulster Unionists gain expected victory in elections to northern parliament.
12 June	Belfast – the police murder gangs strike, killing five nationalist civilians.
22 June	Belfast – the King opens the northern parliament.
24 June	Armagh – Aiken's column derails British military train near Adavoyle station, killing four soldiers and wounding twenty others.
7 July	Belfast – ASU kills James Glover, a member of Harrison's police murder gang.
9 July	Armagh – the Igoe police murder gang kills four nationalists outside Newry.

9 July	Belfast – the Battle of Raglan Street.
10 July	Belfast – Bloody Sunday: Orange mobs and USC burn 161 Catholic homes, killing fifteen people.
11 July	Truce.
14 July	Belfast – an Orange mob led by William Grant (a future Stormont minister) kills two and wounds twenty-eight in the nationalist enclave Ballymacarrett in East Belfast. The mob cheers when it wounds two Catholic RIC.
16 August	The 2nd Dáil is convened.
9 November	Belfast – Chief constable Wickham issues a notorious circular detailing the remobilisation of the USC made up of the 'best elements' of the pogromists.
22 November	Control of security is transferred from London to Belfast, where fifteen are killed and eighty-three dangerously wounded.
6 December	The Treaty is signed, the commandants of Ulster's IRA division meet at a céilí in Clones, where Eoin O'Duffy assures them the Treaty is a trick, leading to the formation of the IRA Ulster Council in early January.

1922

7 January	Dublin – Dáil Éireann approves the Treaty.
14 January	Tyrone – the Monaghan footballers, including Dan Hogan, are arrested in Dromore on the day the Free State government is established.
18 January	Dublin – the Free State Minister of Defence, Dick Mulcahy, agrees to a convention after a meeting with commandants from the anti-Treaty majority within the IRA.
21 January	London – Michael Collins signs his first pact with James Craig.
8 February	Tyrone/Fermanagh – the IRA kidnaps over forty unionists.
11 February	Monaghan – during the Clones Affray, pro-Treaty IRA attacks USC on a train at Clones station, killing four and losing their commandant, Matt Fitzpatrick.
13 February	Belfast – loyalists in collusion with USC throw a bomb at children playing in Weaver Street, killing six. This marks the beginning of a three-day orgy of violence wherein twenty-four people die.

16 February	Belfast – the British newspaper the *Star* describes events as a 'Protestant pogrom against the Catholic minority'.
2 March	Dublin – Charlie Daly is relieved of his command of the 2nd ND by Eoin O'Duffy at an acrimonious meeting at Free State GHQ in Beggars Bush.
18 March	Belfast – USC raid St Mary's Hall, seizing a lot of important intelligence.
19 March	Tyrone/Derry – the 2nd ND raid Pomeroy and Maghera barracks, four USC are killed in separate attacks.
24 March	Belfast – the McMahon murders: six Catholic civilians from a constitutional nationalist family are killed in their home by an RUC murder gang.
26 March	Dublin – the Army Convention establishes the anti-Treaty Executive.
29 March	Armagh – ASU launches the Cullaville ambush, killing HC James Harper and RIC Sergeant Patrick Earley.
30 March	London – the Second Craig–Collins Pact is agreed, under the direction of Winston Churchill.
31 March	Newry – ASU launches Hyde Market ambush, killing USC Allen.
1 April	The police murder gang kills three civilians in Arnon Street.
7 April	Belfast – the northern government introduces the Civil Authorities (Special Powers) Bill.
14 April	Dublin – the republicans establish their HQ in the Four Courts.
2–3 May	Tyrone/Derry – as part of the IRA joint offensive, the 2nd ND attacks barracks in Coalisland, Draperstown, and Bellaghy, and USC patrols at Kildress and Ballyronan (six RIC and USC are killed).
4 May	Donegal – at Newtowncunningham, anti-Treaty republicans, under Lehane and Daly, ambush Free State forces in pursuit of an ASU that had robbed a bank in Buncrana. John McGinley, Eddie Gallagher, Daniel McGill and Edward Murray are killed.
5 May	Tyrone – the USC kills John McCracken in his pub at Dungate, one of a number of civilian reprisals.

11 May	Derry – USC attacks the McKeown family from Ballymulderg near Magherafelt, killing James and seriously wounding his two brothers.
18 May	Belfast – as part of the joint-IRA offensive, ASU attacks Musgrave Street Barracks.
19 May	Antrim/Down – the 3rd ND begins their offensive operations in east Ulster. Planned attacks are called off in Armagh and South Down.
20 May	Dublin – Michael Collins and Éamon de Valera sign the Sinn Féin electoral pact.
22 May	Belfast – the Unionist MP, William Twaddell, is shot dead; the northern regime introduces internment.
26 May	Armagh – a thirty-hour shoot-out takes place between the IRA and USC at Jonesborough.
28 May	Donegal/Fermanagh – intense fighting begins around Belleek and Pettigo between pro- and anti-Treaty IRA on one side and the USC and British Army on the other.
3 June	Donegal/Fermanagh – the British Army expels the IRA from the Belleek–Pettigo triangle with heavy artillery.
3 June	Armagh – ASU attacks the barracks at Crossmaglen and Jackson's house, Drumack.
10 June	Newry – ASU shoots James Wolf Flanagan RM leaving Newry Cathedral.
16 June	The elections take place for the Free State parliament.
17 June	Armagh – USC reprisal against Patrick Creegan and James Crowley; IRA kills seven Protestants at Altnaveigh.
22 June	London – two IRA volunteers, Joseph O'Sullivan and Reginald Dunne, kill Sir Henry Wilson.
24 June	Armagh – USC reprisal against Peter Murray and Michael O'Kane.
24 June	Armagh – the IRA attacks the USC at McGuill's of Dromintee, killing USC Russell.
28 June	Dublin – the Free State attacks the Four Courts, initiating the Civil War.
29 June	Donegal – Free State forces attack Finner Camp, killing Leitrim man, Captain James Connolly, 3rd WD.
16 July	Louth – the Free State army, under Dan Hogan, seizes Dundalk.

2 August	Dublin – a GHQ meeting with Northern IRA officers is held at Portobello Barracks.
14 August	Louth – Frank Aiken leads the attack to retake Dundalk.
19 August	Dublin – the Free State officially adopts a 'peace policy' in the North.
22 August	Cork – Michael Collins is killed at Béal na mBláth.
11 September	Belfast – the northern regime abolishes PR for local elections.
2 November	Donegal – Ernie O'Malley orders republicans to evacuate Donegal; Charlie Daly and his column are arrested.
8 December	Dublin – a Free State firing squad executes Joe McKelvey, Liam Mellows, Rory O'Connor, and Dick Barrett in an extra-judicial killing.

1923

10 March	Donegal – Free State soldier, Bernard Cannon, is killed in Creeslough under dubious circumstances.
14 March	Donegal – the Free State army executes four republicans at Drumboe: Charlie Daly, Seán Larkin, Daniel Enright, and Timothy O'Sullivan.
7 March	Kerry – the massacres begin at Ballyseedy. Seventeen republicans blown up by mines. Overall, thirty-two republicans are killed in Kerry in March 1923, only five in combat.
10 April	Tipperary – IRA Chief of Staff, Liam Lynch, is shot dead in the Knockmealdown mountains.
23 April	Kildare – seventy-one republican prisoners escape from the recently built Tintown No. 1 at the Curragh.
24 May	The new IRA Chief of Staff, Frank Aiken, issues the ceasefire and dump arms orders that effectively ends the Irish Civil War.

INTRODUCTION

FEARGHAL MAC BHLOSCAIDH

The 'cunning of history' describes the way actual results apparently subvert the intentions behind historical actions.[1] Northern republicanism in the early twentieth century might be viewed accordingly. In one of many ironies from the unsuccessful Irish revolution, the northern province, or two-thirds thereof, the birthplace of Irish republicanism, remained within the British state. Most academic accounts of partition portray this as the logical and inevitable consequence of the fact that two nations, one British, the other Irish, inhabit the island. Indeed, the Treaty debates in Dáil Éireann often serve as evidence that many southerners shared this analysis and that Ulster played second fiddle to issues such as the oath, even for those who opposed the Treaty. Similarly, academic history has tended to portray the Irish Civil War as a straight fight between Free State democrats and IRA dictators.[2] The contents of the interviews and letters that follow offer important evidence challenging both perspectives.

Ernie O'Malley's interviews provide insights into the specifically northern aspects of the War of Independence, or Tan War, and more significantly emphasise Ulster's centrality in the slide towards civil war. The 'enormous condescension of posterity' has largely airbrushed northern republicanism from historical accounts.[3] This collection, however, sheds new light on the fundamental importance of partition and the plight of northern nationalists. Similar collections tend to open with a general narrative from the Home Rule Crisis to Civil War. This introduction rather provides the uniquely northern context of the interviews, particularly the sectarianism fundamental to British and unionist strategy and the northern issue's significance in the Civil War.

Notions such as the cunning of history let the powerful off the hook, by ignoring that history 'is nothing but the activity of men in pursuit of their ends' under prevailing historical conditions.[4] Partition was likely – it came to pass. It was not inevitable, however, and emerged from the British imperial élite's determination to secure its interests. Neither did it rely on the existence of two nations – self-determination for an Ulster nation was meaningless; the enterprise subverted self-determination.

Through unionist opposition to home rule, the North began the process that led, by degree, to the Tan War. Even before the formation of Óglaigh na hÉireann/The Irish Volunteers on 25 November 1913, the Ulster Volunteer Force (UVF) had over 76,000 men.[5] Therefore, when the Tan War spread north in the spring of 1920, the IRA operated under specific and very unfavourable circumstances in most of Ulster, due to the large unionist population and residual support for constitutional nationalism, or more pertinently Hibernianism. As Charlie Daly remarked in a letter in this collection, the IRA in Mid-Ulster had 'to contend with a hostile civilian population with superior equipment backed up by regular forces, and the apathy of our own civilian population'.

In 1911, Protestants of various denominations made up 56 per cent of the population in Ulster's nine counties. The fact that home rulers held the majority of parliamentary seats after January 1913 (seventeen, against sixteen seats for unionists) pointed to the fact that all Orangemen might well be Protestants, but not all Protestants are Orangemen. Even in Tyrone, with its history of sectarian antagonism and slim Catholic majority, as late as July 1913 approximately 5 per cent of Protestants supported home rule.[6] Nevertheless, by the First World War, the equivalence between Protestant and unionist generally held, with two-thirds of adult males in the Orange Order, a 'peculiar institution', which 'fostered a sense of community' and 'institutionalised the instinct of racial superiority over the conquered Catholics'.[7] John McCoy described how Hibernian and Orange animosity peaked during the summer marching season, but, generally, 'both parties in the North seemed to get on very well together'.[8] In many respects Belfast replicated the rural pattern, but the close urban environment acted as a catalyst for confrontation, and there the fire burnt much brighter and more intensely, as is vividly captured in these interviews.

The Ancient Order of Hibernians (AOH) mirrored Orange sectarianism, dominating nationalist politics in Ulster. By 1909, the board's charismatic leader, Joe Devlin, whom John Redmond called the 'real Chief Secretary of Ireland', could rely on the support of 64,000 members.[9] Hibernianism demonstrated the evolution of a rural lower-class network within Belfast's religiously polarised urban environment. As Catholic migrants flooded the city's expanding labour market from the mid-nineteenth century onwards, they carried with them their cultural and political baggage, if very little else. In these circumstances, Devlin harnessed the Hibernians to dominate and control Catholic politics in the city, guaranteeing Irish Parliamentary Party (IPP) dominance for a political generation.

This AOH spread rapidly southwards after the 1911 National Insurance Act, becoming an island-wide 'Catholic organisation with a membership of nearly one hundred thousand'.[10] The onset of the Ulster crisis, the First World War, and the Easter Rising, however, derailed Devlin's juggernaut. Many southern Hibernians subsequently found a home in the emerging Sinn Féin movement. In the North, Devlin survived the challenge of the Irish Volunteers by essentially co-opting the movement in May 1914. In September 1914, Ulster contained 60,000 Irish Volunteers. The overwhelming majority went with Redmond's National Volunteers after the split. By the end of the year, only 2,000 remained loyal to the Irish Volunteers or, in effect, the Irish Republican Brotherhood (IRB).[11]

Since its foundation in 1858, the IRB sought an independent democratic Irish republic, adopting a consciously non-sectarian outlook. The Fenians still retained a presence in small pockets of Belfast and among working-class communities in Mid-Ulster. The Dungannon–Coalisland nexus represented the core territory of Ulster Fenianism, which fanned out in a crescent along the south and west shores of Lough Neagh, finding favour among local artisans, labourers, small farmers, and factory workers. By 1916, only Galway, Mayo, Cork, and Kerry had larger contingents of Irish Volunteers than Tyrone, and Coalisland's selection as the rendezvous point for Irish Volunteers from Belfast, East Tyrone, North Armagh, and South Derry on Easter Sunday 1916 relied on the relative strength of local Fenianism.

The Rising, in both ideological and practical terms, owed an enormous debt to Ulster republicanism, which produced its two principal architects, Tom Clarke of Dungannon and Seán Mac Diarmada, who took the Fenian oath while working as a tram conductor in Belfast. Again, by a strange but not infrequent irony, the Rising, which precipitated such a sea change in southern nationalism, did not shake the foundations of northern politics with anything like the same force.

In the North, Hibernianism displayed far greater resilience. At the 1918 general election, Devlin routed de Valera by 8,488 votes to 3,245 in the Belfast Falls constituency. The interviews reveal that most Belfast nationalists did not back the Republic until after the Truce in July 1921. Elsewhere in Ulster, the Cardinal Logue Pact, which McCoy heavily criticised as a concession to sectarianism, complicates an assessment of constitutionalism's relative decline. Nevertheless, the further west you went from Belfast the weaker the Irish Party's residual hold on nationalism. By Easter 1920, when the Ulster IRA began serious operations, Sinn Féin enjoyed the support of around two-thirds of nationalists outside Belfast.

While the IRB maintained an influence over the IRA, the men interviewed in this collection were all comparatively young, with no real track record in the republican movement. Joe Sweeney represents the exception that proves the rule: his attendance at Pádraig Mac Piarais' school, Scoil Éanna, and involvement in the Easter Rising practically guaranteed his appointment as O/C No. 1 Brigade Donegal, where the IRB had just over 200 members prior to the Rising.[12] McCoy recalled how, outside an IRB cell in Newry, the remnants of Fenianism left little trace in South Armagh before the by-election in 1918. While the IRB controlled the IRA Belfast Brigade before the pogrom, the interviews suggest that this actually checked military activity until younger men such as Roger McCorley and Séamus Woods, still teenagers in 1920, took the initiative. A similar situation prevailed in Tyrone, where 'the old [IRB] officers of the pre-1916 vintage ... wanted to retain their influence to cancel or change things'.[13] In general, the Ulster IRA lacked initiative and relied on direction from Dublin. As such, 'the official non-violent policy of GHQ therefore facilitated the development of ever-growing differences in activity between the various counties'.[14] Ulster's fight failed to ignite while brigades elsewhere took the initiative.

The interviews in this collection detail the campaign across much of Ulster, with the notable exception of Monaghan, which remained firmly in the orbit of Eoin O'Duffy. The counties largely acted as organisational boundaries until the IRA divisional reorganisation in March 1921. The interviewees retrospectively applied these divisional boundaries across the period and, in the interests of clarity, a brief outline of the respective Northern Divisions would greatly assist the reader.

The 1st ND comprised four brigades across County Donegal and part of Derry, including the independent Derry City Battalion. The most active No. 1 Brigade, which contained the largest Gaeltacht area, encompassed

Northeast Donegal. No. 2 Brigade brought in East Donegal and the Inishowen peninsula, No. 3 Brigade the central belt, while No. 4 (South Donegal) Brigade ran south from Donegal town. As outlined in his interview, most volunteers in this division went Free State with Joe Sweeney, but its location placed Donegal at the centre of a bitter struggle between Free State and republican elements, which ended with the execution of four republicans in a lonely wood outside Drumboe Castle on 14 March 1923.

The 2nd ND contained four brigades located throughout Counties Tyrone and Derry and did not extend beyond the six counties' border. For most of the period from September 1920 until March 1922, Charlie Daly, executed at Drumboe, occupied the position of divisional O/C and this collection contains significant parts of his correspondence. No. 1 (East Tyrone) Brigade had the strongest Fenian tradition. No. 2 Brigade ran west through Omagh to Dromore, Trillick, and Fintona in the west and also witnessed serious violence. No. 3 Brigade ran along the western shore of Lough Neagh fanning out into South Derry, while No. 4 (Maghera) Brigade did not exist before the Truce and encompassed some of the more unionist areas in Derry.

These distinctions are particularly important in understanding Daly's correspondence with Eoin O'Duffy in March 1922. As a result, IRA volunteers from Tyrone fled west to Donegal, the republicans serving under Daly, the remainder as 'neutral' volunteers under his replacement, Tom Morris. In line with the experience of most active Belfast volunteers, this latter grouping relocated to Keane Barracks, the Curragh, under the false assumption that they would receive training for a subsequent campaign in the six counties. In effect, they either remained inactive until demobilised after the Civil War or joined the Free State army, as was the case with Morris and all the Belfast interviewees.

The 3rd ND had three brigades located throughout Counties Down and Antrim. The No. 2 (Antrim) Brigade and No. 3 (East Down) Brigades covered the areas of Ireland with the largest unionist population and witnessed limited offensive action. Conversely, the No. 1 (Belfast) Brigade bore the brunt of fighting in Ulster. There were four battalions in Belfast, with the third and fourth not organised until after the Truce. The 1st Battalion Belfast Brigade originally had two companies, A and B, which operated along the nationalist Falls Road. As more men joined, C and D

Companies covered adjoining districts in West Belfast. The 2nd Battalion represented nationalist enclaves across the city, with A Company situated in Ardoyne, North Belfast, B Company in the Short Strand, East Belfast, C Company across the Lagan in the nearby Market area of South Belfast, and D Company on North Queen Street, bordering Sailortown. The interviews provide a fascinating insight into the pogrom as well as the process by which the Belfast IRA by-and-large took the Free State side with particular attention on the position of former Divisional O/C, Joe McKelvey.

The 4th ND comprised three brigades in South Armagh, Newry, and North Louth, and the independent Armagh Battalion, which took in majority unionist North Armagh and a small area of East Tyrone. No. 1 Brigade covered North Louth, which would be highly significant during the Civil War. The No. 2 Brigade took in Newry and majority nationalist South Down, while No. 3 (South Armagh) Brigade represented the main operational area and the home place of the interviewees in this collection. The 4th Northern, under Frank Aiken, occupied a unique position. As late as August, Henry McGurran, from Derrymacash in North Armagh, wrote to his mother from their camp at Castleshane in Monaghan that 'we are neither Republicans or Free Staters', but added that 'of course everyone in camp here are in sympathy with the Republicans'.[15] To understand Aiken and his division's role between December 1921 and August 1922 is to understand the complexity of the Civil War. Like their neighbours from Tyrone, many Armagh volunteers ended the war in the Curragh, but as enemies of the Free State in Tintown, and McCoy and O'Hanlon's testimonies provide invaluable accounts from the republican perspective.

Two other divisional areas comprised parts of Ulster, the 5th Northern took in Cavan and Monaghan as well as parts of the Clogher Valley in South Tyrone, while Seán Mac Eoin's 1st Midland Division contained parts of Fermanagh. Again, interviewees mention these areas in relation to the abortive joint-IRA offensive against the North in the spring of 1922. Yet an organisational breakdown cannot convey the particularity and wider significance of this collection. For that, a brief assessment of the pro-British forces and the machinations of the pro- and anti-Treaty IRA before the Civil War are required.

Not only were there very few Black and Tans in Ulster, but northern violence differed significantly from the Tan War in the future Free State (including Donegal, Cavan, and Monaghan), where over 1,400 were killed from 1919 until the truce: 363 police, 261 British army, about 550 IRA volunteers, and 200 civilians.[16] Therefore, southern violence tended to be directed against combatants, with sectarianism barely registering as motivation. This sits in stark contrast to the northern situation. After the Belfast pogrom in July 1920, 23,000 Catholics were driven from their homes and 50,000 left the North before the end of the Civil War.[17] Between July 1920 and July 1922, 557 were killed across the six counties, including 35 IRA and 82 crown forces. Belfast witnessed the vast majority of this violence, in a sectarian conflict waged against civilians. Kieran Glennon has identified 498 killings between July 1920 and October 1922, including 266 Catholic and 181 Protestant civilians, or 90 per cent of the fatalities.[18] As Catholics comprised only a quarter of the population, in real terms, they were around six times more likely to be killed than Protestants.

Yet this emphasis on sectarianism ignores some pertinent caveats. The Belfast IRB and IRA contained some notable Protestants. For example, Archie Herron, a Presbyterian and republican socialist from Portadown, who married James Connolly's daughter, Ina, joined the Fianna in Belfast and served as IRB organiser before 1916. His brother Samuel was secretary of the Belfast Irish Volunteers, while company captain, Robert 'Rory' Haskin, belonged to the Church of Ireland.[19] Therefore, while Tom McNally, the IRA quartermaster, admitted to O'Malley that the fight 'developed into a Catholic versus Protestant business', with the IRA representing 'a small island in this flood', clearly, the sectarian impulse did not emanate from republicans. Indeed, the expulsions that sparked the pogrom were not directed solely against Catholics.

In January 1920, twelve labour councillors gained election to Belfast Corporation, including the Protestant Connollyites, Sam Kyle, who topped the poll on the Shankill Road, and Dawson Gordon in the Docks Ward. These 'rotten Prods', or socialists, numbered amongst the 10,000 expelled by loyalist mobs from workplaces that summer. At the Orange field at Finaghy on the Twelfth, Edward Carson warned his audience:

> those who come forward posing as friends of labour care no more about labour than does the man on the moon. The real object and the real insidious nature of their propaganda, is that they mislead and bring about disunity amongst our own people and in the end, before

> we know where we are, we may find ourselves in the same bondage and slavery as is the rest of Ireland.[20]

Carson proceeded to link socialism and republicanism through an attack on Sinn Féin:

> We must proclaim today that, come what may, we in Ulster will tolerate no Sinn Féin – no Sinn Féin organisation, no Sinn Féin methods … We tell you [the British government] this – that if, having offered you help, you yourselves are unable to protect us … we tell you that we will take the matter into our own hands … And these are not mere words. I hate words without action.[21]

The IRA assassination of Colonel G. F. Smyth in Cork on 17 July provided the premise for loyalist 'action'. After Smyth's funeral on 21 July, mobs expelled 10,000 Catholic men and 1,000 Catholic women, as well as hundreds of Protestant trade unionists from Belfast's shipyards, engineering plants, and factories. When an IRA ASU assassinated District Inspector Oswald Swanzy on 22 August in Lisburn, mobs burnt the town's Catholic population from their homes. Viewing the aftermath, the loyalist hardliner, Larne gunrunner, and James Craig's paramilitary linkman, Fred Crawford, recounted how Lisburn resembled 'a bombarded town in France … there are only four or five RC families left'.[22] The only drawback, apparently, 'some very hard cases in which unionists lost practically everything they had by the fire of a house of Catholics spreading to theirs'. [23] The London *Daily News* described events in east Ulster as, 'five weeks of ruthless persecution by boycott, fire, plunder and assault, culminating in a week's wholesale violence, probably unmatched outside the area of the Russian or Polish pogroms'.[24]

Was there a pogrom in Belfast from July 1920 until 1922?[25] The *Encyclopædia Britannica* defines 'pogrom' as a 'mob attack, either approved or condoned by authorities, against the persons and property of a religious, racial, or national minority'.[26] Belfast certainly witnessed mob violence, which the authorities effectively sanctioned and nationalists violently opposed, as did Russia's Jews during the second, and largest, Tsarist pogrom of 1903–6. At the unveiling of a flag in the shipyards in October 1920, James Craig, Ulster Unionist deputy-leader and soon-to-be northern prime minister, told supporters: 'Do I approve of action you boys have taken in the past?

I say yes'.[27] The previous month, the new security force for the envisaged northern regime – the Ulster Special Constabulary (USC) recruited the mob *en masse*. As Roger McCorley told O'Malley: 'No man could work in the shipyards unless he had a B or C [Specials] card'. Harland and Wolff recognised the loyalist vigilance committee in the unsuccessful negotiations with the Carpenters' Union to reinstate expelled workers.[28] Ulster unionists based their hegemony on a heady mix of incendiary rhetoric, brutal mob violence, police death squads, and financial inducement to loyalty through employment in the yards, factories, and Specials.

On 23 July 1920, Craig told the British Cabinet that the Specials would prevent 'mob law' and stop 'the Protestants from running amok'. General Henry Tudor, Dublin Castle's army advisor, warned that this 'would show that the government did differentiate between rebels and loyalists'. Lloyd George 'remarked that he was not thinking of such differentiation, but of releasing troops and police'.[29] In May 1922, while referring to the violence in Belfast, Churchill remarked: 'Whether it was a case of six of one and half a dozen of the other he did not know. He would be sorry to try and arrive at any other ratio'. Churchill then outlined that the British had nineteen battalions and 48,000 USC in the six counties and that 'orders had been given to accede to Sir James Craig's request for arms and munitions to equip these', because 'at any moment, patience may be ruptured and we shall find ourselves in an atmosphere where people see red'.[30] Apparently, if the unionists weren't armed to the teeth, they might become violent.

The British government created and funded the USC, in the process seriously narrowing the already slim chances of republican success in Ulster. In September 1920, the three principal UVF organisers in Tyrone, Ricardo, Stevenson, and McClintock, issued a secret memo which outlined that the USC would be a wholly Protestant force: 'We are rapidly approaching an absolute crisis and if we turn down this scheme … the powers that be may say "very well you will not help us to help yourselves and you have got to accept the rule of the Sinn Feiner"'.[31] Fred Crawford gave some indication of subsequent tactics: 'where the murder of a policeman or other official takes place, the leading rebel in the district ought to be shot or done away with. If this policy were carried out the murders would soon cease as the whole pack of the rebels are a lot of cowards'.[32]

There were four 'major peaks' of violence in Belfast. The first coincided with the expulsions of the summer of 1920. The second happened in July

1921, when, as McCorley told O'Malley, in Belfast, 'the Truce itself lasted six hours only'. As Glennon has identified, 'A lull in the autumn was followed by another surge in deaths in November 1921 – the month in which the Northern Ireland government assumed responsibility for security and policing and the Specials were re-mobilised'.[33] In fact, Craig authorised UVF remobilisation in October. Crawford wrote how he told Craig 'that if something were not done our people would get out of hand ... they have the feeling that the Ulster Parliament is useless and powerless and that the old leaders have forsaken them'.[34] In essence, Craig let loose the UVF (or demobilised B men) in order to pressure the transfer of security powers to Belfast from London, while simultaneously placating militant loyalist supporters across Ulster. In Tyrone, for instance, Charlie Daly complained to IRA GHQ how

> Orange aggressiveness and cowardly attacks on defenceless people ... are becoming so serious that we must take active steps for their protection ... such cases as this and even ones more serious are becoming so numerous that truce or no truce the volunteers must take action to protect themselves and their people ... The volunteers in the areas concerned are willing and capable of doing so if they are armed.[35]

No arms were forthcoming and the signing of the Anglo-Irish Treaty, unbeknownst at the time, marked the inexorable decline of the northern IRA.

The British government transferred security powers to Belfast in November 1921 and steadfastly backed the northern regime in 1922. Belfast witnessed brutal sectarian warfare between February and May 1922. Indeed, 'the worst of the violence was therefore over before the outbreak of the Civil War in the south at the end of June'.[36] At a notable cabinet meeting on the last day of May 1922, Lloyd George claimed that Mussolini's *Fascisti* served as an 'exact analogy' for the Ulster Specials and that, unlike the Free State, the North was not a dominion. He then claimed that the initial attack and brunt of subsequent violence involved the 'murder of members of the [Catholic] minority,' while, 'we had armed 48,000 Protestants'.[37]

In June, the British civil servant Stephen Tallents arrived to investigate the violence in Ulster in lieu of a public enquiry. General Ricardo reported that in Tyrone the full-time A Specials 'contained a large leaven of a bad type', had serious problems with 'drink and consequent indiscipline', and, overall, represented a 'distinctly partisan force', incapable of 'the impartiality that is necessary in an efficient police force'.[38] The part-time B Specials were 'drawn from the Protestant section of the population and mainly from the more extreme side'. Furthermore, in a period when 'antagonisms, racial, religious and political are at a fever heat ... one section irrespective of its proportion to the other in each locality has been turned into a semi-military police force'. In areas where Catholics predominated, the USC showed the leading nationalist a list with 'his name at the top and he is told that if any B man is touched the list will be attended from the top'. Ricardo then stated that the 'N. Govt. is a very strict party machine which is influenced at the present time entirely by Belfast views of extreme type', concluding that 'the 26 counties are not the only ones that would benefit by a return to the Union and to impartial government by the Imperial Government'.[39] Despite this damning testimony, Tallents' findings were a whitewash. The British government would fully resource the USC for a subsequent two years to the tune of over £6 million.[40]

Partition represented the fall-back policy of an imperial state thrown onto the defensive during the revolutionary period. The manipulation of sectarianism hardly represented a novel strategy. The British employed the Orange Order to defeat the 1798 Rebellion. Sectarian antipathy originated in colonisation but found new expression in industrialising Belfast as a consequence of rapid urban migration in the nineteenth century. At first, the reactionary element in the British political elite backed Ulster unionist resistance to scupper home rule for all Ireland. Partition only emerged as a serious option for securing wider imperial interests and negating Irish independence once some measure of limited self-rule appeared inevitable. Throughout the revolutionary period the Tory establishment offered unwavering financial and military support to Ulster loyalism, even when this entailed a wide-scale and indiscriminate sectarian campaign against Belfast's Catholic minority.

This collection provides first-hand accounts of the scale and ferocity of the pogrom, but, even more unmistakably, the interviewees, pro- and anti-Treaty, give the impression that Free State GHQ bore much of the responsibility for the northern IRA's ultimate demise. A great deal of commentary centres on a period that witnessed little military activity in the South, namely, from Treaty to Civil War. Rather than a side issue, the northern issue appeared crucial during the interregnum in southern violence. Nevertheless, even before the first British shell hit the Four Courts on 28 June 1922, Collins, Mulcahy, and O'Duffy had clearly abandoned any challenge to the Orange State. That they were still in negotiations with the republican garrison about a proposed joint-IRA offensive speaks either to their utter confusion, endemic duplicity, or both.

The Treaty itself apparently offered a non-violent means of ending partition through the Boundary Commission. Certainly this characterised the interpretation of Arthur Griffith, who told de Valera that the Free State would gain 'most of Tyrone, Fermanagh, and part of Armagh, Down,' thereby apparently obliging Ulster unionists to accept unity.[41] On 3 December 1921, de Valera told the Dáil cabinet that the oath and Ulster still required amendment. The negotiators returned to London 'prepared to face the consequences – war or no war', Griffith with instructions to 'try and put the blame on Ulster'.[42] On 5 December, Griffith capitulated on Ulster and the Irish delegation signed the Treaty without consulting Dublin. The following day, Lloyd George told his cabinet that the Boundary Commission 'would possibly give Ulster more than she would lose'.[43]

From the outset, Michael Collins used the IRB to try and sell the Treaty to republicans. While the country at large may have favoured acceptance, even if, as Liam Mellows rightly suggested, the people's fear of immediate and terrible war weighed heavily on their will, the majority of men and women within the republican movement opposed the deal. O'Malley concentrated on the IRB in every interview. There is no doubt that the Brotherhood and Collins' force of personality helped secure a majority in the Dáil. As de Valera later confessed, 'by the "stepping stone" pretence many soldiers of the Republic were led astray until now, having fought against the Republic, they have committed themselves far too much ever to come back'.[44] It is vital to differentiate between the population and republican movement, for, in effect, as John Dillon the leader of the near defunct Irish Party acknowledged in March, 'without Collins, Griffith would not last a fortnight'.[45] The North loomed large in the defeat of the Republic since the issue helped delay conflict between republicans and the Free State, until the latter held the military upper hand.

The Treatyites lost little time in neutralising the northern issue. Several interviews refer to a céilí in Clones on 6 December 1921, when, according to Frank Aiken, Eoin O'Duffy, 'assured us with great vehemence that the signing of the Treaty was only a trick; that he would never take that oath and that no one would (be) asking to take it. He told us that it had been signed with the approval of GHQ in order to get arms to continue the fight'. In March 1922, Collins told the Tyrone IRA that 'partition would never be recognized even though it might mean the smashing of the Treaty'.[46] Before he went to London in May with the proposed Free State constitution, Collins told McCorley that 'he was going to London within a few days to see Lloyd George and he would tell him that he could take his bloody Treaty'. In August, Collins apparently told the pro-Treaty northern IRA that if a political policy failed against the North, 'the Treaty can go to hell and we can all start again'.[47] Yet, after Béal na mBláth, northern IRA petitions met with short shrift, Mulcahy informing Woods in October that 'the policy of our Government here with respect to the North is the policy of the Treaty' and, 'I don't presume to place any detailed interpretations on what are called "assurances that GHQ would stand to the North"'.[48] In effect, this merely confirmed Free State policy since May.

The dominant figure in the northern drama, Michael Collins' role remained unclear, oscillating between tragic hero, villain, and fool. Certainly many within the British establishment held the last view. During the Treaty negotiations, Mark Sturgis described Collins as 'just like a big, young, pleasant prosperous self-satisfied cattle-dealer in a big way of business, with which Ireland is full'.[49] Lionel Curtis called Collins 'a corner boy *in excelsis*', who could 'never quite see the picture through his own reflection in the glass'.[50] Elsewhere, Curtis described negotiating with Collins as like 'writing on water', to which Lloyd George dismissively replied, 'shallow and agitated water'.[51] Both Woods and McCorley appeared to plump for the first option. Woods lamented how the Free State had abandoned the attitude of 'the late General Collins',[52] later complaining to O'Malley that the army constituted a 'mob under Dick Mulcahy's control', while McCorley recounted how, 'when Collins was killed, the northern element gave up all hope'. Nevertheless, from the republican perspective, the evidence points to Collins as Iago rather than Othello.

The stepping stone strategy had several strands, but relied initially on an overly pessimistic view of republican military capacity linked to the age-old constitutional nationalist position that compromise with the British state represented a pragmatic step towards freedom. Collins promised to introduce a republican constitution, which secured an uneasy truce within the IRA and facilitated the electoral pact of 20 May 1922. This envisaged a Sinn Féin coalition cabinet proportionate to the relative pro- and anti-Treaty vote on 7 January being established after the 16 June elections. More decisively in terms of this collection, a joint-IRA offensive against the North operated as the unseen safety net under Collins' high wire political manoeuvring.

Collins partly neutralised partition through the Ulster Council, established by O'Duffy at Clones in January, but headed by Frank Aiken. This included all the Northern Divisions: McKelvey and Daly, the then anti-Treaty commandants of the 2nd and 3rd Northern Divisions, Aiken of the neutral 4th and the pro-Treaty 1st and 5th commanded by Sweeney and Dan Hogan, respectively.[53] In March 1922, Pat McCartan wrote that 'the IRA in the six counties are all anti-Treaty almost to a man. They, however, are out against partition rather than the Treaty. They feel they have been let down'.[54] In short, the northern issue jeopardised the Treaty and, in a counter-intuitive and skilful move, Collins actually manipulated the issue to delay open confrontation with republicans. Free State GHQ at Beggars Bush essentially bought the loyalty of the northern IRA with military hardware and empty promises.

By March, O'Duffy controversially replaced Daly with GHQ loyalist Tom Morris, an episode covered in the letters in this collection and clearly sanctioned by Mulcahy and Collins.[55] Nevertheless, in the same month, and with arms transferred from Liam Lynch's 1st Southern Division, the IRA in Mid-Ulster seized two barracks and killed crown forces, provoking an orgy of reprisals in Belfast. Through the auspices of the IRB, the IRA Coalition Army Council, including Mulcahy, O'Duffy, Mellows, Lynch, and O'Connor, agreed to co-operate in a subsequent cross-border campaign. This precipitated the arrival in Donegal of a contingent of experienced republican soldiers from Munster under the command of Seán Lehane and Charlie Daly in late April, who, according to Rory O'Connor, would 'command both Republican and Free State troops in the area'.[56] As the interviews and letters in this collection make clear, rather than operating in tandem, the relationship between Free State and republican forces in Donegal quickly descended into acrimony.

The republican forces, quickly supplemented by sections of the 2nd ND fleeing the security clampdown after the March offensive, received no co-operation from Sweeney, who 'had no use for the North for I thought they were no good. I got no encouragement from Collins or from GHQ about helping the North, nor had I any instructions to back them up'. The normal Free State soldier in Donegal appeared to resent these southerners, but their own outlook vis-à-vis the Treaty appears particularly significant. On 24 August, Sergeant M. O'Donnelly of Buncrana wrote to a friend in New Jersey:

> Things are much changed since you left here. Then we were fighting the common enemy. Now we are fighting amongst ourselves … Well, Johnny, you over there seem to think, this is a Free State army that is trying to control Ireland at present, but I say, No! When we joined the army in Drumboe in March we told Joe Sweeney that we were not going to serve in a Free State army, but the same army under the same GHQ, and that was before there was any word of a split in the army. Then there came into Donegal a band of blackguards from Derry and the south of Ireland, and started to ambush our fellows … they killed four of our fellows in Newtowncunningham. Two months ago we fought the Specials in Belleek and Pettigo … We would have had Derry only for those fools outside our county. There was only one man in Donegal leading them, that was Peter O'Donnell, but he said that when the Treaty was signed he was going to start a Communist movement … Well, John, do you really think we would fight against a Republic although we are in the National Army? See if we don't get a well-equipped army and then break out and tell England to go to hell.[57]

The myriad interwoven and conflicting loyalties complicate a full understanding of this period, but on some level both Free State and republican leaders agreed to challenge partition militarily, with the former reneging on their commitment.

By May 1922, as Charlie Daly recounted, most northern volunteers remained neutral under Free State command because of false assurances and military assistance: ''Tis in order to be in a position to fight that they have gone to that side. We are certain to have them later when they have got the arms for its well-known that Beggars Bush will not risk the Treaty by carrying on the fight in Ulster'. Crucially, the republicans lacked the resources properly to support the northern IRA. By September, Liam

Lynch wrote that 'it is too bad how the Dáil and olf [*sic*] GHQ let down our people in the North, particularly in Belfast. I fear we cannot come to their assistance financially'. Nevertheless, Lynch confirmed that 'war must go on against those who are preventing our independence in [the] North, especially those who are out to exterminate our people there'.[58] When the second phase of the northern offensive took place in May, among all the southern factions, only the republican 1st ND engaged.

The republicans had the will, but lacked the resources, the Free State the resources, but not the will. By the time they attacked the Four Courts, GHQ had effectively hung the northern IRA out to dry by allowing the 2nd and 3rd Northern Divisions to initiate a general uprising (two weeks apart), while they ordered southern pro-Treaty units to stand down. The inevitable unionist reprisals and the implementation of internment effectively destroyed the IRA in the six counties. By 2 June, the British had rejected Collins' republican constitution and threatened to reinvade, as 'the time had come for them to choose between De Valera and the Treaty'.[59] Suitably chastened, Collins came to heel on 13 June, helped in no small part by the British bombardment of mixed republican and Free State forces at Belleek (18 May–3 June). Whether or not Collins called off the pact on 14 June in Cork hardly mattered, as his acceptance of the, as yet unpublished, imperialist constitution killed the pact. The British government vetoed the Irish people's right to elect a coalition government in a free election involving parties apart from Sinn Féin. In effect, republicanism was once again illegal; as Lloyd George confirmed, the British Government 'could not allow the republican flag to fly in Ireland.' If Michael Collins couldn't deal, 'the British would have to do so'.[60] On 28 June, Collins dealt, four days after the British had cancelled their own attack on the Four Courts. By the first week of July, Churchill felt confident in assuaging Craig's fears regarding his administration's security, now that 'Collins had definitely drawn the sword against the enemies of the British Empire'.[61]

As reflected in the title, *The Men Will Talk to Me*, this collection exclusively speaks to the experiences of male combatants. While O'Malley did interview a handful of women for his project, he did not speak to any female veterans from the Northern divisions. The various roles played by women – as harbourers, messengers, informers, companions, and victims – are alluded to throughout the interviews. Nevertheless, these women are mentioned only in passing and are often unnamed. We do not hear of

Winifred Carney's role in devising the plans for the burning of the Income Tax Office in Belfast in 1920,[62] nor of Eithne Coyle holding up trains and destroying goods across Donegal during the Belfast Trade Boycott,[63] nor of Nano Aiken, who was on the run with the 4th Northern Division from December 1920 and smuggled important intelligence dispatches and arms across the border throughout the period.[64]

However, the interviews that follow deserve special attention for two main reasons. Controversy surrounding Peter Hart's analysis of Cork has meant that for nearly twenty years the only serious discussion of sectarian violence during the revolutionary period has focused on the southwest. By contrast, the irrefutable and exponentially greater resort to sectarianism in the northeast has not received anything like the same scrutiny. Ernie O'Malley understood well the dynamics behind the northern riot, which he noted were, 'generally staged during a time of surplus labour or when the English political situation in its approach to an Irish settlement demanded it'.[65] Violence in Ulster sprang from the summer pogrom and continued through the USC campaign, a state force recruited directly out of the paramilitary UVF, which pursued a strategy of reprisal killings mirroring British conduct throughout Ireland during the Tan War.

The interviews also speak of the Irish counter-revolution. Collins' corpse was hardly cold when the new Free State purged the 'revolutionaries, Irish-Irelanders and most especially the militarist-republicans' from the government.[66] The conservative southern elite singularly failed to challenge partition and, while consolidating the Free State, carried out a proxy war on behalf of the empire against militant republicans and working-class radicals. O'Malley realised the importance of the North. Perhaps this is why he read,

> [Wolfe] Tone slowly. He had been the first to unite Catholic and Presbyterians in the national effort … Tone was the first human note. 'Drunk again' in his diary meant much; it brought him down to mortal level. Too many people had a leader's image in their minds that was a cross between a Calvinist's ideals and a nun's; he must possess the virtues they lacked.[67]

This collection should be read in a similar vein, not to create or consolidate myths and heroes, but to correct the major problem identified by O'Malley himself, namely, that 'Irish history has not been written; it is the history of the underdog'.[68] These interviews give voice to northern republicans and deserve our attention, if only as a corrective to the enormous condescension of posterity, which has attempted to exorcise Tone's ghost. Fortunately for those who desire a non-sectarian future based on republican concepts of freedom and equality, in Ireland still the dead walk around: there is acceptance of their presence, no horror and little dread, the wall remains thin between our living and dead.

Notes

1 The phrase comes from the German philosopher, Hegel, who actually referred to the cunning of reason, but it has entered popular parlance as the cunning of history.

2 For a comprehensive and critical view of the historiography of the Civil War, see John M. Regan, *Myth and the Irish State* (Dublin: Irish Academic Press, 2013).

3 This term emerges from the manner in which the activism of ordinary people is largely written out of history due to their ultimate lack of success; 'the blind alleys, the lost causes, and the losers themselves are forgotten', E. P. Thompson, *The Making of the English Working Class* (London: Penguin Books, 1991), p. 12.

4 T. B. Bottomore (ed.), *Karl Marx: Selected Writings in Sociology and Social Philosophy* (Harmondsworth: Penguin Books), 1979, p. 78.

5 Breandán Mac Giolla Choille, *Intelligence Notes, 1913–16* (Dublin: Oifig an tSoláthair, 1966), p. 33.

6 CI Tyrone, July 1913 (TNA, CO 904/90).

7 J. J. Lee, *Ireland, 1912–85: Politics and Society* (Cambridge: Cambridge University Press, 1989), p. 2.

8 This section of John McCoy's interview was not included in this collection as it is replicated in McCoy's statement to the Bureau of Military History (BMH WS 0492, p. 7). See Appendix to the McCoy chapter for notes on his interviews with O'Malley.

9 *Irish World*, 5 November 1910. See Fergal McCluskey, *Fenians and Ribbonmen: The Development of Republican Politics in East Tyrone, 1898–1918* (Manchester: Manchester University Press, 2011), p. 39.

10 Devlin to J. J. Horgan, 11 October 1911 (NLI, Horgan papers, MS 18271).

11 Mac Giolla Choille, *Intelligence Notes*, pp. 109–10.

12 Ibid., p. 110.

13 W. J. Kelly Jr (BMH WS 893, p. 4).

14 Joost Augusteijn, *From Public Defiance to Guerrilla Warfare: The Experience of Ordinary Volunteers in the Irish War of Independence, 1916–1921* (Dublin: Irish Academic Press, 2006), p. 86.

15 Henry McGurran to Lizzie McGurran, 7 August 1922 (PRONI, HA/32/1/257).

16 Michael Hopkinson, *The Irish War of Independence* (Dublin: Gill & Macmillan, 2002), pp. 201–2.
17 Eamon Phoenix, *Northern Nationalism: Nationalist Politics, Partition and the Catholic Minority in Northern Ireland, 1890–1940* (Belfast: Ulster Historical Foundation, 1994), p. 251.
18 Kieran Glennon, *From Pogrom to Civil War: Tom Glennon and the Belfast IRA* (Cork: Mercier, 2013), Table 1: Who killed and where? Fatalities by status of victim, July 1920–October 1922, p. 263.
19 Robert C. (Rory) Haskin (BMH WS 223).
20 Michael Farrell, *Northern Ireland: The Orange State* (London: Pluto, 1980), pp. 27–8.
21 Geoffrey Bell, *Hesitant Comrades: The Irish Revolution and the British Labour Movement* (London: Pluto Press, 2016), p. 85.
22 Patrick Buckland, *Irish Unionism: The Anglo-Irish and the New Ireland, 1885–1923: A Documentary History* (London: Gill & Macmillan, 1973), p. 445.
23 Ibid.
24 *Daily News*, 1 September 1920. In Bell, *Hesitant Comrades*, p. 86.
25 For an argument that the term is misapplied, see Alan F. Parkinson, *Belfast's Unholy War: The Troubles of the 1920s* (Dublin: Four Courts Press, 2004), pp. 313–14.
26 *Britannica Concise Encyclopedia* (Chicago: Encyclopædia Britannica Inc., 2006), p. 1516.
27 Oliver P. Rafferty, *Catholicism in Ulster, 1603–1983: An Interpretive History* (London: Gill & Macmillan, 1994), p. 211.
28 Bell, *Hesitant Comrades*, p. 88.
29 British Cabinet Conference with the officers of Dublin Castle, 23 July 1920 (TNA, CAB/24/109).
30 British Cabinet Conclusions, 30 May 1922 (TNA, CAB/23/30).
31 'Highly confidential' memoranda on interview with Sir Ernest Clark concerning scheme for calling 'all well-disposed citizens' to come forward to act as special constables, September 1920 (PRONI, Newton family papers, D1678/6/1).
32 Crawford diary, 27 September 1920 (PRONI, D640/11/1).
33 Glennon, *From Pogrom to Civil War*, p. 259.
34 Crawford diary, 27 October 1921 (PRONI, D640/11/1).
35 Daly to Q/M General, 14 October 1921 (UCDA, Mulcahy papers, P7a/26/75–7).
36 Glennon, *From Pogrom to Civil War*, p. 260.
37 Phoenix, *Northern Nationalism*, p. 225.
38 Report of General Ricardo, June 1922 (TNA, CO906/27).
39 Ibid.
40 Mobilisation of the Special Constabulary, 122 (PRONI, FIN18/1/361).
41 Griffith to de Valera, 8 November 1921 (UCDA, de Valera papers, P150/1914/8).
42 Meeting of Dáil cabinet, 3 December 1921 (ibid., P150/1371/179–82).
43 CC, 6 December 1921 (TNA, CAB 23/27/17).
44 De Valera to Luke Dillon, 7 July 1923 (UCDA, de Valera papers, P150/1197).
45 Dillon to O'Connor, 23 March 1922 (TCD, Dillon papers, MS 6744/880).

46 Report of the 2nd ND (NLI, Thomas Johnson papers, MS 17143).

47 Tim Pat Coogan, *Michael Collins* (London: Hutchinson, 1991), p. 383.

48 Mulcahy to Woods, 20 October 1922 (UCDA, Mulcahy papers, P7/B/287).

49 Paul Murray, *The Irish Boundary Commission and its Origins, 1886–1925* (Dublin: University College Dublin Press, 2011), pp. 76–7.

50 Ibid.

51 Michael Hopkinson, *Green Against Green* (Dublin: Gill & Macmillan, 1988), pp. 105–6.

52 Woods to Mulcahy, 29 September 1922 (UCDA, Mulcahy papers, P7/B/77).

53 O'Duffy to Michael Collins, 10 March 1922 (NAI, DT S1801/A).

54 Patrick McCartan to Maloney, 31 March 1922 (NLI, McGarrity papers, MS 17645).

55 Michael Collins diary, 16 March 1922 (UCDA, Mulcahy papers, P7a/62); O'Duffy to Collins, 10 March 1922 (NAI, DT, S1801/A); O'Duffy to Mulcahy, 21 February 1922 (IMA, A/0664/2); Mulcahy to O'Duffy, 27 February 1922 (IMA, A/0664/2).

56 Letter from Rory O'Connor, Mountjoy Gaol, 15 September 1922 (UCDA, Aiken papers, P104/1253/1).

57 Report on the Situation in Ireland for the week ending 2 September 1922 (NAL, CAB/24/138).

58 Chief of Staff to Assistant Chief of Staff, 12 September 1922 (UCDA, Twomey papers, P69/40/113–15).

59 British Cabinet Conclusions, 2 June 1922 (NAL, CAB/23/30).

60 Cabinet minutes, 5 April 1922 (NAL, CAB/23/30).

61 Churchill to Craig, 7 July 1922 (PRONI, CAB 6/75).

62 Letter from Séamus Ua Néill to the Military Service Pension Board supporting Winifred Carney's application (MSP34REF56077).

63 Mrs Bernard O'Donnell (Eithne Coyle) (BMH WS 0750, p. 14).

64 See Nano Magennis (MSP34REF1052).

65 Ernie O'Malley, *On Another Man's Wounds* (Dublin: Anvil Books, 1979), pp. 182–3.

66 John M. Regan, *The Irish Counter-Revolution, 1921–1936* (Dublin: Gill & Macmillan, 2001), p. 259.

67 O'Malley, *On Another Man's Wound*, p. 62.

68 Ibid.

1ST NORTHERN DIVISION (DONEGAL AND DERRY CITY)

PEADAR O'DONNELL

P17b/87, pp. 32–3 (c.1947), P17b/98, pp. 1–5 (3 June 1949)

Peadar O'Donnell (1893–1986) was born into a family of nine at Meenmore, between Dungloe and Burtonport, the youngest child of James Séan Mór and Brigid O'Donnell (née Rogers). O'Donnell's mother influenced his socialist politics as did his uncle, Peter Rogers, an active member of the Industrial Workers of the World, in Butte, Montana. O'Donnell secured a scholarship to St Patrick's College, Drumcondra, where he was exposed to the capital's burgeoning labour movement. Despite lacking real enthusiasm, O'Donnell taught for several years before becoming a union organiser for the Scottish Farm Servants' Union.

He joined the IRA in early 1919, incorporating a company of the Citizen's Army that he had founded while working for the Irish Transport and General Workers' Union in Monaghan town, where he also established a soviet in the local asylum. O'Donnell then formed the first flying column in Derry City, which operated in the 1st ND area of Co. Donegal in December 1920. With the combined forces of the No. 1 Brigade under Joe Sweeney, O'Donnell's column inflicted significant British military casualties during the Meenbanad train ambush of January 1921.

O'Donnell's activism generated conflict with fellow republicans and the British alike. Due to the perceived inactivity of the Derry City Battalion, O'Donnell's column entered the city one night and inflicted seven police casualties causing a clash with Divisional O/C, Frank Carney. Although he escaped, O'Donnell suffered wounds to his arm and hand in a large British military and police raid in the Glendowan area in May 1921.

O'Donnell opposed the Treaty and joined the IRA Executive in the Four Courts. He was arrested following three days of bombardment by the Free State army after 28 June 1922. O'Donnell was held prisoner at various gaols including Mountjoy from late June 1922 until his transfer to Finner Camp in March 1923. During this period, he was elected as TD for Donegal and took part in an unsuccessful forty-one-day hunger strike. He smuggled a note out to his brother Frank, with a list of men to be targeted if he were harmed in prison. Indeed, his future wife, Lile O'Donel, personally informed the Labour Party secretary, Tom Johnston, that he would be shot if Peadar was 'murdered' at Finner.[1]

Following the general order to dump arms, O'Donnell was transferred again to the Curragh, where he walked out the gate on 16 March 1924. O'Donnell subsequently served as editor of *An Phoblacht* and *The Bell*. He wrote six novels and three pieces of autobiographical non-fiction, *The Gates Flew Open* (1932), *Salud! An Irishman in Spain* (1936), and *There Will Be Another Day* (1963). A founding member of the Republican Congress in 1934, O'Donnell fought on the republican side in the Spanish Civil War. He championed radical causes throughout his life, including anti-colonial movements from Vietnam to North Africa, the anti-apartheid struggles, the campaign for nuclear disarmament, and campaigns for disadvantaged Irish communities at home and amongst the diaspora. He died aged ninety-three on 13 May 1986.

This interview was conducted in the company of Joe Sweeney, Peadar's second cousin, who took the opposite side during the Civil War.

(EOM: I brought both of them together so that they could talk and refute.)

[98/1R] (EOM: Joe Sweeney met with Peadar O'Donnell in Bewley's, 3 June 1949.)

Peadar O'Donnell: No more shortage of stuff than there was at any period when our area [1st] ND was coming up to the Truce.

We got 7 mm stuff, ammunition from Dublin from Quartermaster General [Seán Mac Mahon]. I tried it out on a target, but I found that the bullet fell out of the end of the rifle.

March 1921: Frank Carney was appointed Divisional O/C.[2] He stayed in Joe Sweeney's house in Burtonport, but when there was a raid Joe escaped to the dump he had then and the senior officer was captured.[3] He was an IRB man from Enniskillen. He was always in trouble for he was not liked, neither was he any good. First he came to Derry City where he organised Intelligence, he sent out utterly fantastic messages. Later, Paddy Shields of Derry became the Director of Intelligence.[4]

I had told Frank Carney that a British battalion were landing at Burtonport, but he was so hostile to me that he wouldn't even act on the information and as a result he was captured.

[Frank] Carney was IRB. He was in Dublin before the [1st Northern] Division was formed. Seán Larkin [who was] executed by the Free State was County Centre of the IRB in County Derry.[5] Charlie Daly was on the Provisional Council of the IRB. It is strange that important IRB men were killed off. [Richard] Dick Barrett said to me in the Joy, and I think I wrote of it in my book, they'll never let me live, for I was at a meeting and I knew too much.[6] He [Barrett] was a Corkman with a dark Cork mind into which I could not penetrate.

[Liam] Mellows[7] had a low opinion of Doctor [Pat] McCartan.[8] He could not be depended on, he said. He was the only man I could say that Mellows was even bitter against. Mellows had a hard **[98/2R]** time in America for he often told me of it. The Clan [na nGael] had no idea of Mellow's integrity for what they were worried about, when he was [in] gaol in the US, was the fear that he might talk.

In December 1920 we brought 22 rifles out of Derry. We dug them up in a briar in the city. They were in quite good condition with 200 rounds for each of them. In June 1920, there had been fighting in Derry. Paddy Shields [Derry] would know of it.

Peadar Clancy[9] and Seán Treacy[10] were there then, but I never heard of Cathal Brugha being there.[11] The column I had went out to West Donegal.

It shows how hard up they were for leaders when they had to send a man like me out in charge of a column. And I went to West Donegal. Later I was made O/C No. 2 Brigade, which took in Fanad, Inishowen, East Donegal, and Derry.

Derry were not cooperating. Maybe I got their backs up, for a policeman and two soldiers were killed there without permission from the Derry men.[12] Then Derry was made an independent battalion under the Divisional O/C Joe Sweeney. [Winston Charles] McWhinney was in charge of this Derry Battalion.[13] Paddy Shields really wanted to keep Derry quiet for he resented the killing of the peeler and soldiers.

Later a No. 2 [Brigade – 1st ND] column was started in Joe's area, but they had not very much to do for there were few enemy, nor was the column whole time.

Division 1st Northern – No. 3 Brigade, Sam O'Flaherty,[14] No. 2 Peadar O'Donnell, No. 4 Joe Ward.[15] He had rifles dumped, but his area was a fine area. No. 1 [Brigade] hadn't many rifles; Gweedore had block houses only so there was really nothing for No. 1 [Brigade] to hit against. No. 4 [Brigade] had plenty of Tans in Killybegs;[16] also there were posts in Donegal **[98/3R]** town. My headquarters was this side of Derry in the Lagan for that was their [British] main communication route. This was in the 5th Battalion. I was wounded [on the] 10 May. There were about 100 rifles in the Brigade. I had to transfer arms from Fanad to the mainland. Rifles could not be used in the peninsula as it was too narrow. It shows the discipline of the men that I could remove arms from their area.

Frank McKay from Belfast was a good man.[17] He is now in the county council office in Lifford. He is politically minded.

Joe Sweeney did not acquaint his brigades about his decision with regard to the Treaty and this he should have done. Evidently, Document No. 2 had something to do with his decision, but the Sinn Féin Comhairle Ceantair had not. Therefore, he was not telling the truth when he said he had accepted the opinion of the Comhairle Ceantair. (EOM: There were, I said to Peadar, two copies of Document No. 2 which had not been returned at some secret session of Dáil Éireann. These evidently had been duplicated and distributed by the Treatyites. Peadar's idea of holding an area was to make government impossible. Casualties were not as important as making government agents ineffective. This, I said, was the real view of the situation. There was no attempt to drive the British out of Ireland, but the main objective was to make government for them impossible.)

Any fighting that was done in West Donegal around Dungloe was done by my brother Frank.[18] He did not believe in shooting police, but in disarming them for that more mind courage.

[98/3L] The strength of the Hibernians in Donegal: They were very strong. Indeed, they were very active. They opposed our police in Dungloe on the street and the holding of Sinn Féin courts. Their strength was latent, however. They always sided with reaction and were a strength to the Fine Gaedheal [Cumann na nGaedheal – pro-Treaty].

Tan War. Peadar Malone of Clare was brought around in a lorry to see his own house being burned.[19] At the time it looked as if he was going to be shot. A British officer, one of the Cassidy's from Dame Street, was sympathetic, or perhaps he was ashamed, being Irish. He said to Malone, 'Do you want a note brought out for you for you can write to your people and I'll bring it out for you[?]' He brought Malone to the guardroom and left him there. He told the guard to give him anything he wanted, meaning pen and ink. Then Callaghan left. The guard was changed. Suddenly Malone said, 'Where is Callaghan[?]', as he had seen him go out in a lorry. 'He's gone out.' Then Malone said, 'I came in here to see him badly and damn now he's gone!' So he walked out the gate without being seen.

[Civil War] [87/32] Andie Doyle told his unit that an attack was intended but felt he should be there as an attack might take place and [he] would feel ashamed, as if he was avoiding an attack which might not take place outside.[20]

[Liam] Mellows of [Liam] Lynch said, 'He's not thinking of war, but of peace.'[21]

Saw Rory [O'Connor] using an explosive in the court blowing up something.[22]

Colonel Paddy O'Connor was in charge of the prisoners when they got out [of the Four Courts].[23] I told him I was going to go away and he said, 'Good luck to you[!]' and when he went to tell [Joe] McKelvey, he said, 'I think the rest of the [IRA] Executive should stick together.'[24]

Even in Jameson's [Distillery],[25] Paddy O'Connor, he got to charge a sentry and sent word for Andie Doyle, and [Rory] O'Connor held him to the last hoping he would escape.

The attitude of the headquarters staff who would not speak to any of the Free State officers: [Liam] Mellows and me were together and something he said made me say to him, 'You think we'll be beaten then?' and he said, 'There's one thing this will do. They'll save the people from wandering about for a guardian in the wilderness of the Treaty.' Mellows felt the surrender. The shame of the surrender kept me from sleeping for a week.

Seán O'Connor was in charge of the medical mission and was disturbed because they saw men running back and forward to the place where [there] was a Red Cross flag and Paddy O'Connor said, 'Have they arms in their hands[?] [If] they have, then whack away'.[26] (EOM: not long after me.)

Thanks be to Jaysus they're in charge of their own.

Shooting at a window about three weeks afterwards [in Mountjoy Gaol]: Mellows stood [in the window] and had to be dragged down by men and **[32R]** he battered to the attackers and the men who had pulled him down. Colonel Joe Dolan[27] was firing at the windows with the garrison. They took out window frames and ordered them to leave and they refused. Mellows alone stood in the windows. Bugler Kane was wounded.[28] They were on the third storey in the Joy and the angle of fire was very oblique.

Andie Doyle tried to get money to buy a revolver off a sergeant to shoot [Bill] Stapleton and to capture the armoured car, which was inside the gate, and the prisoners were [sitting] on the green refusing to work, they sat down and had to be carried in.[29]

In D wing, they barricaded the Staters, put sentries on it and wouldn't let the Staters in, they put IRA sentries on the stairs. They threatened to shoot up the place. Tom Barry went down and **[98/33L]** saw Diarmuid O'Hegarty, who said they would shoot up the place.[30] (EOM: Rory [O'Connor was] responsible for this.) Then Tom went back and recommended that the men in D [wing] take down their barricade.

Seán and me, looking at men going to confession. Seán smoking a pipe, 'I'd go if I believed in it.'

Melodrama of Rory. Phil Cosgrove[31] and Dan Paudeen [O'Keefe][32] who came in at 2am soused. They were wakened up by Hugo MacNeill and Dan Hogan, who flashed light in their eyes, gave them a form to read and lit it up with a flashlight.[33] Paudeen said, 'Jaysus they can't do that[!]' They got up and dressed and Paudeen and Sergeant Burke brought them [Barret, McKelvey, Mellows, and O'Connor] out at 3.30pm. They phoned up the chaplain before they brought them out.

They were each put in a separate room and each given a note that they were to be executed as a reprisal for the shooting of Seán Hales.[34] Afterwards they were allowed to get together. The chaplain postponed as he was fighting Mellows on the question of confession and GHQ was ringing up wanting to know what the delay was about.

At first there was a complete impasse so that when he wrote his notes he was convinced he was dying without the sacraments.

[Fr] McMahon wanted him to accept the Bishop's Pastoral and **[93/33R]** he refused. Eventually McMahon [said]: 'Won't you admit that you're sorry [for any wrong] you may have done[?]' and Mellows said, 'Of course I'm sorry for any wrong I have done.' (EOM: McMahon told Peadar the story that morning when he was disturbed after the shooting.)

JOE SWEENEY

(UCDA P17b/097, pp. 38–44, April/May 1949)
(UCDA P17b/098, pp. 1–5, 3 June 1949)

Joseph 'Joe' Sweeney (1897–1980) was born in Burtonport, Co. Donegal, and from a young age recognised the failure of the Ancient Order of Hibernians to oppose growing unionist militancy in Donegal. He completed his second level education at Scoil Éanna in Rathfarnham, Dublin, where he received instruction from Mr Slattery in the manufacture of various types of landmines and canister bombs. He was sworn into the IRB by Pádraig Mac Piarais. Sweeney then secured a place at UCD in engineering and became friendly with Charlie Daly.

Sweeney was stationed in the GPO during the Rising, and was later transported to Stafford Gaol and then Frongoch in North Wales. Here he became acquainted with a network of committed activists, including Michael Collins. Soon after his return to Burtonport, he and other local men formed a Sinn Féin Cumann and IRA company.

In the first engagement of the Dungloe company in January 1918, Sweeney led his Company in the rescue of two local men arrested as British army deserters, seizing a rifle in the process. Sweeney then successfully stood as the Sinn Féin candidate for West Donegal in the 1918 elections.[1] In December 1919, as O/C No. 1 Brigade, he led a successful ambush on the RUC at Rampart.[2]

Arrested in a large-scale round-up in March 1920, Sweeney spent a period in Derry Gaol and Crumlin Road, Belfast, before transportation to Wormwood Scrubs in London. On his release, Sweeney was central to the IRA campaign and helped co-ordinate the ambush on the train carrying British military to Dungloe in January 1921.[3]

Sweeney was originally hostile to the Treaty but decided to travel to Dublin to gauge the IRB's thinking, meeting with Eoin O'Duffy and Michael Collins.[4] He consequently took the Treaty side, voting in favour during the Dáil debates.

The anti-Treaty IRA formed the 1st ND to raid the six counties as part of the supposed joint-northern campaign under the understanding that Free State forces in Donegal would support their efforts. Sweeney, however, provided little or no assistance and claimed in this interview not to have received any such directive. Following the outbreak of Civil War, Sweeney sought to rid Donegal of anti-Treaty IRA.[5] He oversaw the execution of former comrades Daly, Timothy O'Sullivan, Daniel Enright, and Seán Larkin at Drumboe in Donegal.[6]

Sweeney remained in the Free State army until his retirement in 1940. He was appointed Adjutant-General in October 1928, Quartermaster General in February 1929, and Chief of Staff in June 1929. He subsequently worked for ten years as an insurance inspector for Canada Life, before being appointed area officer of the Irish Red Cross Society in 1950. He became general secretary in 1956 and held this position until his retirement in 1962.[7] He died in 1980.

[97/41L] Tan War: Douglas was District Inspector in Dungloe. Sergeant Duffy was in charge of Intelligence for Donegal (in Killybegs).[8] They marched into Dungloe one day, held the town and went on a binge. They would have been easy to capture as they were helpless and drunk.

They caught hold of [Donncha] MacNelis, who was there as Divisional Engineer and they beat him so bad he was dying on the street.[9] [Patrick] McCole [O/C Dungloe Company] and his men could have picked all the 20/25 RIC up that day if they had been any good. This was six weeks before the Truce. **[98/4R]** MacNelis, who was Divisional Engineer, never recovered from the beating the RIC gave him. He was carried out on an ass and cart from the [Dungloe] town. The RIC went after the gardener and threatened **[98/5R]** [the] gardener what they wouldn't do to him unless [he] told them where MacNelis was, but the gardener wouldn't talk.

[97/39R] [Frank] Aiken and Joe Doherty were in Burtonport looking for cars to go to Moville for a raid, but they never got in touch with me.[10] There was another man with them. I could have got the cars with IRA drivers. (EOM: This must have been the Moville raid of which I was later in charge.)[11]

[97/39R] At the end of 1920 I tried to get guns from [Michael] Collins, but he wouldn't give me guns.[12] 'Go and capture them', he said. I met Joe Ward next day.[13] He had been able to get me nine Peters [the Painter] and ammunition through Tom Cullen.[14] They're still buried there.

[97/44L] Peadar O'Donnell: There was to have been an attack on Glenties [RIC barracks] during the Tan War.[15] Peadar O'Donnell had got hold of an old cannon. He had arranged that a blacksmith in Lettermacaward make cannon balls for this. The cannon was brought into position with a donkey and cart. It was to blow in the front door of the barracks, but when fired it blew itself to bits and blew the wall backwards. Luckily no one was killed or injured. Peadar on another proposed attack [but] had warned all his friends to clear out of Glenties. Soon the RIC knew about it.

Falcarragh: There was a shoot up but the alert was also given to the RIC.

Costello: Gathered a lot of material once from officers about the Tan War.

[97/42L] Peadar spoiled an attack on [Glenties RIC barracks], [by] warning his friends to leave town so that the RIC knew of it.

Barney O'Donnell from Killybegs worked in Gortahork. He is now in the Electricity Supply Board. He carried out an ambush by himself in the Tan War.

[97/40L] I was always agitating for a division to be formed for Joe Ward in charge South Donegal [No. 3 Brigade – 1st ND] would not create a division to help us. The British threatened to burn the property of Ward's uncle in Killybegs if he moved. That kept him quiet.

In May [1921] [Frank] Carney was appointed Divisional O/C, but Peadar O'Donnell didn't agree with him.[16] Liam Archer was sent down from

GHQ to investigate the matter,[17] but by that time Peadar was wounded and Con Boyle captured.[18] I met Liam Archer in Derry, but just then a girl, who had been up at the [Derry] Gaol, told my brother there that I was in Derry and was asking for them.[19] I got out at once before the raid. I met Archer outside [Derry]. Archer didn't meet Peadar, and Peadar O'Donnell didn't get on well with the local men in Donegal. He had been trying to arrange strikes in the Mental hospitals of Donegal, Letterkenny and Monaghan.[20]

[97/38R] In the escape from Derry Gaol [15 February 1921], [Seán] Larkin, who was a big man, was stuck in the hole.[21] He could not get through it. Afterwards he was the man shot by mistake with Charlie Daly.[22] Frank Carty[23] was sent an ultimatum by Charlie McGuinness, 'Are you going to leave the fucking place or are you not?'[24] Charlie was outside in the only Catholic house (Mrs Heaney) in the terrace. There was an old friendly warden inside who hadn't a drop of Irish blood in his veins. Why I knew was that he had been an old Coast Guard at the station in Burtonport.[25] Afterwards he became my batman.[26]

Derry fighting: (EOM: I thought Peadar Clancy[27] and Cathal Brugha[28] had been there, but Sweeney did not know anything about it save that the Derry men more than held their own.)

[98/4R] I was told to get a Connors RIC who was in Derry, a city commissioner and was connected with the Skibbereen murders, but the Truce stopped that. Charlie Daly was in charge of this area (2nd ND from May 1921 until March 1922). Dan McKenna was second in command.

[97/40L] I was then in charge of the 1st Northern about two weeks before the Truce.

I saw Collins in Dublin before the Truce. 'The long whore is negotiating', he said. I think that when he heard [Éamon] de Valera was negotiating he got into it also. (EOM: Joe Sweeney had never heard of [Alfred] Cope's connection with Mick Collins.)[29]

Once I was in Whelan's Hotel and I was told to move. I moved to Barry's [Hotel] 'Am I not worse here?' I said, but I was told not to leave. There was a move on foot for the whole **[97/40R]** [Dublin] Brigade to have a shoot up. (EOM: This may have been the Dublin hit-up before the Truce at the beginning of July.) I went to Duffy's office where I found that Dev had called the whole thing off. Whilst I was there being very nosey at the time, I heard of trouble between [Micheal] Brennan[30] and [Frank] Barrett[31] in Clare. (EOM: It was Brennan, a very vain man who had the idea of full dress. It was also Brennan who burned all minutes of court-martials in the Civil War, but not the compositions of the Courts.) In these papers was a report of a Court of Inquiry into the differences between Barrett and Brennan.

[98/4R] (EOM: Joe Sweeney was in Dublin before the Truce. He seemed to think that negotiations being on, nothing was being done in Dublin. He gutted an operation which had been put off and suggested that there were others.)

[97/38R] Dan Breen and a crowd went up North after the Truce to fight up in Armagh.[32] They were near Greencastle, but they were chased out of it one night in their shirts with their clothes under their arms.

[98/4R] Paddy Breslin was County Court Registrar in Longford.[33] He was then in Dungloe, Adjutant of the Brigade. He was IRB and had been organising IRB in the area. Joe Sweeney said [the] IRB was not strong in Donegal.

[97/43R] Treaty: Before Dáil met Joe Doherty and Sam O'Flaherty had seen de Valera.[34] He had sent for them I think to find out their attitude to the Treaty. Before I came down from Donegal **[97/44L]** there had been a meeting of the Sinn Féin Comhairle Ceantair at which I was instructed to vote for the Treaty.[35] At the adjournment Dev sent for me but I wouldn't see him. He came along to where I was. 'I hear you are voting for the Treaty,' he said very abruptly, 'Why are you voting for it?' I was a bit annoyed with him. 'I didn't think,' I said 'that the difference between the two proposals would be sufficient to make me vote for Documents No. 2.'[36] He got a bit hot over it. I then met Seán MacBride.[37] I told him what I thought about the Treaty but [he] did not say anything in reply.

Tim Healy[38] did a good turn for J. H. Gallagher, who was once at the bar in Donegal, but had given up his practice and was down and out in London.[39]

[98/4R] A meeting of northern officers before the Treaty at which [Richard] Mulcahy was present in Dublin.[40]

(EOM: I thought Sweeney prevaricated about his attitude to the Treaty. Who had decided [persuaded] him?[41] He seems now to think that there had been a compromise even before the Truce, but that is back-reckoning, I know. Document No. 2 is his reason for his decision. He said IRB never tried to influence him about the Treaty, but when I reminded him about Piaras Béaslaí's book, where he stated that the Supreme Council said that they sent their decision to IRB TD's that they were in favour of the Treaty.[42] 'Yes,' said Joe, 'I remember that.' 'Don't you think that was a lead[?]' I said.)

Civil War: **[97/44L]** I met [Michael] Collins in Dublin the day after [Henry] Wilson was shot.[43] It was two men of ours did it, he said. He looked very pleased. The last time I had seen him so pleased at a shooting was when [the] District Inspector who had kicked Tom Clarke when a prisoner in 1916, and had ill-treated others, had been shot on his orders in Wexford.[44]

Wilson was planning locally as well as internally. 'How do we stand about this shooting of Wilson?' I asked Collins, and that was his reply. Collins promptly issued a denial of his men having taken any part in the shooting.

[97/42R] I remember a meeting in Parnell Square of senior officers in the [pro-Treaty and anti-Treaty IRA]. Liam Lynch was very disappointing for we could all have talked frankly then, but he would hardly open his mouth except for a monosyllable.[45] Joe McKelvey was more or less on our side then.[46] He was condemning [Liam] Lynch and I thought Lynch was too much of a dictator. Joe McKelvey wasn't much good.

[97/39R] Northern Offensive: [Frank] Aiken seemed to have the principal say about northern matters for he took tenders of war flour etc. out of the [Beggars] Bush for the North.[47]

[97/38R] We used a bunker which we filled with drill purpose rifles outside of Drumboe. We got them from Islandbridge, about 200 of them.[48] They were not much good, but they would serve. John Haughey was at that time O/C of the Brigade in County Derry near Magherafelt, or he was V/C.[49] I forwarded them on to him. Haughey represented Derry County at IRB meetings. We sent revolvers and ammunition as well.

Major Morris (EOM: British Army First World War) was in charge of the Division. They raided barracks there and captured a number of them. **[98/4R]** [Major] Morris came in during the Truce [as O/C 2nd ND]. He was ex-British Army.

I had no use for the North for I thought they were no good. I got no encouragement from [Michael] Collins, or from GHQ about helping the North, nor had I any instructions to back them up.

[97/39L] [THE BATTLE OF PETTIGO AND BELLEEK][50]

[Patrick] 'Hun' Doherty[51] and wee Barber Murray of Bundoran were in Belleek then.[52] We had men on the other side of the [Belleek] fort there. I went down there in a car one day to a hill near the fort. I heard shooting. I saw an open Lancia car coming from the Belleek direction and when it was under the fort fire was opened on it. The driver was killed. The other man jumped out and ran towards Belleek. I could see the bullets cutting up the dust around his heels. The car had gone across into our territory.

I was then stationed in Drumboe Castle [Stranorlar]. The Orangemen were very active in Pettigo. I was talking to [Daniel] Gallagher on the street there when fire was opened on the both of us.[53] I told our men to raid houses across the border that night and to burn the houses if they found any arms there; which they did.[54] The British moved in, our men got out, but [Hugh] McBrearty and another man were isolated for a day.[55] They had a Lewis gun. They got out.

Jimmy Hogan of Cork was sent up by Michael Collins to investigate the situation.[56] I was ticked off by Collins. The British then occupied Pettigo until some arrangement was come to between them and the Provisional Government. John Joyce and Joe Rooney were sent up as a Special border force to take charge of Pettigo when the British withdrew.[57]

Collins asked me what I thought of the prospect of a fight in the North when I handed over the drill purpose rifles. I said, 'It's right **[97/39R]** to make those fellows fight.' 'I wouldn't take any joy in it nor would I send in any more', I said.

[97/41L] In Glenveagh Castle were [Donncha] MacNelis and Seán Lehane.[58] At Castlefin I surrounded two Corkmen.[59] There they talked to me and asked me if I would see their O/C in Churchill next day. I agreed with this. Next day [5 July 1922] with an escort, Tom Glennon from Belfast and I went to Churchill.[60] There we met a mob, instead of talking to one or two. I was on home turf, but I could not come to any agreement. It was arranged that the Southerners there could march out with their arms, as they had not been in the area before the Truce. They then wanted a guarantee that Donegal men would not be allowed by me to be used in other parts of the county. **[97/41R]** That I could not agree to. Upstairs I heard Frank O'Donnell's voice say, 'Are you going to let him go?'[61] (EOM: Frank O'Donnell I found of no use.)[62]

[98/4R] There was a dump of Orange rifles found near Castlefin in an Orange house during the Civil War. I had the people tried and they were sentenced to death. Then the pressure was put on Dublin. As a result, I had to release them in a week's time. And at that time we were shooting your [republican] fellows for having arms.

[97/40R] Charlie Daly: One of our officers, Lieutenant Cannon was killed in the barracks at Creeslough.[63] The barracks had been fired at. He went into the hall and was shot dead. We reported it and back came an order to execute four men, one of them [Seán] Larkin. I sent a wireless message back for confirmation. The same message came back to me. Then I sent a message direct to the Adjutant General, Gearóid O'Sullivan.[64] Larkin's name came back again. He was from the six counties and I didn't want to shoot a man **[97/41L]** from the six counties. I was very fond of Charlie Daly. He had been tried shortly after he had been arrested, but the sentence had not been confirmed.

(EOM: I was talking to Peadar and Frank O'Donnell about the shooting of Lieutenant Cannon. All are positive that none of their men were there that night. Nor was there a row in the barracks that night, which I thought there might have been for I examined the soldiers. Outside, behind a wall, we found a heap of cartridges. Whoever had fired had cleared off.)

[97/40L] (EOM: Peadar O'Donnell. I was told by Eoin O'Duffy that he was a spy.)[65]

[98/4R] (EOM: Both Peadar O'Donnell and Joe Sweeney discussed the shooting of [Lieutenant] Cannon in my presence. Frank O'Donnell, Peadar said, told [Bernard] Cannon's father the man who had shot his son and he was Free State. Joe Sweeney said he had investigated the shooting but found that Lieutenant Cannon had been shot through the skylight of the front hall.)

[97/41L] Afterwards I was told a lady was sent to me before [Charlie] Daly was captured to say he was clearing out and would I allow the same conditions to operate as I had previously wanted, but I never met with Daly. I would then have agreed to let Daly leave the county.

We knew where Daly was every night. I had fellows from the old IRA who sent back to their battalion on the '...' and I knew all the information there was to know.

[97/42L] Mutt Walsh, a friend of Peadar O'Donnell, came to me in Arbour Hill.[66] He had broken with Peadar. [He] had gone to Cork but had been shot up for being too friendly with a Free State officer. I saw [Eoin] O'Duffy and I got him a job in the Guards.

[Dan] McKenna was in my area with northern men.[67] They were put in a workhouse. According to orders from GHQ they were not to take part in the Civil War. I traced leakage of information to some of their men. I told Gearóid [O'Sullivan] to take them out of my area or I'd intern them. There were about 200 of them. They were not doing any training. Then they went to the Curragh, where they formed the nucleus of a Battalion. I think McKenna was in charge and [John] Haughey was there. He was a good man.

[97/43L] The best of the Belfast crowd was Roger McCorley[68] and Joe Murray.[69] They were by far the best men there. McCorley lives in Howth. Murray is a carpenter in the Board of Works [now Office of Public Works].

Frank Crummey[70] ran the intelligence system and Tommy McNally was a good quartermaster, a real quartermaster.[71] For you couldn't part him from his staff. Seamus Woods was a bit of an idiot. He was always very mysterious and secretive.[72]

Matt McCarthy of the RIC was in the County's Office in Belfast.[73] He brought the RIC codes regularly to Mick Collins. Later he was a Chief Superintendent in the Guards. I met McCarthy and Collins together in Dublin. The Auxiliaries had just raided the Scotch House in Dublin where both of them were. They were in a snug. McCarthy said he was in the RIC, have you any evidence said the Auxiliary, here said McCarthy, showing his pass and papers. The Auxiliaries then sat down and had a drink with them.

[97/42L] The Mutiny: I met the mutineers, but I couldn't make contact with them.[74] [Seán] Mac Eoin was mixed up with them but he backed out of it.[75] I first **[97/42R]** heard of it when my brother Barney [Sweeney] and Eddie McBrearty were on a battalion officers course at the Curragh.[76] When he came back he showed me a whole wad of papers in which my name was mentioned as being favourable to them and [Seán] Mac Eoin was mentioned as having given them an assurance. I went to Dublin at once. I saw Peadar McMahon,[77] the Chief of Staff, and Dan Hogan.[78] I talked the matter of the mutiny over with them but they pretended to know nothing of it, then I showed them the papers with my name mentioned. I said I wasn't approached by the mutineers for it was promotions in the Dublin area that most affected them. That was the first concrete evidence McMahon or Dan Hogan had seen. Then they told me of the Dublin crowd who were fighting for more control. They went to [Richard] Mulcahy then about the situation.[79] I told [Eddie] McBrearty to keep his mouth shut. It was Hugo MacNeill who finally stopped the troops from fighting when arrests were made later, for I was in Dublin that night.[80]

[97/43L] Peadar McNally,[81] Dan Hogan, McKeown and I got together to suggest a fund of two million to superannuate the officers who were objecting to Britishers controlling the Free State army. We put it up to Gearóid [O'Sullivan] and to [Richard] Mulcahy but for our pains were told to mind our own business.

[97/43R] After the [start of] the Civil War, Michael Collins called a number of us up to Dublin for a meeting, the purpose of which was the reorganisation of the IRB in the [Free State] army. I had chucked the IRB at the time as I had no use for it. I had been sworn-in in 1915 by Pádraig Pearse.[82] Éamon Bulfin had first suggested the idea to me.[83] Then I was asked to attend a meeting in a big room in Parnell Square. Barney Mellows had me thrown out, for I had not been properly introduced to the circle.[84]

Ernest Blythe had been around during the Tan War reorganising [the] IRB it was said, although I never met any people whom he had either sworn in or had meetings with.[85]

At that meeting of the IRB Collins was there, Gearóid O'Sullivan, [Seán] Hegarty,[86] Seán MacMahon,[87] Seán Ó Murthuile[88] and I think [Richard] Mulcahy. Kevin O'Higgins had watched us all go into the meeting and he then put his foot down about it.[89]

[Michael] Collins would not discuss the Civil War at all with me.

Notes

PEADAR O'DONNELL

1 Uinseann Mac Eoin, 'Sighle Bean Uí Dhonnchadha', *Survivors* (Dublin: Argenta Publications, 1980), pp. 30–1.

2 Frank Carney: see biographical sketch.

3 Burtonport, or Ailt a' Chorráin, is a Gaeltacht fishing village four miles northwest of Dungloe and Joe Sweeney's home place.

4 Paddy Shields was a veteran Derry City Sinn Féiner who directed the Belfast Boycott in the northwest with the Divisional Quartermaster, Joe McGurk. O/C Brandywell, Derry City IRA, he was appointed Liaison Officer for Donegal and Derry during the 1921 Truce.

5 Seán Larkin: see biographical sketch.

6 Richard (Dick) Barrett (1899–1922), Quartermaster of the 3rd Cork Brigade. He was arrested following the fall of the Four Courts at the beginning of the Civil War

and executed on 18 December 1922 with Joe McKelvey, Rory O'Connor, and Liam Mellows. In *The Gate Flew Open* (Dublin: Mercier, 2013), O'Donnell describes him as 'easily the most dangerous … of all the minds in the C wing' (p. 24).

7 Liam Mellows: see biographical sketch.

8 Patrick McCartan: see interview in this collection.

9 Peadar Clancy: see biographical sketch.

10 Seán Treacy (1895–1920), from Co. Tipperary, was a member of the IRB and later the Irish Volunteers from its inception. He took part in the Soloheadbeg ambush on 21 January 1919, widely recognised as the first action in the War of Independence. He was active in Michael Collins' Squad and was killed on 14 October 1920 in a shootout with British Secret Service agents in Dublin.

11 Cathal Brugha: see biographical sketch.

12 On 1 April 1921, O'Donnell's column killed two RIC men, Michael Kenny and John Higgins.

13 Winston Charles McWhinney from Derry was active in the IRA during the Tan War and the Civil War, suffering internment in the latter conflict. He was married to prominent republican Linda Kearns, from Sligo.

14 Sam O'Flaherty commanded the Castlefinn Company in 1917. He was arrested in 1918 as part of the German Plot roundup and was incarcerated in Lincoln Gaol, England until February 1919. Following his return to Donegal, he was appointed as O/C of No. 4 Brigade. He also served as TD for east Donegal. While opposed to the Treaty, he played no role in the Civil War and died in 1928 after a short illness.

15 P. J. 'Joe' Ward (1891–1970) solicitor and O/C No. 3 Brigade, 1st Northern Division, TD South Donegal, 1918–24. In March 1920, Ward was arrested and transferred to Wormwood Scrubs, where he went on hunger strike. He supported the Treaty.

16 Killybegs, or Na Cealla Beaga, in South Donegal is the largest fishing port in Ireland.

17 Frank McKay was listed as Adjutant of No. 2 Brigade, 1st Northern Division at the time of the Truce.

18 Frank O'Donnell was vice O/C of No. 1 Brigade, 1st Northern Division and Flying Column. Frank disarmed an RIC sergeant on three occasions and a fourth time the sergeant was unarmed as his superiors had refused to issue him with a new weapon. On that occasion Frank O'Donnell relieved him of his bicycle.

19 Peadar Malone was an IRA volunteer from Clare.

20 Andrew Doyle was Peadar's cellmate in Mountjoy Gaol during the Civil War. He served as Adjutant of the 2nd Battalion Dublin Brigade during the War of Independence and was a member of the Four Courts garrison from 14 April 1922 until the outbreak of the Civil War on 28 June 1922. See Doyle interview with O'Malley, UCDAP17b/96, p. 101.

21 Liam Lynch: see biographical sketch.

22 Rory O'Connor: see biographical sketch.

23 Patrick O'Connor (1901–53) was a member of F Company, 4th Battalion, Dublin Brigade before joining the Dublin ASU and Dublin Guards during the War of Independence. He joined the Free State army in February 1922 and reached the rank of colonel. See his interview with O'Malley, UCDA, P17b/100, p. 101.

24 Joe McKelvey: see biographical sketch.

25 Over 140 men from the Four Courts anti-Treaty garrison were held in Jameson's Distillery from 30 June 1922.

26 This may be John O'Connor of the Dublin Brigade and an officer with ATIRA GHQ munitions, who claimed to have a free pass for the Four Courts Garrison from Seán Lemass.

27 Joe Dolan (1898–1969) served from October 1919 until the Truce with GHQ Intelligence. He served on Michael Collins' staff until December 1922, travelling to London. He served with Free State GHQ Intelligence and resigned with the rank of captain on 27 March 1924.

28 This may be a reference to Captain Thomas Kane, a leading member of the Irish Citizen Army, which opposed the Treaty and provided members for the Four Courts Garrison.

29 William James 'Bill' Stapleton was a leading member of the Dublin Brigade ASU and squad and rose to the rank of colonel in the Free State army before his dismissal for involvement in the failed Army Mutiny in March 1924.

30 Diarmuid O'Hegarty was secretary to the Free State government in 1922. After Collins' death he served as director of Intelligence and commandant general of the Free State army until May 1923.

31 Phil Cosgrave, the brother of the President of the Free State government, was governor of Mountjoy Gaol.

32 Paudeen O'Keefe was the deputy governor. In his prison memoir, O'Donnell described him as 'a restless little man with a fine pair of eyes and a waspish tongue'.

33 Hugo MacNeill (1900–63), O/C 1st Battalion Fianna (South Dublin) 1919–20; Director of Organisation and Training, Fianna, 1920–1, accepted the Treaty and rose to prominence in the Free State army.

34 Seán Hales was a pro-Treaty TD from Cork who was assassinated by republicans on 7 December 1922. His death led to the extra-judicial execution of four republican prisoners, Joe McKelvey, Liam Mellows, Rory O'Connor, and Dick Barrett on 8 December 1922 in Mountjoy Gaol.

JOE SWEENEY

1 Sweeney won by 6,712 votes to 4,116 (*Derry Journal*, 30 December 1918).

2 *Derry Journal*, 15 December 1919.

3 *Derry Journal*, 31 May 1920; Patrick (Kit) O'Donnell, BMH.WS1327, p. 5.

4 Kenneth Griffiths and Timothy O'Grady, *Curious Journey: An Oral History of Ireland's Unfinished Revolution* (London: Hutchinson, 1982), pp. 264–5.

5 Mac Eoin, *Survivors*, pp. 342–3

6 *Derry Journal*, 14–16 March 1923.

7 Ibid. Griffiths and O'Grady, *Curious Journey*, pp. 325–8.

8 RIC Head Constable Duffy was head of an RIC special flying column who controlled a network of spies and informers.

9 Donnacha MacNelis from Malinbeg in the Glencolmcille parish left Donegal as a young man to take up employment in Cork and joined the Volunteers there in 1913. The Cork companies mobilised at Macroom on the morning of Easter Sunday, 1916, but did not engage in any action. Gaoled for the shooting of an RIC Head Constable at Leitrim Street in Cork City, the local IRA effected MacNelis' escape on 11 November 1918. He subsequently returned to Donegal where he took up the position of Divisional Engineer, 1st Northern Division.

10 Joseph O'Doherty (1891–1979), IRB Derry City, was interned in Frongoch after the Easter Rising. On his release he was appointed to the Volunteer Executive. He was the TD for North Donegal, 1921–3, and opposed the Treaty.

11 O'Malley and Frank Aiken (see interview in this collection) took part in a rather disappointing raid at Moville on 2 October 1920 to retrieve only two old rifles and two antique swords.

12 Michael Collins: see biographical sketch.

13 P. J. 'Joe' Ward (1891–1970), solicitor and O/C No. 3 Brigade, 1st Northern Division, TD South Donegal, 1918–24. In March 1920, Ward was arrested and transferred to Wormwood Scrubs, London, where he went on hunger strike. He supported the Treaty.

14 Born in Wicklow, Tom Cullen was IRA GHQ 2nd Deputy Director of Intelligence. He supported the Treaty and was an officer in the Free State army, resigning in 1925. He died in a drowning accident in 1926. 'Peter the Painter' was a small automatic 9 mm pistol reportedly used by Peter Piatkow in the siege of Sydney Street in London in 1911.

15 The IRA attacked the heavily fortified Glenties Barracks on two occasions: 20 April 1921 and 21 May 1921. Both attacks failed to dislodge the RIC and Black and Tans.

16 Frank Carney: see biographical sketch.

17 Liam Archer was a member of F Company, 1st Battalion, Dublin Brigade from 1915 and part of GHQ Intelligence Section, 1920.

18 Con Boyle, IRA west Donegal and Flying Column under Peadar O'Donnell. He was involved in many of the major operations in west Donegal. He was captured in a military raid at Glendowan on 10 May 1921 in which Peadar O'Donnell was shot in the arm, but escaped.

19 Bernard Sweeney was a prisoner in Derry Gaol about that time.

20 In February 1919, Peadar O'Donnell, in his role as ITGWU organiser, set up a soviet in Monaghan Lunatic Asylum.

21 Seán Larkin: see biographical sketch.

22 Charlie Daly and Seán Larkin were arrested for possession of arms and were executed by the Free State on 14 March 1923 in reprisal for the killing of a Free State officer. Sweeney was responsible for carrying out the executions and later commented, 'I didn't agree with it but they were orders and you had to do it.' Joe Sweeney, interviewed in Griffiths and O'Grady, *Curious Journey*, pp. 305–6. See interview with Charlie Daly in this collection.

23 Frank Carty: see biographical sketch.

24 Charlie McGuinness (1893–1947), from Derry, was an experienced sailor and ex-British army, who returned to Derry in 1920 and became involved in the IRA in Derry City. He was arrested and imprisoned in Ebrington Barracks, but later escaped. He was central to the escape of Frank Carty from Derry Gaol. Before the outbreak of civil war, McGuinness also landed German Mauser rifles with ammunition at Passage East and Ardmore, Co. Waterford. He also served in the Spanish Civil War on the republican side. He was drowned at sea in 1947.

25 Burtonport, or Ailt a' Chorráin, is a Gaeltacht fishing village four miles northwest of Dungloe and Joe Sweeney's home town.

26 A batman is a soldier assigned to a commissioned officer as a personal servant.

27 Peadar Clancy: see biographical sketch.

28 Cathal Brugha: see biographical sketch.

29 Assistant Under-Secretary for Ireland and Clerk of the Privy Council, Ireland, 1920–2.

30 Micheal Brennan: see biographical sketch.

31 Frank Barrett from Co. Clare was appointed O/C of the mid-Clare Brigade in 1918. He was active throughout the War of Independence in the mid-Clare Brigade. He was anti-Treaty and served as commander of the 1st Western Division during the Civil War.

32 Dan Breen (1894–1969), from Tipperary, was sworn into the IRB by Seán Tracey. Both men took part in the Soloheadbeg ambush on 21 January 1919, widely recognised as the first action in the War of Independence. Breen led the Flying Column of the 3rd Tipperary Brigade. During the Truce period, Breen went north to help train Tyrone Volunteers at their headquarters in Sperrin Lodge near Greencastle. There is no evidence to substantiate Sweeney's claim about Breen. Breen opposed the Treaty and held a leading position on the IRA Executive.

33 Patrick Breslin was active in the IRB and IRA Company in Dungloe from its establishment in 1917. He was involved with all major operations in his command area and assisted the Flying Column under Peadar O'Donnell in the Meenbanad ambush in January 1921, and also in other operations associated with the Flying Column. Patrick Breslin was Company Adjutant.

34 Sam O'Flaherty commanded the Castlefinn Company in 1917. He was arrested in 1918 as part of the German Plot roundup and was incarcerated in Lincoln Gaol, England until February 1919. Following his return to Donegal he was appointed O/C of No. 4 Brigade. He also served as TD for East Donegal. While opposed to the Treaty, he played no role in the Civil War and died in 1928 after a short illness.

35 Comhairle ceantair (regional council) was the constituency unit of the Sinn Féin party.

36 Document No. 2 was Éamon de Valera's proposed alternative to the Treaty, which still accepted the Boundary Commission and partition, but which proposed de Valera's own concept of external association that Ireland would be independent within her own borders but associated with the Commonwealth in international affairs.

37 Seán MacBride (1904–88), the son of John MacBride (who was executed after 1916) and Maud Gonne. He was a member of the IRA during the War of Independence and

later IRA Chief of Staff in 1936. He entered a Fine Gael-dominated coalition as leader of Clann na Poblachta after the Second World War.

38 Timothy 'Tim' Healy: see biographical sketch.

39 J. H. Gallagher was from Donegal Town.

40 Richard Mulcahy: see biographical sketch.

41 Joe Sweeney first read of the text of the Treaty when the newspapers arrived at Burtonport in Co. Donegal on 7 December 1921. His initial reaction was: 'To hell with this, this is not what we were fighting for', but he decided that he would travel to Dublin to gauge the full extent of the agreement and the reaction of others there before making a decision. See Joe Sweeney, interviewed in Griffiths and O'Grady, *Curious Journey*, pp. 264–5.

42 Spelled 'Beasly' by EOM, Piaras Béaslaí. See biographical sketch.

43 Cavan-born Henry Wilson was assassinated by IRA Volunteers Joseph O'Sullivan and Reginald Dunne on 22 June 1922. Wilson was involved in the Curragh Mutiny in March 1914 and was bitterly opposed to any type of Treaty settlement. He was apparently assassinated on the orders of Michael Collins, but his death actually led the British to pressure Collins into attacking the republican garrison in the Four Courts on 28 June 1922.

44 DI Percival Lea-Wilson was killed by the Squad on the orders of Michael Collins in Gorey, Co. Wexford, on 15 June 1920.

45 Liam Lynch: see biographical sketch.

46 Joe McKelvey: see biographical sketch.

47 Frank Aiken: see biographical sketch.

48 Islandbridge Barracks, beside the Phoenix Park, is now known as Clancy Barracks; named after Peadar Clancy who was tortured and killed by British forces the night of Bloody Sunday.

49 John 'Seán' Haughey was the father of future Taoiseach Charles Haughey. He was O/C of No. 4 (Maghera) Brigade, 2nd Northern Division.

50 Between the end of May and beginning of June 1922, a mixed force of pro- and anti-Treaty IRA fought against the Ulster Special Constabulary and then the regular British army for control of Belleek fort, which lay with the six counties. The IRA evacuated on 6 June after the British deployed heavy artillery. A detachment of Free State forces from Ballyshannon and Bundoran took part.

51 Patrick 'Hun' Doherty was from south Donegal and was active in the IRA throughout the War of Independence, serving as vice O/C of the Bundoran Company.

52 Jer 'Barber' Murray was from south Donegal and was active in the IRA 1st Battalion, No. 3 Brigade, 1st Northern Division.

53 Battalion Commandant, Free State army based in Pettigo in 1922.

54 The boundary border of Counties Donegal and Fermanagh. Pettigo is situated mostly in Co. Donegal and partly in Co. Fermanagh.

55 Hugh McBrearty was from Killygordon, Co. Donegal and a member of the IRA Castlefin Company, No. 4 Brigade, 1st Northern Division. He was active throughout the War of Independence until his capture during the early 1920

round-up. He was interned in Ballykinlar until after the signing of the Treaty in December 1921.

56 James Hogan (1898–1963), born in Loughrea, Galway, was a history lecturer at University College Cork. He served as Director of Intelligence in the Free State army and compiled a file on the Battle of Belleek for Michael Collins (NAI, TAOIS/S1235).

57 John Vincent Joyce (1896–1964), from Dublin, fought at the South Dublin Union in 1916. He was active in some operations of the Squad. He was arrested in 1921 and interned in Ballykinlar until December 1921. He was a commandant to GHQ Beggars Bush and took part in the Belleek–Pettigo inquiry.

58 Originally from Bandon, Co. Cork, Seán Lehane operated in the No. 3 Cork Brigade area during the War of Independence. He served as O/C of the 1st Battalion, Schull from 1920. Lehane was the O/C of the anti-Treaty 1st Northern Division (Donegal) from March 1922. He evacuated from the county and was subsequently interned.

59 Captain Jim Cotter and Divisional Engineer Mick O'Donaghue. In late June 1922, Charlie Daly instructed both to take a column of men to Castlefin, a market town in the Finn Valley, and use this as a base for cross-border attacks. When they were surrounded by Free State troops, the officers on both sides subsequently met at Wilkins Hotel, Churchill on 5 July 1922 to avoid civil war in Donegal.

60 Tom Glennon from Belfast served in the 3rd Northern Division. As Free State Divisional Adjutant he sat on the Military Court panel for the trial of Charlie Daly, Seán Larkin, Daniel Enright, Timothy O'Sullivan, Daniel Coyle, Frank Ward, James Donaghy, and James Lane. The first four men were executed on 14 March 1923, while the others were saved through the withdrawal of the IRA from Donegal.

61 Frank O'Donnell was a brother of Peadar O'Donnell and was vice O/C of No. 1 Brigade, 1st Northern Division and Flying Column.

62 After this meeting, Charles Daly became aware of a plan by a number of Republicans to ambush O'Donnell and Glennon as they left Churchill. Daly prevented this from going ahead, thus saving their lives.

63 See Glennon, *From Pogrom to Civil War* (Dublin: Mercier, 2013). Bernard Cannon was from Leitir Mhic a'Bhaird in the Rosses area of west Donegal. He was a member of E Company, 1st Battalion, No. 1 Bridge, 1st Northern Division of the IRA holding the rank of 1st Lieutenant. He was pro-Treaty and joined the Free State army stationed in the village of Creeslough. On 10 March 1923, shots were fired at the barracks in Creeslough killing Lieutenant Cannon. This incident was the catalyst for the executions at Drumboe on 14 March 1923.

64 Gearóid O'Sullivan: see biographical sketch.

65 Eoin O'Duffy: see biographical sketch.

66 James 'Mutt' Walsh was from Co. Cork. He was a volunteer with the Lyre Company, Clonakilty in No. 3 Brigade, 1st Southern Division. He later transferred to Derry City and joined the IRA command there before joining Peadar O'Donnell in the 1st Northern Division Flying Column. James Walsh also served under Seán Lehane and Charlie Daly during the Civil War.

67 Dan McKenna: see biographical sketch.

68 Roger McCorley: see biographical sketch.

69 Joe Murray from Belfast was a member of B Company, 1st Battalion, 3rd Northern Division. Following a successful operation with men from C Company, the two companies formed an Active Service Unit in the city. They were involved in several operations targeting Black and Tans and Auxiliary Division. They were also tasked with locating RIC District Inspector Ferris, who had also been involved in the murder of Tomás Mac Curtain. Ferris recovered when shot by members of the ASU.

70 Frank Crummey was a school teacher from Belfast, who was No. 1 Brigade Belfast Intelligence and later 3rd Northern Division Intelligence Officer. He had good contacts in military police circles, the post office and the telephone and telegraph sections.

71 Tommy McNally: see biographical sketch.

72 Seamus Woods: see biographical sketch.

73 Sergeant Matt McCarthy was an RIC man from Kerry and an Intelligence Officer for the Belfast Brigade. He passed information on to Collins about the whereabouts of Oswald Ross Swanzy, killed on 22 August 1920 in Lisburn.

74 The Irish Army Mutiny in March 1924 was led by a group of disgruntled Free State officers in the wake of troop reductions and due to apparent dissatisfaction with the Free State government's perceived inactivity on partition.

75 Seán Mac Eoin: see biographical sketch.

76 Eddie McBrearty, from Killygordon, was a member of the Castlefin Company, 4th Battalion, 1st Northern Division. He was a member of a twenty-five-strong unit who were credited with carrying out the first daylight arms raid on the Drumquin RIC barracks, Co. Tyrone, on 26 August 1920. Constable James Munnelly was killed in the attack.

77 Peadar McMahon was a member of the Dublin Brigade of the IRA and had served as training officer in a number of counties from 1919 to 1920, including Kildare and Mayo. He was arrested in 1921 and interned at Rath Camp, the Curragh, Co. Kildare. He was pro-Treaty and was staff officer to Eoin O'Duffy when he served as Chief of Staff of the Free State army.

78 Dan Hogan: see biographical sketch.

79 Richard Mulcahy: see biographical sketch.

80 Hugo MacNeill was from Dublin. He was O/C 1st Battalion Na Fianna Éireann, south Dublin 1919–20 and later Director of Organisation and Training 1920–1. He also played a prominent role in the Free State army during the Civil War.

81 Spelled 'MacAnally' by EOM, Peadar McNally was member of Fianna Éireann, Fintan Lalor circle of the IRB and associate of Seán Mac Diarmada. He was in the Dublin Brigade and later joined the Free State army.

82 Pádraig Mac Piarais (1879–1916), was an educational pioneer, promoting the Irish language and cultural revival through his school, St. Enda's. He was executed following the Easter Rising in 1916.

83 Eamon Bulfin was from Co. Offaly and was the second student to attend Pádraig Pearse's St Enda's school. He was sworn into the IRB at Wolfe Tone's grave in Bodenstown by Art O'Connor in 1912, and later proposed the admission of Padraic Pearse into the IRB.

84 Barney Mellows was active from 1916 and had been involved in the attack on the Magazine Fort, Phoenix Park on Easter Monday 1916, which was carried out by members of Na Fianna Éireann. He was later involved in the battle at the Four Courts. He remained in the Fianna and also served with 1st Battalion south Dublin in 1917, and later as Chief of Staff Na Fianna Éireann in 1921.

85 Ernest Blythe was active as an organiser for the IRB prior to 1916 and had travelled throughout Co. Donegal in the latter part of 1914, speaking to IRB members and encouraging them to organise cells in their areas.

86 Seán O'Hegarty: see biographical sketch.

87 Seán MacMahon (1893–1955) was from Dublin and was an active member of the IRB and Irish Volunteers in 1916. He was interned in Frongoch. He was appointed Quartermaster General of the IRA in 1920 and, as a Free State officer, as Quartermaster and later as Chief of Staff.

88 Seán Ó Murthuile of Cork was secretary of the IRB Supreme Council after Collins reorganised it in 1917. Quartermaster General of the Free State army, Ó Murthuile unsuccessfully attempted to reconstitute the organisation after the Civil War.

89 Kevin O'Higgins: see biographical sketch.

2ND NORTHERN DIVISION (TYRONE AND DERRY)

DR PATRICK MCCARTAN

P17b/89, pp. 22–3 (c. Jan. 1946)
P17b/95, pp. 52–7 (Apr/May 1949)

Patrick McCartan (1878–1963) was born on 13 March 1878 at Eskerboy near Carrickmore, Co. Tyrone, third among two sons and three daughters of Bernard and Bridget McCartan. After learning that Fenianism still existed in America, he became fascinated by the 1798 centenary celebration as a student in St Macartan's seminary.

After two years further study at St Malachy's College, Belfast, McCartan ran away to America with fifteen pounds he stole from his father. He found work as a barman in Philadelphia and was initiated into camp 428 of the Clan na Gael by fellow Carrickmore man, Joseph McGarrity. In 1905, McGarrity provided him with a loan to pursue a medical career in Ireland

and to act as his Irish eyes and ears. With credentials acquired from John Devoy and Tom Clarke in the offices of the *Gaelic American* in New York, McCartan transferred to the IRB Teeling circle and associated Keating branch of the Gaelic League in Dublin.

McCartan established Dungannon clubs throughout Tyrone and became a leading figure in Sinn Féin. In 1914, he returned to America to explain the Volunteer split, raise funds for Pearse's St Enda's, and liaise with Roger Casement before his German mission. He was back in Ireland by December 1914, and was described by the RIC in Tyrone as 'the most dangerous man in the county'.[1]

A member of the IRB Supreme Council from July 1915, McCartan and Denis McCullough failed to carry out orders on Easter Sunday and sent the Tyrone and Belfast Irish Volunteers home from Coalisland. McCartan himself blamed poor communication and Mac Diarmada and Clarke's unwillingness fully to inform him about the Rising.

McCartan went on the run until February 1917, when he was deported to Fairford Gaol, England. In July 1917, he changed an initial plan to go to Russia as IRB representative and sailed to America. He lost the South Armagh by-election in February 1918, but was returned unopposed for Offaly in April. In March, McGarrity made him editor of the newly established *Irish Press*. McCartan then sided with his friend in the Clan na Gael split with John Devoy and Daniel Cohalan, which came to a head during de Valera's US visit.

Much of this interview focuses on McCartan's unsuccessful mission to the USSR between December 1920 and July 1921. O'Malley showed particular interest in his and McGarrity's attempts to reconcile de Valera and Collins.

McCartan lost his seat as a pro-Treaty panel candidate in June 1922 and emigrated to New York. He returned to Ireland in 1937 and finished third as an independent in the 1945 presidential election. A founder member of Clann na Poblachta, McCartan enjoyed little personal political success. He died on 28 March 1963.

[TREATY]

[89/22R] [George] Gavin-Duffy fought hard about delegates going as plenipotentiaries [to Treaty negotiations],[2] he quoted the instances of Alcibiades.[3]

Once Joe McGarrity came over [from the USA].[4] At a meeting in the Shelbourne [Hotel], himself and P. S. O'Hegarty tackled [Michael] Collins and insisted that he meet Dev. 'You'll find he's more a Treaty man than you are', said McCartan. A meeting was held in the Mansion House. Joe McG[aritty] had to frequently get between the door and one or the other of them, as they would alternatively get up in anger to walk out. Eventually they both stayed on. Later, when the meeting was over, Collins put his arm around McCartan's shoulder and said, 'It's true for you, Pat; he believes more in the Treaty than I do.'

At first in the Shelbourne, Collins said to McCartan, 'Dev won't speak to me; wait till you see.'

The shooting of [General Sir Henry] Wilson:[5] McCartan saw [Liam] Tobin when he came back on the train from Cork?[6] He was afraid to see or to meet [Richard] Mulcahy.[7] When he **[89/23R]** met Collins, Collins said to him, 'To Hell with Mulcahy. I'll make it alright [*sic*].'

Just before Collins was killed, D[ick] Mulcahy and Fr [Peter] Magennis were to have gone to Cork to meet Dev.[8] Then, when word of Collins' shooting came they went to Cork, but Dev had already gone to Dublin. Then McCartan was speaking to Gearóid O'Sullivan.[9]

[95/52R] RUSSIAN VISIT [DECEMBER 1920 TO JULY 1921][10]

The IRB secretary, Seamus O'Doherty:[11] I was given plenary powers on behalf of the Provisional Government Irish Republic. [Ivan] Maisky not in London,[12] got in touch with his governess, found Gavronsky [Dmitry] a good friend of Maisky, and he was an agent of the Kerensky government.[13] He said he wanted to keep in touch. [Laurence] Ginnell ([who became a] TD)[14] was a patient as Gavronsky was a medical doctor on the books, as so was Patrick McCartan … Prisoners released then and Wilson's 14 Points published.[15]

[A number of prisoners] had gone before I could see them at the train [in] Dublin.[16]

Supreme Council, Diarmuid Lynch[17] [and] I met and saw Dev who sent for [Eoin] MacNeill and he wrote the document signed by the released prisoners.[18] 'Will I tell Dev about signing the document on behalf of [the] Provisional Government?' [asked McCartan]. Seamus O'Doherty said, 'no he wouldn't understand.'

Liam Mellows was blaming [the] USA in his speeches and they, the Americans, did not like that.[19]

Liam went hungry. He sent money to his mother. When he left the *Gaelic American*,[20] Dev came out soon afterwards.[21] In San Francisco, I got $400 from the Clan [na Gael] and I did it on condition of sharing it with Liam.[22] I gave him $200. Barney Murphy, an old cara, had a pub, also Joe McGarrity, they never would see Liam hungry.

Saw Cathal Brugha,[23] Count Plunkett[24] who were very critical of Cuban statement[25] and Sceilg [J. J. O'Kelly][26] and D[aniel] Cohalan[27] also.

Mick thought, 'well Dev did it', and he was loyal when [Dev] carried the majority of the cabinet with him.

I wouldn't go to Russia unless Dev gave me **[95/53R]** credentials. I thought he was afraid we might get recognition.

Dev signed a printed form later in the US.

'You had better refuse in writing,' he said and I wrote to Dev at once.

Left 20 December [1920]: Litvinov I *saw* 3 weeks, then met [George] Gavan Duffy in Copenhagen.[28] Four months in Russia when trade treaty would be negotiated with England (then our position would be gone into). I met [Georgy Vasilyevich] Chicherin and I said that I don't see that you can give us recognition on account of this English treaty.[29] 'Stay at least another month, it is well worth your while,' Nuorteva was such.[30] Really in gaol as an English spy (Nuorteva), so then I couldn't meet Lenin. 'No,' said the new assistant secretary of state, 'for its no use staying on.' I asked him to stay in touch through the USA. Chicherin [was] quite sincere. Nuorteva wrote a memo for Lenin to grant us recognition. I met an American girl who typed in the foreign office and she said she had typed this memorandum. But that may have been Russian policy.

1921: Then a month in Germany: *Five* of them – [including] [Robert] Briscoe [were] over there then looking for arms.[31]

[The] IRB never asked to vote for [or] against the Treaty. Secret session showed such bitterness that I was not going to vote. Harry Boland wanted me to vote against it and that decided me to vote for it.[32] I told Mick I would vote. 'No', said Mick. Griffith[33] and Piaras Béaslaí [were] at the meeting, but I'm not sure if Piaras [was] there.[34] 'No,' he said, 'don't vote' and MacEntee, Frank Fahey and Malone [possibly P. J. Maloney, TD for Tipperary] **[95/54R]** *were* strong, or they wanted a way out and maybe that was the best way out.[35] I didn't canvass them.

At secret session I suggested a *frank* vote: that our names be put in a hat, [with] no party division. Dev's crowd wouldn't have given me permission for it. Perhaps they were afraid of [the] result.

Meeting with Mick Collins: Mick said neither he nor Dev could control the IRA. 'Can you both together[?]' [I said]. He said that he [wouldn't] speak to me. Harry [Boland], Joe McGarrity [were] to bring along Dev, P. S. O'Hegarty etc. to influence Mick.[36]

Dev, Mick and Joe to meet later and we thought we could get Dev to be reasonable. P. S. O'Hegarty said, 'you must [try] to make terms, Mick.' P. S. O'Hegarty was senior in the IRB.

Dev would hardly speak to Joe at first, when [the] two met there.

The Mansion House: Both would make for the door in turn, but Joe would hold them back one after the other.

'Dev believes in that Treaty more than you do', I said that evening. He looked at me hard and when I met him that night in Mac Laverty's, Mick said, 'Be God, Pat he does believe in it more than I do.' They argued and talked, but nothing came of it. They spent from three until seven arguing and talking, Mick and Dev.

Mick's power of decision and if you beat him in an argument he'd agree, but Dev would change his mind even after an agreement. He'd always ask for a memorandum **[95/55R]**, which he would never ever read. (EOM: During the Truce.)

I suggested that all TDs would go to their constituencies and get [the] editors of papers to put Republic in [the] headlines of papers [or] we might get the people to a position where we couldn't get them back. A verbal reply from Dev in Mansion House.

I told P. S. [O'Hegarty] and both of us cursed him.

After 1916, [John] Devoy[37] [had] sent over [an] order to reform IRB. [John Archdeacon] Murphy from Buffalo and [John] Gill came over for reorganisation and Mrs [Kitty] O'Doherty[38] of the National Aid [Association] was my active and she got her husband [Séamus O'Doherty] and Seán Ó Murthuile to deal with the *county country*.[39]

Mick, when he came home, reorganised the Provisional Committee and when prisoners go out Mick lost contact with Seamus [presumably O'Doherty] who left city after 1916.

Secret session: Brugha said that Document No. 2 was not the Republic but Dev said it was. 'Well,' he said, 'if you say it is I accept it.' Liam Mellows said Tweedle Dum and Tweedle Dee. Séamas Robinson put his hand on his gun when I asked him.[40]

They claim Dwyer was organising the Guards [An Garda Síochána] at the time he was shot [in] Dec[ember] 1922 after Rory and co.[41]

Ben Byrne asked to take charge of [the] execution but refused. Then he got a written order and accepted. I've [to] accept a written order, he said.

[95/56R] Peace moves: Dr [William J.] Maloney and Fr Magennis were here looking to meet Dev. Maloney had great persuasive power and Magennis was a great friend of Dev.[42] Pat McCartan had seen both about peace terms, he was waiting for Mick to come back at 1 o'clock. No news of Mick when I was talking to Mulcahy. D[ick] M[ulchay], when Mick was shot, gave me £100 for them two and Dr Jim Ryan went with them.[43] Dev had come to Dublin in the meantime.[44] They saw Mary MacSwiney and others, I think.[45]

I put it at Mick's funeral. I suggested to Gearóid [O'Sullivan] that the two would like to see Liam Mellows, 'there are a lot of men who would like to see him', he said savagely.

Tom Cullen said if I got hold of Dev that night I would have shot him but I would have been sorry for it afterwards.[46]

Monsignor Rogers [an American priest] then took into us.[47] They met in Farnham's.

Dev and Mulcahy said he couldn't get any peace with him that he was going around in circles. Then Dev stuttered on so far and said nothing could be done.

Liam Tobin in Fermoy.[48] A girl in the Post Office, a friend of Liam Lynch and Tobin, and he used to talk to this girl and send his regards to Liam Lynch and he got a note not to walk out the road all alone.

I saw Mick about peace, not two weeks before, as soon as we get into Cork we can't have peace too soon and it was on that basis I saw Maloney and Magennis.

[95/57] I said to Mick, 'you'll not get them out of the county without fighting and I'm damned if I'd fire on any Irishman. Why not call a meeting of the Dáil, all the TDs for the Treaty, resign and leave the thing completely in Dev's hands? He will be better when in control.' He didn't reply, but I think it was Eoin O'Duffy who told me that it was discussed by the others.[49]

(EOM: [McCartan gives a] repetition of [the] story of Bill [Liam] Tobin's conversation with Mulcahy when he came back from London with the news of Wilson's death.)[50] Mulcahy [was] alarmed and furious. Then Tobin met Collins on the platform when the train arrived later than he had thought. 'Oh I'll fix that alright don't you worry unless you hear from me,' [said Collins].

Wilson was a great friend of the royal family and had great influence on them (EOM: the suggestion [is] that English politicians were glad when they heard of Wilson's death.)

CHARLIE DALY

(UCDAP17b/132, pp. 20–3, 34–7, 46–51)

Charlie Daly (1896–1923), born in August 1896, was the second son of Cornelius and Ellen Daly of Knockaneculteen, Firies, Co. Kerry. He grew up in an area steeped in republican tradition, his younger brother, Tom, became local IRA battalion commandant, while his sister Mary 'May' remained active in republican politics in Kerry for decades.[1] In 1913, Daly joined the Irish Volunteers and mobilised at Castleisland on Easter Sunday, alongside the seventy-five men of the Firies under Dan O'Mahoney.

Charlie was arrested twice between 1918 and 1919, but was released as he was considered to be of no further military danger due to his deteriorating eyesight. He immediately joined the Kerry Flying Column and then GHQ Staff in Dublin in early 1920. In October, he was sent to Tyrone to organise the local units into flying columns on the southern model. A prominent member of the IRB, Daly regularly attended meetings in Dublin, where he was captured two weeks before Christmas 1920 and interned in Collinstown.

In March 1921, Eoin O'Duffy was ordered to organise the 2nd ND with assistance from 'a useful officer [Daly]', who 'already had some experience of Tyrone.'[2] When O'Duffy departed for GHQ that May, O'Daly led the division and accepted the rank of Commandant General from Cathal Brugha in November 1921. He was convinced that the truce 'was only a matter of a few weeks [away]', and the Treaty therefore came as a severe disappointment.[3] On 10 January, he spoke strongly against the Treaty at a meeting between Dick Mulcahy and IRA commandants. Unbeknownst to Daly, he had probably assured his removal as 2nd ND O/C.

In late April 1922, Daly crossed the border into Donegal as republican GHQ organiser and deputy O/C of the 1st ND under Seán Lehane, as part of the second phase of the proposed joint-IRA offensive. As these letters make clear, the northern offensive never materialised in Donegal. In fact, Daly clashed with his old friend, Joe Sweeney, especially after the Newtowncunningham incident on 4 May, the day after two units under Daly and Lehane led raids into the six counties in support of the 2nd ND offensive.

In the wake of the Free State attack on 29 June, the republicans set up headquarters in Glenveagh Castle, and by early August were forced to break into flying columns. Daly's letters during the Civil War provide a harrowing account of the challenges faced by republicans, the growing antipathy between former comrades, and the miserable circumstances of the ordinary people of Donegal.

Daly and his party were captured at John Sharkey's house in Meenabaul near Gaoth Dobhair in November 1922 and were found guilty of possessing arms without proper authority. After the unaccounted-for death of Captain Bernard Cannon on 10 March 1923, Daly was sentenced and executed on 14 March 1923.

[23R] (EOM: Batt O'Mahoney, St Canice's R[oa]d Ballymun, Mrs O'Mahoney, Loch Léin, opposite to the Albert College. Charlie used to stay here in the Tan War and was arrested there and imprisoned in Collinstown [Dublin] as a teacher. He was released after about two months and the British immediately found out who he was.[4]

Seven tried and four executed: three of them signed.[5])

[26R] [Letter from Minister of Defence Cathal Brugha to Charlie Daly]

To O/C No. 2 ND

Your appointment as No. 2 Divisional Commandant has been ratified, also appointment of Frank Stronge[6] as Adjutant and Joe McGurk as Quartermaster.[7]

[Letter from Minister of Defence Cathal Brugha to Charlie Daly]

Director of Organisation,
Dáil Éireann,
Department of Defence,
17 November 1921

To … In view of the possibilities of further fighting and in order to put the army in an unequivocal position as the legal defence force of the nation, under the control of the civil government, the cabinet has decided to issue fresh commissions to officers, and to offer re-enlistment to all ranks. The new army will date from the 25 November, the anniversary of the founding of the Irish Volunteers in 1913.

On the authority of the president and cabinet, acting as the duly appointed executive of Dáil Éireann, I hereby offer you a commission as O/C 2nd ND with the rank of commandant general in the new army.

Cathal Brugha,[8]
Minister of Defence

[Letter from Deputy Chief of Staff Eoin O'Duffy to all Divisional Commandants]

Óglaigh na hÉireann,
General Headquarters, Dublin
30 November 1921

To all Divisional Commandants,

Some time ago, you have, I presume, received a communication from the Minister of Defence [Cathal Brugha] offering you a commission with rank of commandant general. It might be inferred from this document that a new army was being formed, but this is not really so – the idea being to offer fresh commissions to certain officers. The whole situation has been examined into at a joint meeting of the cabinet and GHQ Staff and an understanding arrived at. You should write to the Minister of Defence accepting the commission.

Beir beannacht,
Eoin O'Duffy
For Chief of Staff [Richard Mulcahy]

[26L] [Letter from Charlie Daly to Tom Daly]

Dublin, 12 January 1922

To Tom Daly,

If he likes he (EOM: Liam Lynch)[9] can say that he cannot take orders from certain quarters, but I have to because my area is in a state of war. With the exception of the O/C Second Southern Division [Ernie O'Malley], de Valera and Dick Mulcahy met all the Divisional Commandants and a few Brigade O/Cs at the Mansion House on Tuesday night [10 January 1922].[10] The meeting was called at Dev's request.[11] He explained the arrangements to us. He said that the Republic and the Dáil still existed and while such was the case we were to carry on as the Republican Army. **[27R]** Liam can't see the point – he holds there is no Dáil now. I almost felt guilty of something when I saw Liam cry on Tuesday when making his statement before the President [de Valera]. I am glad however that he (EOM: Liam Lynch) understands me – we have [*sic*] a long chat about this morning … the police and Specials are out to get us. It would not matter one little bit, but it seems curious that we must risk our lives for the sake of a cause that has been handed over to the enemy. Of course the northerners must fight for their existence under whatever government is in power.

[27R] [Letter from Charlie Daly]

Dublin, 19 Jan[uary] 1922

Though I did not sign the document demanding a convention because my views were not representative of my division,[12] I told Rory O'Connor that I was in agreement with it.[13] Duffy came out with this yesterday. Larkin (9 February 1922) and Donaghy, Six-County men had a solicitor to represent them, but we did not, and they asked for a couple of 2nd Northern Officers, who were in the Curragh as internees.

Charlie Daly, born 10 August 1896. 1913 Joined Cullans Company.

1914–1917 Adjutant of Currans Company. 1917 Arrested in August.

November refused to recognise the court, went on the run

1919: Released, adjutant of Firies Battalion. 1919–20 Brigade Quartermaster and then organiser of the Dáil loan.

1920: August: sent by GHQ to Tyrone: 12 January 1921 arrested in Dublin but released in March.

[46L] [Letter from Deputy Chief of Staff Eoin O'Duffy to Charlie Daly]

Office of the Chief of Staff,
General Headquarters,
Beggars Bush Barracks,
Dublin 4 March 1922

To:
Commandant C O Daly
Late O/C 2nd Northern Division,

A chara,

Following the meeting of the 2nd ND and Brigade Officers held here on Thursday [2 March 1922], I have decided to transfer you from the position of division commandant to that of organiser on the Director of Organisation's Staff, which position you held previous to your appointment.[14]

I should state at the outset that it was not my intention at any time to retain you in this position, and on my being called to GHQ from the 2nd

ND, I appointed you temporary in my place, which position you held since.

I desire to take this opportunity to express my appreciation of the work you have done in the divisional area under most difficult circumstances: at the same time, I feel that you are better fitted for the position of organiser than that of chief executive divisional officer.

Furthermore, I always considered that local men were better suited for such positions in every part of Ireland where proper men could be secured. It was not possible to get a local man capable of filling this position in the 2nd Northern Area until the return from Dartmoor of Commandant [Tom] Morris.[15] Immediately on his return I considered that he should be placed in a responsible position on the staff with a view to eventually putting him in charge of the division.

I regret that two out of the three brigade commandants present at Thursday' meeting should have stated that they had not confidence in you.[16]

I think, however, that what they meant by that statement was that they had not confidence that you would be better able to control the division than a local man.

The 2nd and 3rd [Belfast, Antrim and North Down] Northern Divisions will, in my opinion, be the two principal fighting areas in the country, being exclusively inside six-county area. The other Northern Divisions have quite a lot **[46R]** of their territory outside the area.

I did not pay very much attention to the complaints that were made on Thursday [2 March 1922], but I am not satisfied that you experienced sufficient control. I note that you have been (to) the different areas, but it is not enough for a divisional commandant to visit only one or two brigade council meetings in four months; it would not, in a place like the 2nd ND, be much to visit each of the four brigades monthly, it should be possible to visit them twice monthly. Your Adjutant [Frank Stronge] and Quartermaster [Joe McGurk] paid practically no visits at all.

Your answer to this was that your reports furnished by your brigade commandants in so far as they stated that no divisional officers attended are false. If these reports are false, they should not have been passed through your hands and been sent here without some explanation.

Neither am I satisfied that the activities carried out in that division are in proportion to those carried out in other areas with no more arms than No. 2 Northern.

If after a trial I find that Commandant Morris is not equal to the heavy responsibility now placed on his shoulders, I may ask one of the Southern Divisional Commandants to take charge there, as our officers realise they are national soldiers.

Please let me have my reply by return to the matter of your appointment on the Director of Organisation's Staff,

Mise,
Eoin Ó Dubhthaigh
Ceann Foirne

[Letter from Charlie Daly to Chief of Staff Eoin O'Duffy]

Whelan's Hotel
55 Eccles Street
Dublin
8 March 1922

To: Chief of Staff,
IRA,
Beggars Bush Barracks,

A Chara,

I have to acknowledge receipt of your communication (Ref No N/18) of the 4 March 1922.

After what occurred at the meeting of the Divisional and Brigade Officers of the 2nd ND at Beggars Bush on the 2 [March 1922], **[47L]** this communication has given me no small amount of surprise. If the statements made by you there were accurate, I should not be fit to be offered any position of responsibility in the Army.

After hearing all sorts of ridiculous complaints, which you tried to make the most out of, you accused me of being the only divisional commandant in Ireland who brought politics into the army; of being insubordinate; of trying to obstruct GHQ and of imputing my removal to what you called traitorous motives of GHQ. Notwithstanding all these grave accusations you now offer me a position on the Director of Organisation's Staff.

In this communication you give a different reason for my removal to the ones you gave at the meetings at Beggars Bush. There you tried to make it appear at first before my Staff and Brigade Officers that it would be because of certain complaints which you received. When these, as a means, failed, you stated 'twas because of my youth and inexperience. Now you gave an altogether different reason. I will deal with the one about divisional control further on. You state here that my appointment as O/C 2nd ND was only temporary, and that 'twas never your intention at any time to retain me in that position.

'Tis very strange that this should be the first time that I have heard that the appointment was only temporary. Neither at the time that you handed over command to me (last May I think) nor any time since have I heard that this was so. If it were, or if I was not capable of commanding the division, I should have been changed last October or November when we were threatened with a resumption of hostilities. That was the time when the very best officers that could be procured should have been put in command of such an area as the 2nd ND – a division which was expected to witness, and which you say is to witness, the horrors of war more so than any part of Ireland. Concerning your complaint about sufficient control and supervision not having been exercised in the division, I **[47R]** have admitted that there was not. From the time I took over command until last October, I, with an Adjutant who you stated at Beggars Bush was useless, and Divisional Quartermaster administered the division. There was no complaint then, that we were not doing our duty. If any dissatisfaction were expressed, it was never suggested that we were to blame. There is no complaint about the month of November. During the month of December, I was not able to visit all the brigade councils as usual, though I did manage to visit those in Tyrone. This was because of my having to come down to Dublin to attend meetings which used up a good deal of time.[17] But even though I were absent myself I saw that the other divisional officers constantly and regularly visited each brigade area. I seldom or never had the brigade councils visited by other staff officers; for I always made it a point to visit them personally. I kept the other divisional officers strictly to their own departments, so that the Divisional Training Officer [Edward Conway], Divisional Adjutant [Frank Stronge], Divisional Quartermaster [Joe McGurk], Divisional Engineer [Tom Kelly] and Divisional Medical Officer [Edward King] and other officers only visited brigades to attend meetings, give instructions to the officers of their respective departments.

Since Christmas it was impossible to carry on with the same regularity or exercise the same supervision. In the first place it was out of the question to keep the Divisional headquarters any longer established owing to the increased activities of the armed forces of the 'Northern Government'. In December two brigade camps were raided and several arrests made. Next to the Divisional Training Officer, Divisional Medical Officer, Divisional Transport Officer [Joseph Donnelly] and several brigade and battalion officers were arrested at a brigade review in No. 2 Brigade area in the first week in January.[18] These with the arrests in December meant a loss of twenty important officers to the division since upwards of twenty-five men in all have been arrested in the area.

Since then the small remnant of divisional staff consisting of the O/C, Adjutant, Quartermaster, Assistant Adjutant, Assistant Engineer, Assistant Quartermaster and Supply Officer have had **[48L]** to work under what were practically war conditions. To make matters worse the Divisional Adjutant [Frank Stronge] fell ill in the middle of January and has been away from the division since; and I contracted an attack of pneumonia at the end of the same month while doing a tour of the division on a bicycle. Since that time though I have been in constant touch with GHQ and my brigades through the Assistant Divisional Adjutant. I have been unable to take an active part in the affairs of the division. Previous to my illness I was delayed a whole fortnight in Dublin in January to attend meetings.[19]

Having practically no divisional staff, no divisional headquarters; illness of divisional officers; constant enemy activities; it is any wonder that meetings of brigade councils were not visited as usual and that the same supervision was not exercised over the division. Added to these, [this sentence was restructured] increasing demoralisation and slackness which set in, in almost every unit in the area as a result of partition and disappointments about supplies of arms. Another problem with which the division was handicapped was a lack of funds. Latterly the divisional staff have had to use up their own salaries in order to carry on at all.

Despite these obstacles I made the best use I could of the staff at my command. I established the Assistant Divisional Adjutant in a house near to the old divisional headquarters. His position was known to all brigade commandants and he was also in close and constant touch with me until I was removed from command. At the same time, I started a tour of the division intending to visit meetings of battalion councils in each brigade area. I had got through Nos. 1 and 2 Brigades when I fell ill. The Divisional Quartermaster, Assistant Divisional Quartermaster and Supply Officer established separate headquarters in another part of the division, and carried out work as usual. The Assistant Divisional Engineer supervised Engineering, and at the time I left had brought that service up to a standard not hitherto reached.

About the monthly report forms – the report forms in question **[48R]** did not pass through my hands. Those for December were sent in by the Divisional Adjutant and those for January by the Assistant Divisional Adjutant.

As regards the complaints made by O/C No. 4 Brigade [Seán Haughey], though it proved that there was nothing in them, they might never have been made, had you not diverted the arms sent to Dundalk for my division into Monaghan. I told you before anything occurred that I feared that this might cause trouble, as the officers had been much dissatisfied over the question of arms and supplies. What I feared happened. The O/C No. 4 Brigade to whom I had promised this supply thought that I was responsible for the arms being sent into Monaghan and immediately communicated with you. He got together all the complaints possible against me and the divisional staff. You denied at the meeting that he made the complaints after the transference of the arms. I have looked into the matter and have found that the Divisional Quartermaster [Joe McGurk] acquainted him of the fact of the arms being sent to another [5th Northern] Division on 17 February and it was on 19 February he made the complaints. I saw this Officer (O/C No. 4 Brigade) a few days before I came to Dublin. When he stated that 'twas 'only all a cod' trying to carry on without arms and that he would supply no more reports to divisional headquarters until he got them. I am not at all surprised that one or two brigade commandants should lack confidence in me. They found that I had deceived them about arms. On the strength of promises made by you I had told them time after time that supplies were coming. I quite agree with you that a local man may be better able to control the division and may perhaps receive more confidence than I did. Major [Tom] Morris will have a better chance than I had in that respect. I was a stranger – a southerner – the principal characteristic of most northerners is their suspicious attitude towards all strangers.

While admitting this I can I think at the same time claim that, for a stranger, who did not very well understand the temper **[49L]** of the Ulster people, I had and still have the confidence of my officers and men as much as many divisional commandants, that I know, have in divisions of which they are natives and that I can claim more confidence from my junior officers than some officers on GHQ Staff can claim from theirs.

I am glad you say you did not pay much attention to the complaints made, but to me and to the majority of the officers present it appeared that you did until I proved that there was nothing in them, or if there was, the blame did not altogether attach to the Divisional Commandant and Staff – instance the complaints about grenades without necks or detonators, signal lamps supplied without bulbs, broken revolvers, and cheddar which proved to be pot chlorate. After I had met and quashed these complaints you would not allow me to proceed any further tho' you promised to do so at the beginning. You also went back on your promise about allowing me to see written complaints which had signatures. When I protested against this unfairness I was accused of insubordination and threatened with the guard room. I am glad of the opportunity of dealing with these matters now, without being accused of insubordination or threatened with arrest. I take this opportunity also to state that I was in no way insubordinate on that occasion. Though given good reason, I was not so because I fully realised our relative positions.

You state that you are not satisfied that the activities carried out in the division are in proportion to those carried out in others with no more arms than in No.2 Northern. In reply to this I hold that more activities were carried out in the division – which in this respect means only the part of Tyrone which I commanded and a small portion of South Derry (I had nothing to do with Derry until a few weeks before the Truce) than in some of the Eastern and Midland Divisions. Tyrone and Derry did more **[49R]** in the war than several of the counties now included in these areas. I, by no means want to claim that the division did its share in the fight but taking into consideration the fact of having to contend with a hostile civilian population with superior equipment backed up by regular forces, and the apathy of our own civilian population, this area did far more than several southern counties situated under far more favourable circumstances.[20]

Before closing I wish to repeat the statement I made at the meeting at Beggars Bush – It is this, that the reason or motive for my removal are not the ones which you state. My reasons for this statement are these; you knew my attitude towards the Treaty and where I would be in the event of a division at the Convention [scheduled for 26 March 1922] (I informed you what side I would be on) a dual command existed in the division; your having interviewed junior officers and civilians at Beggars Bush from my area without my knowledge; your being in direct communication with one of my Brigade O/C's, also without my knowledge; and because of the way the meeting of Divisional and Brigade Officers was conducted as well as the matter in which I was treated there.

It is because of these facts that I have taken up my present attitude. I hope that you will not take it that I am writing this in any spirit of insubordination or that I want to obstruct GHQ – if I wanted to do this I could go about it in a more effective manner than in writing a communication like this or making statements at a meeting at Beggars Bush.

Had you given the reason that you give in this communication or the one you gave at the end of the meeting instead of handling the case as you did, we would both have spared a good deal of trouble. At Beggars Bush you practically kicked me out of the command and twice threatened me with the guard room in the presence of my junior officers. I am certain that the late **[50L]** Chief of Staff [Richard Mulcahy] would have acted in a different manner.

The rank by the way if I remember rightly, before being appointed Divisional Commandant was Divisional Vice Commandant but this does not matter for as I told you the other night I was not in the Army for a job or for any salary connected with one. If it were not otherwise I would only be too glad to be relieved of a dangerous position in the North – no matter with what circumstances my removal was attended – for the safer and more comfortable one which you offer me at Beggars Bush. I joined the Volunteers in 1913 through patriotic motives and for an ideal and have held different ranks in the Army since. While I remain in the Army, I hope that unselfish considerations will make me forget that or work for selfish motives.

The reason that I have written at some … [length] many details is that because I expect that this document will go before the other officers of GHQ Staff some of whom are not acquainted with the circumstances of my removal by you.

If the administration of the division has not been satisfactory an impartial inquiry should be held and the responsibility attached to the responsible persons. I will be satisfied with the result of that.

Mise do chara

[24L] [Letter from Charlie Daly, possibly to Tom Daly]

Whelan's Hotel,
20 March 1922

… I felt it very much to have left the fellows (EOM: in the 2nd ND) up there now when the trouble is just commencing. There are a good many decent fellows there and I would have liked to have taken my chances with them. A very successful job was taken off in Tyrone yesterday morning and a couple of others were to be done last night in Derry.[21] Rather hard luck for me to leave there when my work was just commencing to bear fruit. I have heard nothing from GHQ since nor don't expect to. O'Duffy was very disappointed I believe that I did not take up the job of chief organising officer on the staff. His disappointment I am sure was more for his own safety than for mine.

[50L] [Letter from Charlie Daly to Richard Mulcahy]

Dublin,

To: Minister of Defence [Richard Mulcahy],
Dáil Éireann

22 March 1922

A chara,

Enclosed are copies which I have sent to the Chief of Staff [Eoin O'Duffy]. I have received no reply to the one of the 8 [March 1922] and unless the manner of my removal from command of the 2nd ND is dealt with in the way I have asked in to-day's I may be reluctantly obliged to put the whole matter into the hands of the press.

Mise le meas,
Cormac Ó Dálaigh

[50L] [Letter from Charlie Daly to Chief of Staff Eoin O'Duffy]

Whelan's Hotel,
Eccles Street,
Dublin,

To Chief of Staff [Eoin O'Duffy],
IRA,
Beggars Bush Barracks,
Dublin

22 March 1922

A chara,

Since I stated at the meeting of the officers of the 2nd ND at Beggars Bush on the 2 [March 1922] and later in my communication of the 8 [March 1922] to you that the reason for my removal from command of the division was because of political motives, I have received information which proves beyond very little doubt that that statement was correct.

On my journey to the North on the 11 [March 1922], I met the O/C No. 4 Brigade [Seán Haughey] at Portadown [Armagh] (11th instant). He expressed regret for his part in the affair, and said he has now realised that he had been fooled. He told me that at an interview that he had with you that morning you informed him that you were not responsible for my removal but had to do it on instructions from the Minister of Defence [Richard Mulcahy] who had taken exception to some statement I had made at a meeting of Divisional O/Cs in Dublin [10 January 1922].

I can quite understand why it was that you did not give this reason – which is the real one – to me and why you should have gone to so much trouble in finding other.

I met the O/C No. 3 Brigade [Patrick Diamond, but EOM writes Seán Larkin] the following day. He informed me that you told the new Divisional O/C [Tom Morris] that you had only been waiting for an opportunity to remove me. This officer (O/C No. 3 Brigade) said he 'was disgusted with the whole business and that if he saw anymore of this crookedness he would make a clean breast of what he knew.'

In view of the fact that you have yourself given plenty to show that my statement was correct, is it not strange that you should have threatened me with arrest on the first occasion that I made it. It is strange also that this information should have been supplied by two officers whom you said had not confidence in me.

The least that you can do now in justice is to supply my brother officers and the officers of the Northern Divisions with the same reason for my removal that you gave to the present **[51L]** Divisional O/C and the O/C No. 4 Brigade. Unless you do this I feel that I may be compelled to submit all this correspondence, with a statement of the events which proceeded my removal, to the press.

Mise le meas

[Letter from Chief of Staff Eoin O'Duffy to Charlie Daly]

Office of the Chief of Staff,
General Headquarters,
Beggars Bush Barracks, Dublin

Commandant O'Daly,
Whelan's Hotel,
Eccles Street,
Dublin

24 March 1922

A chara,

In reply to yours of the 8 [March 1922] and 22 [March 1922], I have only to state that you have been transferred from the position of Commandant, 2nd ND, to that of organiser with the rank of commandant because I consider you better suited for the latter position. I gather from your letter of the 8 [March 1922] that you do not accept this position.

As regards your publicising the correspondence in the press, I would not be surprised at anything I might see there nowadays and neither will it annoy me.

Mise le meas,
Eoin Ó Dubhthaigh
Ceann foirne

[Letter from Secretary to the Minister of Defence to Charlie Daly]

In reply please quote (ref A 1476)
Department of Defence,
Cormac Ó Dálaigh,
Whelan's Hotel,
Eccles Street,
Dublin,
25 March 1922,

A Chara,
The Minister of Defence desires me to say that your letter of the 22 [March 1922] has been duly received.

Beir beannacht,
Rúnaí

[22R] [Letter from Charlie Daly]

Dublin, Monday morning [8 May 1922]

I came down here yesterday by car with the O/C Seán Lehane and a few more of the lads ... we are going back tomorrow ... 'Twas a very tragic affair but the blame lies wholly with Joe Sweeney the Free State Divisional O/C. Like some of the other Free State crowd he has been interfering with our men up there. He had arrested a couple of men for carrying out the [Belfast] boycott and on a few occasions had held up and had disarmed some of our fellows. If we are to do anything against the Specials [Ulster Special Constabulary] this should end. So Lehane and I went over to him this day week. We told him that we were not in Donegal to fight him and that if his HQ were not going to fight in the Six Counties neither it nor he should interfere with us who were. He told us that he did not recognise us at all and went on about his army being the army of the 'govt.' (government) and so on. We wanted him to face facts or there would be trouble, but he said he did not care and would carry out orders no matter what happened. I knew Joe well so I did my very best to try and make some arrangement so that we would not have the same things happening as there were in 'other parts'. 'Twas no use and more than this his [Adjutant], a Belfast chap named [Tom] Glennon, said that we were their enemies.[22] On account of this attitude 'twas inevitable that there would be trouble of some sort. On Thursday morning a small party of our men raided about Buncrana [Inishowen, Donegal].[23] As they were taking the car to a motor garage **[22L]** and rifle fire was opened on them from the surrounding houses without a moment's notice.[24] One of our fellows was shot through the lung and a little girl was shot and some civilians of the Free State [at the same time as this happened around fifty of our men were on hand in Newtowncunningham[25] near the Border where they were billeted that morning after a couple of raids into the Six County area the previous night].[26] On hearing of this cowardly attack in Buncrana, they decided on going there and giving the Free Staters ten minutes to surrender their barracks there. Just as they were about to start out 'twas reported that lorries were coming. Being near the border, 'twas thought that they might be Specials, so the order to take cover was given. When 'twas seen who were in the lorries some of these men came out on the road and called on the lorries to halt. Instead of halting the Free Staters opened fire and the row began with the result as you have seen in the papers. None of our men were hit although there [were] some close shaves. The press of course made it appear that there was a deliberate ambush.[27] It was lucky that there were not more killed.[28] This party of Free State men on their way to Buncrana to attack our fellows who they thought were … [USC] at least the officers were, for the men were told when starting out that they were going to the Border to fight the Specials.

Since this affair I understand [Joseph] Sweeney is very anxious for peace, but had he been half as anxious a few days earlier no lives would have been lost … I don't like though about Florrie [O'Donoghue] and the others stating that because the majority of the people being in favour of the Free State that we should accept it too.[29] There is great danger that this may cause a split in our part of the army … On account of the Press and the murder verdict in the Donegal affair … When I get back I will see Sweeney **[23R]** and try to come to some understanding with him. A great old friend of mine in Tyrone has been murdered by the Specials [on 3 May 1922]. It is [John] McCracken, 'twas in his house I was nursed when I had the flu. He was a fine old man and we were great friends. The poor man was about eighty …[30]

Besides being a GHQ organiser I am Deputy O/C to Lehane (If both Free State and Republicans might concentrate on Ulster there would be no fighting among themselves in the South but a few amadáin like McEoin (Seán) who are the cause of the whole trouble.[31]

[25R] [Letter from Charlie to Tom Daly][32]

HQ 1st ND,
Raphoe,[33] Donegal
20 May 1922.

Dear Tom … I wanted to see you badly about getting men up from home. Cork has already sent up about a dozen picked men and others are coming.[34] There is only one Kerryman here so far … Our side is losing ground here every day because we are unable to do more. This is the case especially within the border. We have only one brigade now in the old 2nd Northern.[35] One of the four brigades there went at the start. The others held out for a long time, but when they saw that the Free State Brigade was getting more assistance from GHQ than we were able to give them they went over. The last brigade that went, 'twas only last week, remained loyal to the Executive until 'twas almost impossible to carry on.[36] It had three or four flying columns of about one hundred men who were being hunted for their lives. Their own people, that is the civil population, would not feed them. The doctors and hospitals had refused to attend to the sick and wounded without payment. The men were without boots or clothes. We could give them practically no help so it is no wonder that they should go over to Beggars Bush, from which hard cash they are being supplied with arms.

The fact of the fellows in the Six Counties going Free State does not matter a big lot for they will fight anyway. 'Tis in order to be in a position to fight that they have gone to that side. We are certain to have them later when they have got the arms for its well-known that Beggars Bush will not risk the Treaty by carrying on the fight in Ulster. It may make things hard there for a little while. Its shows by the way that **[25L]** they have an interest in the people there and for practical reasons. The Free State business within the border is altogether different for what 'tis outside. In the rest of the country the majority of the fellows have gone Free State for the sake of pay and an easy time, but in the six counties they have gone Free State for the sake of arms and financial assistance. Propaganda and arguments don't count there and as far as I can see we may as well go back home if more assistance is not forthcoming. So far we have got little help from Dublin. They have given a few rifles and a little ammunition which does not go far so much now in the North. Our only help now is in the First Southern Division. If ye could send up about 50 or 100 rifles a couple of machine guns and some good men, we could go ahead without looking either to the Free State or republicans within the border for co-operation. At the moment we can do nothing. By Beggars Bush orders the fellows within [the border] are keeping quiet for the present and 'tis out of the question for us to act alone, although Seán Hegarty has plenty of stuff the damn clerk refused to give us anything and as for Florrie [O'Donoghue] he is waiting to see how his negotiations will go. [37] The Free State crowd has given us no trouble, since the Newtowncunningham affair [4 May 1922] has worked out better than I expected. Even though an agreement is not reached we don't fear them very much up here.

(EOM: Charlie Daly was sent to Tyrone in the autumn of 1920 as an organiser. Later he was appointed vice O/C of the 2nd ND. In June he was appointed O/C 2nd ND. Eoin O'Duffy was then at GHQ. Fresh commissions were issued in November 1921 and Charlie was then appointed the O/C with the rank of Commandant General. The O/C of the No. 3 Brigade referred to in March 22 of 1922 was the late Seán Larkin.)

[P132/23R] [Letter from Charlie Daly]

Clarence Hotel, Dublin
Tuesday [20 June 1922]

… there was a Convention in Dublin on Sunday. The Army question is in a worse mess than ever, and everybody is sick and disgusted.[38] The worst of it is that people on our side have made a muddle of the whole thing. We don't know where we stand at present and so far as we in Donegal are concerned I don't see that we have any business being there any longer. We will probably go back there for a few days to wind up things and then go home for some time.

(EOM: Seán Hoy Coalisland [Tyrone] in Donegal or a column) Drumboe Castle.

[20R] [Letter from Charlie Daly]

Glenveagh Castle[39] [Donegal],
13 July 1922,

I found things completely disorganised when I got back and they were not much better when the rain came on unexpectedly. [Seán] Lehane[40] [O/C Republican1st ND] and most of the responsible officers were in Dublin at the last convention.[41] A few of them got back about a week later, but nearly all the Corkmen are still away.[42] Lehane got here a couple of days ago.[43] He went first to Cork and then came up through the West. He had to walk from Sligo to North Donegal. I had no intention of attacking the Staters and they knew it, but still they attacked us treacherously when they thought that they had the advantage of us.[44] Afterwards when we got into the mountains and we had the advantage of them. Joe Sweeney[45] [O/C Free State 1st ND] came by begging to me for a settlement. His terms were that we would evacuate all positions, our men could retain their arms, and men who had come from the South would have been allowed to return home with arms which they brought up with them. I wouldn't agree on any account and Sweeney went away in a desperate fix. I gave him to understand that we would fight just as hard as ever we fought against the Tommies or the Tans.[46] We held back from taking life as long as we could, although we got plenty of provocation, but remaining passive too long would have been dangerous. So we started out a couple of days ago. Eight of your men consisting of Kerrymen and a couple of Cork men tackled over twenty Staters, killing two and wounding two others.[47] All the Free State troops in Donegal have got the wind up a 'twas only a matter of little time until the business is over. Most of the followers here (Free State) are a low crowd. They raid houses and abuse prisoners and civilians exactly as the Tans did.

The Kerry lads we have here are very good men, and are doing fine. Eleven others from Firies' Brigade were coming up to me but the war over took them in Galway where they are on active service now.[48]

[20L] [Letter from Charlie Daly]

Tír Chonaill [Donegal],
8 September 1922

I can never think of firing a shot against an Orange[man] Special or any English man while a Free Stater remains. Up here we have had a pretty rough time. Greatly outnumbered by the other side we were almost smashed at the start. There isn't much fight in the local fellows we had and they allowed themselves to be captured, our lads were mainly composed of our own fellows, has more than held its own against all the odds. No column in all Ireland has been up against more or has endured more hardship. Thankfully we now are again on a firm footing and are confident about our future. 'Tis is a grand job that the material up against us could not be worse or else we were encircled long ago. One evening a small party that I was in charge of was surrounded by about 150 of them. We got through under a hail of rifle and machine gun fire with only four of our men taken prisoner, while we killed two of theirs, about a week ago eight of our fellows were surrounded by over one hundred.[49] After eight hours fighting they got away without a scratch. We have only lost one man who died of wounds, so far as they have lost five killed and several wounded – nine killed altogether counting those at Newtowncunningham in this county … If [Joseph] Sweeney had only come to an arrangement like the ones in the S[outh], I would have been glad to come to an arrangement before he took action against us. We started an offensive a couple of days ago. A small section of our own column consisting County Kerry men and two Cork men ambushed over twenty Freestaters and wounded two others. On the same day two Free State Captains were wounded during a search in Inishowen [Donegal].

Besides not showing very many sympathies this county is very bad for columns on account of the poverty of the people. You have no idea how very poor most of this county is. We hate to have to billet on them, but they are very generous. Everybody even their own **[21R]** friends are disgusted with the Staters, especially on account of their cowardice and their Black and Tan tactics. There are only twenty of the boys from the Kingdom now left. [Patcheen] Clifford, [Martin] Quille and [Hughie] Brady were taken out of hospital and Patsy McElligot got run down in health and went home.[50] There is no respect for Red Cross here either. Our hospital raided several times and patients and staff made prisoners … We always manage to get enough grub and sleep even though we hardly ever see a piece of meat and we rarely sleep at night. Rough as times are here I would suffer this place to the Six Counties … I do hope that my friend Owen [O'Duffy] will get his wings clipped in the South … he is one of the most unscrupulous of their side …[51] However, we managed to find a priest a month ago to hear our confessions … a good priest up on a mission Fr [William?] Hackett S. J. of Limerick, when this business started.

Do you know who was up here to me on a message a few days after fighting started? Nora Brick [University Branch, Cumann na mBan], Seán Lehane was away and I was in charge at the time. I did my best at the time to avoid trouble here, but Joe Sweeney attacked the men without the least motive. He afterwards asked for an interview with me which I granted. He realised that we would be able to give him a certain amount of trouble and hadn't much heart for fighting.

[Note from Charlie Daly]

Drumboe Castle, Stranorlar
[20] November 1922

For one thing anyway, I am having a good rest

[Note from Charlie Daly]

[Drumboe Castle,]
8 December 1922

We had something over one hundred men at the start, but most of them were very poor stuff, word came that some of them were spies and traitors … in the course of a few weeks we were left with only thirty men and nearly all of them were strangers to the county. 'Twas that we got it in earnest we could only keep to the wildest and poorest houses, constantly on the move over mountains and bogs in all **[21L]** kinds of weather, and worse than all with little or no local assistance and very little sympathy. The few people that were on our side though were very loyal, but the action of the clergy told on most of these in the end. There were always more people on the look out to betray us than were otherwise. The county is so [ac]cursedly poor that we could hardly get enough to eat. We were often glad when we could get potatoes and salt or a bit of bread and a drop of tea … no matter what side their sympathies were with they were always hospitable. Often and often we wanted to make a stand and have done with it in one decent scrap … as the thing was becoming more hopeless every day, we made up our mind to get out of Donegal before 'twas too late, but before deciding on it finally, we thought that we would give it one more chance. Some divided into small groups and went to different areas. One group got captured within a few days and I had been out for little more than four weeks when the same thing happened [to] me. I just had a dispatch from Seán Lehane a few days before informing me that Ernie O'Malley had authorised him to evacuate and asking me to meet him.[52] I was on my way to meet him when I got captured. On account of my being about to leave, I was not quite careful as I might have been otherwise. Anyway, I considered that we were in a very safe place, and for the first time omitted putting on a guard.[53] The spot was safe enough alright, but we were tracked by local spies … we could have got across Donegal Bay into Sligo at any time, but we didn't want to give up here if there was the faintest chance of carrying on …

That's a good sign that they are in no hurry to deal with our case … I would far rather any day to be as the **[22R]** eight poor fellows who have been recently executed than to be in Dick Mulcahy's or the firing squad's boots.[54] They tried the high hand with us for a time in order to try to humiliate us, but that failed and we are being treated decently now. One or two of the officers and nearly all of the men with whom we are in contact are on the best of terms with us … kind as they were to us outside they are even kinder to us in person.

[24L] [Letter from Charlie Daly from imprisonment]

17 December [1922] Drumboe: one of the priests from the town came and heard our confessions last night, and we were at Holy Communion.[55]

February 1923: When have heard nothing from them since (the trial) and are waiting the result as calmly as if it weren't the important thing that it is to us (EOM: three times the rumour went out that they had been executed.)[56]

Drumboe Castle, 25 February 1923 (This man was working for a cousin of ours (EOM: what man?) in Dublin. Twelve full cartridges and blank cartridges [were given out], [there were] supposed to be three Ulster Specials and one Stater at the firing squad.)[57]

[24L] Drumboe Castle, 25 February 1923 … However, I think that the crisis is as good as over and with God's help we will all meet again.

Notes

DR PATRICK MCCARTAN

1 CI, December 1914 (TNA, CO 904/95).

2 George Gavan Duffy (1882–1951) was the son of the Young Irelander, Charles Gavan Duffy, and a prominent lawyer who defended Roger Casement in 1916. He was elected Sinn Féin TD for South County Dublin in 1918 and went to the Paris Peace Conference on behalf of the Dáil. As one of the Irish plenipotentiaries, he signed the Treaty, but resigned from the Free State government because of its conduct during the Civil War.

3 Alcibiades was an Athenian statesman (*c.*450–404 BC) who served Athen's arch-rival Sparta, before returning to Athens.

4 Joseph McGarrity (1874–1940) was born in Carrickmore. After emigrating to Philadelphia, he became the treasurer of the Clan na Gael. He played a central role in the Easter Rising and helped organise de Valera's American tour, eventually parting with long-term ally, John Devoy, in the process. He opposed the Treaty and engaged in a two-month tour of Ireland beginning on 12 February 1922. The event mentioned was a lunch in his honour in the Mansion House organised by Patrick McCartan.

5 Henry Wilson: see biographical sketch.

6 Liam Tobin: see biographical sketch.

7 Richard 'Dick' Mulcahy: see biographical sketch.

8 Born in Armagh, Fr Peter Elias Magennis was the general of the Carmelites in New York and supported Irish independence in America and Rome.

9 Gearóid O'Sullivan: see biographical sketch.

10 McCartan's pessimistic memorandum of his mission to Moscow to seek Russian support for Irish independence is available in 'Documents on Irish Foreign Policy, No. 89' (NAI' DFA ES Box 14 File 96).

11 Seamus O'Doherty (1882–1945) joined the IRB in Dublin in 1910. He and his wife, Katherine (or Kitty), were involved in republican politics prior to the Easter Rising.

After the Rising, Seamus played a role in reorganising the IRB. He was interned and went to Philadelphia, returning to Ireland when the Civil War broke out. Elsewhere, McCartan related how the idea of the Russia mission emerged in O'Doherty's home while they discussed international affairs with another Tyrone man, Kevin O'Shiel.

12 Ivan Maisky (1884–1975) was a Russian diplomat and was Ambassador to Britain when McCartan went to Russia.

13 Dr Jacob Osip Gavronsky (1878–1948) was a Russian-British physician and Provisional Government high commissioner in London before the Bolshevik revolution on 7 November 1917. Alexander Kerensky (1888–1970) was a Russian lawyer and politician who served as the second Minister-Chairman of the Russian Provisional Government between July and November 1917.

14 Laurence Ginnell (1852–1923) was an Irish nationalist politician, lawyer, and IPP MP for Westmeath North. He stood as an independent and was elected as a Sinn Féin TD in 1918. He opposed the Treaty.

15 Thomas Woodrow Wilson (1856–1924) was the twenty-eighth US president and the author of the fourteen points in a speech on 8 January 1918, which would form the foundation of peace based on the principle of self-determination.

16 On 22 January 1918, the British released republican prisoners on hunger strike in Mountjoy Gaol under what was known as the Cat and Mouse Act.

17 Diarmuid Lynch (1878–1950), from Co. Cork, was a member of the IRB Supreme Council for Munster and a staff captain in the GPO during Easter Week 1916. He was TD for Cork Southeast. He was the head of the Friends of Irish Freedom in America and fell out with de Valera when the President toured the USA. Lynch played no part in the Civil War, but remained neutral with other key figures such as Seán O'Hegarty.

18 Eoin MacNeill: see biographical sketch.

19 Liam Mellows: see biographical sketch.

20 Under the control of Clan na Gael leader John Devoy, the *Gaelic American* was the most prominent republican newspaper in America. Mellows had worked with Devoy in its offices, but increasingly distrusted the veteran Fenian, especially when he backed US involvement in the war.

21 After his election as President of the Irish Republic at the second session of Dáil Éireann in April 1919, de Valera went on an American fundraising and propaganda tour between June 1919 and December 1920. Although he managed to raise $5,500,000 from American supporters, de Valera also fell out with various Irish-American leaders, such as John Devoy and Judge Daniel F. Cohalan.

22 The Clan na Gael was formed after the failed IRB rising of 1867 to act as a replacement for the Fenian Brotherhood in the USA, which had split disastrously between the O'Mahony and Roberts factions. The Clan also acted as the means by which John Devoy reasserted his control on republican politics in America and came to exert significant financial influence over the IRB, its sister organisation in Ireland.

23 Cathal Brugha: see biographical sketch.

24 Count George Noble Plunkett (1851–1948) was the father of Joseph Plunkett, one of the seven members of the 1916 provisional government. He won the North

Roscommon by-election in February 1916 on a Sinn Féin abstentionist policy, although the renewed party itself did not formally exist until October that year. He was Minister of Foreign Affairs in the First Dáil. He opposed the Treaty and remained with Sinn Féin after the formation of Fianna Fáil in 1926.

25 On 6 February 1920, de Valera gave an interview to the *New York Globe*, which stated that Britain could treat Ireland as America treated Cuba, which under the Munroe Doctrine was not permitted to enter into a treaty with a foreign country. He was immediately criticised by Devoy and Cohalan. He sent McCartan back to Ireland to explain his position to the Dáil cabinet, whose more republican members, Brugha, Plunkett, and Markievicz, heavily criticised de Valera.

26 John Joseph O'Kelly, Sceilg or Seán Ua Ceallaigh (1872–1957), was a writer, journalist, republican, Irish-language activist, and member of the First and Second Dáil for Louth. Born 7 July 1874 on Valentia Island, Co. Kerry, he was editor of the influential pro-Sinn Féin *Catholic Bulletin*, president of Conradh na Gaeilge, and Dáil Minister for the Irish Language. He bitterly opposed the Treaty and was Sinn Féin president after de Valera founded Fianna Fáil.

27 Daniel F. Cohalan (1867–1946) was a prominent Irish-American politician, a New York supreme-court judge, and a close associate of John Devoy within the Clan na Gael.

28 Maxim Maximovich Litvinov (1876–1951) was a prominent soviet diplomat who served as soviet representative in Britain after the October Revolution. After his arrest in Britain, he served as roaming ambassador and his name was given to the Litvinov Pact of 1929, recognised as an eastern version of the non-aggression Kellogg–Briand Pact.

29 Georgy Vasilyevich Chicherin (1872–1936) was People's Commissar for Foreign Affairs in the Soviet government from March 1918 to 1930. The Anglo-Soviet Trade Agreement was an agreement signed on 16 March 1921, which ended the British blockade of the USSR.

30 Spelled 'Nuratova' by EOM, Santeri 'Santtu' Nuorteva (1881–1929) was a Finnish-born journalist and soviet diplomat. He had signed a proposed Treaty between the USSR and the Republic of Ireland with McCartan while in New York in May 1920. He was the head of the Anglo-American Division of the People's Commissariat of Foreign Affairs when McCartan visited Russia in 1921, but was arrested and imprisoned in June 1921, although subsequently released.

31 Robert 'Bob' Briscoe (1894–1969) of Leeson Street, Dublin, was the IRA's gunrunner in Germany as well as a Zionist. He served as a Fianna Fáil TD from 1927 to 1965.

32 Henry James 'Harry' Boland (1887–1922) was an IRB member who fought in Easter Week 1916. He was elected TD in the First Dáil for South Roscommon. As special envoy to the USA, he accompanied de Valera to Amercia. He opposed the Treaty and was killed, while unarmed, during his arrest at the Skerries Grand Hotel on 2 August 1922.

33 Arthur Griffith (1872–1922) was the originator of the Sinn Féin policy of abstention. He led the party by the same name prior to the Easter Rising. After 1916, he made way

for Éamon de Valera and held the position of vice-President. One of the signatories of the Treaty, he was President of the Second Dáil, but was largely subordinate to Mick Collins in the Provisional Government.

34 Spelled 'Beasly' by EOM, Piaras Béaslaí. See biographical sketch.

35 Francis Patrick 'Frank' Fahy (1879–1953) was the TD for Galway and served for nearly thirty-five years for Sinn Féin and then Fianna Fáil, before serving as Ceann Comhairle for nineteen years.

36 Patrick Sarsfield O'Hegarty (1879–1955) was born in Cork, but operated in republican circles in London. Writing as Sarsfield, he made significant contributions to the Dungannon Clubs and later the IRB paper *Irish Freedom*. He initiated a young Michael Collins into London republicanism and prior to the 1916 Rising acted as IRB Supreme Council delegate for southeast England.

37 John Devoy (1842–1928) was a leader of the 1867 IRB Rising. Exiled to America, he took control of the Clan na Gael, launched the New Departure with Davitt and Parnell and then reasserted his leadership of Irish-American republicanism after the Parnell split. The owner and editor of the *Gaelic American*, he was central to the 1916 Rising and also played a role in the War of Independence, eventually backing the Treaty.

38 Kitty O'Doherty née Gibbons was the wife of leading IRB man Seamus O'Doherty. She apparently was the ghost writer of Dan Breen's *My Fight for Irish Freedom*. She took a leading part in the Irish National Aid Association and Volunteer Dependents' Fund. Kitty related how, in mid-June 1916, the Irish Relief Fund of America sent John Archdeacon Murphy of Buffalo as a representative of Clan na Gael and John Gill of the Bronx as a representative of labour to deal with the issue of dependents of the Easter Rising. John Archdeacon Murphy was also the Buffalo delegate to the Clan na Gael Executive and later occupied the role of chairman.

39 Seán Ó Murthuile, of Cork, was secretary of the IRB Supreme Council after Collins reorganised it in 1917. Quartermaster General of the Free State army, Ó Murthuile unsuccessfully attempted to reconstitute the organisation after the Civil War.

40 Séamus Robinson (1888–1961) was an IRA leader from Tipperary who led the Soloheadbeg ambush on 21 January 1919. Elected as TD for Waterford–Tipperary East to the Second Dáil, he voted against the Treaty and was O/C of the ATIRA Southern Division. He later joined Fianna Fáil.

41 (James J.) Séamus Dwyer (1882–1922) served as Intelligence Officer for the IRA Dublin Brigade and a Sinn Féin judge. He was elected unopposed to the Second Dáil for Co. Dublin and supported the Treaty. He stood as a pro-Treaty Sinn Féin candidate at the 1922 general election but was not elected. On 20 December 1922, he was shot dead in his shop at 5 Rathmines Terrace, Dublin by the anti-Treaty IRA after the execution of Rory O'Connor, Liam Mellows, Joe McKelvey, and Richard Barrett.

42 Born in Edinburgh to Irish parents, William Joseph Marie Alois Maloney (1882–1952) was a neurologist and a member of the Irish independence movement in the USA. After the Easter Rising, Maloney resigned his commission in the British army and befriended many prominent supporters of Irish independence. He joined the

Clan na Gael and wrote a great deal of propaganda. He was a close associate of Patrick McCartan and much of McCartan's correspondence sits in the Maloney collection, NLI.

43 Dr James Ryan (1891–1970) from Wexford was a founding member of the Irish Volunteers and delivered MacNeill's countermand to Cork in 1916. He was elected to the First Dáil for Wexford. He later served as minister in several Fianna Fáil governments, most notably as Minister for Finance (1957–65) with Seán Lemass. See his interview with O'Malley, UCDA, P17b/91, 92, 94.

44 Collins was killed on 22 August 1922. He was transported by sea from Cork to Dublin and lay in state for three days. Half a million people purportedly attended his state funeral.

45 Mary Mac or Máire Nic Suibhne (1872–1942) was an educationalist and leading member of Cumann na mBan. She was elected to the Dáil for Cork Borough after the death of her brother, Terence, on hunger strike in 1920. She opposed the Treaty and became Sinn Féin president after de Valera formed Fianna Fáil.

46 Born in Wicklow, Tom Cullen was IRA GHQ 2nd Deputy Director of Intelligence. He supported the Treaty and was an officer in the Free State army, resigning in 1925. He died in a drowning accident in 1926.

47 Spelled 'Rodgers' by EOM, Monsignor John Rogers was pastor of St Patrick's Church, San Francisco, and a leading supporter of Sinn Féin.

48 Liam Tobin: see biographical sketch.

49 Eoin O'Duffy: see biographical sketch.

50 Henry Wilson: see biographical sketch.

CHARLIE DALY

1 Tom Daly was also interviewed by O'Malley. See UCDAP17b/132.

2 Mulcahy to O'Duffy, 14 March 1921 (UCDA, Mulcahy papers, P7a/17/111).

3 Charlie Daly, 'General report of training, 2nd ND', September 1921 (IMA, A/0664/8); Daly to battn commandants, 13 August 1921 (IMA, A/066/9); Daly to each brigade O/C, 27 August 1921 (IMA, A/066/10); Daly to each brigade adjt., 30 August 1921 (IMA, A/066/11); Daly to each brigade QM, 30 August 1921 (IMA, A/066/12); Daly, Training syllabus, August 1921 (IMA, A/066/13).

4 Charlie Daly was arrested in Dublin two weeks before Christmas 1920. He gave the name of a Kerryman, Moriarty, whom he had met on the train down to Dublin. Moriarty was the teacher at Ballygawley National School and had helped get medical attention for RIC wounded in an attack led by Daly at Ballygawley on 23 November 1920. He was told to remain in Kerry until Daly's release. Through the agency of Moriarty's school manager, a local 'loyalist' Catholic priest, Daly was released in early March 1921.

5 The four executed 'Drumboe martyrs' were Kerrymen Charlie Daly, Daniel Enright and Timothy O'Sullivan, and Derryman Seán Larkin. Dan Coyle (Donegal), Frank Ward (Donegal), James Donaghy (Derry), and Jim Lane (Cork) escaped execution.

6 Spelled 'Strong' by EOM. Vice O/C, Frank Stronge.

7 McGurk was a volunteer from Carrickmore, Co. Tyrone.

8 Cathal Brugha: see biographical sketch.

9 Liam Lynch: see biographical sketch.

10 Richard 'Dick' Mulcahy: see biographical sketch.

11 Éamon de Valera: see biographical sketch.

12 On 18 January, Minister of Defence, Richard Mulcahy, chaired a meeting of the GHQ Staff, divisional commandants, and some brigade commandants at which it was agreed that an IRA convention would take place within two months.

13 Rory O'Connor: see biographical sketch.

14 Major General Eamon 'Bob' Price was IRA Director of Organisations before the Truce and a Free State general stationed in Portobello Barracks.

15 Tom Morris: see biographical sketch.

16 The confusion regarding the number of brigades stems from the fact that No. 4 [Maghera] Brigade, O/C Seán Haughey, had only been created after March 1922. No. 3 Brigade (South Derry) was commanded by Patrick Diamond, but it appears clear that Seán Larkin, who later died with Daly, held this position before Morris' appointment and lost it as he went republican. Morris and his associates were adamant in the pension files that Larkin did not hold this position, but it appears he attended the meeting as Brigade O/C. The O/Cs for No. 1 (East Tyrone) and No. 2 (West Tyrone) Brigades, W. J. Kelly Jr and Michael Gallagher, supported Daly.

17 Daly was a high-ranking member of the IRB and attended Supreme Council meetings.

18 On 21 December 1921, the Specials broke up the IRA camp at Cranagh Hall. On 6 January 1922, they raided an IRA brigade review at Dromore, arresting most of the officers in the No. 2 Brigade in the process.

19 These were the series of IRA and IRB meetings surrounding the IRA's attitude to the Treaty.

20 By April 1922, there were some 4,300 B Specials in Co. Tyrone. There were over 1,500 RUC and A Specials. In addition, there were 650 men of the Rifle Brigade in Strabane, a military depot in Omagh and, after the Anglo-Irish Treaty, a battalion of the North Staffordshire Regiment at Clogher.

21 On 19 March 1922, twenty IRA volunteers raided Pomeroy Barracks. The same night, the South Derry Brigade raided Maghera Barracks.

22 Tom Glennon was a Belfast Volunteer, the son of an IRB man from a nationalist enclave in South Belfast. He was appointed full-time IRA organiser for Antrim in November 1920. Glennon escaped from the Curragh internment camp during the Truce and then made Adjutant of the 1st Northern Division in 1921. He supported the Treaty and generated a certain antipathy among republicans due to his role during the Civil War in Donegal.

23 Buncrana is a town on the Inishowen Peninsula, fourteen miles northwest of Derry City.

24 On 4 May 1922, five republicans under the command of Divisional Quartermaster, Joe McGurk, were attacked by Free State troops under the command of Joseph

McLaughlin while robbing the Ulster Bank. One republican was wounded while Esther Fletcher, a nine-year-old girl, died of her injuries.

25 Newtowncunningham is a village in the Lagan district, ten miles west of Derry City.

26 On 3 May 1922, two columns, one led by Seán Lehane, the other by Charlie Daly, carried out unsuccessful cross-border attacks, the former against a British installation between Burnfoot and Derry, the latter against a USC platoon at Molenan House, less than five miles southwest of Derry City.

27 This was contested by Tom Glennon at the inquest, but it appears that Free State forces did fire first, despite their own weak position.

28 Corporal John McGinley and Volunteers Eddie Gallagher, Daniel McGill, and Edward Murray were killed, while Packy Bryson, Jim Dawson, McCool, Sharkey, and Johnny Grant were wounded.

29 Florence 'Florrie' O'Donoghue: see biographical sketch.

30 John McCracken, a publican from Dungate, Kildress, was sixty-six according to the 1911 census, but he had only aged five years between the 1902 census and the 1911 census. He was killed by five USC on 6 May 1922 as a reprisal for the killing two days earlier of Special Constable William Thomas McKnight in an IRA ambush two miles east of his pub and farm.

31 Seán Mac Eoin: see biographical sketch.

32 This was Charlie's younger brother, Tom, who was Adjutant and then O/C Killarney Battalion, Kerry No. 2 Brigade, 1st Southern Division.

33 Raphoe (population in 1910: 804) is a town five miles west of Strabane close to the Tyrone–Donegal border.

34 Seán Lehane had already recruited veterans from the Bandon area in April.

35 This referred to the No. 2 (West Tyrone) Brigade, whose O/C Michael Gallagher was a member of the Executive and which operated close to ATIRA positions at Finner and Bundoran. The No. 3 (South Derry) and No. 4 (Maghera) had gone to GHQ in order to get arms and because of Daly's replacement as Divisional O/C with Tom Morris from the No. 3 Brigade area.

36 This specifically refers to a meeting in early May of the No. 1 Brigade where the Carrickmore and Dungannon Battalions sent word to Daly to get support, but received word back that he was unable to provide any, at which point the latter contacted GHQ while the No. 1 (Dungannon) Battalion remained with the Executive, many going on to fight with Daly and Lehane.

37 Seán O'Hegarty: see biographical sketch.

38 This is an apparent reference to the 3rd IRA Convention of 18 June 1922, when a split appeared to take place between the Four Courts Garrison and the 1st Southern Division.

39 Built in 1870 by local landlord John Adair, of the Derryveagh evictions, Glenveagh Castle sits within the eponymous national park on the border of Donegal's northwestern Gaeltacht between Churchill and Gaoth Dobhair. It was used as the headquarters of the anti-Treaty 1st Northern Division after their retreat following an attack by Free State forces under Joe Sweeney on 29 June 1922.

40 Seán Lehane (1897–1938) was born in Keilnascarta, Bantry, Cork. An Irish Volunteer from 1917, Lehane was a member of the 3rd Cork Brigade Flying Column and eventually commanded No. 3 Brigade of the First Southern Division under Liam Lynch. He was appointed divisional officer commanding the anti-Treaty 1st Northern Division in April 1922, which was eventually made up of anti-Treaty volunteers from the old pre-Treaty 1st and 2nd Northern Divisions (Donegal, Derry, and Tyrone). Lehane left Donegal in October 1922. For his interview with O'Malley, see UCDA P17b/108.

41 Just after the Sinn Féin pact election, a third IRA Convention met on 18 June 1922. It led to disagreements between the Four Courts garrison and Liam Lynch's 1st Southern Division, which were healed ten days later with the Free State attack on the Four Courts.

42 Executive Forces in the Four Courts had instructed leading IRA commanders from Cork to form the nucleus of a republican division that would attack the North in co-operation with the Free State forces, including Brigade commanders Mossy Donegan, Seán Fitzgearald, Séamus Cotter, as well as Denis Galvin (Bandon), Jim Lane (Clonakilty), Denis O'Leary, Billy O'Sullivan (Bantry), Tom Mullins (Kinsale), and John O'Donovan (Dunmanway); Seán O'Driscoll to Florence O'Donoghue, 11 April 1962 (NLI, MS 31301/9).

43 Lehane was at the Four Courts in anticipation of a northern offensive when the Free State attacked with British artillery on 28 June 1922 precipitating civil war, although the republican garrison actually believed a further joint-IRA offensive had been agreed (Moss Twomey to Florence O'Donoghue, 5 July 1952, NLI, MS 31423/6).

44 On 29 June, Free State forces surrounded the republican base at Finner Camp. After a two-hour gun battle in which two republicans died, the garrison surrendered. Buncrana Barracks surrendered the next day without a fight. Ballyshannon and Bundoran also surrendered with 200 republicans taken prisoner. Joe Sweeney wrote to Dick Mulcahy on 3 July 1922: 'Daly, late O/C 2nd Northern Division, is in Glenveagh. He informed us he does not wish to fight and will leave the area if ordered.' On 5 July 1922, Daly and Sweeney met in Churchill to discuss the terms outlined in Daly's dispatch to ATIRA GHQ.

45 Joseph Sweeney: see biographical sketch.

46 A reference to the British Army and the auxiliary police force, the Black and Tans, first deployed in March 1920 during the War of Independence.

47 On 11 July, a car carrying five Free State soldiers was ambushed at Drumkeen, near Stranorlar. Two Free State soldiers, McGinley and Jack Sweeney, were killed outright.

48 This was Daly's own area.

49 By early August 1922, Lehane abandoned the Divisional headquarters at Glenveagh with eighty men and formed four flying columns. Two columns of eight and fifteen men were captured in the south of the county. Free State forces captured the northeast column and the northwestern dumped their arms and were subsequently arrested.

50 Patrick Joseph McElligott was a long-term member of the IRB in Listowel and later Battalion O/C IRA. On 28 July 1922, Free State forces under the command of 1st ND

Adjutant, Tom Glennon, arrested six injured republicans from the Red Cross Hospital at Churchill. Martin Quille later claimed that the prisoners had been ill-treated.

51 Eoin O'Duffy: see biographical sketch.

52 Seán Lehane sent Daly a dispatch just prior to his capture on 2 November 1922: 'I have received an order from E. Ó Máille authorising us to leave Donegal at once and withdraw our men. I believe our work here is impossible.'

53 Daly and his column were staying in John Sharkey's house at Meenabaul near Gaoth Dobhair.

54 At the time of writing, eight republicans had been executed by the Free State: James Fisher, Peter Cassidy, Richard Twohig, and John Gaffney were killed in Kilmainham on 17 November 1922; Erskine Childers, Joseph Spooner, Patrick Farrelly, and John Murphy in Beggars Bush on 24 November 1922. That very day, and unbeknownst to Daly, Joe McKelvey, Dick Barrett, Rory O'Connor, and Liam Mellows were also shot.

55 This letter appears at the bottom of the page in O'Malley's notebook, but has been moved to maintain the chronology of the collection.

56 Charlie Daly was arrested on 2 November 1922 at John Sharkey's house. His court martial did not convene until 18 January 1923, when eight republicans were found guilty of possessing arms without proper authority, a sentence that carried the death penalty under the Army Emergency Powers Order. Sentence was not passed until after the unaccounted-for death of Captain Bernard Cannon on 10 March 1923. Daly, O'Sullivan, Enright, and Larkin were shot, Coyle, Ward, Donaghey, and Lane were not.

57 It appears that Commandant Sheerin was detail officer and the firing squad was made up of ex-British army. Joe Sweeney left Drumboe Castle before the executions were carried out.

3RD NORTHERN DIVISION (NORTH DOWN AND ANTRIM)

SEAMUS WOODS

(UCDA P17b/107, pp. 1–11, Nov./Dec. 1949)

Seamus Woods (1900–1978) was born near Downpatrick in 1900 and was a member of the local branch of the Irish Volunteers from 1914. In 1918, he moved to Belfast in search of work. After being forced out of Mackies in the Springfield Road because of his religion, he became a trainee accountant. He joined the IRA C Company, and one of Woods' first operations, commanded by Joe McKelvey, was the burning of the Income Tax Offices in the Custom House in the city centre. He also helped organise the execution of Swanzy in Lisburn, although he took no part in the operation. Woods formed part of the ASU that killed two members of the Auxiliaries at Roddy's Hotel, Belfast on 26 January 1921. The same unit killed three Black and Tans (RIC) and one plainclothes Special Constable in February/March 1921, as well as killing two Auxiliaries at Donegall Place on 23 April 1921. He also formed part of the party that shot dead murder gang member, RIC Constable Glover, on 10 June 1921.

Woods was at first unsure about the Treaty, but joined the Free State army on 1 February 1922 and succeeded Joe McKelvey as O/C 3rd ND, after the latter's removal by Eoin O'Duffy by March 1922. The Free State secured the Belfast IRA's loyalty through the creation of the City Guard, a salaried sixty-man unit, with fifteen men from each battalion, headed by Woods, which effectively replaced the existing ASU. Woods represented the Belfast IRA in a significant meeting with Collins and Mulcahy on 2 August, when the northern pro-Treaty IRA were stood down. He became disillusioned and critical of the Free State treatment of northern nationalists, especially after Collins' death.

Nevertheless, by September and October 1922, Woods still operated a Free State army recruitment centre out of the Hibernian Hall at the bottom of Clonard Street, West Belfast. He was active in Kerry in the spring of 1923, during the atrocities carried out by the Dublin Guards. A Free State colonel, Woods was arrested during a visit to Belfast, charged with the killing of William Twaddell MP (22 May 1922) and then interned on 14 November 1923. He was the last prisoner to leave the *Argenta* when it was decommissioned in January 1924 and secured his release on 17 April 1924. Woods took no real part in the Army Mutiny, although he appeared to sympathise with some of their grievances. He left the Free State army on 15 July 1926, while serving at the rank of colonel, and established a successful bookmaking business. He died on April Fool's Day 1978.

[1920–1]

[3L] I was born in Downpatrick. I came into Belfast where I joined C Company. Before the order to burn the customs and excise offices was issued, I was called to a meeting of the officers of the Belfast Brigade.[1] Seán O'Neill,[2] a tall, strongly built decent fellow was there and Seán MacEntee.[3] They considered that shortly they would be arrested. For this reason, they asked me to undertake the destruction of the outlined offices. I agreed to this. Then when I was about to leave the meeting I was told that I would have to submit plans of these offices. I refused. 'If you expect to be arrested,' I said, 'then why should you expect me to ask to control my activities?' I refused absolutely to give them any information about my plans, **[4R]** but in the end they asked me to carry out my own plans. The Customs House was one of the places we had to burn [on 4 April 1920], so we met there '...' of us in postal uniform. We used petrol and when I flung the bottle, the blast from the ignition full flung me out of the room and singed my eyebrows. At the time I knew nothing about the proper use of petrol. Then we went to Danny McDevitt's to change into civilian clothes.[4] He was a tailor in Musgrave Street and there's a story about that. There was a fellow present when we were changing clothes. He wasn't belonging to the Irish Volunteers but anyone who came into or who stayed to talk in McDevitt's must be right, I thought, for he was a socialist and all kinds of reds came in there.

[7L] A one-night hit-up; then we were surrounded. We didn't do a lot that night. 75–80 [per cent unionist] against 25–20 [per cent nationalist] in Belfast.

We had good lads but we wouldn't tackle a job unless it was successful.

Then there were arrests and a number of our fellows were in for a long time after that. In July 1920, rioting broke out after [James] Craig had made a speech to the [Queens] island that they didn't want any Sinn Féiners working on the island, and Catholics working there had to swim for it. Then the factories took it up. Was there labour trouble at the time?[5]

[8R] In the County Down we burned empty barracks attacking Ballykinlar and attacked Crossgar Barracks.[6] We blew it in with explosives between two and four [a.m.] and walked back seventeen miles to Belfast and got in at seven. In our days there were no friendly people on the way back. Crossgar took place in May 1920.

Then the pogroms started. The Catholics organised in their own areas and a defence force had to be organised so we took in the ex-soldiers into the Irish volunteers.

There was a nominal split in Belfast. Paddy Thornberry, who was in a teaching College, [St] Patrick's, came up as a cadet, was divisional adjutant.[7] I suggested they'd take a vote in every company and the numbers abide by the majority. I think we took the vote and the vote result would have been overwhelmingly for us.

Roger McCorley would get a vote no matter what. They did [not] stop operations. Christ, they hadn't started.

Easter Saturday 1920.[8]

Ballynahinch Barracks [Co. Down] occupied [March 1920].[9]

Crossgar Barracks [Co. Down] [June 1920].

Income tax offices misfired [4 April 1920].

Pogrom June 1920 to 1922.

Sept 1920: Disarming police.

Murder of the brothers Duffin Pat and Dan,[10] [Ned] Trodden [and] John Gaynor (Seán Gaynor).[11]

[8L] 26 January 1921: Auxiliaries escorted the Kings to give evidence on Michael Grey for shooting Sergeant Fallon in Ballymote.[12] He was awaiting trial in Belfast Gaol.

[In] February, three Black and Tans who had come in from Gormanstown [Co. Meath] to drive back an armoured car or Lancia.[13] That was the night the three boys were killed. About [a] hundred yards from Musgrave Street Barracks between a pub in Arthur Square and Musgrave Square three of them were got. I had two guns on me and I was a hundred yards, 220 and 440 yards' champion sprinter. It was 9:30 and you had to run up the street as it is dead centre of the city. The Castle junction is the dead centre. A man followed me but he was tripped up by Macready. It was when he was tripped up he was a quarter mile sprinter. There were two or three other lads with me but they got **[9R]** frightened.[14]

February or March 1921: District Inspector Ferris.[15] Roger was there with three fellows who fired and ran but Roger waited until he was sure the job was completed. (EOM: What was Ferris connected with? Was he from Bandon?)

Connor was transferred.

Swanzy the County Inspector [was] transferred to Downpatrick and I went there to get him and I was all set when he moved off on the 6:15 train.[16] He was there only a short time when he was transferred.

April 1921: (EOM: Auxiliaries came up to Belfast. Did he get a letter about their coming or did Collins tell us about them?) They came up for a quiet weekend and there were three of them sailing around. We followed them in uniform after dinner and it was near 10 o'clock in Donegall Place when the three were got.[17] Roger and I had three guns each and forty rounds between us. Up Fountain Lane near the Falls Road, we got round the hoarding, but every civvy we saw pulled a gun, but we were covered by unarmed men. We fired back on the civilians who were pursuing us. We used not more than eight rounds, forty-seven rounds used in all.

[9L] (EOM: Was this the night the two Duffin brothers were shot?) A publican McBride was taken up Antrim Road; his battered body was found after curfew in Nixon's area.[18]

Mac Coill[19] '…' Yes, the two Duffins were shot after the Auxiliaries job. Gaynor, Trodden [and] Mac Fadden shot [in] one night.

On the day the king opened the northern parliament, three men were on for Glover who was shot half way up the Falls Road, he had eleven bullets in him.[20]

21 June [1921]: He was the last of the four who had been responsible for those murders. We had a copy of the sworn enquiry in which Glover swore that he had shot [Seán] Gaynor **[10R]** in self-defence.[21] He hadn't come out for a long time, for we had two lads on constant watch for him, but he didn't come out in the daytime and curfew was on until June of 1921.

Swanzy: Tom Fox and Roger McCorley on that.[22] He was shot as he was coming from church. Lisburn was the safest place in Ireland for there were five per cent Catholics in it. Jack Leonard, who drove the taxi, came from Ballymote and he has a garage now.[23]

(EOM: Father Hassan's book on the Pogroms in Ulster was stopped by the Provisional Government.[24] Perhaps they thought they were going to negotiate. The *Capuchin Annual* also published something.)

June 1921: Kennedy the warder. I left Belfast in April 1923 and I was dealing in cars for four to five months in the army. I went to the motor show in London and then I went home. There was a Belfast Reception Office, I had notes in my sock. A warder said to me when I was in gaol, 'It's alright Seamus, you know me. I am Kennedy … remember the gate.' Then it dawned on me who he was. When we were trying to hold up the gaol once he fell in a faint and lay there so that he would not have to get up to get the master key from the governor.

Seán O'Neill [was] a very nice big fellow. In 1918, he **[10L]** got, as he thought, a crack of a baton but he had been hit with a hurley. Before 1914 he had been an old regular British soldier. He was a good influence and no bickering was allowed.

We were dressed in uniform [and] when the stunt failed we went into three houses, but we could find no clothes so we got out the back doors and we invaded Donnelly a shoemaker and Irish Volunteer. He put me in a snazzy blue suit, too small for me, and gave me a little bowler hat which I stuck on the side of my head.

Intelligence: Nellie McGuigan in the telephone exchange in Belfast who was married to Micky Carolan.[25] She was good on intelligence.

Micky in 1920 was a vice-commandant of Battalion 2. He went to Dublin in **[11R]** the autumn of 1920 and he was caught in boycott work. It was easy enough to spot him for he had bright red hair, so we had to [move] him to Dublin for his own safety.

Dr Arthur Ryan's brother was in the Post Office in Belfast but wouldn't take him on jobs and we were to disarm a Military Policeman at 7 am.[26] He was finished that evening. Joe McGuinne[27] was on that job also.

No spies shot. Many years afterwards a lad was shot in 1930; Turley, a lad who had been in the Irish volunteers after 1916.

Belfast was a close circle (for we had to be very careful). On other jobs, all a man was given was a couple of hours' notice for Barracks attacks. We never thought of espionage on our own side.

[TREATY]

[3R] Dennis McCullough, after the Truce and before the debates on the Treaty, met '…' He was very fair.[28] He sounded a note of warning for he said there was no alternative to the settlement as the IRA was not in a position to go back to a fight. I had seen the men in Dublin drinking and I knew they would not go back to fight. Until the Treaty was signed, we regarded ourselves as on a war footing. Denis McCullough was, I think, Chairman of the [IRB] Supreme Council; he never tried to influence me. 'You're the fellows who have borne the brunt of the fighting as I have been in gaol and I have had a soft time of it.' That was flattering to me if you like, but it was fair and just.

[3R] Collins and Pogroms: I came down from Belfast as a result of the McMahon murders.[29] Curfew was at 12 in Belfast and at 12.30 the murders took place. Nixon, the District Inspector, must have closed a blind eye. He personally didn't ill-treat prisoners although he might take a '….'

[4R] General [Arthur] Solly-Flood succeeded Wilson and he got all his reports and Wilson's work on the Ulster police and the Specials would be in that.[30] I have a report in which Solly-Flood referred to burnings prior to [the] Civil War and he pointed out that police and military could not guard any place, but in another report he referred to the protection of the Orangemen in Catholic districts. Wilson was military advisor on the

North in London and he was in his job there. In June 1921, the northern government in office didn't know **[4L]** about Wilson, but I have duplicates of Solly-Floods records. There was a lad who was private secretary in '…' [and] was given £220 to get it. He had to clear out from the North then as he would be suspected.[31] It frightened them to have their secret stuff known. Later this lad was appointed a commissioner in the Civic Guards.

The only point I impressed on Collins was the disarming of the 'B' Specials. I put this up to Collins when I went up to see him. For this would breed sectarianism. They couldn't act save they were called upon by the police, for as there was no martial law proclaimed in the North the military could not act on their own.

We were there for about 3 or 4 days and Arthur **[5R]** Griffith was there also.[32] I was prejudiced against Mick Collins also, for I thought they were politicians and I thought he would be better than the politicians, for when he came back here he would be preoccupied.

People were on deportations.

But the pogroms did not stop.

We were friendly and I had been to a couple of Mansion House conferences at which were Frank Aiken, Dick Mulcahy, Cathal Brugha,[33] Liam Lynch,[34] Michael Collins, Liam Mellows,[35] A/C '…' Then I was twenty and I felt awkward. I said to Liam Lynch, 'There is only one thing I dislike in the Treaty. I'm afraid that if the northern government takes shape every day will make it more difficult for us to do anything.'

Our tolerance.

The pogrom stopped. We were in the middle of burning in March, April, May 1922. The *Belfast Telegraph* at the time estimated the damage at 3½ million pounds. At a meeting of the Belfast Corporation, Sir Crawford McCullough, the Lord Mayor, made an appeal for a truce. I came to Dublin where I saw Liam Lynch and Liam Deasy.[36] I saw then there was no hope and I told them both that when fighting began between republicans and the Free State we would be **[5L]** wiped out in the North. When I went back I found this appeal for a truce. I was to get Roger McCorley alright and other fellows. Why should we accept this now? It was hard to stay on our own men. If the Civil War starts we will all be bunched, I knew, but if we have forty-eight hours of peace it might work. Then there was a peace. We stopped burning and that really saved us, for the Civil War broke out below and if the Orangemen had been quick they could have wiped us out.

We would have had to evacuate the North at once and nobody would have heard of it.

[11R] In the spring of 1922 we meant to get the armoured cars from eight to ten of them attached to Musgrave Street Barracks [18 May 1922].[37] We had boys who had been trained in the British army to drive armoured cars. There were twenty-two men in a school. We had a friendly policeman who was orderly for the night and Roger went up to disarm the armoury. We had some armoured cars running at the time. **[11L]** This was during curfew and McKenna was the policeman and he had to establish an alibi, [so] I had to bump into him to get the password, which was 'Belfast'.

Seamus Timoney, who was in charge of the Irish speaking battalion, succeeded Roger as the O/C of C Company.[38] They had guns drawn to shoot McKenna and we had bolt cutters with which to cut our way in.

[5L] [William] Twaddell, an MP, made a harangue at an open air meeting in the Pre-Truce times: at 11:15 am he was shot in Royal Avenue.[39] That stopped the big wigs from **[6R]** going out in public to exhort the mob.

[CIVIL WAR]

[1R] I met Frank Aiken in Dublin when he came back from Limerick.[40] (EOM: This was in July 1922 when Aiken was trying to arrange for the cessation of hostilities.) He told me about his visit to Dublin, that he had seen [Richard] Mulcahy who had asked him to write a long memorandum, which Aiken intended to do when he reached Dundalk that night.[41] Dan Hogan, on Eoin O'Duffy's instructions, raided the barracks in Dundalk and took Aiken and his men prisoners.[42] I read about the capture of the barracks [the] next day in Dublin.

I came down to Dublin having written an account of my opinion of Mulcahy. I had a girl in the same train who later gave in my report and when Mulcahy [read] it he was interrupted by an account of Aiken's escape from Dundalk. It was an outrage I wrote to Mulcahy. He should release Aiken at once, for Dan Hogan is a mutineer. If you didn't order Hogan to surround Dundalk barracks, then O'Duffy did: either that or Hogan acted on his own initiative. The army then, I wrote, was seemingly a mob under Dick Mulcahy's control.

Mulcahy couldn't say 'yes' or 'no' in any known language, but he carefully surrounded himself with 'yes' men.

Three weeks later I was in Portobello barracks and I went into the mess. Piaras Béaslaí was pulling away at a cigarette (EOM: Piaras always sucked a cigarette); rather sucking away at it and in front of him was a large dish of jam.[43] This **[1L]** was at tea time. Hogan was at the head of the table. I couldn't resist it. I said, 'That was a marvellous military operation of yours the other night,' meaning the sudden capture of Dundalk. Now, Dan Hogan was jealous of me because O'Duffy had brought me up previously to Beggars Bush. Why O'Duffy brought me up then I do not know. 'I wish you had been there,' said Hogan, meaning that he wished he had been able to take me prisoner, you might have got it.

Hogan put his hand on his gun and drew it and I put my hand on mine. Piaras Béaslaí (EOM: expecting the worst) dropped his head into the plate of jam. I didn't speak to Hogan for a long time after that.

22 July [1922]: A month later Seán King, who was chairman of **[2R]** the County Down GAA, in August or September came down with me to a match in Croke Park, around in front of us were O'Duffy and Hogan. So O'Duffy suggested that we have tea in the Wicklow, us four. Hogan and I talked then and Hogan invited me to drive to Dundalk with him and he was very pressing. I didn't want to go for I was going to Belfast in connection with the White Cross, I think, and I wanted to get back at once. Seamus McGoran, O/C Cavan, was there and '…' so Hogan wanted us to have a game of solo but I wouldn't go.[44] The early train was always safe for me to get into Belfast anyhow. Hogan went to Dundalk at 11.30. The other boys had waited and had they gone to Clones, which I think was Divisional HQ; but that morning, at 2 a.m. Aiken took Dundalk and I'm certain that Hogan thought that I knew about it, and perhaps that is why Gearóid [O'Sullivan] later called me an 'irregular'.[45]

In March of 1923, or perhaps at the 'cease fire', I left Belfast. I was offered the post as Deputy Adjutant General and when I came to Dublin I found that Bob Price [was also] to be Deputy Adjutant General. There were to be two of us.[46] Tom Cullen asked me to a meeting to discuss the foundation of a kind of ex-service men's organisation.[47] I knew at the time that old IRA men [were] being pushed out of army jobs, but they were undisciplined, the old IRA, in the army, I knew, and were not fit many of them, for discipline or continuous regular army work. Tom **[2B]** Ennis[48] was there and Liam Tobin and a number of others.[49] At the time I knew nothing about a mutiny. I was asked by Cullen to outline or propose a policy, and I told them that as army officers they could not take any political move without authorisation. That seemed to be news to some of them. Then Paddy Daly got up and said that it was time to shoot a few cabinet ministers.[50] Later, Gearóid [O'Sullivan] accused me of being an 'irregular' and he said I had become one at the time.

I nearly sprung at his throat for that. Then I left the army.

[3R] At Christmas 1923, I was on the *Argenta* and I was taken off at Larne on the last day of January.[51] I was the last to leave. Nixon was in charge of the escort and I was in charge of two police. [He] offered me a nip of brandy. 'No, thanks,' I said. We nearly got him once and I had a hole through. He used to attend the Orange Lodges and at 8.30 he made an Orange speech, which **[3L]** was reported in the press, so he was humped out of the police.[52]

[4R] (EOM: Lord Glentoran called Nixon the District Inspector a murderer, but he had to take the words back.)[53]

[6R] 'Twas years later, in the holy week of 1924, I was arrested.[54] In November 1923 I was on the *Argenta* [and] on the 31 January I was brought to Belfast Gaol, and [a] few mornings later I was paraded for identification. [Kevin] O'Higgins was in London at a Boundary Conference and he told me later that he raised my case first as I was a commissioned officer in the Free State army in which I yet was and was on leave.[55] I was leaving the army and at that time our head office was in Belfast. I went to a motor show in London and then went to see my people who lived in the County Down. I drove up in my own car, and at that time the curfew was at 12:00 all over the six counties. I ran out of petrol. I hired a car in Belfast and I arrived home at 12:05. We were three miles from one barracks and seven miles from another, but there was a posse of the RUC in behind me when I reached home.

One morning on the *Argenta* I was paraded. He paraded seven fellows and I said to the Governor 'must I be on this parade and if I was I should pick the other six or you'll be a party to a miscarriage of justice and I'll refuse to go on parade?' I picked six of my own height and build. I was always addressed as Colonel Woods and they '…' give a damn about my rank. I picked two dapper men amongst the others **[6L]** [and] didn't the crown witness pick on one of them. George O'Kane, who was picked out, went to the governor's office.[56] He had been arrested on 21 May 1922. So when he went to the office, the governor [A. D. Drysdale] said to him, 'you can go, you're the wrong man.' I got O'Kane to tell me what had happened to him on that interview. A few days later all the witnesses were brought to Derry. A month later I was brought to Belfast where I was charged with murder in the crown court. I heard the crown witness give evidence. He swore that he had identified me. I got an interview with the governor and I was going to call him as a witness to say that another man had been identified instead of myself and that he knew it. You asked me my name, my address and my sentence. **[7L]** The governor got the wind up, so he came in voluntarily as a witness. I was afraid I would have to bring in my warders, whom I was bribing, and he was afraid they could prove it. At 5:45 I asked for my solicitor to put the statement on paper. 'Look here, Woods. You are an officer of high rank will you give me the right to think it over?' '...' He went to the Home Office and at 10:30 he came as a witness and the Attorney General [Richard Best Unionist MP for Armagh] had kept him. The Attorney General asked him why he thought it was necessary to come in as a witness and my council jumps up, 'I object and this is a very proper attitude and the judge is with him.' Willie Beatty was my senior council and I said to him that if I ran through this case from A to Z. 'I don't want a bloody word,' he said, 'I have never been so completely briefed in any case I have ever been given.' I had the evidence of the sworn inquiry into what happened in my case. Ryan is a district inspector, a military and police officer in India and he walks out and picks a man last, he identified men also. I was third from the right; he had a lay man told him that was a lay man but an officer numbers from the right, always.

I had O'Kane also as a witness. I was acquitted, but **[7L]** I wasn't released. I was held on remand. You couldn't get food sent in and they would give me the tea.

ROGER MCCORLEY

(UCDA P17b/98, pp. 6–13, June 1949)

Roger Edmund McCorley (1901–1993), born in Belfast in 1901, was the third child of Roger and Agnes McCorley. His older brother, Felix, was also a leading member of the Belfast IRA, with both men particularly militant during the War of Independence period. He joined Na Fianna with Felix while a teenager, rising through the ranks to become a leading officer, serving as a Battalion Officer Commanding, Brigade Vice Officer Commanding and Brigade Officer Commanding in the IRA.

McCorley took part in the burning of the Income Tax office in Belfast in April 1920, and the attack on Crossgar RIC barracks on 2 June 1920. McCorley operated as look-out with Tom Fox and two Corkmen, Dick Murphy and Seán Culhane, during the killing of DI Oswald Ross Swanzy in Lisburn, on 22 August 1922. He was a member of the ASU that killed two members of the Auxiliaries at Roddy's Hotel, Belfast on 26 January 1921. He took part in the attack on a British military guard at the Reform Club, Belfast in April 1921 and the killing of two Auxiliaries at Donegall Place on

23 April 1921. McCorley shot the notorious DI Ferris at Cavendish Square, Belfast on 7 May 1921, but the murder gang member survived. He also shot dead another member of the Harrison gang, John Glover, on 4 June 1921.

Although he attended the anti-Treaty IRA Executive, McCorley backed the Treaty. In January 1922, he was appointed 3rd ND Director of Training. On 18 May 1922, during the joint-IRA offensive, he took part in the raid on Musgrave Street barracks. On 31 May, he was shot and seriously wounded by USC and had to be smuggled out of the North to Dublin via Glasgow, while still recovering from his wounds, to prevent his capture. McCorley went to the Curragh as a supposedly neutral northern IRA commander, but received a salary from the Beggars Bush Director of Organisation and joined the Free State army in November 1922. He was in Kerry at the time of the Ballyseedy massacre, but scarcely mentions this to Ernie O'Malley. In retrospect, McCorley claimed that he accepted the Treaty only because it gave Ireland an army and that after Collins died the Free State government had no interest in the six counties. McCorley served throughout the remainder of the Civil War and retired at the rank of Major on 31 March 1928. He settled down in Clontarf, outside Dublin, and lived until into his nineties, dying on 13 November 1993, survived by his wife Rita.

[THE POGROMS 1920–2]

[6L] The pogroms of 21 July 1920 divided our attention for we had then to defend the nationalist groups.[1] The brigade in Belfast had about 1,000 men, two battalions which became therefore four battalions at the Truce. We were out of contact with Dublin for stuff and we had to find our own way. Our fighting was based on rifles not on revolvers and bombs, as in Dublin. We did not use bombs to any extent. We had to hold large areas on a long front. If armoured cars with netting wires came into the areas, we used rifles from the top of windows. We were only afraid then of the armoured cars (Pierce or otherwise).[2] Sometimes an area would be cut off for three days or so; then often areas were cut off from each other. In the early stages, the British were quite free with regard to shooting but when the Specials got into working order there was a certain antipathy.

Pogroms. The intention was to drive our people into certain areas. At first mobs operated [alone] then they met rival mobs. We stood by at the beginning. Then the Orangemen were organised into Specials. There were a few hundred rifles, Steyr rifles, very good rifles; they were with an inscription insert 'For God and Ulster'.[3] About 60 of them we had, Martini–Enfields also. After the first week of fighting we got hold of them. They belonged to the National Volunteers. We had fairly good supplies of ammunition belonging to Seán Cusack who got them about 1918.[4] It was UVF stuff. The Martini Enfields belonged to the Redmondites. We go them the first week of the pogrom through a priest.

[6R] The Martini Enfield's took mark VI cartridge[s] with a mark VII bullet. About 1922 we had from 400/500 rifles.

The men were supplied with Peters about 20/30 and with Peter ammunition.[5]

Carrickfergus Castle: then been all the conscription arms taken from shops and from private individuals in 1916 (also Dublin Castle held the store of such material). We had a line with Carrickfergus Castle so got out stuff by degrees.

The pogrom lasted two years.

Specials:[6] A [Specials]: full time £4 per week.

B [Specials]: so many patrols per week. Arms kept in the individual's house. These were the main instruments for sniping on Nationalists['] houses.

C [Specials]: called on for special missions. He had a revolver.

Roughly in all [there were about] 20,000 to 30,000 men. No man could work in the shipyards unless he had a B or C card.[7] Against [these] numbers of men it was always easy to find a target. The more they increased, the easier to inflict casualties. A few months prior to the Truce the nationalist areas were not **[7R]** patrolled [the] same by armoured cars used by the police. When shooting started doors had been kept open for a while to allow our fellows freedom of movement.

When I was wounded in May 1920, I was brought in an ambulance. I was stopped on the way by the Specials. The driver said to me 'close your eyes and pretend you're dead' for there were two dead men in the ambulance already. I shut my eyes keeping a lid of one [of] them open when the specials flung open the door. 'They're all dead, the three of them', said the driver. 'That's a good job', said one of them, 'or we'd so and so make sure of them.' That meant that they had made a habit of shooting the wounded. Just then came a very burst of fire, the Specials flattened themselves against the walls of the houses and the ambulance moved off. I thought it was our fellows who had opened fire but later I found out it was not so. The British military had fired on the Specials.[8]

The Truce [11 July 1921] itself lasted six hours only.

Sniping into our areas was the form of activity. We kept the mob under control at first when they were trying to attack the Orange people in our area and then they went off.

We had advanced information about the first pogrom. The shooting of Swanzy.[9] We asked to be headed off for a while, as the Orange crowd were only waiting for an excuse to start a pogrom and throw the blame on us. A District Inspector Smith [Gerald Smyth, 17 July 1920] was shot in Cork who had Belfast associations and then [Oswald] Swanzy was shot in Lisburn [22 August 1920].[10] The beginning of it was the driving out of workers from the shipyards then the pubs of nationalists were looted and burnt out. Orange mobs would then attack nationalist **[7L]** mobs. We would ward off or keep order then until fighting began. There was great poverty in the nationalist areas as a result of the fighting, for many of [the] men could not go to work, or [had] been driven out of work. No rent was paid. The White Cross was of great help to all.[11] There was a starvation level for the ordinary class of worker. I found that roughly 450 had been killed and 2,000/3,000 wounded during the period. Then comes a northern government established by Lloyd George who handed over this area to a murder gang, those who had caused the pogroms. It would be interesting during that period to compare the rival papers. Sometimes the nationalist press was splashed with large headlines. The Orange press of the same day would have a small sentence tucked away and vice versa.

Irish News	Nationalist
The Newsletter	Orange
The [Northern] Whig	Orange

After the Truce we started a bomb factory to make a form of contact bomb, but we didn't use any large quantity of them. We had a very fine intelligence system. We called men by their initials so much so that the man's real name was not known to many. T. I. for instance was McCarthy.[12] David McGuinness (12 Leoville Street) was Brigade Intelligence Officer.[13] In March 1921 there were three Brigades in our Division, the 3rd Northern:

Belfast No.1; Antrim No. 2; East Down No. 3. Divisional O/C was Joe McKelvey,[14] Seamus Woods **[8R]** was adjutant. Tommy McNally adjutant.[15] At the beginning of 1922, Woods was O/C of the [3rd Northern] Division. I was second in charge. Seán O'Neill [was] in charge of No. 1 Brigade.[16]

IRB: Séamus Dobbyn would know about this.[17] He was there on the Brigade staff of No. 1, but he was an organiser for [the] IRB in Ulster. He lives at 2 Rathlyn Road, [Glasnevin]. [Joe] McKelvey used to come down regularly to Dublin. Once he phoned me about the terms of the Treaty debates. 'The Treaty has been rejected by three votes,' [he said], 'Three days' notice was to be given of the termination of the Truce.' Then he came up again later to say that his first idea of the voting was wrong. (It appeared to be that these men, if '...' represented the feeling, were not very particular whether the Treaty was agreed to or not.)

The day prior to the Truce was known as 'Bloody Sunday'.[18] We had a required system to signal with coloured lamps of enemy movement. Police had been shot on Friday but they had not yet died. A reprisal party of 10–15 were killed as they tried to get into one area and reinforcements were attacked. This was a Sunday morning. By that evening the city was a sea of fire and I heard from the Carrick Hill area, which was entirely cut off from us, that three of the large armoured cars were trying to break their way in, and that our men there were short of ammunition.[19] A man who came out with the word said that it would not be possible to get back again. Then two of the local clergy came up to me to say that McGrath, a local RIC sergeant, wanted to know would I withdraw our outposts if they withdraw theirs in the Falls Road. But we refused unless it, the Truce **[8L]** extended to the whole city area. Then we agreed to it for the city. They would have to escort our couriers through and we would escort their escorts through our lines until an hour prior to the Truce. The British after the Truce were prepared to shoot at any sniper, for we didn't then interfere with them.

[12R] In Belfast we broke down back yard walls from working class houses were placed back to back. We broke down the walls in a zig zag pattern.

District Inspector Nixon was involved in all the reprisals.[20] 'Take no prisoners of any reprisal gang,' was part of our orders.

On 'Bloody Sunday' I saw a gang hold up a tram with hatchets **[12L]** and rifles. A patrol of the RIC stood by, but they did not interfere. At times a gang would use sledgehammers against people. They were utterly savage.

In 1924 there was a book printed from the Catholic angle, but it was never distributed: *Facts and Figures of the Belfast Pogroms* printed in Dublin.[21]

We had a system of signalling along the electric mains. We used a 12-volt battery, a one flash system for we had HC mains. We used it to get in touch with isolated areas that way and keep in touch with them. A chap named O'Grady invented the apparatus which was a very simple apparatus indeed.[22]

[CIVIL WAR]

[8L] 1922: I was shot on the 31 May and I left Belfast via Glasgow for Dublin at the end of June. We had issued an order that all able-bodied men were to come to the Brigade area even for a day. That was why I was surprised when I was passing the Fowler Hall [10 Parnell Square] to see Belfast refugees in it.[23] They came from the slums, for we knew nothing whatever about them. **[13R]**

Fowler Hall: I was walking by there when someone said, 'There are Belfast refugees inside.' That was the first time I had ever heard of refugees in Dublin. I found they were [from] the slums of Belfast. The same thing happened in Donegal, Joe Sweeney told me. Collins–Craig pact: The Catholics according to it were to get representation on the police force.[24]

[8L] The attack on the North: We started off with the idea that it was to be a fight to the finish. We were to attack barracks and a date was set for [a] further general attack prior to the arrival of arms from Dublin. The first cargo came **[9R]** to County Down. There were 150 Lee Enfield's, which came by boat to the County Down coast. Tommy McNally, or Woods, would know of this. The next cargo was for County Antrim in an oil tanker. It got through alright, but it broke down at Carrickfergus outside the house of the colonel in charge of the military in Carrickfergus Castle. There was a crew of three: my brother, adjutant of County Antrim, Seamus Timoney,[25] adjutant of the 1st Battalion and [Paddy] Downey.[26] They all worked at it for a time but the axel [*sic*] was broken. The colonel invited them in for tea, but they knew they could not get into Belfast before curfew. The local barracks would not open for the colonel so that he could not get a police pass. Then he gave our men a military pass and they got through alright.

To County Antrim arms, 150 rifles were sent, grenades of the Mills type, piles of war flour, which we didn't want as we had plenty of it in Antrim and in Belfast we manufactured it ourselves.

We weren't prepared for the date outlined. We called up [Eoin] O'Duffy by phone.[27] He had to speak very carefully of course on the phone, but he had no other option then. The Second Division went off too soon but the 4th ND didn't go off at all. [Daniel] McKenna[28] was second in command under [Tom] Morris[29] of the 2nd Northern. On 22 May we went off. Either 19 or 20 [May] was the day. We burnt out a number of barracks and we completely isolated Belfast. We blew up bridges there and in County Antrim and we nearly took their chief barracks in Musgrave Street, where they kept their armoured cars, also.

We received in all 520 rifles. All of our rifles were first class. There were about 100 rounds per rifle [and] in addition we had 150 service revolvers for Belfast. We had a good supply of bombs but we didn't **[10R]** particularly need them. To make sure that the whole of County Down would go off, Aiken and his staff from the Fourth Northern met us. It was important that one area would be followed by troops if the other area didn't act and it seemed that Aiken thought that his area would be flooded on account of us. We expected him to off at a particular time and it happened the other way around, for our part of County Down was overrun. Hugh Jack was O/C East Down.[30] He said that if a man didn't come soon from the 4th Northern, they couldn't stand up to the situation in East Down. I saw O'Duffy and I explained the situation to him. He said, 'I can't do anything with the 4th Northern. They have more arms than any place in the North; also I cannot get anything done [from] them.'

We heard that the border was to be attacked in local raids from the South. There came into Belfast everyday three train loads of Specials. We were burning Belfast right, left and centre. They, the Orangemen, had reached saturation point and we were pleased, for when they were in the city it would [make] things easier for the 4th Northern. A good number of Specials had been drawn from Fermanagh, where there had been little of our activity. We felt very sure later that the 4th Northern did not in any way help us.

There was a conference held at GHQ during the Civil War. Men from the six counties came there. We saw Mulcahy, Gearóid O'Sullivan and Collins.[31] I do not know if [Diarmuid] O'Hegarty and O'Duffy were there.

Joe Sweeney was not there.[32] Morris, Woods, [Thomas] Fitzpatrick O/C Antrim and myself were there. [Patrick] Casey from the 4th Northern, but I didn't know him, he was a chap from Fermanagh area.[33] The purpose of this **[11R]** meeting was to discuss the situation in the North. County Antrim was shaky but effective. Belfast was still going strong, but we could see no point in the casualties we were suffering. East Down by that time was pretty bad. It had nearly scuppered out. Our problem was how could our men live on a peace footing. Collins said he was going to London within a few days to see Lloyd George and he would tell him that he could take his bloody Treaty. Nothing further happened in the North then. Men were withdrawn from 2nd and 3rd Northern areas, men who could not live there under peace conditions or men who would not put up with the government of Northern Ireland. **[13R]** Woods would have come to Dublin on various occasions. I think he was in on conferences held between Beggars Bush and the Four Courts.

[11R] The idea in our May 1922 attack was to smash the northern government completely. As far as we could help it we didn't attack the British. There was nothing to indicate to us that we couldn't trust GHQ about this operation.

Henry Wilson was military adviser to the northern government.[34] We got hold of his files at police H.Q.; the private secretary to the head of the police service, under Wickham, was one of our agents. He was an Intelligence Officer on our staff before he was appointed. He was a civilian. This was in 1922. He got files and in them a scheme for the defence of the six counties against an attack from the South. Seamus Woods would know about this material. I never saw it nor do I know whether it was taken out before or after Wilson's death. **[12R]** In the Curragh, the men were first put into Keane barracks. I was O/C of the 2nd and 3rd Northern crowd, about 400/500 there. Then we were moved to the Hare Park Camp. We stayed in the Curragh until after Collins was killed. **[11R]** Men were brought to the Curragh, but they did not go into the army, nor was any pressure put on us to go into the Free State army. We were there until about October. When Collins was killed and the northern element gave up all hope. **[12R]** We held a meeting, then the divisional O/C's and staffs and we decided that any man was free to go when he wanted, either to go home to the North or join the Free State army. If anyone wanted to join the Free State army, he could join. There was no pressure brought to bear on us whatsoever.

I was sent south to Kerry with a unit which consisted of half Belfast men and half 2nd and 3rd Northern men. We went to Kenmare until March [1923].[35]

[13R] Kerry: When Murphy was in charge of this area everything was alright.[36] I was there from November to March in Kerry. A sergeant, a northerner, told me a story. He was in charge of a guard there. Some officers, Dublin men, he said came in, demanding prisoners. The sergeant said he would not turn them over without authority. Then he suddenly called out the guard, 'I'll shoot', he said, 'If you attempt to come any further.'

[12R] Then I was fed up. I came back to the Curragh. I wanted to get out of the Army or get out of Kerry. The unit was then formed into [the] 17th Battalion and sent to the workhouse in Tralee. Joe Murray, a Belfast man, was in charge of it there. When I went to the Curragh I was attached to an Officers Training Camp there.

In pre-Truce times I offered Dublin to exchange a number of officers to take advantage of the different systems. We were producing officers as fast as we needed them. I thought it would be a good idea to find out what Dublin fighting was like. This did not materialise, however, for GHQ didn't take up the idea.

TOM MCNALLY

(UCDAP17b/99, pp. 88–93, Sept. 1949)

Thomas 'Tom' James McNally (1894–1958), born in 1894, was the eldest of three sons to Thomas and Catherine of the Falls Road, Belfast. His earliest memories were of rioting, burning, Orangeism and brutal sectarianism. At fourteen, he joined the Mitchel's GAC who had an old military hut for clubrooms in the mid-Falls area, where they held céilithe and Irish classes. After a spell in Derry with the Great Northern Railway, McNally returned to Belfast and joined O'Donovan Rossa in 1918, a strongly republican GAA club made-up of many IRA Volunteers. From there he joined B Company, Belfast Battalion.

During the War of Independence, McNally served as a Belfast Brigade and then 3rd ND Quartermaster with the IRA. He took part in the burning of Thompson's Garage and attacks on British barracks at Crossgar (2 May 1920) and Broadway. He also used his position within the Great Northern

Railway Company to assist the work of the Belfast Boycott. Although he did not officially join the Free State army until 19 February 1923, his service was recognised from 1 July 1922 for pension purposes. McNally himself claimed that he coordinated the transfer of IRA volunteers from Belfast to the Curragh Camp after June 1922 and facilitated their entry into the Free State army. McNally served throughout the remainder of the Civil War and served in the army until 1 February 1947, having reached the rank of Colonel. McNally investigated the IRA raid on the Magazine Fort, Phoenix Park, Dublin in December 1939. During the Second World War, McNally was O/C at the Curragh with responsibility for internment camps housing IRA internees. He then worked in a civilian capacity with the Department of Defence in the 1940s and 1950s. He died on 27 October 1958.

[88L] He was in 'B' Company of the Belfast Battalion. It was known as the 'collar and tie' company.[1] Woods was the O/C of this company when it was of any value.[2] I was the Brigade Quartermaster. I was transferred out of the city as I was working on the railway, then Woods decided to make me full time as Divisional Quartermaster. We were attached to the 3rd [Northern] Division, which was then the second best armed division in Ireland, for they told me at GHQ when I was pleading for stuff that only Liam Lynch had a better armed command. In the beginning, Seán Mac Mahon [at] GHQ gave us preference for stuff.[3] At the Truce we gave the Minister of Defence [Cathal Brugha] a guard of honour with 24 Enfield Rifles.[4]

Steyrs, the Austrian rifles and Lee Enfields could be bought for £7 a rifle.[5] We had more than 200 rifles. I didn't come south after the planned attack on the northern government, for Collins said he wanted lads who held the threads of the organisation together.

Before this attack, Seán Mac Mahon and [Eoin] O'Duffy [Free State Chief of Staff] were to give us six hundred rifles, Free State rifles. I brought some up the coast and landed them in Gunns Island [Ballyhornan Beach], near Seamus Woods' place in County Down, in a little twelve-ton motor boat – about two hundred rifles and 30/40,000 rounds of ammunition. We swapped two Lewis Guns for Thompsons.[6] I brought five Thompson guns by rail. Frank Aiken had the stuff in Barracks in Dundalk.[7] We were to receive two hundred rifles for each of our brigades – six hundred in all.

The two hundred for Belfast went to Antrim. They should have gone **[89L]** by boat but Felix.[8]

Stuff was sent on a tanker oil, from Thompson's (here in Dublin).

Rory Mac Nicholl was the driver and he is now a sergeant in the Guards and a fine fellow.[9] They filled up the tanker up first with arms then put enough oil to feed the taps. The tanker broke down near the military barracks in Carrickfergus. The driver went in to see the local colonel and was given a tow outside with an army lorry for he was on his way to Antrim. The British towed it until the car started again.

We got sufficient .22 ammunition from Carrickfergus Military Barracks to supply the remainder of the Divisions in Ireland from the military. We were getting stuff from Dublin, revolvers and machine guns. Seán McMahon was particularly good at the time. We made tons of explosives. We had a very good divisional chemist '…' who was experimenting with gun cotton. They stored the explosives all over the place. Before the truce, the McArdles made contact grenades in Belfast.[10] My brother worked in the fitting shop. They made about 45,000 grenades. The grenade had a contact rocker. We had one serious accident, but our people then had no faith in them. They were the same as a Mills grenade (EOM: The British always used 'grenades' for their explosive weapons and 'bombs' for ours) as far as the case covering was concerned, but the rocker arrangement was very good indeed. There were several thrown during the riots, thrown into a crowd. There was an element of doubt about them as the lads weren't exactly happy with them. This bomb was invented by McArdle **[89R]** our divisional engineer. The men were working in the Foundry, Tommy Gilling, a moulder, the best in Ireland. None of these bombs went to any other brigade. (EOM: why?) We had little assistance outside of ourselves, and we had no faith in other areas.

Roger Mc Corley and Séamus Woods were both fine fighters. Seamus Woods was a very close friend of mine. He was very nervous in the sense that he was sensitive. Roger was cold like a fish. He had no nerves. Woods overcame his nerves and now he is alright.

Colonel Tom Fox was on a job with two fellows from Cork.[11] Leonard, a Sligo man, drove the taxi.[12] He was sentenced to death. Fox, Roger McCorley, Dan Donovan and '…' shot Swanzy in Lisburn.[13] They made two or three goes at him. Joe McKelvey organised it. Joe was a great lad, a good man for giving confidence but he was not a soldier. He had a very good manner and was a gentle type of fellow. (EOM: Fox did not help to shoot Swanzy.)

[90L] Tan War

We organised a flying column for Cavan. Joe McKelvey did, that didn't do well at Lappanduff [Cootehill].[14] Colonel [Seamus McGoran] (now A[djutant G[eneral]) was on it. The O/C was [Patrick 'Paddy'] Smith now a TD.[15] He escaped. Fox and the other men were caught. Ten of them, and they were sentenced to death. There were four or five Belfast men in this column. They were trying to stir the area up. Mc Goran would know about this column in Cavan. In 1918, I came in to the Volunteers but McGoran was in from the early days of Sinn Féin.

[Seamus] McGoran (Colonel Commandant) was a captain organising Cavan after Gallagher, a Dublin chap sent by GHQ who just sat down and drank.[16]

At the end of the Truce we were in very good form but we got very demoralised later. They held together men. Two lads went up as cadets to join the Free State army and both were called back to their area, but only one came back. Seamus Woods was satisfied that when our plan for burning out areas in Belfast was finished with, he felt we would be secure.

1921: There was not much doing except the shooting of lads who were giving evidence against some of our lads.

The Hibernians were of no use to us. Indeed, they were a menace through their weakness. I was reared through the GAA and I had no contact with the Hibs. We had to rely upon the Irish Volunteers and on some of the ex-soldiers.

[90R] Intelligence: Frank Crummey was in charge of it.[17] Old Frank was good but Donegan second in command was in charge.[18] He got a lot of information from inside the RIC (they would have been mostly from outside of Ulster and Catholic).

McCarthy, who was in the RIC, was giving us a lot of information about murder gangs who went out in lorries.[19] They got their names. He even tried to go out with them so that [they] would know them better.

Murder gangs: These men [were] purely RIC at first then when the Tans came in they joined up.

Following night, three prominent Sinn Féiners were shot in bed. We got a fair few of the murder gang. Check on this with Roger McCorley and Seamus Woods. I cannot say that the shooting of members of their gang interfered with them. Their murder gang never came to a house when they thought there would be a fight. Often enough our lads waited for them, but they never came to a house when men were waiting for them.

[91L] Woods had plenty of energy. This helped during the Truce. The division was not satisfied with Joe McKelvey.[20]

Joe was pro-Treaty just at the time the Treaty was signed. There was a meeting held in Clones. Eoin O'Duffy was there from GHQ. Joe McKelvey was there. I was at Clones but I wasn't at that meeting. Dan Hogan was present and Frank Aiken also.[21] Joe McKelvey came out of the meeting saying even the Falls Road can vote itself out. (He must have been told that any majority unit in Ulster would have the right to vote itself out of the northern government.) He told us that all our areas could vote themselves out so there would be little left of the northern government, and as a result they would have had to come in with the rest of Ireland.

When I came out of Clones I was tremendously happy, for I felt that even in Belfast we were secure. Woods and I were at this concert in Clones, but we were not at the meeting.

A divisional meeting was held at which Woods was appointed Divisional O/C. Woods has a good memory and he also has a diary.

Fighting in the North, 1922 May: We had been sent on some revolvers from the Kells area [Co. Meath], which I refused to take for they were rusted and in terrible condition.

[91L] We were told we were to get loads of stuff from the First Southern Division.[22] Seamus Woods carried out all the personal interviews with Collins. I was told about the details then, but I do not remember them now. I remember coming down with Aiken about the attack on the [Four] Courts and he wanted to stop the fighting.[23]

I was on a conference with Aiken in Dundalk Barracks. He gave me a hand in getting the rifles for our division out of Dundalk. He closed down on two hundred rifles which had been brought up from Dublin and which men were waiting for the organisation of their transport. There were two hundred rifles which were to go via Donegal for Antrim to come in at Red Bay [a townland in Co. Antrim]. They did not come in by sea, but they came in by tanker. That accounts for four hundred but there were two hundred yet to come.

We had more faith in Johnny McCoy than in anyone in that Fourth ND.[24] They sent stuff across the border to men and the Quinns in Newry helped.

[92L] Our plan for Belfast was to burn out the centre of Belfast. We were to destroy all [of the] High Street and destroy them industrially. In Antrim, barracks were to be attacked. Seamus Woods was the man. The operation wasn't so successful.[25] Two or three jobs went well. Then we were into it but it was a failure. It developed into a Catholic versus Protestant business. There was a lot of defending areas, organising the IRA to save the Catholic positions, but there was really no nationalist fight. A lot of your own you couldn't trust. The IRA were a small island (in this flood) by reason of their activity and drive, but the Catholic population with their Hibernian background would let you down suddenly at the time.

The 2nd Northern: I don't think they did a damn thing that time that I know of. They were to come out too and fight with us.

(EOM: Did the 3rd Northern go off before its time?)

Ben Donegan in Belfast now was intelligence officer.

Tommy Flynn was a good fighting man but talkative.[26]

The Ulster crowd had us completely demoralised when our fighting was of no avail. The northern men could no longer stay in the North. They went up to reorganise in the Curragh. A lot of local volunteers moved from Dublin to Belfast escapists. In the Curragh, they hoped there would be a chance to reorganise. Roger McCorley was there and McKenna, who had never been of any use for anything.

I came along in February or March 1923. Your life had been **[92R]** made impossible by raids. The IRA there never recovered.

(EOM: What did the North think of the joint plan between Four Courts and Beggars Bush against the North?) Seamus Woods objected to men coming in to fight. What we wanted he said was guns and ammunition, for we can get around the difficulties of our areas but they could not.

Felix Devlin: He was no use. He was on my staff and he wouldn't know much.[27]

McGoran: He would know. He was a good soldier and politically minded.

Dumps: They were very well organised. I had my house as a clearing centre. We kept our stuff in convents often. The late Cardinal was very good.[28] There was a fair amount of stuff for a while in Saint Malachy's. We built the dumps into houses. We did not use concealed rooms.

[93L] Joe Murray, a carpenter, a foreman now in Portobello, would know about dumps.[29] He was a good soldier, one of the best.

Seamus McKenna: in the civil service. He was in a lot of the shooting jobs.[30]

Joe McNally: I have a brother who was working on incendiary jobs and explosive jobs with war flour.[31]

Tom Fox: Director of Training now.

We finished up with seven or eight Thompson guns. But we were never able to use them. All the Mills bombs we had we used early [in] the pogroms.

The first contact bomb we threw hit a lorry but didn't explode. Then the British wired the lorries. Then in a test with the contact bomb a young fellow blew his hand off. My brother, Joe, would give information about these grenades. He lives out at Clondalkin [Co. Dublin].

Woods was a great friend of Kevin O'Higgins,[32] Seamus Hogan and the political end of it.[33] He was very inquisitive and ambitious. He could talk most of any of us and he is accurate.

JACK 'SEÁN' LEONARD[1]

(UCDAP17b/136, pp. 26–85 Nov. 1951)

John 'Jack' Leonard (1896–1976) was born in 1896 at Toorlestraun, Sligo, the seventh of eleven children to John and Margaret. Like many others from North Connacht, Jack migrated to Belfast, where he secured work as a driver in a loyalist-owned garage in North Belfast, lodging at 21 Bedeque Street near the Mater Hospital. Leonard joined the volunteers and, like his comrades, translated his name to the Gaelic, Seán.

Although not a prominent volunteer, Leonard helped organise the hijacking of motor cars from his place of work and possessed a good knowledge of the roads in and out of the city. As a result, he was selected to drive an ASU comprised of Cork and Belfast volunteers to assassinate DI Oswald Swanzy in Lisburn. As the interview makes clear, the first attempt ended in failure when the taxi broke down. The following Sunday,

22 August 1920, Leonard drove the taxi and acted as getaway driver. Seán Culhane of Cork, who carried out the attack with Dick Murphy, Roger McCorley, and Tom Fox, gave a detailed account of Leonard's part in the Swanzy shooting, noting, 'I had asked Seán Leonard to accompany us and promised him a job in Fords Works in Cork. He preferred, however, to take his chance and said if apprehended he would say he had to do the job under compulsion with a gun to his body.'[2]

Unfortunately for Leonard, an eyewitness identified the car registration plate, leading to his arrest. Leonard was charged with murder on 27 August 1920.[3] During his court-martial at Victoria Barracks in February 1921, the famous constitutional nationalist barrister, Tim Healy, acted in Leonard's defence. Leonard pleaded not guilty and told the court, 'I am innocent … I had nothing to do with those men.'[4] Despite the contradictory nature of much of the eyewitness testimony, which wrongly identified Leonard as one of the gunmen and claimed that he had a dark moustache, Leonard was sentenced to death. He was later reprieved on St Patrick's Day and his sentence was commuted to fifteen years. Leonard served in Portland and later Dartmoor prisons until the general amnesty after the signing of the Treaty. He then joined the Free State army and operated as a driver in the 1st ND, seeing action during the fighting in the Belleek–Pettigo triangle in late May and early June 1922. After the war, Leonard opened a garage and auctioneers in Tubbercurry, where his wife was postmistress on Main Street. Leonard later emigrated to Huntington Beach, Orange County, California, where he died on 16 November 1976.[5]

[28R] Murphy was there first.[6] Culhane and 'Stetto' came down and they stayed in a 'C' man's place in the Quays in Belfast.[7] The next time they stayed in a hotel in Royal Avenue. Culhane stayed in this hotel and he was there under an assumed name and he was ordering breakfast and an attendant said, 'What'll you have Seán,' said the girl, who was from his own place. I understand that trains at the time they were returning to Cork … had been held up in Belfast. But Matt McCarthy (EOM: who was in the RIC in Belfast and who was working for Mick Collins) escorted them to the train and he said to the RIC, 'Them fellows are alright and get them into the train.'[8]

The first day in which they were to go to Lisburn they held up a hire taxi. We were to get a Minerva privately for a funeral.[9] Turner was a funeral undertaker and we ordered the taxi for [four] but evidently it was ordered for big bags as they sent us a taxi instead [for six] and the lads got into it. The driver was then held up and he was tied up, but on the road on the way out the taxi broke down so that we had to abandon it. Next Sunday was not my day off, but the lads wanted me to drive them and so when the taxi was ordered I **[28L]** went.[10] We drove to Lurgan.[11] I kept the car running for a while. Fox and McCorley were there to watch Swanzy's movements so that they knew he had gone to church.[12] The car was not running then, but while I was waiting a woman, who was looking after a child, had scratched the number of the car on a panel and that is how the RIC got the number of the car I was driving. On the way into Belfast we stopped and John McDevitt took the guns from us.[13] We went into the city by the Cave Hill which was an unfrequented route.

Later on I was told by a Greek, Mepras, who ran the garage that the police wanted to see me. Mepras was friendly with the RIC and I went up to the barracks. I remember I saw beside '...' the driver of the '...' taxi and he told me what had happened when he had been held up and tied up. I listened to him sympathetically, but this was the day after he had been tied up. Tim Healy mentions me in his book.[14] Leo[nard], a first class mechanic in Tubbercurry.

[26L] (EOM: Seán Leonard, wife has [a] post office in Tubbercurry.)

County Inspector Harrison was in charge of the Specials, and later he was a commissioner.[15] Edwards, the District Inspector, was released when I was brought away.[16] The County Inspector was hitting me with a Colt automatic. Igoe was a policeman in Belfast from Bunnyconnellan, and he was offering me farms in Canada if I would give information, or £15,000 down, and he would come to the cell to talk to me.[17] I think Harrison would have shot me then for I was down on my knees. I said that I had been tied up on the way out and that I had been released on the way back. I was brought up for interrogation and I was brought to the Central Police Station and I was taken up to an officer. I didn't know what they knew then. They found *An tÓglach* in my digs.[18] Edwards told me, as a hint, that it was better to keep me alive afterwards for they [could] get the rest through me. There was a Mrs Finn, an RIC man's wife, and the man afterwards gave me rifle and revolver stuff in Belfast. He is dead now, and I mind to call at his house for he was a native of Sligo.[19] Turley in Bunnyconnellan was married to Mary Carolan, and I was in gaol then some time in Belfast. Both happened to clash. Mrs Turley and Mrs Mary Finn came to see me for '…' sake. Mrs Turley was coming in. Do you know what she said to me, she asked Mrs Finn, 'Hanging wouldn't be good enough for me.' There was then a teacher who I asked to put down the record that I had been called out on this Saturday and he put it down in the book.

The first Sunday that I went out it was my day off.[20] I had a day off every two weeks. They held up the driver of the Hackney Taxi and then I took over but after a number of miles the pin of the accelerator sheared off and I couldn't go.

I was in Belfast gaol.

[27R] '…' to look at me or is he connected in any way. I was two months there awaiting trial. I was taken twice to the civil court to the court and it was adjourned, and I was then handed over to the military for court martial. McCrudden, who worked in the Belfast Post Office, was arrested for he resembled some of the men who were with me, but maybe he was a spy![21] Later he was a Super in the Guards in Boyle and he is now dead. He had me persecuted to tell him who was with me, and get him out to his wife and children. At a court martial people gave evidence. I was brought to Victoria Barracks.[22]

At the court martial witnesses. When I made a statement [I said] I was held up. They took me out to point out [where] I was held up, but it had poured cats and dogs and I think at first that they said that they didn't see. These girls came in later and they said that they did see a car which was held up. The next day the County Inspector [Harrison] was with me and I believe that they meant to do me in.

I was nearly lynched in Lisburn another day when I was there with the military, and they had to protect me or I would have been lynched. When I was being tried, Tim Healy and Campbell defended me: and a man, Donnelly, took up my case. Barney Donnelly took it up later, and Barney Donnelly's nephew came in to see me. I said I had £75 in King Street Savings Bank. I said, 'Draw it and use it for my defence.' But I found that this £75 was never used for my defence, but that he went off to Australia, this nephew. They found out that it was drawn. Barney was responsible to prove the case. He offered me £44 and I accepted it. The trial lasted six days in Victoria Barracks. I was found guilty. Tim Healy was good. I was sentenced to death by the military. I was six weeks in the condemned cell and I thought that I would be hanged when Kevin **[27L]** Barry was hanged.[23] I was in Crumlin Road Gaol for a month. A warden or an RIC man was with me day and night. I was in one of the padded cells. I saw the carpenters who had come in to repair the scaffold. I didn't give a damn but I didn't like the thought of the Belfast quicklime. There was no hope for me. The chaplains were awful nice to me. Dr Healy was so friendly that he sent in Dr McGurran to hear my last confession. On St Patrick's Day I was reprieved and the governor came out and he shook hands and he said, 'Leonard I'm glad that you're not going to be executed.' And I was brought in. A major read out the sentence and then he said at the end, 'That is now commuted to penal servitude for life.' I have a great old regard for St Patrick and St Joseph and I was doing a novena to them. Always on St Patrick's Day, we have a celebration with the children here. You could get whatever you wanted to eat when you were in the condemned cell and then I neither smoked [n]or drank.

At Toorlaustrane, 100 yards from the church, my mother for these six weeks which I was in the condemned cell, crawled on her two knees up to mass, and I feel that this was responsible for her death.[24]

I was sent to Walton in Liverpool. And I went once on a mail boat chained to five Black and Tans who had committed robbery and arson and we were in criminal clothes. From Walton to Portland I was chained – to Black and Tans. We were in jails going in the ordinary mail boat from Belfast to Liverpool. I was a month in Walton and then I went to Portland. I was always hungry with a lively sea breeze. Then I was brought on a warship to Portsmouth and Dartmoor. Portland was closed down and it was turned into a borstal: and we were brought on a warship a **[28R]** number of Irish lads from Cahirguillamore in East Limerick.[25] They had been surprised at an IRA dance there. Tadhg Crowley, Robert Ryan a TD from Loughgur [Limerick].[26] Dartmoor was depressing for there was fog there all the time and I was kept there until my release when the Treaty was signed. I was on bread and water there. Frank Thunder was there.[27] A great singer he was. And Potter, who had been sentenced to death for Bloody Sunday.[28] Milk and water he was and the appetite! But he was never a volunteer. Conway was also there from Tipperary and he had been sentenced to death for 'Bloody Sunday'.

[BELLEEK–PETTIGO TRIANGLE, MAY–JUNE 1922]

[26L] Dinny McCullough didn't want **[26R]** to be captured in Bundoran.[29]

Their rifles were slung on their backs but they left the camp in single file. Martin Bernard McGowan, then in Ballinvally [Co. Sligo], was there.[30]

Pettigo.[31] Twelve Irish Volunteers from here [Bundoran] and so many from Belleek were at this operation.[32] A Belleek man was in charge. I drove the lorry and in part of the barracks had a woman in it. John James McGonigle, the barber, lives here now (in Bundoran) and we came from Belleek.[33] John Joe Stevens was an ex-British soldier and was afterwards shot in Dublin in the civil war.[34] I think he was in charge of it, or if he was not he was one of the leading men. I think it was burned then. Paddy Gallagher of Donegal town was there and Phil Timoney.[35] They both live in Donegal town.

Notes

SEAMUS WOODS

1 The Income Tax office was raided and burnt in April 1920.

2 Seán O'Neill was a Belfast man who joined the British army to fight the Boers but while there joined McBride's Irish Brigade and fought against the British. He was O/C 1st Battalion, Belfast. He became a Commandant in the Free State army.

3 Seán MacEntee: see biographical sketch.

4 McDevitt was a sympathiser who allowed the IRA to use his shop on Rosemary Street for intelligence-gathering. It later operated as headquarters for an ASU, which included Woods.

5 This was the start of the pogroms when more than 10,000 workers in the shipyards and factories were driven from their workplaces. On 14 October 1920, Craig unfurled a large Union Jack at the shipyard, and said, 'Do I approve of the action you boys have taken in the past? I say "yes".'

6 Crossgar (population in 1910: 600) was an equally mixed Catholic and Protestant village fifteen miles south of Belfast. An IRA ASU from Belfast, including Seamus Woods, Roger McCorley, and Joe McKelvey, attacked the barracks at Crossgar on 2 June 1920. While they did not seize the barracks in the two hour siege, two RIC constables, Fitzpatrick and Carey, were wounded. It was stated that the IRA gave commands in Irish.

7 Patrick Thornberry was a national school teacher at St Matthew's on the Newtownards Road and prominent anti-Treaty republican. Interned on 11 October 1922, he led republican prisoners on the *Argenta* as well as directing a hunger strike on the ship. He was released unconditionally on 28 November 1924.

8 During Easter weekend 1920, volunteers across the country burnt between 300 and 400 old RIC barracks and twenty-two tax offices.

9 Spelled 'Ballinahinch' by EOM.

10 Spelled 'Duffy' by EOM. Volunteers Dan Duffin and Pat Duffin were killed by the RUC murder gang apparently under the command of DI Ferris, on 23 April 1921.

11 Murdered by Harrison's murder gang on 26 September 1920. Only Gaynor was a volunteer, although Trodden was a republican – as was another victim that night, John McFadden.

12 Sergeant Patrick Fallon was killed in Ballymote, Sligo, on 3 November 1920. Michael Grey, although a volunteer, did not commit the offence but was found guilty and sentenced to death only to be spared by the Truce.

13 The Italian-made armoured automobile used by the British army.

14 This refers to the killing of three Tans on Victoria Street on 11 March 1921 by an ASU containing Roger McCorley, Seamus McKenna, Seamus Woods, Seán Keenan, and Seamus Heron.

15 DI John Patrick Ferris had been involved in RIC reprisals in Cork and was transferred to Belfast, where he operated out of the Springfield Road barracks and allegedly took part in reprisals against the nationalist population. The IRA failed to assassinate him in May 1921, when Roger McCorley wounded him in the stomach and neck as he left church.

16 Oswald Swanzy was transferred to the North after his involvement in the murder of the Lord Mayor of Cork, Tomás Mac Curtain, on 20 March 1920. See biographical sketch.

17 On 23 April 1921, two Auxiliaries, Ernest Bolim and John Bailes, were shot dead in Donegall Place in central Belfast.

18 Perhaps a reference to Alexander McBride of 28 Cardigan Drive, who was taken from his home and murdered on 11 June 1921 by an RUC murder gang, apparently led by DI Nixon.

19 Most likely a reference to Felim Mac Guill, the Brigade Intelligence Officer in Antrim.

20 Glover was part of the murder gang that killed Gaynor, McFadden, and Trodden on 26 September 1920.

21 Thirty-one-year-old Constable James Glover was shot on 7 July 1921.

22 Originally from Norfolk Street on the Falls Road, Tom Fox (BMH WS 365) was a member of the ASU that killed District Inspector Oswald Ross Swanzy on 22 August 1920 in Lisburn. Fox was an officer in the Belfast IRA, he also held the rank of quartermaster in the 3rd Cavan Brigade as part of an unsuccessful attempt to get Belfast fighters to stimulate activity in west Ulster. He joined the Free State army after the Treaty.

23 Tom Leonard: see biographical sketch.

24 G. B. Kenna (pseudonym of Fr John Hassan), *Facts and Figures of the Belfast Pogrom 1920–22* (Dublin: O'Connell Publishing, 1922; reprinted Belfast, 1997).

25 Carolan was interned in Frongoch along with twenty-three other republicans from Belfast in the aftermath of the 1916 Rising. He escaped from the Curragh Camp in 1921 and shared a report of his 'thrilling escape' with the *Freeman's Journal*.

26 Dr Arthur Ryan was Medical Officer for the Belfast Brigade.

27 Joe McGuinne was later shot and wounded by the British army. When imprisoned on the *Argenta*, he was known for playing the melodian and the Uilleann pipes.

28 Denis McCullough: see biographical sketch.

29 On 24 March 1922, six Catholic civilians from a constitutional nationalist family were killed in their home by an RUC murder gang, apparently led by CI Harrison and DI Nixon.

30 The son of Major-General Sir Frederick Richard Solly-Flood, Arthur succeeded Sir Henry Wilson as military advisor to the northern regime after Wilson's assassination on 22 June 1922. Cavan-born Wilson was involved in the Curragh Mutiny in March 1914 and was totally opposed to any type of Treaty. He was apparently assassinated on the orders of Michael Collins, but his death actually led the British to pressure Collins into attacking the republican garrison in the Four Courts on 28 June 1922.

31 This was John Stapleton. He was ex-British army.

32 Arthur Griffith (1872–1922) was the originator of the Sinn Féin policy of abstention. He led the party by the same name prior to the Easter Rising. After 1916, he made way for Éamon de Valera and held the position of vice-President. One of the signatories of the Treaty, he was President of the Second Dáil, but was largely subordinate to Mick Collins in the Provisional Government.

33 Cathal Brugha: see biographical sketch.

34 Liam Lynch: see biographical sketch.

35 Liam Mellows: see biographical sketch.

36 Liam Deasy: see biographical sketch.

37 This was the final act in the unsuccessful joint-IRA northern offensive.

38 Originally from Coalisland, Co. Tyrone, Timoney was Adjutant No. 1 (Belfast) Brigade. He shot two Specials dead during the pogrom.

39 William Twadell (1884–1922) was a unionist politician and northern MP for Belfast West. He has a street named after him near Ardoyne in Belfast. He was a mob orator and a notorious anti-Catholic who formed the Imperial Guards, a loyalist mob. He was assassinated by the IRA on 22 May 1922, an action that precipitated the introduction of internment.

40 See EOM's interview with Aiken in this collection.

41 Aiken's 4th ND were nominally neutral regarding the Treaty. Aiken himself commanded the Ulster Council, a body formed in Clones in January 1922 to co-ordinate the joint-IRA northern offensive. Michael Collins, Richard Mulcahy, the Minister of Defence, and Eoin O'Duffy, the Free State Chief of Staff, co-operated with Aiken in regard to this body. After his arrest by the Free State, on O'Duffy's orders, Aiken then went anti-Treaty. Aiken did indeed write this 'long memorandum' promised to Mulcahy when he was imprisoned in Dundalk gaol and it is included in this collection.

42 Dan Hogan: see biographical sketch.

43 Spelled 'Beasly' by EOM. Piaras Béaslaí: see biographical sketch.

44 Seamus McGoran was a leading Belfast republican and an active member of O'Donovan Rossa GAA club and GHQ Organiser for Cavan.

45 Gearóid O'Sullivan: see biographical sketch.

46 Eamon 'Bob' Price was captain of C Company, 2nd Battalion Dublin Brigade in 1916 and was in the Jacob's Factory garrison during Easter Week. He was IRA Director of Organisation (1920–1).

47 Born in Wicklow, Tom Cullen was IRA GHQ 2nd Deputy Director of Intelligence. He supported the Treaty and was an officer in the Free State army, resigning in 1925. He died in a drowning accident in 1926.

48 Tom Ennis was O/C of E Company, 2nd Battalion, Dublin Brigade in 1916. He was Battalion Commandant during the War of Independence and O/C of an ASU in Dublin city, 1920–1. He led the burning of the Custom House on 25 May 1921. He later supported the Treaty, commanding Free State forces during the Battle of Dublin in July 1922.

49 Liam Tobin, see biographical sketch.

50 Paddy Daly, see biographical sketch.

51 Under the Special Powers Act, the unionist government interned 700 republicans between May 1922 and December 1924. They were housed in Larne Workhouse, Derry Gaol, and most notoriously on board the *Argenta*, a prison ship moored off the coast at Larne. Woods was interned on 14 November 1923 as a Free State Commandant. He was the last prisoner to leave the *Argenta* when it was decommissioned in January 1924. He was released on 17 April 1924.

52 John Nixon: see biographical sketch.

53 On 6 May 1941, during a heated debate on the floor of the northern parliament, Herbert Dixon MP, Lord Glentoran, the chief whip, rebuked criticism from Nixon, then an independent Unionist MP, that he had sung the Soldier's Song at the Curragh, by stating 'you cannot murder me, my lad'.

54 Woods was arrested, while interned, for the killing of William Twaddell MP in May 1922.

55 Kevin O'Higgins: see biographical sketch.

56 Spelled 'Kain' by EOM, George O'Kane was a postman from Rostrevor, Co. Down. He was actually interned on 5 October 1922. According to their records, one of the other seven internees with the surname O'Kane on the *Argenta* was arrested before the introduction of internment, which appears to undermine Wood's recollection.

ROGER MCCORLEY

1 Pogroms have a long history in Belfast: in 1828 before Catholic Emancipation, 1843, 1857, 1864, 1872, 1880, 1884, 1886, 1898, and 1912.

2 The Pierce-Arrow armoured car was an anti-aircraft armoured lorry built by the British during the First World War.

3 The Steyr Mannlicher M1895 rifle was an 8 mm bolt-action rifle made by the Austrian firm Josef und Franz Werndl, which was smuggled into Ireland before the war by the UVF.

4 Seán Cusack was an important military IRA officer in the years 1920–2 and went on to become a senior officer in the Free State army. He was deeply hurt by the lack of

interest in the North shown by Cosgrave's Government and resigned his commission in 1924.

5 For 'Peter the Painter', see above, p. 30.

6 Founded in September 1920, the full-time A Specials were disbanded in 1925 and the C Special reserves never remobilised after 1922, leaving the part-time B Specials only.

7 In July 1920, 8,000–10,000 Catholics and socialists were expelled from the Harland and Wolff shipyards and from other workplaces by unionist mobs. The Ulster Unionist leadership was directly implicated, while the employers acquiesced to the demands of the loyalist vigilance committee that no Catholics be reappointed.

8 According to McCorley's witness statement (BMH WS 389), during this period there was bad blood between the Specials and the British army and incidents like this occurred regularly.

9 Oswald Swanzy: see biographical sketch.

10 Lt Colonel Brice Ferguson Smith gave a speech in Listowel in June 1920 which led to the resignations of RIC men in Kerry when he advocated shooting IRA suspects on sight.

11 The Irish White Cross was established on 1 February 1921 as a mechanism for distributing funds raised by the American Committee for Relief in Ireland. As a result, Amcomri Street (an acronym of the committee's title) was built off the Falls Road for expelled Catholics.

12 Sergeant Matt McCarthy was an RIC man from Kerry and an Intelligence Officer for the Belfast Brigade. He passed information about the whereabouts of Swanzy on to Collins.

13 Spelled 'Mac Jinnes' by EOM, McGuinness was an early member of Na Fianna Éireann in Belfast, having joined in 1910.

14 Spelled 'Mc Elvey' by EOM, Joe McKelvey. See biographical sketch.

15 Spelled 'MacAnally' by EOM.

16 Seán O'Neill was a Belfast man who joined the British army to fight the Boers but while in Africa joined McBride's Irish Brigade and fought against the British.

17 Séamus Dobbyn was present at the foundation of the Irish Volunteers in Belfast in 1913. Dobbyn was later a member of the Supreme Council of the IRB, 1917–21. He shared a cell with Éamon de Valera in Lincoln Gaol and helped coordinate the escape in 1919.

18 Belfast's Bloody Sunday took place on 10 July 1921. In a reprisal for an IRA ambush on a police raiding party, which caused in the death of RIC Constable Thomas Conlon, the RIC launched attacks on several majority Catholic neighbourhoods. This sparked clashes between republican and loyalist paramilitaries resulting in the destruction of over 150 houses and the deaths of fifteen civilians (ten Catholics and five Protestants).

19 Carrick Hill is a nationalist area at the bottom of the Shankill Road in Belfast.

20 John Nixon: see biographical sketch.

21 *Facts and Figures* is an important record of the Belfast pogroms, 1920–2. Written by a priest, it gave a day-to-day account of the actions of the Orange mobs, the RIC murder gangs, and the Nationalist defence of the areas under attack. See above, p. 118 n. 24.

22 O'Grady was an IRA volunteer.

23 Fowler Hall was the HQ of The Loyal Dublin Volunteers, a Dublin version of the UVF, and was used as a drill hall for them up until the First World War.

24 There were two Craig–Collins agreements, the first in January, the second, referenced in the interview, was signed in March and failed like its predecessor. See the chapter on Joe Sweeney in this volume.

25 Timoney was an active IRA volunteer in Belfast, originally from Coalisland. He shot dead two Specials during the Pogroms.

26 Patrick Downey was listed as Adjutant to A Company, 1st Battalion, No. 1 Belfast Brigade, 3rd Northern Division.

27 Eoin O'Duffy: see biographical sketch.

28 Dan McKenna: see biographical sketch.

29 Tom Morris: see biographical sketch.

30 Hugh J. Murray was listed as captain of the Castlewellan Company, No. 1 Battalion. 3rd Down Brigade, 3rd Northern Division.

31 Gearóid O'Sullivan: see biographical sketch.

32 Diarmuid O'Hegarty was secretary to the Free State government in 1922. After Collins' death he served as Director of Intelligence and Commandant General of the Free State army until May 1923.

33 Patrick Casey was a leading Volunteer from the Newry area (BMH WS 1148).

34 Henry Wilson: see biographical sketch.

35 McCorley was in Kerry during the worst of the fighting. In March 1923, twenty-three republican prisoners were murdered in the field and five executed in four weeks. At Ballyseedy, on 6/7 March, nine republican prisoners were tied to a landmine, which was then detonated. Stephen Fuller miraculously survived. Two similar incidents subsequently took place at Countess Bridge and Cathair Saidhbhín.

36 William Richard English-Murphy was a decorated British army officer from Wexford. He was known as W. R. E. Murphy (1890–1975) and was a soldier and policeman. He served as an officer with the British army in the First World War and later in the Free State army. He was in charge of the Kerry Command during the Civil War and was second in overall command of the Free State army from January to May 1923. He enlisted in 1922, having taken no part in the War of Independence.

TOM MCNALLY

1 They were so described as the company was made up of many clerks and shop assistants.

2 See interview with Seamus Woods in this collection.

3 Seán Mac Mahon (1893–1955) was from Dublin and in 1916 was an active member of the IRB and Irish Volunteers. He was arrested and interned in Frongoch then released under amnesty in December 1916. He was appointed Quartermaster General of the IRA in 1920, and as a Free State officer as Quartermaster and later as Chief of Staff.

Internees at Ballykinlar Internment Camp, Co. Down, in 1921. (Mercier Press)

Séamus Woods, Tom McNally, Joe McKelvey and Frank Crummey of the 3rd Northern Division shortly after the Truce in July 1921. (Jimmy McDermott)

Buncrana barracks during the Truce period. William O'Doherty is in uniform on the right. (Mercier Press)

British military evacuating Letterkenny in March 1922. (Niall McGinley Collection)

Members of the Liscooley/Killygordan IRA Company no. 4 Brigade, 1st Northern Division. The photo was taken outside the home of local volunteer John McGroarty, who is at the end of the front row on the right. (Mercier Press)

Eithne Coyle, a native of Falcarragh, Co. Donegal, bearing arms for a photo shoot in 1921.(UCD Archive)

Crowds gather during Michael Collin's visit to Armagh on 4 September 1921. Collins is seated at the centre of the back row of the car. (UCD Archive)

The command of the Anti-Treaty IRA 1st Northern Division, March 1922. In the picture are Seán Lehane, Charlie Daly and Jack Fitzgerald standing from left to right.

Over fifty Sinn Féin prisoners from County Fermanagh being escorted to Belfast Prison under armed guard in May 1922. (*Belfast Telegraph*)

A large quantity of arms and ammunition were found in the an attic above this house on Park St, Belfast, during a military raid in June 1922. (*Belfast Telegraph*)

Searches on pedestrians during the Belfast Riots 1922. (*Belfast Telegraph*)

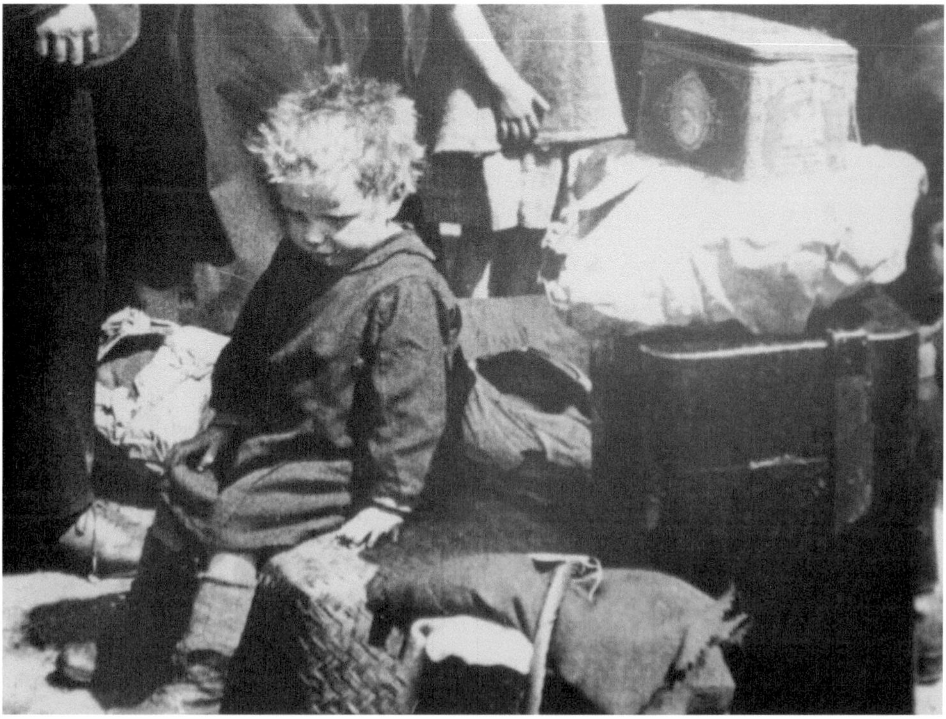

A refugee child fleeing Belfast during the Northern Pogroms.

IRA in Carndonagh, Donegal, in 1922. (Mercier Press)

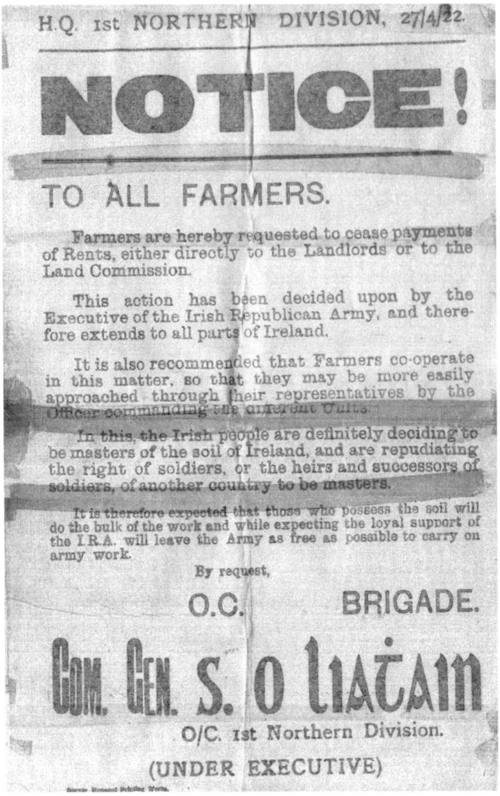

H.Q. 1st NORTHERN DIVISION, 27/4/22.

NOTICE!

TO ALL FARMERS.

Farmers are hereby requested to cease payments of Rents, either directly to the Landlords or to the Land Commission.

This action has been decided upon by the Executive of the Irish Republican Army, and therefore extends to all parts of Ireland.

It is also recommended that Farmers co-operate in this matter, so that they may be more easily approached through their representatives by the Officer commanding the different Units.

In this, the Irish people are definitely deciding to be masters of the soil of Ireland, and are repudiating the right of soldiers, or the heirs and successors of soldiers, of another country to be masters.

It is therefore expected that those who possess the soil will do the bulk of the work and while expecting the loyal support of the I.R.A. will leave the Army as free as possible to carry on army work.

By request,

O.C. BRIGADE.

COM. GEN. S. O LIAĊAIN

O/C. 1st Northern Division.

(UNDER EXECUTIVE)

Notice from the 1st Northern Division requesting tenants to cease payments of rent. Dated 27 April 1922. (Mercier Press)

IRA Executive Volunteers on the Donegal–Tyrone border, May 1922. (*Belfast Telegraph*)

Peter Boyle, Frank Aiken, Mick O'Hanlon, John McCoy, Pádraig Quinn and Ned Fitzpatrick of the 4th Northern, circa 1922. (UCD Archive)

Frank Aiken in a boat, circa 1922. (UCD Archive)

Frank Aiken in Sandyford circa 1925 with two unidentified women. (UCD Archive)

Frank Aiken, Mick O'Hanlon, Pádraig Quinn, Seán McBride and Pa Murray at Derrycamma House outside Castlebellingham, Co. Louth, during the Civil War. (UCD Archive)

Wedding photo of Nano Aiken and Felim Magennis in Sandyford on 29 October 1930. In attendance were May Aiken and husband Heber Magenis, and Pádraig and Malachy Quinn of the 4th Northern. (Eoin Magennis)

A Free State soldier outside the hole breached in the wall of Dundalk Gaol through which about 50 men from the 4th Northern Division escaped on 27 July 1922. (UCD Archive)

Éamon de Valera's arrest in Newry in October 1924 as he entered a meeting in support of Michael Murney, the anti-Treaty Sinn Féin candidate for Down. (Irish Academic Press)

Paddy McLogan in conversation with Fr. Harris. (Len Costello)

4 Cathal Brugha, see biographical sketch.

5 The Steyr Mannlicher M1895 rifle was an 8 mm bolt-action rifle made by the Austrian firm Josef und Franz Werndl, which was smuggled into Ireland before the war by the UVF. The Lee–Enfields were most likely Standard Mark III bolt-action rifles, also widely used by the British Army during the First World War.

6 The Lewis gun (or Lewis automatic machine gun or Lewis automatic rifle) was a First World War light machine gun of US design that was adopted and mass-produced in Britain. The Thompson ('Tommy') gun was an American submachine gun first produced in 1918.

7 See interview with Frank Aiken in this collection.

8 The passage ends abruptly here. It would appear to refer to either Felix McCorley (brother of Roger) or Felix Devlin, Divisional Communications Officer.

9 Rory McNicholl was part of an ASU with Thomas Flynn, Captain D Company.

10 Johnny McArdle, the Divisional Engineer, invented his own type of grenade.

11 Originally from Norfolk Street on the Falls Road, Tom Fox was a member of the ASU that killed District Inspector Oswald Ross Swanzy on 22 August 1920 in Lisburn. The Corkmen in question were Dick Murphy and Seán Culhane.

12 Tom Leonard: see biographical sketch.

13 This would appear to be a mistake by McNally. O'Donovan did not come up for the second, and successful, attempt to assassinate Swanzy.

14 In May 1921, GHQ ordered a Belfast Flying Column to an abandoned farmhouse on Lappinduff mountain. Thirteen men from the four companies of the 1st Battalion of the Belfast Brigade, under the nominal leadership of Joe Magee, operated in the 3rd Cavan Brigade (Cootehill). They were quickly surrounded by around eighty RIC and Black and Tans and forced to surrender. Volunteer Seán McCartney was killed.

15 Patrick 'Paddy' Smith (1901–82) was O/C of the Cavan Brigade. He opposed the Treaty and went on to become the longest serving TD in Irish history.

16 Seamus McGoran was a leading Belfast republican and an active member of O'Donovan Rossa GAA club and GHQ Organiser for Cavan; Seán Gallagher occupied the roll before McGoran and was apparently arrested drunk in his bed.

17 Frank Crummey was a school teacher from Belfast. He was a member of No. 1 Brigade, 3rd Northern Division and held the position of No. 1 Brigade Organiser. He was then part of No. 1 Brigade Intelligence and later 3rd Northern Division Intelligence Officer. He had good contacts in military police circles, the post office, and the telephone and telegraph sections. He was interned on the prison ship *Argenta*, and supported the Free State.

18 Benedict Donegan of the Springfield Road was 1st Battalion deputy Intelligence Officer. His brother, Thomas, operated as Battalion Medical Officer.

19 Sergeant Matt McCarthy was an RIC man from Kerry and an Intelligence Officer for the Belfast Brigade. He passed information on to Collins about the whereabouts of Oswald Ross Swanzy, killed on 22 August 1920 in Lisburn.

20 Joe McKelvey: see biographical sketch.

21 Dan Hogan: see biographical sketch.

22 Liam Lynch's 1st Southern Division arranged an arms transfer with the pro-Treaty GHQ at Beggars Bush as part of the proposed joint-IRA northern offensive in spring 1922. Lynch exchanged IRA guns for rifles with the serial numbers chiselled off, which Beggars Bush had received from the British.

23 The beginning of the Civil War, on 18 June 1922, when the Free State army attacked the republican Four Courts garrison with British artillery.

24 Spelled 'McKay' by EOM. John McCoy: see biographical sketch.

25 This refers to the Belfast Brigade's attack on Musgrave Street barracks on 18 May 1922, which formed part of the second and last joint-IRA offensive in the spring of 1922.

26 Tom Flynn was a very active IRA man from Kashmir Road, Belfast. He took part in the Raglan Street ambush, on 10 July 1921, when the murder gang led by Nixon was repelled from the Falls Road area. At the time of the Truce, Flynn was captain of D Company, 1st Battalion, No. 1 (Belfast) Brigade, 3rd Northern Division.

27 Felix Devlin was Divisional Communications Officer. He served as Deputy Quartermaster General in the Free State army.

28 Joseph MacRory (1861–1945), was Archbishop of Armagh from 1928. He was Bishop of Down and Connor during the Belfast pogrom and was reasonably sympathetic to Sinn Féin.

29 Spelled 'Murry' by EOM, Joe Murray was O/C 3rd Battalion, Belfast Brigade during 1921.

30 Along with Seamus Woods, McKenna was an officer in B Company. He fought in Cavan and was part of the ASU, along with Murray, McCorley, and Woods, who carried out the killing of three RIC at Roddy's Hotel, beside Musgrave Street barracks, in January 1921.

31 Spelled 'McAnally' by EOM, Tom's brother worked in the IRA engineering department.

32 Kevin O'Higgins: see biographical sketch.

33 James Hogan (1898–1963), born in Loughrea, Galway, was a history lecturer at University College Cork. He served as Director of Intelligence in the Free State army.

JACK 'SEÁN' LEONARD

1 Ernie O'Malley mistakenly named Seán 'Tom' Leonard, perhaps a case of the author failing to read his own terrible handwriting.

2 Seán Culhane (BMH WS 745, p. 11).

3 *Cork Examiner*, 28 August 1920.

4 *Freeman's Journal*, 3 February 1921.

5 *Sligo Champion*, 11 March 1977.

6 Dick Murphy, Captain G Company, Cork City Battalion.

7 This was Dr Leo 'Stetto' Aherne, a Cork IRA man and a good friend of Seán Culhane.

8 Matt McCarthy, an RIC man from Kerry and an Intelligence Officer for the Belfast Brigade. He gave detailed information to Collins about the Harrison/Nixon murder gang.

9 A popular type of car of the period.

10 Leonard, who was called Seán by the Belfast volunteers, was selected to drive the volunteers to shoot District Inspector Oswald Ross Swanzy in Lisburn on 22 August 1920 as he was a taxi driver and a motor mechanic.

11 Lurgan seems to be mistaken for Lisburn here.

12 Originally from Norfolk Street on the Falls Road, Tom Fox (BMH WS 365) was a member of the ASU that killed District Inspector Oswald Ross Swanzy on 22 August 1920 in Lisburn. Fox was an officer in the Belfast IRA, he also held the rank of quartermaster in No. 3 Cavan Brigade as part of an unsuccessful attempt to get Belfast fighters to stimulate activity in west Ulster. He joined the Free State army after the Treaty.

13 A Belfast IRA volunteer, Seán McDevitt was 1st lieutenant C Company, 1st Battalion, No. 1 (Belfast) Brigade.

14 Leonard is indeed mentioned in his Healy's memoir, *Letters and Leaders of My Day*, vol. 2 (New York: Frederick A. Stokes Company, 1929), p. 622. Timothy 'Tim' Healy: see biographical sketch.

15 According to a report by the Free State in 1924, County Inspector Richard Harrison colluded with a twelve-man police murder gang operating out of Brown Square Barracks in the Shankill area, including Harrison's close associate District Inspector John Nixon. The gang was responsible for a series of reprisals against Catholic civilians, including the infamous McMahon family murders on 24 March 1922.

16 District Inspector Joseph Edwards was stationed in Omagh RIC Barracks. On 13 December 1921, the Unionist MP for South Tyrone, William Coote, asked questions in the northern parliament stating that 'he did associate with Sinn Féiners'.

17 Head Constable Eugene Igoe was born in Attyma, near Ballina. Bunnyconnellan, spelled 'Bunnycoolan' by EOM, was the place name of his birthplace. He led an RIC secret team who fought against Collins' Squad in Dublin after the assassination of the Cairo gang on 21 November 1920.

18 *An tÓglach* was the newspaper of the Irish Volunteers from their inception in 1913.

19 Thomas Finn, who was forty-six in 1920, was a native of Sligo. He was married to Mary, a native of Leitrim. Both were Roman Catholics.

20 This section of the interview refers again to Leonard's involvement in the Swanzy shootings and his subsequent imprisonment in Belfast gaol.

21 Obviously a loose-talking volunteer who took the Free State side in the Civil War.

22 A major British army barracks in Belfast in the New Lodge Road area.

23 On 1 November 1920, IRA Volunteer and UCD medical student, Kevin Gerard Barry (1902–20), was the first Irish republican to be executed by the British since the Easter Rising.

24 Spelled 'Toorlistrane' by EOM, Toorlaustrane is a small village in Kilmactigue parish in south Co. Sligo. Leonard was present when his mother, Margaret Leonard née Feeney, died on 12 January 1926 at their residence in Tourlestrane, Sligo.

25 On 27 December 1920, the Black and Tans raided a Sinn Féin fundraising dance at Cahirguillamore in East Limerick, killing five IRA volunteers.

26 Tadhg Crowley was O/C Ballylanders Company, Adjutant East Limerick Brigade, and member of the East Limerick Flying Column. He was arrested on 19 October 1920. Robert Ryan was also in the Limerick IRA and subsequently won election to the Dáil as Fianna Fáil TD for Limerick in 1932.

27 Frank Thunder was a singer and harmonium player and is believed to have led a choir in Dartmoor prison.

28 Bloody Sunday referred to 21 November 1920, when thirty-one people were killed, including eleven British soldiers and police from the Cairo Gang, sixteen Irish civilians, and three Irish republican prisoners. Frank Teeling, Edward Potter, and William Conway were sentenced to death at their court martial in February 1921 for the assassination of the Cairo Gang. The evidence against Potter in particular appeared very weak. Teeling escaped from Kilmainham before his sentence could be carried out and Potter and Conway were reprieved.

29 This section of the interview refers to Leonard's involvement in the Belleek–Pettigo triangle. He was released during the general amnesty after the signing of the Treaty and joined the 1st ND of the pro-Treaty IRA. Like Leonard, Denis McCullough also supported the Treaty. See biographical sketch.

30 Martin Bernard McGowan (BMH WS 1545) was a national school teacher and anti-Treaty IRA Commandant in Sligo. He was elected to the Free State parliament in 1923 for Sligo–Leitrim as an abstentionist Sinn Féin candidate.

31 Pettigo is a small village on the Donegal–Fermanagh border.

32 Between the end of May and beginning of June 1922, a mixed force of pro- and anti-Treaty IRA fought against the Ulster Special Constabulary and then the regular British army for control of Belleek fort, which lay with the six counties. The IRA evacuated on 6 June after the British deployed heavy artillery. Leonard was among a detachment of Free State forces from Ballyshannon and Bundoran who took part.

33 A Volunteer from Ballyshannon, McGonigle was involved in the fighting at Belleek.

34 John Joseph Stevens was taken from his lodgings in Dublin by armed men on 2 September 1922 and shot dead.

35 Timoney, Gallagher, and Stevens were active volunteers in Donegal during the War of Independence.

4TH NORTHERN DIVISION (LOUTH, ARMAGH, MONAGHAN AND SOUTH DOWN)

MICHAEL O'HANLON

(UCDAP17b/106, pp. 71–86, April 1950)

Michael Rodger O'Hanlon (1898–1968) was born in Mullaghbawn, Co. Armagh and was the eldest of Bernard and Sarah O'Hanlon's nine children. He received his secondary education at Blackrock College and remembered climbing up onto the school roof during the Rising to watch the city burn and listen to the roar of the cannons.

O'Hanlon joined the Mullaghbawn Company, Newry Brigade in January 1918. He canvassed for Patrick McCartan in the Sinn Féin South Armagh by-election in February 1918. His two brothers, Peter and Bernard, were also active throughout the period. As the eldest son, O'Hanlon was afforded the opportunity to study medicine at UCD in 1917 and during his time in Dublin was active in C Company, 3rd Battalion Dublin Brigade. Notably, he helped carry out the directives of Michael Collins' Squad on Bloody Sunday on 21 November 1920. He was subsequently sent to Cavan where he operated as an IRA organiser and ran training camps.

After the signing of the Anglo-Irish Treaty in March 1922, O'Hanlon rejoined Frank Aiken's Fourth Northern Division as Divisional Intelligence Officer. When the pro-Treaty 5th Northern Division occupied Dundalk on 16 July 1922, he was interned in Dundalk Gaol. He escaped on 27 July along with 105 other men, when a mine was detonated at the gaol wall. O'Hanlon was later caught and imprisoned in the Curragh in November 1922, and escaped once again through a tunnel in April 1923.

O'Hanlon resumed his studies at UCD in 1925 and practised medicine in Shrewsbury in England for five years from 1927. He returned to Ireland in 1933 and became a captain in the Army Medical Services, serving in Mallow hospital during the emergency and later as O/C of Athlone Military Hospital. He also served as medical officer to the Disability Pensions Board until his death in 1968. O'Hanlon's mother, Sarah O'Hanlon, although not mentioned in this interview, was active in Cumann na mBan and acted as an intermediary between members of the IRA and O/C Frank Aiken. As a consequence, the O'Hanlon's home and business premises were often raided. As Sarah notes in her military service pension application, 'I had a very hard time.'[1]

[1920–1]

[71R] I joined C 3 [Company 3, 3rd Battalion] when I was studying Medicine [at UCD]. Tom Burke[2] was in my company of which Paddy Flanagan was the O/C.[3] At the beginning of 1920, Frank Aiken made me join.[4] We had about twenty students in the company. Andie Cooney;[5] Seán Flannigan, a good chap who went as Medical Officer to the Dublin ASU; Seán Dunne, now in Grangegorman,[6] Paddy Quinn,[7] [Jack] Egan[8] of Kiltimagh [Co. Mayo], Jerry Davis[9] [of Roscommon].

When Balbriggan was burned they pulled us out on patrol one or two days afterwards.[10] I was doing an exam at the time. Our patrol went along by the [Dublin] Castle, Dame Street, Tara Street, Quays, and I was on this for a week, three or four hours at a time. I had a grenade, and there were eight to ten of us. Paddy Flanagan was with us all the time. We started at five o'clock [p.m.] mostly as we were fellows who could be free. We went on both sides of the street, round about ten men. There were some men in front of me. My instructions were to rush off the path, throw a grenade at the target and rush back again. Below Healy's [store][11] the lads stopped and they said they missed [Seán] Connelly who was from East Galway. He was taken out by the Auxies. He had a grenade on him. He got a good beating from them and thirteen years.

Mick White was a pal of mine and he was as happy as a lark when on patrol.[12] He was on the King's Inns job. Peadar Clancy[13] had decided that morning that on account of a sudden shower of rain the soldiers would not lie out on the grass in front of the place. He lived on Swift's Row near the Hal'penny Bridge. His place was a dump and the mother was very good. The Auxies had taken over the Central Hotel that evening, and we didn't know they were in it.

Seán Connelly, I think , was killed on our [anti-Treaty] side in the Civil War.

I was on a job in South Richmond Street on which there were **[71L]** supposed to be two lorries. The second lorry was attacked before the first came up to us. We had our stuff in Holles Street. The first lorry stopped when the second lorry was attacked. The wheel of the second lorry was broken with a grenade, I found.

Bloody Sunday.[14] Dick Sweetman,[15] Joe Carroll[16] and I had a room at the back of Vincent's [Hospital] almost at the corner of '...' [Street]. On Friday night Paddy Flanagan told us to go in and shoot a man in a room. We were told that these lads might fight so we had better bring an axe to break down doors, and a grenade. There were a number of them in the one room. We were given no description of the man save that he was sleeping in a particular room. There was a bedroom and a sitting room and we were to go on in through the sitting room into the bedroom and the sitting room opened on to the landing. We were told we would find trouble there. When we got in we found that our man had a gun and that he was covering the door to the landing, but we came in **[72R]** by the door of the sitting room and none of us fired for there was a girl in bed with him, and she put her arms around him. One of us lifted the gun, so we thought on account of the girl we had better bring him down to Paddy in the hall. Paddy Flanagan gave us a terrible look. Paddy asked him his name and he clicked his heel. I was covering him and the shot blackened my hand. Paddy fired twice but I don't think the man was killed. He wrote his experiences in the *Daily Sketch*.[17] I had admiration for him. We got his revolver only. We did not get his papers.[18]

We had nothing to do with the lads covering off the house. There were three of us for each room and there were three or four of the British in this double house.[19] The porter there got two years for letting us in to the house, a poor old man he was.[20] Seamus Gaugin was outside the house, and Jack Egan from Kiltimagh. When we had finished we went off to 86 [Grafton Street] to dump our arms, and just as we were near 86 we saw Jerry Davis and the other lads making for 86, so we went to the Ha'penny Bridge (which could not be crossed by lorry) and then went amongst the people coming from mass. Mick White was at home when we got to his house. 'I don't know where I'll put this stuff,' I said, and Mick said, 'I'll keep it.' He was on a job that morning and he shot an old Major, and he ate the Major's breakfast when he came out of the room. He was always as cool as a cucumber.

You [Ernie O'Malley] gave us a lecture after your escape [14 February 1921][21] about automatics, on Eden Quay. Peadar O'Donnell was in that class,[22] and Jerry Davis, for we were being trained before being sent down the country. I was to have been sent first to Wicklow but Ginger [O'Connell][23] sent me to Cavan. Charlie McAllister had been sent up there before me.[24] He had **[72L]** had about a week's lecture. Charlie [McAllister] and Emmet Dalton and you [EOM] lectured us.[25] Then I told them I knew nothing about a rifle for I had never handled one, so they sent me down to one of the dumps to see both a rifle and a machine gun. Leo Duffy, the Quartermaster of the 3rd Battalion was with me.[26] We were in a dump when [Oscar] Traynor[27] was caught in Brunswick Street, a dump in an old coach house, and Duffy gave me a run on a Lewis gun.[28] Ginger [O'Connell] said I had best go to the North. There were conferences about the formation of Divisions. The northern men came up on a Saturday to Monday conference. [Richard] Mulcahy said, 'you should go into this conference.' 'I have no business there,' I said. 'You should go in,' he said, 'for it will be of use to you.' Someone got up and ridiculed Fermanagh, and Mulcahy said that 'little [Frank] Carney[29] was the only good man in Fermanagh and the best thing to do with that area was to take that man out of it.' Rory O'Connor, had just escaped from the Curragh, came in to the conference and he got a great reception.[30] There had been six IRA men executed [6 March 1921] **[73R]** that morning in Dublin whilst the conference was on.[31] The conference did not last long that morning. All trams stopped in the city, workers came out for two hours and the whole city closed down and was packed with its people who were all walking around and no one was talking.

Tom Burke went to Offaly to the Birr end and Jerry Davis went to Athlone. Tom Lawless went to Wexford,[32] Charlie Daly to Derry,[33] Peadar O'Donnell to Donegal, [Michael] McCormick to the Second Southern Division.[34] I had put down my name as an organiser. I was a squad leader at the time. At a company parade I was to have been appointed section leader, but Holy Joe [O'Connor][35] said before I was to be sent away as an organiser. I was told to go to Lower Gardiner Street to see Mr Baker. We waited, a number of us, six hours for [Richard] Mulcahy ('Baker') and then [Oscar] Traynor saw Pádraic O'Connor[36] and I … he was a great talker. Traynor examined us on what we knew. He told me to go back to my Company O/C and tell him what he, Traynor, thought of him for my not knowing about the rifle. Ginger [O'Connell] after the Truce [in July 1921] took me out to Camp in Glenasmole to learn about a rifle.

Cavan: I went to Shercock and Bailieboro [Co. Cavan], where there were no organisations of any kind. There were four fellows in Bailieboro who were keen. There were two good companies in Kilbride [Mountnugent], East and West; Paddy Smith came from there.[37] I got a company going in Shercock. There was a conference for the 1st Midland Division. There were from five to six good companies in the Virginia Battalion. In May [1921] I came up for it and for the 1st Eastern Division formation, so the 1st Eastern [Division] took over Bailieboro and Virginia [Co. Cavan], but I don't think they made anything of Bailieboro.

I was sent to Michael Collins for a run on intelligence **[73L]**, but instead he gave me four or five pages of a memo to read, and then I was to burn it … He read out lists to me, but as he went like a steamroller and as I wasn't accustomed to the West Cork accent, I didn't get much from his talk. I have a certain notion it was the Engineer's Hall in Gardiner Street in which I met him. I was sent to Seán Boylan,[38] and I told him I was going to Bailieboro. Diarmuid O'Hegarty[39] told me to get off at Virginia Road Station that a Volunteer, Benny Lynch,[40] drove the sidecar and he was to leave me at Fitzsimmons, who was the Battalion Adjutant in Virginia and who was a returned American. I was to say to Benny, 'I'm the man from Dublin' but he didn't turn up so here I was walking along the road with Collins' papers on me. The Tans were beating up a drunk in the village. I stayed in the hotel that night and it was next door to the barracks. I had a note also on me for Fitzsimmons. I was given a bicycle and I remained there until the Truce. Then Meath took over Virginia and Bailieboro and I was pushed to **[74R]** Cavan town Battalion, Crosserlough Battalion. I was pushed on to Ballingar [Ballinagh] which had been taken over by the 4th Northern [Division]. It had eight of the nine companies, all of the men were of a good age, who had been in the volunteers since 1915 … decent fellows they were, but too old. They had six or seven rifles, but they never told me about them. Frank Aiken would agree with us joining the IRB and he said it wasn't necessary. In Ballinagh [Co. Cavan] the old fellows used to go to an old IRB man for advice, so I joined the IRB. Peeny Smith was then the centre.[41] He was a publican.

Eoin O'Duffy was the Director of Organisation before the Truce. Once I came up [to Dublin] to see D[iarmuid] O'Hegarty, but I saw Eoin O'Duffy and Joe McKelvey.[42] O'Duffy asked me if I knew of any safe digs in Dublin. He questioned me up and down, but I didn't then know he was the DO then for the two areas, which I then told him were good areas, he took in to the 5th Northern [Division] – Cavan and Crusherlan [Co. Cavan].

[TRUCE]

When the Truce [12 July 1921] came I told Ginger [O'Connell] I was going to do medicine. There was an Officers Training Corps in the college, and I joined it. The others jeered at us, and Andie Cooney also, so I left the Officers Training Corps. Frank Aiken then began to organise in the North and I went up to him.

Evacuation. [Jerry] Davis and I met Emmett Dalton, Chief Liaison Officer, and I took over Greenore, Sligo, Westport. In Room 56 in the Gresham [Hotel] I met fellows who were walking out because they were not satisfied with the present GHQ.

They offered me a job in the Adjutant General's office, but by this time Frank Aiken had taken over Dundalk and I went up to him.

Tom Rogers, who had been Divisional Quartermaster, got **[74L]** hurt so Frank A[iken] sent out for me, and he made me Acting Quartermaster.[43] I said I could not act as I had left Beggars Bush, and then Paddy Quinn became Quartermaster and I became both Assistant Quartermaster and Assistant Adjutant.

We had a Column in South Armagh and had an ambush arranged for Mullaghbawn [Co. Armagh], twenty of us who had rifles and a Lewis gun as well. We had several mines laid down but on this particular day we had none in position. We went into an old factory to wait. Specials had gone to Jones' Cross from N[orth] Armagh. This was in May or June 1922, and we were waiting for them to come back. We left the '...' outside and the countrymen went into the factory which had a high wall. We had to get ladders to get in. The Specials didn't come back until one o'clock in the morning. We fired but I don't know what happened. In all, the action lasted about twenty minutes. No one fired a round from the Lewis gun and both of our parties skipped it. **[75R]** We found one drum of Lewis gun ammunition left behind and rifles, grenades as well.

The rifles came in to us from Beggars Bush Barracks. We got the rifles in Beggars Bush, and one Crossley tender went to the Four Courts and exchanged these rifles for other rifles, and then brought the exchanged rifles back to Dundalk from there they were issued to the 4th ND.[44] There was a tender full of rifles, about forty of them. (EOM: 'What led up to this?') Well, we were supposed to file off the numbers from the Beggars Bush rifles in Dundalk barracks before we were to issue them to northern units. Our fellows one evening brought down a consignment of rifles from Dublin, and I was in the stores when the rifles came in. The O/C of the Banbridge Battalion [Co. Down] and his men had been waiting a day for their rifles which were to have come from Dublin. They had to go back at once and we gave them the rifles before we had filed off the numbers. I think these men had to get back to their area for there was a curfew on then. The British had only handed these rifles over the day before and they were caught in the Banbridge Battalion area in a dump, and the British got back at Michael Collins over it.

As a result of this mishap an exchange of rifles was arranged. I expect the Banbridge men had promised to file off the numbers as soon as the rifles had been dumped. John Henry Burn [Byrne] in charge of the Banbridge Battalion, is now in the USA.

Seamus Woods'[45] men from the 3rd Northern Division came down for rifles which had been sent from the [Beggars] Bush to us and they got the rifles. They stayed one night in Dundalk. They **[75L]** had the rifles in an oil lorry. Felix McCorley[46] was in it and MacNicholl, Rory, with the lorry also.[47]

Our rifles from the [Beggars] Bush went to our own men in the division. We must have got a couple of hundred rifles from the Bush. When the break was coming Paddy Quinn and I sent sixty rifles to the South Carla Battalion area close to Dundalk.

Frank Aiken had been instructed by the [Beggars] Bush to attack Anne Street Barracks Dundalk, which was held by republicans belonging to his division, but Frank refused. He went to the Bush then with all his officers except P[addy] Quinn and I. John Quinn[48] and Johnny McCoy went up with him.[49] They returned on a Saturday night and the men [were] instructed to return to Dublin on Monday morning. We sent out the sixty rifles that day. The fellows we could rely on were across the border and we sent word to [Charlie] McGlennan of Armagh Brigade to send us reliable men to guard our prisoners.[50]

Frank wouldn't raid for hostages. He argued when we **[76R]** brought back hostages that we were making the border. If you wanted to scrap, he thought, you could always go across the border and fight there.

Frank Aiken was chairman of the Northern Divisions and I always understood that he was to take charge of any joint action if there was a fight in the North. Peadar Mac Mahon[51] was to be sent down, about Woods' period,[52] to be O/C [of] the 4th Northern and Aiken was to be chairman of the 5th ND. We thought it was a way of getting rid of Frank and that he would be used politically as a scapegoat. In the barracks in Dundalk, we were sure that Mac Mahon was coming.

Belfast area [1922]: 'Chuck' Byrne was very active and he was a great scrapper like a captain of the ASU.[53] At the split [in late June 1922] he was with [Joseph] McKelvey and the Four Courts men. Some police came to a corner of the Falls Road and Chuck's men ambushed them there. The Free State crowd also heard of this and Roger McCorley rushed down with his crowd, but Roger was late and was wounded and captured. It was lucky they weren't both wiped out. 'Wish' Fox,[54] O/C of the Brigade that took in

Down. He is somewhere in Belfast. He was outside of things in the 1922 period.

Charlie McGleenan: a good man, a Battalion O/C from Ballytrodden, Blackwatertown [Co. Armagh]. He ran that area. Wish Fox was also from Blackwatertown, Armagh.

Another Battalion O/C was Seán McConville[55] who is still there, and who lives in Derrymacash. His Adjutant, John Joe Murray, has a furniture shop in Lurgan.

[Charlie] McGleenan sent us down fourteen prisoners, who had been **[76L]** picked up. McMurrin,[56] County Commandant of the RUC [USC] had been picked up in Newtownhamilton and others were picked up who had been accidently [*sic*] run into things. They were a nuisance to us for we had to feed them and guard them. Frank was always being ordered from Beggars Bush to let them go. We kept the prisoners away from the Barracks and they were guarded with North Armagh rifles, the only rifles we had.

Frank Aiken, with the exception of Johnny McCoy and [Paddy] Quinn, returned from Dublin and Frank was to return again to Dublin on the following Monday. That night after supper we were standing outside and we were wondering where we could hold our explosives in safety. We had Catholic ex-soldiers as a garrison in Dundalk. They were the scourings of towns and always a nuisance, for our good men were on the border. There were one hundred of these ex-soldiers, but we didn't even trust them to look after the prisoners. Frank Aiken said nothing. Paddy Quinn said he wouldn't trust them in Dublin in Beggars Bush.

[IMPRISONMENT IN DUNDALK GAOL]

That Saturday **[77R]** night at four in the morning we took out a five-ton lorry to Cooley with explosives and we had none of these ex-soldier lads with us. We met some of the garrison of the barracks when we were coming back in the morning and we were arrested in bed by our own men, the garrison.[57] An hour afterwards, and by the 5th ND men as well. Dan Hogan,[58] Acting O/C 5th N[orthern], from Clones [Co. Monaghan] was in the barracks in Dundalk. They held seven or eight of us and they wanted to leave us in the officers' quarters. They allowed Frank [Aiken] up on parole to see [Richard] Mulcahy on Sunday morning and as far as I can remember from subsequent talks with Frank, Mulcahy said he knew nothing about the arrests in Dundalk. Frank came back with documents which Dick Mulcahy had given him to put up to us to sign stating that we would be of good behaviour. The Beggars Bush crowd expected us all to sign the documents, but everyone refused to sign. The next day we were all flung into the gaol, which was a mile and a half away at the opposite end of the town. Frank Aiken demanded to be sent to the gaol with us and he was sent there next day.

The Armagh fellows came in and they made a hole in the wall, a good lot of them had Free State views.[59] Johnny McCoy was in charge of that operation. When it was over they went off home again to Armagh for they didn't agree with our views. [John] Hanratty and [Frank] Mallon,[60] who were both on the brigade staff, are in a firm in Armagh, a provision business. You [Ernie O'Malley] had better question the figures as to what rifles we got from the [Beggars] Bush. Perhaps one hundred rifles might be correct.

[CIVIL WAR][61]

Frank Aiken drew up the plans in Dundalk **[77L]** for dumping arms. He held a divisional meeting and he put it up to all the officers. Both sides were to dump arms and to concentrate on the North itself.

Two Louth Battalions had gone over to the Four Courts Executive. The six-county end were under Beggars Bush. All the divisions were split except our division, for even those who were Free State in our Division never broke away from us. Frank Aiken brought me and Tom Rogers to Dublin and he went first to Dick Mulcahy.[62] O'Connell Street was burning when we arrived and Cathal Brugha was yet alive.[63] Frank thought that Mulcahy would arrest him, so he gave me a copy of the stuff he had on him and in case he was arrested I was to go through to the South [to] see [Liam] Lynch; and Rogers, if Frank was arrested, was to go to Liverpool and get back to our area to inform our men. Frank came back with three passes for us to go to Limerick, passes signed for a general and two colonels.

The last Free State post was Maryboro [Maryborough, Co. Laois]. There were no signs of anyone in **[78R]** Templemore. We found that the Staters in Maryboro [Maryborough] were disciplined but we were first held up in Tipp[erary] by fellows who were playing pitch and toss, and the man who held us up had a revolver in his pocket. There was really no defence of a line or of an area of country. We were trying to avoid Jerry Ryan in Thurles.[64] We reached Tipperary without being held up then we thought that republicans wouldn't hold out for a week, for there was very little sign of activity between Tipperary town and Limerick.

[Michael] Brennan[65] was in Cruise's Hotel and [Liam] Lynch[66] was in the new barracks and there was a truce on. (EOM: 'Did [Dick] Mulcahy allow [Frank] Aiken to go down so that republicans would be thrown off their guard and so that Free State could intensify their effort to start the fight in Limerick?') Frank Aiken went back and forwards between the two barracks, and he thought he was making progress. Our attitude, of course, was coloured by the Northern situation. A GHQ man came down, Free State, and he criticised [Michael] Brennan's defences. Frank Aiken pleaded with Brennan not to put up barbed wire and additional defences as it could only cause ill feeling. Frank Aiken was there also … At some point the Cork men who occupied it had fired at men who were putting up barbed wire and then the firing began again, and it lasted all night. We got the impression that Brennan was being pushed from his GHQ and we heard that it was [Dan] Hogan who had been sent down.

The following morning we went up to [Liam] Lynch, but he had gone away. We followed him on to Clonmel. We ate there, but we found he was terribly annoyed. The Free State had used the Truce to land troops on his coastline. We were in Limerick on 12 **[78L]** July [1922] and it was then we heard that Cathal Brugha was dead. Liam Lynch was very sore that day at lunch when the four of us were there. The road from Clonmel to Kilkenny we found active. I had a pass from Liam Lynch. There was no petrol in Kilkenny and I was sent to get petrol from the QM in the Barracks, representing ourselves as a crown of Dan Hogan's men from the 5th Northern. The Free State had sent out 250 men the previous night to attack Templemore and the QM had stayed in bed, 250 cut throats he said they were.

Frank Aiken, when he reached Dublin, reported back to Portobello to Dick Mulcahy.

Within a week all the other things happened. Dundalk and the whole countryside was full of refugees; houses were being burned in our area across the border and fellows were shot dead. They took up the old men and they shot them when we had placed mines, one [man] in each mine hole, so [we] were up against terror in Dundalk.

Whilst we were in Dundalk Gaol for ten days the 'B' Specials came in and took over houses in South **[79R]** Armagh, in Mullaghbawn, but the day Frank Aiken escaped they never came back again, the Specials.

Frank Aiken was pushing Peter Hughes,[67] the TD, as hard as he could, and on the Saturday before we attacked the town he sent Tom '...'[68] in to see Hughes in Dundalk to say he would have to do something about the situation. The [Dundalk] Town Council held a private meeting, and later Dan Hogan arrested them and put them all in gaol, but only two of them were republican so he released them so they couldn't come out in public.

The Free State evacuated Dunleer next day [Sunday] in Louth. The men wanted to attack Ardee, but they were only a mob, I felt. Cavan had a very fine crowd who were enthusiastic, but very unlucky. For Tom Sheridan got killed at the start in an ambush in daylight at which proper precautions were not taken.[69] He was killed, a few of the lads were wounded and that disheartened the men. This was in Ballinagh district. Andy Reilly was Free State. He was caught soft in the Tan War; a Cavan man, he used to drink.

We sent some of the stuff we had captured in Dundalk to South Armagh. John Quinn wanted to entrench around Dundalk and fight the Staters as they came in, but Frank [Aiken] was yet in hopes of peace. We had a plan for the capture of Cavan Barracks. We were to put a mine against the gate and when it had gone [off to] rush in with petrol tins, but the Staters had barbed wire behind the gate and it held us up, and besides the plan of peace we had been given was all wrong. Our intelligence was very bad at the time.

Eiver Monaghan,[70] our Divisional Engineer, farms at Point's **[79L]** Pass. He is now back from the USA. He stayed in Monaghan and he got caught there. We went to Owen Meegan's house, and Meegan wanted Eiver to go somewhere else, but they were caught together that night.[71]

I got caught at Virginia in my way back from '...'

I had arranged for an attack on Killashandra. I called at Paddy Baxter's house, as the Baxters lived near the Leitrim border, and Paddy said the country was finished forever.[72] It would only end in a stalemate, he said, so he sat up and we talked. They did attack Killashandra but they didn't take it and I wasn't there. They had not many rifles. The best of the Cavan men had gone into the Free State army. The Ballinagh men had attacked.

I was caught and I was brought to Oldcastle. We had arms in Dundalk gaol. Jimmy Goodfellow was in charge of prisoners there and the prisoners were to fight their way out.[73] Between my trips to Cavan I was outside [the prison] with a party for we were to engage them when I would hear a shot from inside the prison, but the escape didn't come off. After four or five weeks I reached Kilmainham **[80R]** Gaol. I had been caught with arms in December [1922]. I was moved by mistake to Hare Park and the Free State tried to bring me back from Hare Park,[74] but the lads hid me in the cook house, blackened my face, but it was hopeless to hide me. MacNicholl from Belfast was waiting for me in the Curragh, and whenever he saw me he winked at me although he was in charge of the PAs [Prisoners Assistant]. Then at last I was brought back, but it was none too late for court martial. I was kept in 'the condemned wing' in Kilmainham with the Leixlip column, Mick O'Neill and the others.[75] Six were executed there. I came back with Seamus Maguire, and we all changed our names on the way down.[76] There were twelve of us. I was to take the name of Mallin, but going to the camp one of the officers recognized me, Johnny MacAllister '...' 'I'm sorry you're here, Jerry,' he said. Also they knew Maguire from Castlepollard [Westmeath]. Pat Farrelly from Kells,[77] Seamus Maguire, Mick O'Neill were not know to the Staters so they remained behind. Pat Farrelly got out in a Cork fellow's name. He had been Brigade O/C of the Kells Brigade. I went back to Kilmainham with six Cork men who had taken the names of six other men who were due for execution. They were waiting for the, the Staters, all day until they found me. Whacker MacCarthy took the place of a man from Ballina; Murphy from '...' and when he was asked where he came from he said to me, 'is it in Mayo or Sligo?' There was a seafaring fellow from Cork who took the place of a fellow from 'H...' who was [at] the Post Office in Mullingar and who had been caught with Maguire. He had a very long face one morning. 'What's wrong with you', I asked. 'I'm the father of twins', he said. A fellow [named] Hoolihan from Cork took Pat Farrelly's place.

[80L] Pat Farrelly's brother was a priest and he came up on Christmas Eve to say that his brother had been shot as he had not written a letter, and no one had heard about him. He kicked up a row outside of the gate. The commandant came in and outlined the duplicate to send out a note to his brother, but I told him not to send a note. We had sent a wire to his wife when we were told that she had had twins. The lad refused at first then he sent out a note, but that only made matters worse for his brother did not recognise the handwriting and then he was sure it was a Free State trick and that his brother had been executed. Then the priest kicked up a violent scene. He said his brother had surely been executed and that the Free State had forged the handwriting. Hoolihan was the man whom the Cork men had sent over to [Terence] MacSweeney's funeral in London.

There was an old sentry box in Kilmainham which had a plank sticking out about a foot in the **[81R]** bottom of the box. There was a dummy in that sentry box for we threw stuff up at the figure and were convinced that it was a dummy, but at night we thought there was a live man there. We stove a hole in a ventilator. You know the kind of '...' there was there and we got a pair of blankets from which we made a rope. The ventilator faced out on to the yard. There was a sailor there who said he would get up a rope ladder on to the second storey. The hot pipes were unused, and the sailor had convinced us that he could get a rope around the block which was sticking out and then climb up to it. He was busy making a rope ladder and he was cutting the blankets fine and was testing the result. On Christmas Eve [1922] when it was dark we were to make an attempt, but a number of men came in who were in more danger than we were. They had a contact outside, and they asked us to postpone the attempt for a day or so. I was moved suddenly. I was picked out of a crowd by myself and I was brought to the Joy. A few days later I was called out and was given the form to sign, but I dodged it.

There was a solicitor in Newry, [John Henry] Collins,[78] and when he saw that [Henry] O'Hanrahan was to be executed the following morning in Kilmainham, he and a few others came up to see [Richard] Mulcahy about me.[79] When I came home from internment he told me what had occurred. Dick Mulcahy had told him that there was no danger of my being executed and he showed a letter from Dick Mulcahy which stated that if I signed the form, I would be released.

Kilmainham. The men were in fairly good form. We were locked up when we entered the prison. The food was **[81L]** handed in to us but they didn't interfere with us. O'Hanrahan and a Dublin lad were executed. Usually they were brought to our part of the wing when they were sentenced. The deserters in Mick O'Neill's column were kept apart. One of them tapped with his toe pointing downwards as he passed us at exercise and that men [meant] they were for the grave. They were shot as deserters. There was not as much tension as you would expect. In Tintown I felt the morale was too soft. Men were better when things were hard, when parcels were being stopped and when they had to put up a resistance. I got two hundred cigarettes in the office when the lads were cut off.

The Joy. I was in B Wing. Andie Cooney came across to me. Andie wouldn't touch [Dr] Loftus who had been in practice in Thomas Street, Dublin.[80] He told me to take a fit and that he'd be hanging around the circle, and he came in; and in a few weeks' time I took another [fit] but he wasn't there. Only a few orderlies came in to me and I was put on a special diet. I wanted to get back to the Curragh so that I could escape. If Dr Loftus recommended me I would be changed to the **[82R]** Curragh. Both Andie and I knew [Dr] Loftus for he had been in the 4th Battalion, [Dublin No. 1 Brigade]. He gave me cigarettes and everything. There was a strained feeling in the Joy, and a bitterness against the Staters due to the shooting of Rory [O'Connor] and the other three.[81]

There was a tunnel there. Peadar O'Donnell said there was a way of getting out through the roof to escape as they were afraid that I would be taken back again to Kilmainham, where I would be executed.

The Cork men didn't come to the Joy when I was there. There was an old officer of Maguires from Castlepollard (who was in the Free State army) and he knew all the fellows who were wanted and he knew one right man, little Titch Maguire from Castlepollard.[82] 'What were you doing with the Lewis Gun?' he was asked when he had been captured. He was a kocky [cocky] little lad. 'I had it for shooting crows', he said, and they nearly killed him. This officer knew Titch. Of course, the others had Cork accents. Hoolihan from Douglas has an awful Cork accent. I heard [Pat] Farrelly try to practice [*sic*] the Meath accent, but the Meath speech is very flat.

In January [1923] I was moved to Tintown 1. Peadar O'Donnell was O/C [of prisoners] of it and he was a good O/C. There were four huts in it and a medical hut. There were 120 in each hut, which was really a zinc stables. Peadar ran the camp well. On the way down from the Joy, Peadar got around the different groups as we went down by train. Peadar slipped through the crowd and told the men to pick twenty-five from each group for this particular hut – twenty-five Mayo men – Jim Rush, Johnny Mullen; twenty-five from Limerick, West Limerick (Paddy Hegarty, Crossmolina).[83] Peadar had **[82L]** men in a group of twenty-five from Dublin, a nondescript crowd. Each hut elected an O/C. Mayo and Limerick had a falling out about this election. Peadar O'Donnell wanted me as a neutral to become O/C [in] this hut as the feeling was hot. The only way to keep the matter secret was to tell everyone in our hut. Johnny McCoy was brought over from Tintown 2 to the 'sentries hut' in Tintown 1 for isolation so that he could be near to us. Old Doc Ferran was in charge of the medical hut.[84] Peadar wanted to run a tunnel from the hospital and he wanted to put me into the hospital, but [Dr] Ferran would not allow us to take advantage of the hospital.

We decided to start the tunnel from the doorstep at the entrance to the hut because the Staters never searched the doorstep. The Mayo men had made three unsuccessful attempts in Athlone previously so that they had bad escape experience. [Michael] Kilroy had been in gaol in England in the Tan War, and he was a stonemason by trade. The floor was formed of six inch squares.[85]

[83R] We picked off bits of cement, and we dressed them into the shape of a set with old nails until the mixture looked like a set, which he then put on a three by two board. There was soap and dirt put in between the squares and a '...' piece of '...' wire stuck through it. When the wire was pressed down the soap would hold the wire, which would then be held down by the cement.

James Kilroy was a little fellow. Paddy Connor, a school teacher who was in that Mayo bunch. Big Paddy Connor also and Willie Malone,[86] a cousin of Paddy's. The wire went through the board and the nail would help to lift up the false set.

Then he had to cut out a set just inside the door. The Mayo fellows did most of the tunnelling. Four to five did orderly officers on our turn. They worked at night and they were nearly killed with work. They would prize [*sic*] away loose board and pack in the earth behind them. Tom Mullins of Castlebar, a teacher in Howth, was very able. He was Vice O/C to Peadar O'Donnell. There were two switches at the door. One switch covered three lights at the far end where the manure was put for horses. There were from twenty to thirty lights on the other switch. On the first evening the men broke the bulb at the end of the hut. We appealed for bulbs but they were again broken.

[Tom] Scanlon from Sligo put the wire into the tunnel and when the switch was pressed the fellows would stop their work below for this switch controlled [all] the bulbs in the tunnel.[87] The Free Staters were worn down in time so they would give us any more bulbs and that corner was darkened. They made dummy beds in the corner in case men working on the tunnel could not get up in time (for a sudden inspection or for a raid). A sculptor could not have done **[83L]** it better than these men [who] made the figures. Two men worked at a time below, one digging and the other hauling. They made bags out of sheets and the bags were brought back filled to the shaft and there they lay until night came. It took twenty-four hours to make a yard. Our tools were a carving knife and it was so well used that it looked like a needle in the end.

At night there was a system of guards. They would put their beds in under the window and put their shirts over their clothes. The[y] knelt up and watched the outside. They clicked their fingers according to the number of PAs who were coming. Then the orderly officer would switch off the light in the tunnels. The PAs would count the dummy beds; several times they would do this. When the signal came the lads below ran to the mouth of the tunnel and waited there. There were three of our fellows on each side of the hut spotting sentries or PAs at night. Ours was the end hut. At 3 a.m. the PAs went for tea and it was at this time that we packed away stuff. There was one fellow, an artist, who **[84R]** could pack away stuff at night like Rory O'Connor. He was an East Mayo lad, very deft at packing stuff at night, and he never made a sound. He would put a strip of cardboard to replace the board he had taken out when he was packing. So he moved silently from place to place at night whilst he packed away the earth.

There were as well a few picked footballers outside the hut in case a ball came which would hit the hut (if a football hit the hut hard it might cause an avalanche). The other huts could not be told to keep off. Once a handball hit the hut and it knocked out clay from partition boards.

Little Jimmy Donnelly was in here also.[88] The tunnel took about six weeks at the false lid – about twelve weeks in all for the 42 yards. The tunnel ran into Tintown 3. There were hard shingly stones in the clay which was fairly dry.

Ventilation: Between the stalls were square posts which had been kicked by horses, and timber had been nailed over the places which the horses had smashed. The lads took down one post, ran a red hot poker through it and so made a passage for ventilation. Paddy Hegarty of Crossmolina got very white as a result of tunnelling, yet he had been an athlete in his younger days.

The PAs would raid during the daytime, but there was always a fellow hanging about who would use the switch. One day the Free State found clay in one of the stores so they raided the place inside and upside down and they threatened me for I was O/C of the hut.

In Tintown 2 there were 1,400 to 1,500 men. Seán Gormley of Dundalk[89] and Tom Bourke (Squint) kicked up a row for parcels.[90] Our tunnel was nearly finished at the time so we couldn't join **[84L]** in with them as we were near the wires. Seán Gormley wanted to kick up a row but I said it would mean a hunger strike and I wouldn't go on with it. The governor sent down parcels for us and we wouldn't take them, so the governor scratched his head and said, 'them fellows are on strike for parcels and you won't take yours.' We had spring beds and plenty of food, good mattresses. The governor was Billy Byrne, [Dublin No. 1] Battalion 2, a very decent man.[91] When he threatened you, you knew he did it because he had to do it.

One of our lads below in the tunnel put up a rod so that we could test the length of the tunnel had gone and the rod came up inside the wire. I had a £5 [note] in those days. We gave a workman a £1 for a wire cutters and a £1 for a cold chisel, I think. We got a wire cutters. Workmen with a PA came in to do something and one of the workmen 'lost' his wire cutters. We were to go out in tens; certain fellows were in charge of each bunch of ten and we were to start off between ten and eleven at night. On Thursday, Johnny McCoy came in to our hut: 'Anyone would know there was something on,' he said, 'for the **[85R]** lads are shaving and getting ready.' We tried the rod and it came up beyond the wire. I asked Billy Byrne to find out what time mass was to be on the following morning. The lad who was in charge of each ten stood by until nine of his men were gone, watching the sentry who walked up and down, and when his back was turned to the tunnel he switched on the light and when the sentry turned round he switched the light off again.

The lads were feeling some fun for they had surrendered without a fight and they got very sore as the executions continued and in the end they'd do anything. Owen O'Brien, a creamery manager from Kilmallock, a good man who kept the Limerick City men in order.[92] He was the best of the two Limerick bunches and he died of pneumonia before the tunnel was finished. A fair-haired, very nice man and a dead loss as far as Limerick City men were concerned. He was the man put up for the hut [O/C] against a Mayo man, small man, Reevey, who worked in the tunnel. Either he or Kilroy went that night through the tunnel and cut through the wire of the new Tintown Camp which was ready for prisoners. When he had cut the wire he tied a handkerchief which flapped in the wind so that the men would easily find the hole. Jim Boyle of Foxford, a battalion O/C, was also on that and he put up a good fight the time he was caught during the civil war.[93] He had got in a few Joyce [*Concise*] *History of Ireland*s for each of them had canals and railroads marked on it. One bunch hit off for the Wicklow Mountains.

The Mayo men went west for the Cardwell's at Celbridge for Mrs Cardwell was an aunt of Frank Aiken. One of them, however, was in Mulally's column and one of the girls was accidently [*sic*] shot by one of our fellows.[94] Paddy Mulally's men were staying there.[95] About seventy-five **[85L]** men got out. One of a group of the Dublin fellows at the end of the tunnel wanted to get back and he held up the men. Old Jimmy Gunn and Micky Wade, ICA, and Brian Fagan, a lean man and a great man. They were old men and there were fine characters. They remained behind reluctantly. Burke, ex-Lord Mayor of Limerick, was also there. We got broken up and I was with Jim Boyle of Foxford, Jim Colbert, Liam B. J. Callaghan of Cork. I was on the Curragh when Jim Boyle caught up with us. We could see the lights of the Curragh and we waded across the Liffey catching each other's hands. Then we lay in the furze and slept. We found that the Kildare people were good whenever we called in for food. We came to a cottage and the sons of the house were in the Free State army, but they gave us milk and bread and told us where our supporters lived and the people who weren't so good. We found later on that we were in a trap for we were on the Dublin Road. We left it, crossed Black Church **[86R]** Road and we went on a rock, slept in the furze and then came down to a [shep]herd's house where there were a couple of old men. An old mother came in from shopping. She had rashers and eggs and she gave us a great feed. We had just come down to them on chance. They told us to go to Art O'Connor's, and they brought us to an outlying house. The Mayo fellows got to Caldwell's and it was raided while they were there. The house was on the north side of Celbridge and we were on the south side of Celbridge. Tom Mullins was caught there. Jim Boyle and I went north. Johnny McCoy and Jim Rush caught up with us in O'Connor's, where we got guides for Dunboyne. Louis McGee was always friendly and he put us up. [Tom] Scanlon of Sligo, Jim Rush, Kiltimagh, who was in [Michael] Kilroy's column, and is now dead. A school teacher from Ratoath came to us on a wet night when we were to cross by fields so we decided to go by the road. Jim Boyle was away behind arguing about

'…'. We saw the flash of shot, for the Staters were raiding the house of the girl and they heard us. Johnny McCoy took a rifle from a Stater and we went to fire at a fellow covering '…' and they were captured.

The three of us went back to Louis McGee, and I went home by car. McGee brought us to MacCarthy's of Dunboyne. He had been a Fenian in his young days and had then gone to Australia. For a fortnight we were kept in Nugent's farm. They were the family of Molly Nugent.

Peadar [O'Donnell] really picked his men before we went into Tintown Camp that time. A bunch of Kerrymen came into the hut later. Some of them were Cahill's men.[96] 'I would do anything for **[86L]** him,' they'd say of another Kerry man who was down the tunnel. I won't relieve him. Both Kerry sides worked hard and both had fine men. Cahill – Humphrey Murphy were the two sides.[97] Cahill's men used to boast that they had met the Staters in Kerry before Free's [Humphrey's] men had met them.

MICHAEL DONNELLY

(UCDA P17b/116, pp. 43–6, 23 Oct. 1950)

Michael Donnelly (1895–1984) was born in Carnally, in the parish of Lower Creggan, Co. Armagh. His parents, Patrick and Anne (née Fearon) Donnelly, were both Irish speakers according to the 1901 census. Donnelly is believed to be the only South Armagh native to mobilise during the Easter Rising, serving as a volunteer in the Dundalk Battalion under Seán MacEntee. Due to his involvement, he was captured and imprisoned in Wakefield Gaol, and later in Frongoch.

On his release in December 1916, Donnelly travelled to Liverpool, and from there set sail to New York. He worked in a pharmacy in Manhattan, and in May 1917 registered for the US Army, noting that he had two years' military experience as a 'corporal' in the 'infantry' of the Irish Republican Army.[1]

Donnelly returned to Ireland in the spring of 1918, and quickly became involved with the republican movement. He was an active member of A Company Dundalk Battalion throughout the War of Independence. He was shot in the right leg during the Cullyhanna shootings of 6 June 1920, in which the IRA assailed a group of RIC men at the local Aeridheacht. During the Civil War, Donnelly was involved in the attack on Dundalk Gaol on 27 July 1922, which resulted in the freeing of Frank Aiken and his men who had been imprisoned by the pro-Treaty 5th Northern Division under Dan Hogan. Donnelly was subsequently imprisoned by the Free State and was transferred to Mountjoy Gaol on 2 August 1922. He participated in the Civil War hunger strike in the Curragh in October–November 1923.

Donnelly went back to the USA in 1926, where he worked with the A&P Grocery store chain. He returned to Dublin in 1939 and set up the Lilmar Pharmaceutical company.[2]

[EASTER RISING]

[43L] I was attached to the Dundalk Battalion in 1916. Arrangements had been made for the Rising, and on Easter Sunday morning the main body left Dundalk and seized the rifles in Ardee RIC barracks [Co. Louth]. I was to remain in Dundalk. There were eight of us there under Seán MacEntee, who was then an engineer in the Dundalk Power House.[3] We remained indoors in the old Gaelic League Rooms but we were to seize the old National [Redmondite] Volunteer Rifles in Dundalk afterwards and we were to be picked up by cars.[4] We were there all day, hidden. We saw [Eoin] MacNeill's countermanding order but an order came in the evening to countermand it … and we were then to get in touch with the main body who were on their way to Slane [Co. Meath].[5] Paddy McHugh of Dundalk was with us.[6] MacEntee set out to check on this countermanding order by motorbike. Joe Boyle (dead) went off on the Ardee Road and three of us cycled.[7] Paddy Hughes (consul San Francisco) and I and at Slane we came up with the Volunteers, who were then confused as a result of the different orders.[8] They had about one hundred men and they had brought on men from Dunleer and Ardee. Donald O'Hannigan and Paddy Hughes were in charge.[9] We gave them the countermanding order, so we were ordered to go back the three of us and to await further instructions. On [Easter]

Monday evening word came through that fighting had started in Dublin. These men who were in Slane didn't return to Dundalk again. We were at a loose end there so we went on into Dunboyne [Co. Meath] for they had some rifles.

When I was arrested I was brought to Wakefield and there I was kept in solitary for a month, but then their prison regulations eased off.[10] Jimmy Hanratty, of the Tempest Press,[11] Terence MacSwiney[12] and Séamus Dobbyn **[43R]** were there.[13] Then I was sent to Frongoch 2 Camp (the Distillery Camp).[14] Denis McCullough was there,[15] Henry Dobbyn (dead),[16] 'Comrades' (Seán O'Mahony) and they were active in the IRB.[17] I got out early out of the camp, but I went back to visit it when there was a bust up there. There was some kind of a mutiny in the camp, and in Dublin they were anxious to get a report of what was happening, so I got this report and brought it on to Liverpool, where I met Neil Kerr and the IRB command, so I gave them my report.[18] I was asked to take a job on a boat, the *Celtic*, as a fireman (trans-Atlantic ship). I often wished that the damn ship would sink. There were a hell of a lot of lads who were evading military service in England there. I brought the report to the office of the *Gaelic American*.[19] [John] Devoy was there then, and Liam Mellows.[20]

I remained on in America until the conscription campaign began in Ireland [April 1918], when I returned home. There was a registration at the time at the end of 1918. In September, I came back with a cargo of mules from Missouri. There were six of us in the party. Duffy was with us. All of us signed up in New York, and we went in on a convoy of thirty-eight vessels. We had to feed the mules. There was [Spanish] flu on board, and Duffy, who was from Clonaslee [Co. Laois], died aboard and was buried at sea.

[44R] It took us nearly a month in convoy to reach London. We jumped the ship, stayed a day or two around London. Some of us stayed in a Salvation Army house, and then we broke up. At that time a travel permit was required for Ireland, but Neil Kerr put us in the crew's quarters at Liverpool.

I was attached to A Company Dundalk, from 1919–20.[21] Most of our officers were older men then. There was a raid on Ballyedmond Castle [Killowen, Co. Down] for arms and [Frank] Aiken was in charge of it at the end of 1919 [May 1919].[22] We got a couple of small pieces only in that raid. In early 1920, there was the demolition of the evacuated barracks in Louth [Village], Castlebellingham [Co. Louth]. In Dundalk, the RIC held posts at Bridge Street and Anne Street and Clanbrassil Street, but I think it (the last) was evacuated.

(EOM: to go in after the evacuations) On Saturday night I was in charge of a party that raided the Income Tax Office and burned it in Dundalk. (That could be about Easter, 1920).[23] These activities were all new and strange to the older men who were more cautious. My idea then was to carry out operations in the evening.

At Cullyhanna [Co. Armagh], we held up the RIC, who surrendered but the sergeant who had his hands up, took down one hand and pulled his gun and he backed down the street. I kept firing and I got him, but he wounded me in the foot. I had wounded him a couple of times and I counted my rounds as I fired. The lads got a car to Dundalk and I was picked up by some of the party as I was coming in to Dundalk. I got as far as Drogheda, for I wanted to get on to Dublin and I put up at the White Horse Hotel [Newpark, Co. Dublin]. Seán Gormley came up with me and he contacted someone in Pearse Street, and I was brought to the Mater [Hospital], where I spent two months.[24] This was about the middle of 1920. My name got around as being concerned with the shooting of the sergeant so I was then on the run. One RIC man was killed and one wounded in that scrap.[25] It was late in 1921 when an ASU started.[26]

I went to London where I got .45 ammunition and .45 revolvers and they came in through Dundalk. I got about two dozen revolvers or so. The GHQ price for stuff was very high.[27] **[44L]** Dick Walsh (of Ballina, Co. Mayo) was then in London, where he got some rifles.[28] Early in 1921 we got some explosives as well through Liverpool. There was a reorganisation at the Truce and Paddy McKenna, who had been sent down from the GHQ, was appointed Brigade O/C.[29]

John McGuill on a Monday evening, which was the market day in town, raided the Inland Revenue Office and he put it up in smoke, although there had been an unsuccessful attempt there on the Sunday.[30] My home was on the border in South Armagh, and I was working in Carroll of Dundalk.[31]

Newtownhamilton RIC Barracks.[32] This attack was carried out by Newry and South Armagh. The barracks was attacked from houses which were adjoining. The barracks' door was sprayed before the attack, for Johnny McCoy came up the street with a potato sprayer.[33] The Newry group, of whom [Frank] Aiken was in charge, attacked from adjoining houses and we in front used covering fire.

'Surrender,' Frank Aiken said, 'or we will blow you to hell.' The barracks was **[45R]** partly blown in. The barracks was burned but it was not captured.

At the Truce I was appointed liaison officer. Craig was the C/I [County Inspector, RIC].[34]

[46R] Liaison work: There was no question of the bill you sent in when on this work, for you were always asked if you wanted money – that is anyone who carried on in a paid capacity. Evidently there was no control of money, and you were seemingly encouraged to spend money. There was a definite attempt to sap morale. [Emmet] Dalton and [Bernard] McAllister were in the Dublin office.[35] There were a lot of fellows who had been having a rough time for a few years, and I realised what the fellows on top were at.

[45R] Spies: A fellow in the Post Office was shot for a report came down about him from Dublin. It was very difficult to get good information.

IRB. There was a circle in Dundalk of about twelve. I was a delegate to the Leinster Council meeting which was held in Gardiner's Street [Dublin].[36] [Michael] Collins, Martin Clarke, Seán Ó M[urthuile], Gearóid O'Sullivan, P. S. O'Hegarty, Diarmuid O'Hegarty, Dick McKee, [Seán] Mac Eoin, Liam Toibín, Frank Thornton. There were about twenty-five there. There was nothing of importance discussed.

[TRUCE]

At the Truce there were a number of the IRB crowd in [Dundalk] Gaol.

North Louth Brigade was the First Brigade in the 4th Northern Div.

O/C [Paddy] McKenna — Adjutant Seán Gormley
V/C Mick Donnelly

There were two battalions in the Brigade. Jim Kennedy was O/C of the 1st Battalion.[37] Felix Dawe was in charge of the 2nd Battalion. This Brigade went republican [in the Civil War]. I was a delegate to the first [IRA] convention as was Jim Kennedy.[38] We never let a clash develop between us and the 4th Northern. I was liaison officer and as such I took over Drogheda Barracks [from the British]. We had already taken over two

RIC Barracks in Dundalk and the republicans were there. There was a divisional council to be held and he pulled up, Frank Aiken, with Dick Mulcahy[39] and Eoin O'Duffy[40] at the barracks to read the minutes of the previous meeting and we called the roll. No. 1 [North Louth] Brigade was called. McKenna and I said that we did not intend to take part in the proceedings as there were two men present who should not have been present unless two republican officers were there. Then the 1st Brigade officers left the meeting and Frank Aiken was very bitter about that.[41] I suppose **[45L]** Mulcahy and O'Duffy came there to talk us over. (I expect all this screwing up to leave the Beggars Bush crowd meant a disrespect for authority, for first of all you had to disagree with all the members of the staff you would have been familiar with as a senior officer: Chief of Staff, Adjutant to the Chief of Staff, Deputy Chief of Staff, Director of Intelligence, Adjutant General, Duty Officer, Quartermaster General.) After that meeting we carried on and we recognised the Executive. We cooperated in the northern attacks. There was an attack on Urker, near Crossmaglen, in our brigade area and an attack on a patrol. Very early in March [1922], I brought down twenty to thirty rifles from Beggars Bush to Dundalk (this was not the swap for the attack on the North).[42] In the 1st Battalion area there were a few 'B' Specials, but in the 2nd Battalion [area] there were none.

(Johnny McGuill from the 2nd Brigade has a saw mill in Meath near Gibbstown.) Before the Truce we had about twenty rifles.

Civil War. McKenna, McGuill and I left for Dublin to get instructions, but we ran into Eamon Rooney and a patrol in Dublin, and we were taken prisoner at a bend of the road.[43] We were on parole and so as we passed in and out the guards were used to us. We withdrew on parole, slipped out and got from Dunleer to Dundalk. When the Dundalk Military Barracks was captured by the Free State, we got out of the RIC Barracks, took to the country and formed an ASU.

[46R] In the assault on the military barracks, I had a party to blow up the bridge, cover the military barracks and to isolate it.[44] We commandeered a train and we put it under the bridge, but no explosives turned up. We attacked the Free State by the railway yards but we were surrounded. Their armoured cars surrounded the place. I was knocked out by a rifle because I accepted full responsibility for the men when the Staters were threatening. Aiken and his men got out but Johnny

McCoy got caught. We were brought to Portobello [Barracks] where Joe Griffin and Johnny McCoy were in the gymnasium; then we went on to Maryborough and from there to Tintown 2. We made contacts with one of the guards there, a lad called Bergin, to get out.[45] Then Tom Gough, a medical student, was released having signed a form for he was suspected of being a spy.

T2 [Tintown 2]: There was a tunnel in No. 16 hut. Mick Sheehy, a nephew of Parkinson, an engineer from Offaly, was connected with it.[46]

JOHN MCCOY

(UCDAP17b/116, pp. 1–21, 1951)
(UCDAP17b/94, pp. 90–105, 27 Feb. 1949)
(UCDAP17b/90, pp. 46–51, Sept. 1948)

John McCoy (1889–1971) was the eldest of five siblings born into a staunch nationalist family at Tullymacrieve, Mullaghbawn. He was a founding member of the Mullaghbawn O'Rahilly's Gaelic football team, which in later years formed the nucleus of Mullaghbawn Company 3rd Battalion 4th Northern Division, in which he held successive positions as Company Captain, Battalion, Brigade and Divisional Adjutant, and as Divisional Officer Commanding.

McCoy took an active part in the organisation of the Volunteers during the South Armagh by-election in January 1918, in association with Harry Boland and Peadar Clancy. In April 1919, he helped organise the raid on

Ballyedmond Castle, Co. Down for the Ulster Volunteer rifles. He also took part in important Volunteer attacks on Newtownhamilton Barracks in May 1920 and on Camlough Barracks in December 1920.

In March 1921, with the formation of the 4th ND, McCoy was appointed Divisional Adjutant. In a British military and Specials raid on 24 April 1921, he was critically wounded and captured by the troops. He was released in August 1921 prior to the general amnesty because the British considered him incapable of further military action. McCoy then served as a Liaison Officer for Armagh during the Truce period. He adopted a neutral position regarding the Treaty, in line with Frank Aiken, O/C 4th ND, but clearly sympathised with the republicans.

On 16 July 1922, after the outbreak of the Civil War, Free State Forces captured Dundalk Barracks, imprisoning Aiken and many of the 4th ND. McCoy led the attack on Dundalk Gaol and released Aiken and 105 of his men, even though, as O'Hanlon notes in his interview in this collection, many of the men who led the escape were on the Free State side and didn't necessarily agree with Aiken's views. Later, in the return from Dundalk, he was himself captured and interned in Port Laoise and subsequently in the Curragh Camp. He escaped through the tunnel from Tintown on 23 April 1923 but was wounded, recaptured, court-martialled, and sentenced to a long term of imprisonment. He took part in the general hunger strike in November 1923 and was released from the camp in June 1924.

After Fianna Fáil came to power in 1932, McCoy was appointed Chairman of the Disability Pension Board, and later as a member of the Advisory Committee on the Military Service Pension Act, 1934. He subsequently worked as an official in the Department of Defence Bureau of Military History. He died, aged eighty-one, at 73 Monastry Drive, Clondalkin, Co. Dublin, on 17 January 1971.

As John McCoy's first entry in the notebooks **[116/1–21]** largely mirrors his Bureau of Military Witness Statement (BMH WS 492), the editors have selected extracts from the McCoy interviews, such as his account of imprisonment, which is unique to this collection.[1]

[CIVIL WAR]

[116/14L] But the split in the south meant a Beggars Bush force and an Executive force.[2] The northern government idea was to strike terror so that republicans would be unable to operate against them militarily or politically, also they had to repair the damages of the **[116/15R]** boycott. The Belfast trade boycott was having a strangling effect on northern business and it had been the strongest weapon used against the British interests in Ireland.[3] Unionist traders whose names had been put on the black list for selling Belfast goods in a northern town and who had been fined went to the boycott committee and had paid substantial fines and had given undertakings, which they honourably kept, not to deal with boycotted firms during the boycott campaign. Then came the Collins–Craig Pact and Collins called off the boycott.[4] Sir James Craig promised to give the Catholics of the North equal status in matters of employment etc., but the bargaining effect of this boycott weapon was enormous and could only be appreciated by the people living on the spot in Northern Ireland. An end was to have been put to the Belfast pogrom by Craig and attacks on the Catholic population in Belfast were to cease. Under the articles of agreement, the northern government was given [status] by recognising its existence, which it had otherwise lacked. The anti-Treaty side could see that an agreed effort to prevent the northern government from functioning could unite all the former republican elements in the country. It was agreed that all the old IRA arms that had been used during the Tan campaign should be collected all over the south and handed to the men in the North. An issue of arms which were handed over by the British under the terms of the treaty were to be handed out to replace the arms sent to the North. It was considered inadvisable in the spring of 1922 for the pro-Treaty party to allow arms under their control to be used in attacks on British forces in Northern Ireland.[5] This exchange of arms was made in many southern brigades and a dump of stuff was got together in Dublin for despatch to the North. Both sides agreed on an attack on the North, but who was to take **[116/15L]** charge when the fight began, and what help, if any, was to have been sent to Northern Ireland[?] The northern units would not have been capable of dealing with the forces opposed to them. By surprise at the beginning they would have an initial success, but they would have had no reserves to throw into the fight later. Would these reserves have come from southern Ireland[?] After first enthusiastically approving the idea of the northern operations, the pro-Treaty party seemed to suddenly realise that operations in the North might and possibly would cause a complete smash up of all the treaty plans with the British. The anti-Treaty party were anxious to encourage an attack on the North as the only evident means of getting the pro-Treaty forces to take a line of action that would smash up the treaty position … to most northern republicans, that the treaty was the last straw as far as they were concerned and any rumpus that might break up the treaty position was good policy for them.

Arms which had been collected for use in Northern Ireland (EOM: why not Ulster?) were made available at Beggars Bush, headquarters of the pro-Treaty section of the army and at the Four Courts, where the anti-Treaty forces had their headquarters, at this time our division was attached to the Beggars Bush headquarters.[6]

All **[116/16R]** the large quantities of war material were received and safely dumped in the areas for which they were intended – the 2nd, 3rd and 4th Northern Divisions. The date for the rising was 19 May [1922] and plans had been completed in each area. At the last moment, the rising on 19 May was cancelled. Orders to us (EOM: from where?) with only sufficient time to enable the operations to be called off. In some areas, notably Tyrone, Derry, Belfast, County Antrim and East Down, the cancellation did not reach the men in time and operations commenced. I am not in a position to define how this muddle of the orders cancelling the rising occurred. I believe that in the case of the 3rd ND the fault lay with the pro-Treaty headquarters in not providing alternative means of notification which would ensure the order arriving by at least one route.[7]

[TAN WAR]

[94/90R] John McCoy[8]

[I was] wounded in April 1921, I thought we were doing fine then. Division formed in March, a paper division the 2nd Brigade was formed: the Newry Brigade:

South Down;
South Armagh to Poyntzpass;[9]
North Armagh, some units;
and, North Louth.
In March, North Louth handed over: Divisional officers
O/C [Frank] Aiken,

Adjutant John McCoy.
2nd Brigade: Newry Brigade
Archie Hale O/C,
Quartermaster Seán Quinn.[10]

1st Brigade not formed until after the truce. [Patrick] McKenna, a GHQ 'Tiddly', came down as brigade O/C, but I think he was acting as brigade O/C before the Truce.

Louth, the Armagh area, Armagh–Lurgan were two independent battalions – then three battalions during the truce.

– Brigade there was organised but no other.

1922: 3rd Brigade formed. All North Armagh–Lurgan and a little of southeast Tyrone round Blackwatertown.[11]

Prison – April [1921]: Victoria Barracks Belfast: [I was wounded].[12] They looked after me well, and did as much for me as ever they could. A Kerryman, Daly, was then in charge of RAMC [Royal Army Medical Corps] in the North and I think he was a republican.

When I went there first I had a local reputation as **[94/91L]** a person to be got. 18–20 IRA men in an isolation ward … the day before I arrived they put up barbed wire around a venereal hospital before I got there. Hugo MacNeill was there from Ballykinlar with a cut knee.[13] When I got better this colonel [Lieutenant Colonel J. Duggan], said he thought I was going to live about four weeks, then when I got up and was walking about feeling in good form. I got septic again and they thought I was going to die but I got better. The British side always treated their officers right. It looks like we were fixing you up to do away with you. It's up to yourself as soon as you get better it's a court-martial.

On [the] day of [my] release, I talked to a man who I found was General Carter-Campbell, General Officer Commanding Northern Command, in civvies. He said he was told by the medical authorities that I would be of no further military use, but costing them money. He gave me advice to mind my own business. He had been a few years in Ireland, liked the people and said he would settle in Ireland. How would he classify the IRA? He laughed, the IRA are bloody silly from the military point of view, a few thousand scattered all over a province, poorly armed and equipped, how could they hope to beat the British Army who had won a great war **[94/91R]** (EOM: what was Frank's position in the IRB?)

1st August [1921] released, I communicated with Eoin O'Duffy in St Mary's Hall but no supplies from him.[14] A Dr Martin [was] very friendly and sent messages. Paddy Rankin [was] Brigade O/C of Newry Brigade up to November 1920. He went to Dublin [and] fought in '16. He wanted me to join IRB in 1919 and he was told from HQ in Dublin I could hold rank as brigade adjutant. I told him to give me time to consider. Then I said I wouldn't join. My grandfather was mixed up and he had a very bad opinion of secret societies. He was in some society which led up to Fenianism. He had a famous No. 1 who organised in the North before the Fenians.[15]

I said that I didn't mind if I lost rank that I'd fight. Frank Aiken asked me did I join the organisation. I told him I refused. Frank said nothing. I said, 'Are you in the organisation?' 'You shouldn't ask me that question,' he said, 'Johnny'.

'Then you have answered it,' I said. 'Mullaghbawn cares.'

'I'm thinking of all these bloody IRB men in Newry, they're all gone,' he said.

'And I was thinking of the same thing,' I said. Rankin lost his nerves for he wasn't fit, then Frank replaced him and Johnny was adjutant to both.

Seán Quinn, a fine man tipping but not a good officer as he trusted men too much.

[TREATY]

[94/92L] Northern feeling was against it. When fellows were released from gaol they came on to me leading men too. All were against the treaty from our area as the North was let down. I thought that the Treaty gave some status and certain freedom and if we were from twenty-six counties we would have had a different opinion.

The Treaty split the good men and divided the effort. (Mick Collins came over in Marlboro) ... a bunch of local officers from the garrison came in with guns in their hands and were driving officers out of [the] bottom landing and none of us knew what was the reason.

A lot of fellows ran out and I was on bottom landing in pants and shirts. Some officers ran past me, dodging them I walked in opposite direction.

Mick came in and he was in uniform.

'Hello Seán, is this where you are?'

'Yes,' I said.

He held out his hand, I kept my hands in my pockets. It wouldn't be a good policy to shake hands, and there was also a lot of suspicion and I didn't know.

'Take your hand out of your pockets, you're talking to your superior officer.'

'No you're not, Mick', I said, 'you were once'.

[94/92R] 'You're here and you're going to be kept quiet.' He went out amongst the prisoners, out of the compound. He talked [to] Tom Burke of Portumna and Paddy McDonnell, O/C North Tipp in 1922 … I think.[16] The result was that Tom Burke was also sent into the other.[17]

Paddy McDonnell had an ambush at the Bower and Paddy Mac D turned a machine gun on them and shot some when the priest was attending to them, and he fell out with some of his men because he didn't shoot prisoners. They sent two Crossley tenders as an escort and Paddy Mulcahy sat in the tender to protect him, and between Tullamore and wherever he was taken first our way to Maryborough.[18]

Charlie Childie, an English soldier in weights and scales.

Connaught representation of Avery, he was badly wounded in an ambush where Collison was killed.[19]

[TRUCE][20]

Appointed liaison officer in Armagh, October 1921. I went to Dublin for instructions to GHQ. I saw Charlie McAllister but got no instructions.[21] He asked me what cash I had and I said I hadn't any I was on [the] sick list. He appointed me acting captain McCoy.

[94/93L] Armagh 1st and 2nd with a major and [RIC] County Inspector and liaison officer from Armagh. He trusted me a good deal, accepting my word. The first serious thing was a crowd in Keady, County Armagh, they held a Sinn Féin court, also Sinn Féin on a local robber, where they kept prisoner and he escaped. The RIC and military arrested six to eight men. They sent for me. The County Inspector gave me authority to visit them. I couldn't get them released. The County Inspector said he was a bad criminal, but RIC would not stand for arrest. I reported to GHQ, but nothing was done about it they all got sentenced.

Breaches of the truce, the carrying of arms. Auxiliaries in Newry, Specials and IRA. Some in Dundalk, but they went away after the truce.

The Yank, an American, carried two guns all during truce – a swaggerer. John [Seán] Quinn complained that he held up people, asking them if they were IRA, hitting them. Then County Inspector said he had no control over auxiliaries. I was to go to Newry, verify facts and then write to him. John confirmed the stories. On our way to [the] pictures, end of December [1921], John and I met the Yank who recognised John: 'Hello, Mr Quinn, what about it? Who's your pal?' I turned. 'I have you, John *Mac* wounded in *Grants* … f*** the Truce, I'll carry those as long as I'm here.' He wanted us to have a drink **[94/93R]** but we weren't drinking and then he said, 'you won't drink with a f***ing Auxie[?]' John tackled him about holding up men. 'He's alright,' said John, for he said [to] the Auxie, 'I knew they are IRA and they deny they're not.'

I was in Armagh when the stand-to came. I had attended [the] divisional brigade meeting in Newry. I was examined by a cousin of Frank and it was felt I was …

We were to attack [the] stronghold of Colonel Warren (EOM: Waring) South Down near Hilltown, county commandant of B Specials, and he had a block house there.[22] I was called to Newry for there were plans drawn up for resumption of hostilities. I went to Newry in a hurry as John Quinn and I were to be on the job with two South Down battalions. Frank Carney (later TD in Donegal) and I met as messenger from GHQ.[23]

(It was possibly a general plan this attack on the block house.) (Seamus Monaghan, 3 Charlemont Street was divisional adjutant then, he would know that period.)[24]

Frank Carney, Quinn and I had tea (he was O/C 1st Northern 2 – a TD). There was no stand-to that night. I went back to Armagh as Frank wanted me in the division, as he heard the liaison officer was in danger.

Seamus Connolly of Armagh appointed liaison officer – arrested a week later by the county inspector.

[94/94L] There were a few liaison officers arrested at the same time – liaison officer for Derry–Shields also.

First job, an attempt to capture commissioner of Armagh City Council, a brother of Colonel Warren [Waring]. Malachi [Malachy] Quinn was to get in at Warrenpoint with the man and opposite Edward's Street Station, Newry, to wait for Malachy's signal.[25] We had a towing car with 5–6 men, we were to take him at Goreywood if we got the signal. We meant to go to frontier at Drumgooley. We didn't get the signal.

The Armagh City Council was nationalist majority. Éamon Donnelly wanted books taken by IRA.[26] We didn't want to lose them for a job like this. The seizure was partly political, to show we were trying to prevent the northern government from functioning.

We had headquarters in Newry, [a] secret HQ, but everyone knew it, a Mrs Bailiey's in Newry. I wanted Frank to leave it. Frank is hard when you want him to change his mind, as it was too dangerous, but we shifted to Dundalk. Northern government put on [a] curfew in South Armagh and had curfew patrols, this was in February [1922]. I [did a] good bit of IRA activity in the area and I suppose this was their reply.

We lay in ambush one night, four or five lorries, but they didn't come that night. Their activity was a bit of a problem, for one day they would jump on local companies **[94/94R]**[27] and arrest the men. Every company was to have a local house put bedding into it and the company was to sleep in or around the house at night … All company arms were to be taken to the house. It was to be the rallying point during the day as well. I checked up on this order and visited companies at night to check up. The battalion officers would go to the local companies at night. In some areas where there was a big Orange population this '…'

In the barracks we had a column, a big problem to organise the barracks. We tried to train local fellows from our division late February/early March. We had Gerard Tipping, a divisional signaller, [set-up] a chain from Lurgan to Dundalk Barracks with Lucas daylight signalling.[28] We tested the chain at least once. We went in a lot for engineering.

After the Executive was formed, it caused an awkward position. I wasn't keen on staying with GHQ. Frank was very keen on remaining where he was, as by leaving he was adding to the gravity of the situation. We held a divisional meeting before [the] banned convention [26 March 1922]. Frank put forward his views. [Paddy] McKenna, 1st Brigade was anxious for division to go over to Executive at a vote; this was the decision.[29]

1st Brigade only had two battalions then, one complete, five to six of the other, that caused friction in Dundalk as they had two **[94/95L]** police barracks. We had a lot of ragamuffins in the 'Yank' barracks to keep them from harm. It looked like friction, many a time. I got in touch with Seán Gormley (see Carroll's Moore & co lines Hilton House Stapleton Place. He would have a go[o]d deal of information.)[30] Seán was a command adjutant under the Executive, also adjutant of 1st Brigade, 4th ND. We kept liaison with each other, so that there was no trouble.

After Executive formed, Frank and I had a row about taking a car to Castleblayney with girls.[31] Dan Hogan sent his adjutant, O'Carroll (later a colonel), with soldiers, some drunk, to stop us.[32] The girls were in the way. They wanted to search us for arms – they said we had no authority to come in there. I defied him. Dan wasn't there. We went to the dance. Carroll came in later to Lord Hope's Castle and was following me around so I stopped him.[33] He went away. Dan rang up Frank, Frank said I was in bed. Then he found his own sister was there. Dan Hogan had told Frank that McCoy was a prisoner. Frank said, if you don't release him we'll go in and take him out. Frank and I had a row and it seemed to be whether he'd believe Hogan or I.

I was to be three days as divisional adjutant and three days with a column **[94/95R]** in [the] north, two every week. I said I'd have to be in complete control of the column. I told Frank he'd have to apologise or I wouldn't return as adjutant. I trained sixty men able to use M[ilitary] C[orp] signallers. Engineers transport. We went to the mountain house, put down three mines on [the] road (the Mountain house was a drinking house Redmond … as well as a district).[34] We waited two days nearly, my days were up then. That night two Catholics [were] take[n] out and shot where the mines were. They were from wider apart districts the men, [Patrick] Creggan [and] [Thomas] Crawley.[35] We heard of it in the Dundalk Barracks. Then Frank said I could operate unless steps be taken for reprisals and we decided to take hostages.

There was a divisional order – a camp at Castle Shane in Co. Monaghan [for] 3rd Brigade, a camp for Newtownhamilton Battalion at Bridge-a-crew in County Louth and a camp for Camlough Battalion at Dungooley and Ravensdale, County Louth.[36] Every camp was to make out a list of hostages and submit for approval. List was approved, simultaneous raids on a Sunday. In all thirty to forty prisoners taken into Dundalk, some prisoners in Castleshane and in Military Barracks Dundalk.

At same time, Mac Eoin raided Fermanagh on an operational basis and then a capture of hostages?[37] Some of his officers captured.

[94/96L] No miss on our part I think … we put them into a cage, treated them well. Then we started operations. Lislea County Armagh was our next operation. We put down mines, waited [with] sixty-five men [in] a vacant house on side of Slieve Gullion with half [the] men and we stayed at a farmhouse, I was told every four hours main road between Newry and Forkhill, etc. … we concealed ourselves, nothing happened and no news from signallers … about five or six o'clock a signaller told us a car was coming from south, from Forkhill, and then we heard five or six lorries from north. This car came first, six men in trench coats … I couldn't see arms. They were going slow, watching me carefully. We had a machine gun in a trench set on the road and mines down and had a switch in my hand. We decided they were the murder gang – Igoe's gang – 10 x from mine. I decided on firing the machine gun.[38] Ex-soldiers said later they forgot to take off the safety catch … the car went through, the lorries were coming. A quarter of a mile away the car stopped: two armoured cars and two armoured lorries, two open tenders. Men got out, shook hands and talked. Our position [was] on [the] side of a rock and we had to get back up. We cut white bushes and got up slowly then I got other half of [the] column down. We started ten or fifteen minutes. **[94/96R]** The armoured car went up a back road to enfilade.[39] We went up across [the] road, a lot of lorries came from the south and it looked as if it was an enveloping movement. We were trying to cross the Mullaghbawn Valley in a kind of bowl. We'd drop a screen of 10–12 men from time to time to hold up the others. We reached a main road, scouts in first. We crossed this at Mullaghbawn, then lorries came up the road two miles from [our] position. They were using [a] machine gun coming up the road. Riddled houses in Mullaghbawn.

We got back across.

An ambush in Mullaghbawn at night. Our lads panicked [and] ran away. No one injured on either side. One night (Jerry Davis knows)[40] an ambush in Newry – six killed.[41]

Royal Magistrate Wolfe Flanagan, ex-Major, shot dead on cathedral steps in Newry.[42]

Jonesborough: a fight for three–four days in out of it a couple of hundred men in that. We were mining to blow up the barracks, digging tracks in advance to move on.[43]

No casualties, I think police had some.

It was of use for training purposes for the lads as it was in the frontier but it was no real value.

Frank ambushed with his column – Dromintee.[44] He **[94/97L]**[45] was to go there. Frank wounded an officer there in a duel, but some of the men threw away their rifles. He had men with him who were never in jobs before. Frank Aiken was going to shoot some of these men.

We were looking for northern transport four men to get a lorry in Newtownhamilton, two lorries – car of Specials came up the road ... they stuck up the car, Captain Mac Murrin [*sic*] was in the car, surrendered.[46] The four brought the two prisoners to the frontier. The lorries missed [a] private car [that] followed it and came to [the] frontier. McMurrin was then put in the cage.

April or early May [1922]. Never any big scrap. Murder of men in mine holes – along a lane. We were 40 men we were in bogs – swamps – with only one road for us to get out. I felt that after twelve hours we'd have to shift. (This had been mentioned before.)

[THE JOINT NORTHERN OFFENSIVE]

(Plans of invasion of north: southern arms and hand grenades sent north.) Some came through Dundalk and Donegal and some maybe through Clones.

All Tyrone and Derry through Donegal.

Down, Antrim, Belfast, Armagh and South Tyrone supplied through Dundalk.

[94/97R] O/C Adjutant 3rd Northern, Seamus Woods, [and] Tom McNally, Divisional Quartermaster 3rd Northern, were in Dundalk looking after [the] packing of stuff.[47] They were packed into oil tanks – Thompsons, revolvers, grenades, ammunition.

Rory McNicholl was in charge of packing the stud, a captain or commandant (EOM: now a dairy in Sherough Street in Tom's Directory.)[48]

Paddy Quinn, Divisional Quartermaster, had a big say in handling the stuff.[49]

One big tanker, 7–8 ton, packed full went at least three times to Belfast.

There was great disorganisation after arrests, March 24 1922. Tyrone not much as a time, a jealous kind of people, and perhaps Fermanagh.

Dumps captured in South Down. Some fellows gave the information about our area. They left the country afterwards.

Chairman of northern officers: Frank Aiken instead of being called the officer in charge.

2nd, 3rd and 4th [Northern Divisions] really involved.

Men from the south were to come up, but it was called off before the civil war. Word was to be sent to North Armagh. Frank Aiken asked me to [go] down to brigade adjutant Armagh to call it off. Malachi Quinn (93749) was with me (EOM: in charge of Pay and Take in Dublin, 70 Moyne Road, Ranelagh,[50] Quinn Ltd.)

Brigade Adjutant Newry and Down 2nd Brigade, only a boy at the time.

[94/98L] It was called off, Mallon brigade adjutant Armagh.[51]

No action in any of our area, but in 2nd Northern there was an abortive rising; in Derry, Antrim they went out and started to fight and in East Down also there were casualties.

They got such hell afterwards [from] opposition in local areas as there was a general evacuation afterwards.

Casualties in the Glens of Antrim.

A well-organised round-up of known IRA [were] put in the *Argenta* in Belfast Lough and remnants crossed [the] frontier from Antrim and Belfast under our officers in the Military Barracks under their own officers.[52]

When civil war started, 27 of these fellows in Military Barracks, I think, [were] sent to Curragh and refused to join the army. Seamus Woods,[53] Tommy McNally, Dan McKenna (ex-CIS)[54] [and] Tom Morris all divisional officers.[55] Some didn't join [the] army and on Christmas 1922 there was a crisis there. Some joined [the] Free State and rest went home or (EOM: Seán Corr messenger Malboro Street would know about Tyrone Brigade adjutant or Brigade Quartermaster)[56] rather they emigrated.

Cause of smash up [of] Collins and Craig agreement would have helped to smash the unity of the attempt on the North. **[94/98R]** Churchill kicked up a row about hostages in House of Commons. It put Collins in an awkward spot as barracks in Dundalk was used for hostages. Churchill threatened to send down British Army. Our GHQ tried to make us release prisoners. They sanctioned operations, the GHQ, the hostages were our attempt to protect civilians. At time of capture the question of hostages was not raised.

We refused to release prisoners. O'Duffy was Deputy Chief of Staff (he was actually Chief of Staff) and Mulcahy also put pressure and individual pressure on Frank. Kevin McMurrin was specially mentioned by Churchill. We had threats from both sides. The Civil (EOM: O'Duffy's area was very poor: he talked about the only area in the North that had auxiliaries was

Castleblayney when they were in Newry. He had a flair for organisation, but not for fighting. Monaghan people a queer bloody people, but they are bloody thick) War saved the situation for us. When it broke out we had a meeting, but we knew war was coming as we were in touch with Beggars Bush. I felt that the crowd in Four Courts were making no effort to avoid war and making no preparation for it. (Joe McKelvey was appointed to his command because he was IRB.)[57]

[CIVIL WAR]

[94/99L] September 1921 (EOM: A County Tyrone PP said that [there was] a dance in Clones the evening after Collin's meeting in Armagh [with] Divisional officers. [The men] met at a ceilidh on the night after that meeting. Once O'Duffy told the priest all the O/C who attended were in favour of the treaty:

Charlie Daly 2nd Northern;[58]
Joe McKelvey 3rd;
Frank Aiken 4th;
Dan Hogan 5th.

(This was not true, says Frank Aiken to John McCoy.)

The arrest of the liaison officers in the North [was] the first sign of war, so after February 1922 the truce did not apply to the North.

[94/99R] 29 June [1922], some of 1st Brigade [Paddy] McKenna, O/C, Mick Donnelly,[59] vice, Phil Daly, civilian, left for Dublin and were captured by Free State troops under Eamon Rooney.[60] They rang up Military Barracks Dundalk to say they were in trouble. Frank and I went up to get them out and we had an understanding that if there was a civil war that they'd be neutral (I am not sure if this was an actual agreement).

He, Rooney, consulted with O'Higgins by telephone and they got parole and skipped, so that they made free after it had been agreed that they would be released.[61]

We held a divisional meeting, I think that evening if not before it … 1st Brigade agreed to there in lot with division to keep a neutral area. Frank Aiken, 29 [June 1922], said he was going south to make peace. Frank Aiken away ten days. The following Monday, Frank Aiken went on peace mission. He saw Collins, Mulcahy, went to Limerick, saw Liam Lynch came back again to Dublin, a long discussion with Mulcahy, following Saturday 15

July all divisional staff, battalion and brigade staff officers O/Cs to go to Dublin to see Mulcahy.

We met Mulcahy in Portobello for one and half hours, Frank Aiken said only hope was to be neutral, that he had hopes of an agreement. Mulcahy said there wasn't much of a chance but to put his proposals (Frank Aiken) the basis of agreement.

[94/100L] Agreed on before the set-up. Frank's idea was that the republican constitution would be a basis for unity. Where Free State could be used as a stepping stone was the basis on which agreement could be come to. Also if there was a proper election held then the decision of the result should be upheld, that is if people went Free State.

I was in charge while Frank was away. As soon as Frank Aiken left Dublin to travel south, Owen [Eoin] O'Duffy got on to me on the phone and ordered me to attack the two Executive posts in town. I told him that there were no Executive posts there, he said he would insist on it. He used threats but I said no outside troops had better come in. He said he would send order on as a dis[patch]. I saw Seán Gormley and his crowd and told them. This went on for a few days – the order arrived to attack posts and report in a few hours and they'd send on help. If captured names – numbers of prisoners also to be sent on.

Another order to release the hostages from O'Duffy, who was in charge of the north and eastern command. Sometime about Friday, Paddy Quinn was in Dublin. He always visited both parties when in Dublin. He came down a bit tight, he wanted to help M/B, Court House and two barracks RIC in town. I didn't know if Paddy had any support from the other fellows in division. I told him he would depart from our neutrality, also that we were too cowardly to hold them. Then later he said release McMurrin (I was going to release them for they were a danger) from South Down. I told Paddy to take up McMurrin who came up. He asked me why I sent for him – I don't think I said we can't keep you much longer in case there is fighting. I think it best to release you. [He said] 'I was to be kept as a hostage why am I being released now[?]' We couldn't carry on war in the North with our trouble in the south. He wouldn't trust us, he said, as we might shoot him. I said I'd send for his wife and she could come down and see him.

Frank said he would end on his memo on the basis of agreement when he got home from the Mulcahy meeting and he was in good humour. Frank Aiken and Mulcahy very great and I didn't trust him then. Frank

Aiken and Collins weren't speaking at the time; Collins was in the barracks that day. He seen us but he didn't come near us. The rest of the boys didn't trust Mulcahy either. We had a feed in the Red Bank. Frank Aiken said we'd all meet for a certain train and shift all our stuff. I told Frank I'm not going down. Malachi Flynn stayed with me. Frank Aiken went up later shifting **[94/101L]** stuff. A few killed or wounded in the Anne Street Barracks, but they walked into the barracks. They had secured the co-operation of Dominic Doherty, a twister always, was barrack O/C and I always knew it. Frank didn't attempt any fight there.

When we arrived at Dundalk there was a guard of twenty men and an officer on the station. We got out our line on opposite side then and went out on station doorway. We met Eddie O'Hare on the street and he told us to clear out.[62] Then we were told that the barracks was captured. We walked out to Dungooley Camp, over one hundred men there. The boys didn't know what to do as they drew stuff from Dundalk … I went to Ravensdale Camp then … I agreed to call a division meeting on 22th [*sic*] on Sunday in a graveyard over Robert [Edward] Bruce's grave.[63] We decided to go to war.[64]

A new divisional staff appointed. I was O/C, John Quinn adjutant or quartermaster, with a Headquarters at Omeath.

I called off all the fighting as the 1st Brigade was fighting. We would have to send an ultimatum giving Free State forty-eight hours' notice to clear out. We drew up a fine document. We were not going to let area be used by either party during war, but would maintain order. On Thursday 27 [July] ultimatum expired.

[94/101R] We were in touch with English warder in gaol, ten past seven on Arder, prisoners at exercise who would take up position so as not to be hit by splinters. Hand grenades to be thrown to keep guards quiet. Thirty pounds of war flour [over] four square feet, two bags cheddar against wall we had blown all the old walls – Eiver Monaghan – all over the country now in Poyntzpass.[65]

We wiped their eye: Greenore Post Office there State 11c of post, we tapped wires between Dundalk and Carlingford about us [and] we listened in about capture of our headquarters.[66] We thought of getting Dan Hogan away from Dundalk. This officer was to ring up Dan Hogan on a night to tell Dan how he could get us. Wednesday at ten. We cut wires at 9 o'clock kept eye on Boyle and we rang up Dan Hogan with a portal and we told him if he arrived at Omeath at 9 he'd get us all. Our lads were to let him in the peninsula then cut walls out.

The military barracks was masked.

Old column attacked gaol.

Roads cut before Dan reached area, he took ten to fifteen lorries to cut trees. He heard explosion there and came in, thus he could easier surround us. We had three cars but Frank Aiken wouldn't go our planned way. We were a kind of a rear guard – 112 prisoners – we tried for cars. **[94/102L]** We took a car. Staters or lorries, we'd fire a few shots at them, a lorry got out in front of us at a crossroads. We got into fields. They surrounded us. I didn't want to fight as I didn't know that men had been shot. We put up our hands and they fired. Then we picked up our rifles and fired again. Then they came on again, O'Beirne in charge. They treated us rotten.

Maryborough [Gaol – Portlaoise] February 1923. Mick Sheehy in charge of tunnel from Leix [Laois]. They blocked it and threw tins and spoons on top of [the] blockade but we had to go fifteen feet under wall (started a new tunnel from another cell) we ran out of timber.[67] Stuff disposed of in cellars and ventilators. Another wall outside of prison wall. Work ceased because I think we hadn't material for shoring.[68]

Tintown 2, about February 1923: They shot Geraghty and two others in Maryborough and one of our fellows saw him.[69]

Some of the lads saw him that night before he was shot. Some lads in hospital wing they met these lads.

Some of our men saw them being shot.

They were taken into Maryborough the night before, a priest brought in, then shot in the morning.

[Liam] Deasy: fellows condemned him and there were rows amongst Cork men.[70]

August: We burned the prison. Jack Twomey in charge of military[71] – a military government.

[94/102R] Joe Griffin decided on his own to burn the prison without election[72] … we got out in compound.[73] There was hellish smoke and the boys began to dig a hole through the outside wall: a corner pill box and soldiers behind lashed ever who could fix on them. Soldiers told them to get away from [the] wall … a waxed-moustached soldier warned and fired but it was [the] opposite side of compound – bullets went towards Free State on other side.

(EOM: A crowd of senior officers protested against Griffin before this.) [John] Hickey shot dead … two fire brigades came down from Dublin.

Twomey had nothing to do with the shooting as far as I know. I think he was trying to keep men from firing.

Mac Rory was an MP [PA written above] and he was in touch with Johnnie McCoy. Peadar asked me to get a certificate for scabies to get over – this note from T. I. You couldn't be kept only for a while. Dr [J. J.] Comer certified me. I went to T. I. … Peadar [O'Donnell] took me to Dr [Francis] Ferran and told me to show me to the Free State men that I was a hospital case.[74] Dr Lavery came in – a northerner – and he'd order me to be kept in hospital under Ferran.

Tom Mullins [from] Mayo, now teacher in Howth [was] in charge of tunnel.[75] They thought the tunnel was far enough out but they[76] **[94/103L]** couldn't get the right distance. They put up a wire and found they needed ten feet to clear the wire. They told me a few days before. Peadar taken up as a hostage to Donegal a few days before. It was a bloody fine camp, Peadar was in charge. A fine crowd – Kerry[77] and the west some of them. Ferran knew the tunnel was underway. I said I was going back and he said I must go back to T2. He held that if I was a hospital case I couldn't go out our tunnel. I went out our tunnel, over one hundred got out – I was the twelfth. It went 70–100, very small crawl along on hands and knees, air very bad stoppages when guard's back was turned. A light was switched off when the guard was in the way. No planking. Jimmy Grace was in hospital from that hut.[78]

Brennan from Killcullen (a brigade O/C) he ran away they were to cut the wire.[79] He went into Tin 3 where there were no prisoners. They were to cut the wire but I couldn't find the hole Brennan and Mullins were to cut. Brennan ran away at wire and left Mullins. Mick O'Hanlon next and he got stuck.[80] I waited for ten minutes and he lost one of his boots. A fellow called Rush (Westport) was out in front. We went together. We walked fifteen miles that night. At Hill of Allen and at daylight we were within sights of Curragh … We knocked up a man in Rathgarvan [Athgarvan].[81]

[94/103R] Boiler White's father, who wasn't on any side, but he gave us food and the wife. We were through Liffey at Kilcullen that night … he wouldn't keep us in house, but left us in hay loft.[82] Staters came an hour later as we had ladders above. Some soldier said the house had been raided.

Servant boy there two weeks didn't betray us but they only took him four miles, left him on the way.

We went to MacDonnell's, a milk contractor to the camp, and he put us up. Paddy Brennan was to have stayed with him. He said, 'is that Paddy[?] I have the beds fixed for you.' He was backing horses for us, he gave me five pounds and I won thirty pounds. A Protestant and not a republican … fired on our night territorials in civvies … got in touch with Rory Kiely of Celbridge Malones – a farm house, neutral IRA, for a bed they sent us to a cattle shed.[83] House raided that night but not cattle shed. We started for Cardwells of Celbridge, half way over and machine gun fire started at Caldwells as there was a raid on.[84] Then we went to Rory Kiely, he took us to an old lad's place near Maynooth whose son was in the Free State army.

We met Mick O'Hanlon near Hazelhatch [Park], Tom Mullins and twenty or thirty men – an hour on canal they stayed and they were having a dance that night, Jimmy Colbert near Kill there.[85] They had taken drink from William's boats and tinned food liquors.

[94/104L] Mick O'Hanlon and Jim Boyle, Foxford Brigade O/C.

Jim Rush,[86] Tom Scanlon from Sligo[87] with Rory as guide to Dunboyne [were] going north by Slane and Ardee … we went into Louis McGee, vet[erinary] surgeon.[88] Mick O'Hanlon knew him well. He was damn nice to us and kept us for a long time. A girl, Doolan [from] Ratoath, took us away … she went up to [the] house and we heard her laughing so we went on towards us … Scanlon and I were in front … we ran into two soldiers, a soldier rushed with a bayonet … another fellow shot me high up in thigh and I fell down … two years brought to Tin, April–August – in T3 in August. Paddy Mullins in charge T3.

I was in charge of tunnels. Three tunnels overseen. Nearly all minors on tunnels. Some better than others, twenty men on tunnels.

We made flower beds, walks and hollows in [the] landscape garden to get rid of stuff. Trap doors in both our hut and a steel door on top of [the] tunnel underneath.

Hungerstrike … They found [the] tunnel during hungerstrike. When there was low morale there was always danger.[89] They began to dig trenches around [the] camp and fill them with water. Tunnels in every camp there.

I got down a few men, got men out of it, [to] make [a] chamber to hold a lot of clay half [the] size of room L moving huts.

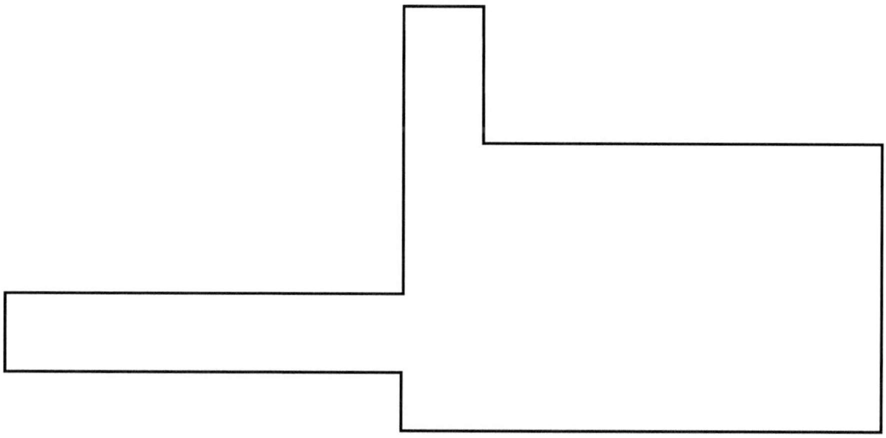

Sketch by EOM of the L-shaped huts.

[94/104R] Have breakfast, [a] working party would go down. Every second day clay would be brought out in little bags, a few pound of clay at a time … [The] clay was gravelly there and it stuck together [in] lumps of stone and sand.

Hungerstrike: [It was due to] an Order from GHQ. Tommy Mullin's instructions [came] from outside from headquarters. I was in communication with Frank Aiken for a long time to call it off. Tom Derrig from Mountjoy went around the camps in the Curragh to call the strike off.[90]

Joe Bergin would take anything out. He was talking too much about it. I was trying to put sense in him but he was as mad as a hatter. His girl was working near the Curragh and they were taking it out on him, so he said, as he wanted to get him away to Dundalk then he'd clear out. But I couldn't help him as I knew no-one alright and he seemed to be very upset by that. He was the only safe contact we had.[91]

McClean (an A/P, not his name) and Maryborough was handing out stuff to Costello. Also Costello had Joe Griffin's man in Maryborough.[92]

We could have taken the guard – Mick O'Keefe Portumna, a civil engineer, made a lovely plan of Maryborough [a] coloured plan … Frank Carty, divisional adjutant, in on this, Paddy McDonnell, Thomas Malone;[93] Joe Griffin not **[94/105L]** in favour. If we could get arms in … Plans sent out with McLean (to Costello really) … Tommy asked me to join the Free State with rank of colonel to take money as from June. He showed me the papers and said that I would be court-martialled and shot for it.

Hare Park: [in] two minutes I got in touch with Andie Cooney O/C.[94] Lady O'Donoghue in charge, no food before this.[95] McHugh, [a] teacher from [the] west, a Free Sate officer, he used to give me information about P.A.s. A priest there on Christmas Day got drunk after mass, [he] went on a raiding party and shot a man.

[TRUCE]

[Fourth] ND: end of March [1921], appointed divisional adjutant and the division was worked out. We held the first divisional meeting. No one from GHQ came up, or ever came up as far as I know.

Treaty debates: I was liaison officer in Armagh city.

4th ND;

1st North Louth: Cooley peninsula/South Armagh;

2nd South Down;

3rd North Armagh and a part of Tyrone and Antrim very small.

Army kept clear of politics. I was approached to go to a Sinn Féin Ard Fheis to consider the treaty but I refused, Frank Aiken's attitude was the same [and] that was the attitude of 90% of the men.

Frank sent for me in December when there was a danger of things breaking in London. Frank Carney, divisional O/C **[90/47R]** Donegal, came to see us and Frank Aiken sent for me and I was to take charge of County Commandant of 'B' men in Down with Seán Quinn. A gunboat and a few light tenders in Carlingford Lough and *peninsula* with machine guns in them very fast. That was called off then.

A very intensive training during the Truce. Byrne and an ex-Irish Guards' man down from Dublin, not much use, to train us. A number of officers went to GHQ to train. No proper divisional headquarters. Frank Aiken set up headquarters in Newry. Seamus Monaghan was divisional adjutant and I don't think Seamus and him were pulling well. Seamus was to take charge of Newry Brigade O/C and I was to be adjutant. We had a guard night and day in Newry in our headquarters. I couldn't get Frank to shift and I prevailed in Frank Aiken to ship papers to south. Later we set up headquarters in Dundalk. Tommy Rogers Divisional Quartermaster and Seán Quinn went to 3rd Brigade as Quartermaster.

This go[t] a bit of an edge and we decided to attack. The northern government set up an armed patrol [of] mixed military-police and it was hard to attack 5/6 of our area in N. Ireland. We were doubtful of being able to protect our civilian population, only a certain [number] of northern area men were to evacuate the area and we started camps [at] Dungooley, Ravensdale, Bridge – in County Louth, near the frontier. A camp near Castleblayney in Monaghan and Castle Shane. Camps, the local northern battalion O/C was in charge of camps usually.

[90/48] We attacked or attempted to attack patrol of three to four lorries and an armoured car. It didn't come off. We decided on capturing influential unionists as hostages and if reprisals occurred they would be shot. We had about twenty-three hostages in May [1922]. We got 80% of what we wanted. Captain McMurrin amongst them – a county commandant in Armagh. We took him from behind his escort of two lorries, himself and his driver, both armed.

We had him there until Staters came. Churchill raised the question of why Dundalk, under Provisional Government, was used (Mid-June 1922).

May [1922]: Exchange of arms: plan of attack for six counties drawn up. I know nothing of the exchange of arms for our division. We sent cars. One burnt out in Banbridge.

Dundalk used [as] a jumping-off place for transport and another around in Donegal, around Lifford. Part of County Tyrone, Down, Armagh, Antrim went through Dundalk. Army went through Dundalk.

Donegal: North Tyrone and Derry

*Larkin closely associated with Daly. A North Tyrone man, Mossy Donegan, up with Charlie Daly for a while. He was a teacher in model school in Cork.[96]

Seamus Woods would know about the Belfast.

Tommy McNally (Quartermaster division but not approachable).

*Sheriff Street: Rory McNicholl packed stuff for Belfast and he packed it into oil tankers and none of them were ever captured. Peter Boyle was in charge of transport. He is **[90/49R]** now driving Frank Fahy.[97]

Paddy Quinn, Divisional Quartermaster, would know a great deal about this.

Malachi Quinn, runs Pay and Take in Rathmines himself. He is general manager and he might know something. I don't know his rank at the time. He was only a youngster.

We had planned operations for [the] north and Frank Aiken was to take general control. He was chairman of the board of northern officers to save military control being found out. The whole thing was called off when Collins/Craig Pact was made and the boycott called off. Dundalk was the base and I was busy. Dispatches calling it off sent from the Military Barracks in Dundalk. One of the Walsh girls carried the calling-off orders. Some areas didn't get it. Tower head in the Glens, some IRA killed there. A general evacuation of the areas where a start was made, a couple of hundred in the barracks in Dundalk. Apparently the N[orth] … knew of the plan and the northerners knew a great deal about it and captured a lot of prominent men.

Seán Corr: Department of Education Marlborough Street, messenger in Education, quartermaster of a brigade there. He was there in connection with them arms to Tyrone.

Wilson made an inspection of all barracks in frontier line (We attacked Camlough in December 1920, but nothing happened) week before I was wounded, 16 April–21 April. Wilson and Wickham, divisional commissioner of RIC in Belfast.[98] Wilson, inspector for or military advisor to the North.[99]

[90/50R] Wickham. Igoe spent a week or ten days in the North and shot two O'Reillys and fellow[s] called Quinn and McGinnty outside Newry, all on the same night [9 July 1921]. He was recognised in Armagh and Newry. I was also divisional intelligence officer as well as adjutant. Two O'Reillys shot in one house, Quinn in another house and Mac Ginnity.

After boycott was called off we felt badly. The boycott was having a wonderful effect. The northern exporters were feeling the pinch as were the local Orange traders. We were fining them hard in Newry (Bill Kelly, 16 May Street, Newry would know of this. He was also in the IRB, one of the old crowd through the Fenians). The northern opinion, I think, never consulted about calling-off the boycott. The North was a kind of embarrassment to everyone. Seán Gormley of Dundalk was in charge.

See MacCarroll [MacArdle] Moore and Co. Dundalk – almost stone deaf – (Wilton House, Stapleton Place, Dundalk) he was under the Four Courts Executive there.

In June we had certain military activity but we were discouraged from it. I had touch with Eamon Price and Seán Mac Mahon for money – arms.[100] I drew arms down on lorries and was afraid the Court would attack us. Frank Aiken told to release the hostages from headquarters but we refused. The civilian population used to sleep in crowds across the border during trouble, a three-day fight in Joneborough RIC Barracks – the fight went on for three days and three nights, but it was good training for the boys. A hell of a lot of arms wasted.

[TAN WAR]

[90/51R] Frank Aiken's attitude was that he couldn't protect the civil population. After [the] attack on Camlough Barracks (12 December 1920) there was a reign of terror in South Armagh. The military came out from Newry that night. We had our boys on the Egyptian Arch, the whole thing was a fiasco. Seán Quinn showed 3–4 bacon boxes supposed to be full of arms and there was no arms in them. The British burned the Sinn Féin Hall in Newry, 4–5 killed at the attack.[101] The road [was] not blocked and the military got through. We were harried then in Corry's outside Newry, a fight in which Frank Aiken was concerned – five or six of our fellows who got away and killed some of the British.

Attack on Courts: some of the officers from Dundalk, ex-forces Phil Daly, Mick Donnelly, here in town [in Dublin] they have a factory near Santry Court [Lilmar Manufacturing Company] – [were] captured by Rooney in Drogheda on way to the courts. Frank Aiken and I went up to negotiate release, Eamon Rooney was very nice and friendly. He promised Frank Aiken good behaviour. They had broken parole and had escaped. (I could have escaped out of Tintown in the Civil War by Seamus McGurran if I gave parole.)

APPENDIX: NOTES ON JOHN MCCOY

UCDAP17b/116, pp. 1–21

John McCoy's first entry in the notebooks largely mirrors his Bureau of Military Witness Statement (BMH WS 492). Indeed, O'Malley wrote, 'John McCoy … from his written notes' in his index. Thus, to avoid unnecessary duplication of material already in the public domain, McCoy's material in notebook **[116]** has not been included in this collection.

However, there are a number of noteworthy comments made by O'Malley on McCoy's written statement. In one instance, O'Malley noted the difference between signal training in rural and urban areas **[116/2L]**, 'only in cities did it seem that the Battalion Vice Commandants organised their special service classes, for throughout the country could be found signallers, musketry instructors, doctors for field aid, mechanic for cars for transport, but these services were never fully organised'. In addition, O'Malley commended the Brigade intelligence system during the abortive northern campaign of spring 1922 **[116/17L]**, 'Evidently the brigade intelligence system was carefully thought out for **[116/18R]** in each of these two instances, and there was a third, … the brigade was not surprised.'

Elsewhere, O'Malley commented on the defensive precautions taken by the RUC against IRA attacks on barracks: **[116/6R]** 'When Forkhill barracks, which they intended to attack, was evacuated they found when they burned it the following night that sand had been spread on the floors and the walls had been loop-holed inside. O'Malley also questioned McCoy's claim that **[116/15L]**, '26,000 to 30,000 people had left the six counties between March and June 1922. Some of these IRA joined the pro-Treaty forces. Others, smaller in number, became associated with the anti-Treaty forces.' O'Malley opined, **[116/18L]** 'what of the northerners joined up with the republicans[?] It must have been a very small percentage – less than 1% I should think?' On another occasion, he corrected McCoy for calling Richard Mulcahy the Chief of Staff in 1922 when he was Free State Minister of Defence **[116/20R]**.

McCoy's own testimony points to the non-sectarian character of Irish republicanism. He was highly critical of the sectarian nature of constitutional nationalism, or Hibernianism,[102] and described the AOH as 'definitely sectarian and anti-Protestant and in its policy it has no doubt played a most sinister part in all northern counties' **[116/1R]**. Elsewhere, McCoy presented the Orange and Hibernian organisations as almost equally hostile to republicanism in South Armagh. After 1916, and in line with developments elsewhere in rural Ulster, GAA clubs in South Armagh largely split along a republican–Hibernian divide, with the formation of a host of Easter clubs, typically named in honour of republicans killed or executed in the Rising. Indeed, McCoy outlined how unionists agreed to **[116/1R]** 'support the candidacy of Patrick Donnelly' of the IPP in the South Armagh by-election on January 1918.[103] Furthermore, he related how, **[116/1L]** 'in a few cases, Hibernians and Orangemen joined up to attack us' during violent electoral confrontations, noting how the IPP victory relied on unionist votes and that 'Sinn Féin must have got at least a majority of the nationalist vote' in South Armagh.

Unsurprisingly, McCoy criticised the subsequent Logue Pact during the December 1918 General Election.[104] McCoy recounted how, **[116/2L]** 'on 3 December 1918, Cardinal Logue allotted four seats to Sinn Féin and four to the IPP.[105] The interference of Cardinal Logue in political affairs had **[116/3R]** the most unfortunate results. The IPP got a representation which they could not otherwise obtain.'[106] McCoy continued that, 'the worst aspect, however, was the effect this had on a considerable volume of opinion – non-nationalist – in the North who did not see eye-to-eye with the official unionist crowd.' In McCoy's opinion, 'this small band of intellectuals had a following some of whom would go the whole gamut of working for a republic for all Ireland and others were interested in the labour movement.' Yet, they 'had no use for the Irish Parliamentary Party as they saw that the parliamentarians were steeped in sectarianism, which all lovers of freedom detest and which had been the bane of northern Ireland politics for over a hundred years.' As a result of the pact, these

> former unionists with republican inclinations got such a revulsion of feeling that some reverted back to unionism and others became so suspicious of republicans in general that they could not be got to take any further interest in our politics. I do not believe that any responsible northern republican who then knew the real situation in the Orange districts in the North, would have agreed to such an arrangement about nationalist seats.

While McCoy clearly identified with republicanism's non-sectarian ethos, he held a more equivocal attitude towards the IRB, despite his own grandfather's earlier affiliation. McCoy claimed that Paddy Rankin, the local IRB Centre from Newry, had been contacted by 'GHQ to the effect that I was not a **[116/3L]** member of the IRB and as I held an important rank in the IRA, I should be asked to join the IRB.'[107] Rankin was apparently 'afraid that if I refused to join the IRB, headquarters might not sanction my appointment as Brigade Adjutant.' Nevertheless, McCoy refused to join 'a secret oath-bound society' due to 'certain moral scruples about joining it, and secondly that there was no need for a secret society then seeing that the IRA had a well-organised army in existence.' Apart from demonstrating McCoy's own principled position, this testimony also indicates the Brotherhood's considerable influence over the northern IRA across the piece.

McCoy also identified the formation of **[116/5R]** 'the Special Constabulary' as a significant turning point.[108] He made it quite clear that in majority nationalist areas, 'an attack [from] the Ulster Volunteers had to be allowed for as a potential enemy force to guard against even though they were not active'. Clearly, then, the creation of the USC, with British support, facilitated the spread of loyalist authority into previously unaffected areas. McCoy again reiterated that 'the participation of the Ulster Volunteers in military action against the Irish Volunteers would have given the resultant action the appearance of a sectarian struggle, which the IRA would have been very anxious to avoid. The British failing to make use of the Orangemen on a voluntary basis decided to get the Ulster Volunteer units into uniform as paid auxiliaries.'

On his release from prison hospital, **[116/13R]** 'about October 1921, Frank Aiken told me I was being appointed liaison officer for County Armagh'. McCoy claimed that **[116/13L]** the failure to embed the republican counter administration represented a significant lost opportunity. While he clearly noted hostility from the RIC, McCoy was equally scathing of what he deemed southern incompetence, or even deliberate neglect: 'This matter was not further pursued as the republican police and courts were so badly let down by our GHQ that similar activities were abandoned.'

As is the case with other testimony in this collection, McCoy provides important detail on the proposed joint-IRA offensive during the interregnum between the Treaty and Civil War.

MICHAEL MURNEY

(UCDAP17b/116, pp. 22–5, 19 Sept. 1950)

Michael Murney (1893–1973) was born in Killowen, Co. Down. He came from a strong Republican family. Aodh de Blácam paid special tribute to his mother, Rose Murney, when she died in 1943, noting she was the 'true mother of the Maccabees' and that 'her strong songs deeds in the service of Ireland are known to all who know the North.'[1] Indeed, Michael's older brother, Peadar Murney, was a well known abstentionist MP for South Down from 1945 to 1949.

Murney took up a post as a teacher in Lurgan and served as Battalion O/C of Lurgan Battalion from around 1920. He was active in the burning of the Birches Barracks near Portadown in December 1920, and was involved in the holding up of a train up between Portadown and Lurgan in February 1921. Murney was arrested in March 1921 along with Bernard McCann, Battalion Adjutant, and Hugh McShane, Battalion Quartermaster, after a list of officers' names was seized in a raid on a GHQ office in Dublin. Murney was imprisoned in Crumlin Road Gaol, Belfast, and later in the Curragh, where he attempted an escape in September 1921. He was subsequently transferred to Kilkenny Gaol where he participated in one of the most remarkable prison breaks of the period, when forty-nine men successfully escaped after burrowing a tunnel out of the prison with a table knife.

Murney resumed IRA activities after his release and was an active member of the 4th Northern Division. He was rearrested in the early hours of the morning of 14 February 1922, along with Seamus Monaghan and John Murray, when they were stopped by B Specials at Liscaree as they cycled from Kilkeel and Newry. They were held in Kilkeel before being transferred to Newry. Seamus was charged with possession of a revolver, while Murney was charged with carrying seditious literature, namely a copy of the *Irish Republican Brotherhood* newspaper. Murney refused to recognise the court and protested to the Truce not being observed.

After completing his prison sentence, Murney was interned on the *Argenta* for most of 1923 and was later detained at Larne workhouse. He was selected as the anti-Treaty Sinn Féin candidate for Down at Newry Convention in October 1924. Although he was defeated, his campaign galvanised significant attention. On 29 October, Éamonn De Valera was famously arrested as he entered a meeting in support of Murney in Newry.

Murney later resettled in Dublin and served as Chairman of the Disability Pensions Board. He was also President of the Antrim and Down Association. He died in 1973 and was survived by his wife, Annie (née Duignan), who was a leading figure in Cumann na mBan from Leitrim.

[22R] Murney N[orth] Armagh, Pensions' Board, St Brian's [Hospital].

The North Armagh Battalion was formed about 1919 and it consisted roughly of North Armagh. I was in charge of Lurgan and Portadown but we did not go into Armagh city, which was linked to the Newry Brigade, and so it went in with the 3rd Northern. There was the operation, the burning of a courthouse at the Birches close to Portadown, as a try out.[2] There were seven men from the North Armagh Battalion and at 10:30 in daylight we carried it out. We raided houses for arms, and we had to raid for petrol and paraffin, and we had to hold up for hay so as to burn the place. All the men engaged got away.

The 'B' men were formed in September 1920.[3] The Ulster Volunteers had their Ulster rifles in their houses. Some of them were good rifles? The 'B's used to patrol with the [Royal] Ulster Rifles. The Ulster Volunteers used to practice [*sic*] in the local Orange Halls. The house of the Birches, [the base] of the Commandant of the Ulster Volunteers, was guarded day and night by Ulster Volunteers and 'B' Specials. In December 1920 there were raids on the mails.[4] In February of 1921, a train was held up between Portadown and Lurgan, which was a fairly good operation as the train was held up and no one was arrested as a result.

In the first week of March [1921] I was caught and was brought to Belfast to Victoria Barracks, which was then a dumping ground. In Lurgan there were strong forces of RIC – fifty men in the Ivy House [Barracks] and eight or nine in another barracks. The biggest reprisal close to us was Lisburn, as a result of Swanzy, the district inspector, being shot there.[5] There was a veiled threat in our area that the local convent would be attacked.

In Belfast, the Crumlin Road Prison was crowded out with prisoners from the southwest and all over. The governor's son from this prison is now in charge of Port Laoise[6] and the O/C prisoners there was **[22L]** Paddy McLogan, who is also in Port Laoise, where he owns a pub and he's a right good fellow.[7] About forty-nine to fifty of us were brought by the train to the Rath Camp in the Curragh, and by lorry also, and we were kept the whole day without food. We spent the summer in that camp and at the end of the summer we had about one thousand prisoners, so they had to open a number two camp, which had five hundred in it. The O/C of number one was Peadar McMahon.[8] I didn't meet Rory O'Connor there.[9] Dr Peter Conlan of either Waterford or Carrick escaped in a linen cart and two or three escaped in the same way. Tom Glennon, Belfast escaped[10] and Lawless from North Dublin escaped.[11] They never found out how these men escaped, but afterwards the swill cart was always pushed with a bayonet.[12]

About the end of September, we tried to escape from the isolation camp for *some* disease, about eleven of us. The O/C camp knew of the attempt and GHQ sanctioned it and there were eleven men picked [including] Dave Gibbons from Armagh City;[13] Seán O'Kelly, Offaly; [Bill] Donoghue, Carlow; [Tom] Hyland, Laois; Seán Graham, Kildare; [Tommy] McCarrick, Sligo.

We were in number two and we were to escape from the one hut. It was arranged that my bed would be made up for the check so that would pass. We were in the isolation (hospital) waiting to cut through the wires that night and we had pliers. We sheltered in a vegetable shed and we intended to move **[23R]** out between 11:30 and 12:00. At about ten o'clock we must have been given away by fellows who were afterwards known to be spies. The British gave us a good hiding and dumped us in the clink. They were held by a Major Vinden, the adjutant of the camp, in this beating up.[14] We were taken two-by-two up to the clink by men with crash helmets and we were beaten with rifle butts and truncheons and boots on the way up. Then we were taken to Keane Barracks in the Curragh where we were sentenced to twelve months' imprisonment by a field general court-martial.

We were then taken by lorries to Kilkenny, the eleven of us, and there was a bit of a journalist from North Dublin with us. Kilkenny Gaol was guarded by Tans and Auxiliaries. The warders were inside. The governor was Boland, who had been a deputy governor in the Joy when Thomas Ashe died.[15] Things were tolerable enough, and I think the Auxiliaries had quarters in the gaol. They used to be in the circle in the daytime. At this time there were only two wings occupied, 'A' and 'B' wings, and there were about one hundred prisoners there. Brennan from Kilkenny was in charge of the prisoners and it would be then about October, 1921. We got the papers and it looked as if negotiations were going to break down and, that being so, we decided to get out of gaol. On the ground floor there was a double cell. It was [a] treble cell really and it had a wooden floor to it. We cut a hole through this floor into an old underground punishment cell, these cells then were closed up and the doors to the yard was made up close above it from the outside. We thought the window was facing the gaol wall, which should be roughly seven yards away. If the depth of soil was sufficient we could easily bore a tunnel. The Auxies **[23L]** patrolled around, and, as we bored, we could hear them. We had no tolls. We got a hack saw blade smuggled in, as Fr Delahunty was a prisoner, but in the hospital, and he got it cooked in a cake, and also we had a bottle of whisky for you got a tot when you went in and when you came out.[16] I was pretty string at the time, but I would say that fifteen to twenty minutes was as much as I could stand and then you would change back, for we worked two at a time. We started off with an old poker, then we used knives and spoons. The earth was soft. It was a fairly damp autumn so there was a seepage and we propped the tunnel with head boards which we cut with hack saws. Things were tolerable inside and there was no check on our movements. The earth was put back in the disused cells. There was no soil on our boots or on our clothes when we came up from the tunnel. I would say that eleven of us knew of this tunnel for we didn't know the others and we were not sure whom we could trust. One time, fairly close to the wall, we came across a fairly heavy rock and we wondered would it hold, for it was so big that we had to dig down under, and if the rock slipped or came down we would be crushed. Our fear was would the rock come down[?] Or would it fall in on the clay in front **[24R]** later[?] We had candles at first and then two electric torches which came in, all of them through Fr Delahunty, for he was a privileged [prisoner] being on account of his collar.

We were three weeks on this tunnel and we worked constantly on it. We couldn't work at night so well as we were locked up at night. One or two did collapse and [we] revived them, so maybe it was brandy we had and not whisky[!] We got as far as the wall and we could hear the feet of guards above us, and so the question was how far we were below the surface[?] But we never could check properly.

When we came to the wall we had to sink a shaft against it to get ready to go under the foundations. That was both an awkward and a heavy job, but we bored right down and then we bored up again. Outside a street ended. At any rate it was pretty soft right along the gaol wall, so we worked up until we guessed that we were near the surface. We used our poker, and in coming up we made steps like badgers along the wall, and the stairs would serve as an easy way of getting up.

Finally, one fine night the poker went through to the outside world and we saw a star. We got our props and we secured the exit as best we could. We never mixed with the men in 'B' wing and we were about fifty of us in 'A'. There had been a big transference of prisoners from Spike [Island] and some of them were put in either wing. Ned Punch from Limerick was O/C of the gaol.[17] We thought we would have to let the prisoners from Spike and Jimmy Murphy from Limerick know, so that they could use their own judgement as to whom they would tell the information to. We made one getaway. Fr Delahunty was supposed to be the biggest man and we asked him if he would go first. He got across to us by some trick and at half past seven we started. The fellows would slip out one-by-one without any fuss **[24L]** or any dressing up. When we got out the first, second, third, and fourth had to stand and help the others get up quickly.

We had to arrest a young lady who was coming along. But she screamed so we had to commandeer a house across the road, a house named Armstrongs, who were north of Ireland Orangemen, and we held them up by using our pipes in our pockets. The chief warder was to come along inside, so we had to get him also. We had contact with GHQ in Dublin, who wanted to send down a fleet of cars, but this we turned down. There were one or two in Kilkenny who knew all about it, but they didn't know how many men [were] on it – forty-nine escaped. The forty-ninth man was out when the bell went inside, the warning bell. The fiftieth man got stuck in the tunnel in some way or other. The Auxies fired a few shots and the bell was wrung then.

We broke off into groups of six or seven and each went their own way. We walked through an old fox[hole] cover, walking by the stars. We were all strangers. The night turned wet and we could see the searchlights in the roads. We were walking for four hours when we chanced on this road or by-road and we saw a house, a little farm house, and I think we spotted a Sacred Heart light so we guessed that it was alright. One young lad had got weak on our hands.

Teehans of Barrackhill [Barton]: It was in Barrackhill and it was only three miles from Kilkenny City. The boys were **[25R]** in the IRA and the girls were in the Cumann na mBan. The young lad who had the weakness died afterwards. We got a guide, then *paid* a young lad [who] came along with us: at four in the morning we left this house and we went on through Tullaroan to another house where we stopped for a day and night, then on to Gortnahoo [Tipperary] and the next move was to Templemore to a big house belonging to Fogartys, and there was only a caretaker in it. [Jerry] Stapleton, a grain merchant in Thurles, gave us clothes and there was a big black hat included and money. He advised us to get back to Dublin by train, one-by-one. At the Curragh they looked in at us carriage by carriage, and we got out at Lucan. Three of us had to go north by train, and we got off at Dundalk. None of the forty-nine were recaptured (EOM: the courthouse was combined with a barracks, but only the courthouse was then in use.)

Seamus Monaghan has an antique shop in Charlemont Street [Dublin City].[18] Their house in Banbridge was surrounded by a mob but they fought, the Monaghan family. He was the brigadier in reorganisation at [the] time of [the] Treaty. We set out to do a bit of organisation and we saw things were happening below and we thought if we could start a fight.

We had a battalion meeting but the place was raided by specials on 14 February 1922, but we came back and we had our meeting and we went on by road on bikes: [Patrick] Murray, Monaghan and I, but after the Specials had made the raid they flung out 'B' patrols. For the first time since the truce, the *Argenta* battalion near Kilkeel (Ulster Volunteers) [were] up in the hills, flung out patrols, and we walked into them. So we got a milling and we were brought to Newry Military Barracks and then to Belfast Gaol.[19] At that time, there were Johnson and MacShane who were to be hanged, and they were transferred on their way to Peterhead [Gaol, Scotland]. Five or six lads, Tom Hyland, Laois, Belfast **[25L]** who tried to run a military camp were caught. That was the end of February [1922].

The aftermath of the pogrom in Belfast. We were still attached to the 4th Northern Division. We were tried by a civil court at the sessions in Downpatrick. I got off with twelve months. Monaghan got seven years, for it was against the truce (EOM: ?) and Murray got six years for having the breech of a rifle bolt. We thought we'd be in for only a month or two. I got out 24 December 1922. Monaghan and Murray in March 1925.

I was in Belfast and in Derry in more or less solitary confinement for three months in Belfast. I got two or three hidings in Derry Gaol from warders. The 'B' Specials were on guard in the night time and the governor knew of this. He was a little pup, a Captain Stevenson, and I'm quite sure he was up to the neck in it.

Belfast: prisoners came in every night in sixes and in tens and by July 1922 there were maybe one [hundred] prisoners there, in Derry there were a good number of prisoners also, but no one group was left too long there for fear of trouble. There were between fifty and sixty prisoners. In Larne Camp, which was an old workhouse, there were between four and five hundred prisoners. When my gaol sentence was finished, I was interned.

When we were on the Kilkenny escape we had to tie up the night warder who was on duty, but he didn't hold that against us. He raided my cell in Kilkenny and he got a lovely pipe and he showed it to me, for **[26R]** Auxiliaries and warders raided there in that gaol to see what they could pick up. Tom Crany from Armagh was the decentest warder I ever met.

PATRICK MCLOGAN

(UCDA P17b/132, pp. 51–5, Oct. 1951)

Patrick 'Paddy' McLogan (Pádraig Mac Lógáin) (1899–1964) was born in Clady, Co. Armagh, in 1899. In 1913, he joined the IRB in Liverpool under the influence of his uncle. McLogan was purportedly in the GPO during the Rising and imprisoned in Frongoch. After his release, he helped organise the IRB and Volunteers in Belfast, before fighting under Desmond Fitzgerald in Bray. He was recaptured and imprisoned in Mountjoy, where he participated in the September 1917 hunger strikes during which Thomas Ashe died after being forcibly fed. McLogan was released due to ill health, returned to the North, and actively campaigned in the Sinn Féin elections in South Armagh in January 1918. He was imprisoned once again during the Belfast general election in 1918. After his release, he became O/C of the Antrim Brigade and he cycled across Antrim to organise and form companies.

McLogan was appointed by IRA Headquarters as brigadier of a new Brigade formed of North Antrim and some East Derry Battalions in 1920. However, he was arrested shortly afterward at Toomebridge in the company of leading IRB man, Séamus Dobbyn. He served two years hard labour in Walton, Liverpool, and Preston prisons and attempted a foiled escape from Mountjoy. On his release, McLogan worked as an IRA Evacuation Officer under Beggars Bush before returning to Antrim to take part in the abortive northern offensive of May 1922. He went to the Curragh with the 'neutral' Volunteers of the 2nd and 3rd Northern Divisions but left to join the republican side in December 1922.

In 1925, McLogan applied for a licence to run a pub on 34 Main Street, Portlaoise. He served as Secretary of the Portlaoise branch of the Gaelic League from 1927 and was also Chairman of the Portlaoise Branch of the Republican Prisoners' Release Association. He was elected as an abstentionist MP for South Armagh (1933–8) and maintained a position on the IRA Army Council until the 1950s. As a result, McLogan was interned again during the southern emergency in 1940, but was again let out on health grounds.

After the general release of internees in 1945, McLogan worked closely with Tony Magan and Thomas Óg MacCurtain to reorganise the post-war republican movement. McLogan was elected as the President of Sinn Féin in 1950. Together with George Harrison, he ran guns from New York in the 1950s and was arrested in 1957 after the Garda Special Branch raid on the Sinn Féin Ard Chomhairle. McLogan opposed the order to dump arms in the wake of the unsuccessful border campaign and tendered his resignation as President of Sinn Féin in 1962. McLogan died under mysterious circumstances in 1964, having sustained a gunshot wound in his home.

[CIVIL WAR]

[51R] Roger McCorley <u>had his Battalion</u>.[1] [It] contained [an] ex-British Army man IRA from <u>Down</u>, [it was] a small unit. They left the Curragh and they went to Dublin, the Salvage Corps. I used to go back and forward, but I left the Curragh in December [1922]. The first break came on 8 December 1922, as far as I was concerned. A number of fellows left with me and they drifted back to the six counties. Some of them were arrested and interned: some made their peace by handing over arms to the Northern Government. He [I] tried to hand over a dump in Martinstown Barracks to the RUC.[2]

Those who joined the Guards had a record of their activities from their Battalion O/C and from their Brigade O/C or Divisional O/C who endorsed them. Reed asked me to endorse records and I did. When I found Reed had done this, I took it up with O'Duffy and I had a file, but O'Duffy said that he was in the Guards because we had all endorsed him, but the O/C Battalion found that it was a fake and we all withdrew.[3] Then I told O'Duffy, he said that a certain tenure of office existed in the Gardaí and he could not do anything. This was my only contact with Woods.[4]

There was a meeting in the Curragh (Portobello). Gearóid O'Sullivan, [Michael] Collins, Dick Mulchay. Roger McCorley ranked as Battalion Commandant and he attended that meeting.[5] O'Duffy was not present and at it there were Brigade and Divisional Officers from the 3rd Northern only. This would have been before I crossed the border to the Six counties on 12 July [1922]. I was there two weeks. The meeting was held in the last week of July, and then I crossed the border again, and I was arrested. I was a week in Larne and two weeks in Belfast and then I was deported across the Border.

Before 1920 I was attached to the organisation Department in GHQ as an organiser. I was organising Antrim. I was first sent from the Brigade **[52L]** Staff in Belfast, and then later I was attached to GHQ. I was also attached to Derry in 1920. I was only about a month in charge of it; Major Morris had been organising on his own.[6] IRB had contact there, but GHQ had no touch. He was organising with the Larkin family.[7] I reported that Morris was operating on his own; and I was asked to report on him and ask him if he would be a whole-time organiser in Derry. He had only been two weeks appointed when he was caught. He was given two years. Charlie [Daly] and I met Diarmuid O'Hegarty to discuss Derry.[8] Charlie was having a hard time in Tyrone and he asked me if I would manage Derry, and I did.[9] There was a meeting in Lavey [the meeting was in Guladuff] in October of 1920 of all officers as I intended to meet the Derry officers and arrange with them to attend parades of the area. On Sunday, I attended the meeting, and I was arrested in Moneyglass with Séamus Dobbyn next day in Antrim.[10] Séamus Dobbyn teaches in Dublin and he teaches in No. 2 Rathlin Road, [Drumcondra].[11] He had no rank in Belfast. He was an organiser for the IRB up to that time. This was in October, 20 October 1920.

We were in Victoria Barracks and MacSwiney died on a Thursday [25 October 1920].[12] I got two years. I was on a faked charge for a copy of *An tÓglach* was planked. From October to June [1920], I was in Belfast;

and then for attempting to escape I was deported to England to Walton [Liverpool] and then I was in Preston.[13] The Six County men were there (EOM: What to hell does he mean? The 'Six Counties' did not begin?) in Liverpool, I was a week there. In Walton, I met three of the 'Connaught Rangers', the Mutineers.[14] Some of them were doing fifteen years. Walton was a huge big place, a clumsy place.

After release, I was on the organisation staff under Price.[15] Then I was transferred to Evacuation[16] under Dalton and from February to June 1922, I was in the 26 Counties.[17] **[52R]** I did the evacuation of Goresbridge and Gowran [Barracks] in Kilkenny. Then Portlaoise, Portarlington, Banagher and Tullamore. Then I did eight with Hugo MacNeill, and I went to Cork to take over Ballincollig and Victoria Barracks and we got eight days to do it.[18] I did an old fort. The Tans or Auxies were in Fort Elizabeth, the transport shed in Victoria Barracks. The last job was the Freemasons' Hall in Molesworth Street [Dublin] and it was handed over to Sir John Keane.[19] I went over it with Charles Keane, and I got his views on the damage which had been done there. I could not assess the damage as I had never been in the place previously. I was asked to go to take charge of the Antrim Brigade and I was to cross the border the morning the Four Courts was attacked [28 June 1922].

I was in Dublin at the time, and every morning I reported to Emmet Dalton who was then in the College of Science. Charlie McAllister had a bulletin.[20] And [an] officer who had broken his honeymoon to take up active service, and that was Charlie McAllister.

On 19 May [1922] it had been arranged that there would be an attack on the North. By arrangement with the Provisional Government six divisions were to take part in a general attack. The 1st to 5th Northern Division were concerned in it. In the 1st Joe Sweeney, 2nd [Joe] Morris for the Provisional Government Forces and Charlie Daly for the Republican forces.

3rd Northern: Seamus Woods succeeded Joe McKelvey.

4th [ND] [O/C] Frank Aiken.

5th [ND] [O/C] Dan Hogan.[21]

Then there was the First Midland [Division] in which Seán Mac Eoin was in charge.[22] In the six counties, there were only two divisions whose areas were there confined – the 2nd and the 3rd Northern. The 1st, 4th and the 5th were on the border and so was the 1st Midland, which took in a part of Fermanagh. There six divisions were to co-operate.

The attack was to have taken place during the first week of May. The second of May. Then, as the date approached, Woods was **[53L]** involved with Brown Square Barracks.[23] He had an RUC man there for this was the Headquarters in Belfast, the Transport Headquarters. There were two armoured cars there and this RUC man proposed to hand over the Barracks, but he had to be on duty on a certain day, and from week to week he could not say when he was to be on duty. Woods wanted these armoured cars for the job. He went to Dublin and the general attack was to be postponed in favour of the handover of Brown Square. This was to be the beginning of the attack. Two days were to be allowed to elapse before the general attack would begin. On 17 May 1922, and on 19 May, the 3rd Northern attacked and burned Shane's Castle [Co. Antrim]; this outpost was to be occupied by Specials Ballycastle, Martinstown Barracks.[24]

A week or ten days before, the 2nd Northern Division attacked and no one else made an attack. The active men within the six counties were, prior to the attack, to be purposely formed into columns. Collins supplied the arms, the allocation to Antrim was Thompson guns, rifles, revolvers and ammunition. Half the allocation came through from Derry to Antrim through Joe Sweeney in oil tanks and the other half came around by the coast. They were never sent on by Sweeney, and they were used by him against the Republicans. Was Sweeney entirely responsible or not?

The men who [were to] take part in this attack were to be formed into companies and to be put on the payroll of 24 [shillings] per week as for the private in the Provisional Government troops. They were then to be supplied with their salaries by the Provisional Government. In Antrim, as a result of that, they could return to their homes, but they were missing from their homes. There was no police activity for two weeks and then they began to close down. This put men on the run. There were 1,500 men in Antrim, and I could give them fifty rounds a man when I took on.

There was an intensive course of training at the end **[53R]** of June or in the early part of July but '...' came on 11 July when I met in Dundalk with over one hundred men from two divisions, [who] nearly filled Hare Park Camp and the numbers increased daily.[25] They were to go back after two weeks, and while they were in Hare Park they were officered by their own officers. Roger McCorley was O/C of the camp. Then Hare Park was required for Republican prisoners and the Northerners were sent to

Keane Barracks in the Curragh.[26] Peadar McMahon was then O/C of the Curragh, and he was also a member of the Organisation Staff before 1922.[27]

There was a mutiny in Portobello Barracks first, after the 11th of July men came down. Terms: 1) you were neither asked nor were you compelled to take part in the fighting in the twenty-six counties; 2) In the Curragh, our men were under our own officers and not under the Provisional Government Forces, except in so far as the general orders in the camp were concerned. There must have been from 400 to 500 men there. Each Brigade of the 2nd and 3rd Northern occupied a line of huts. Dan McKenna was the Vice Commandant.[28] He was a Derry man and he had been vice O/C to Morris of the 2nd Northern Division. A Northern man in the Curragh had equal pay with that of Provisional Government troops in addition to full maintenance: so that this 24/- could be sent home. After the transfer, Dan McKenna was the O/C of the Northern men and I was the Vice O/C. The Battalion O/C, and others not of the 3rd Northern Division officers in Hare Park, before we left we (had begun to) consider if the Northern men would or would not be allowed to take part in the fighting (in the twenty-six counties). It was debated and only three there present were against it (Pat McCormack, Liam Lynn, Ballycastle, who was O/C Battalion 2 of the Antrim Brigade and myself). Briefly we said that we had left the six counties where fighting should be done and that if our men **[54L]** should be lost they should be lost in the North and that if we did fight here (against Republicans) it would make things more difficult in the North, having run away from the North, we fought in the South. That was the first tangible break then. Before this it was coming, but now it came.

Collins stressed at the Portobello meeting that in two weeks or three the fight would be finished and they would resume the fight in the six counties, and as a way of resuming the fight they wanted these men to have an intensive course of training. After this meeting, McCorley organised his Kerry draft and then McKenna became O/C of the North in Hare Park Camp and there we were. McCorley was recognised as O/C. Felix [McCorley], my Brigade Adjutant, was a line captain in Hare Park and the line was composed of Antrim men alone.[29] He was forced to resign as line captain for three other men refused to attend. He was a scurrilous cur. He ordered men (up) for a medical examination and three men refused. It was a venereal disease parade and [there was] a penalty for breach of rules … or a man was given a voucher and had to leave.

I was in Dublin and I came down and asked Roger to withdraw the vouchers; and then I said we would all go, all the Antrim men. Dan McKenna and himself and I were as court-martial officers and he gave the decision against his brother that day. The Antrim men wrote me a letter asking me to dismiss Felix as Brigade Adjutant. Then Felix resigned and he was sent to Naas.

About November, or at the end of October, we went to Keane Barracks; and the first batches of internees came in. Roger's draft left for Kerry. Dan McKenna ordered our lads out that evening to fix bandoliers. At first they refused, but then they decided they would and they found at Newbridge that they were 750 rounds short. We offered to hand over the Curragh to the Republicans. Joe Wilson was in Dublin attached to intelligence under Micky Carolan, but nothing happened (EOM: I never before heard of this officer. Then I was in Dublin. **[54R]** To whom was the offer made?) The Republicans burned an officer's house near Kilcullen. An establishment was burned out, and an order was issued to everyone to turn out, but our fellows cheered that night. After December, all out before Christmas 1922. At that stage, we were taking sides. You were Free State or Republican. All Republicans would have gone by Christmas 1922 and I don't think there would have been many left there by then.

The vast majority of the men who had come down were the sole support of their families: they couldn't remain at home. They sent back money. If we went back it would only be a short time until they would be picked up. Dan McKenna was O/C of the Northern men in Keane Barracks when I left and then McKenna was commissioned in the Free State Army.

During the Truce, the 3rd Northern Division had a Headquarters in St Mary's Hall [Belfast] and Collins heard that it was to be raided. Joe McKelvey was then O/C of the 3rd Northern Division, and Woods was his Vice O/C, but Joe McKelvey ignored the advice (or the order) and it was raided.[30] They captured a complete list of all the men and all the ranking officers in the 3rd Northern Division.[31] McKelvey was to be cashiered. The [IRA] Convention then was proclaimed. All the 3rd Northern officers who attended the Convention [March 1922] were automatically dismissed and all the others went over to Beggars Bush the morning after [to] the Provisional Government and they made their peace. McKelvey stayed in the Four Courts and I always felt that McKelvey, knowing that he was being cashiered, may have determined him. He would not acknowledge his mother. He worked in a Factory and he lost his head and he wouldn't cross the word.

[TAN WAR 1918]

Austin Stack, Terry [MacSwiney], John Dunne and I were in Belfast gaol and we were working on an escape which came up through St Malachi's College.[32] The rope was to be thrown over and got to 'A' wing. There was a passage from Crumlin Road which leads up a **[55L]** gaol wall and a lower wall. We went in through Malachi's College to throw the rope over. This was in the General Election of 1918. I was in charge of a group with a ladder. I had seven men with me, two with bludgeons to knock out the sentry. At six or at nine the escape to St Malachi's College was to have taken place, dependent on Stack's arrangements. At six a signal and at 6:30 it was off. Collins at three o'clock had sent a man to Winnie Carney, Carney was a contact, to call it off.[33] [There was] a contact between Seán Cusack, the brigadier, and she went in and told Stack that evening and the Brigade O/C didn't tell us about it. One bludgeon was left behind in the retreat and it was picked up by someone who took it to Micky Carolan, and he began to talk about the escape and that he didn't know about it, and how hard it would be on the election results, and that he was threatening to tell the police; so I was told to interview him. I drew a gun and I told him I'd shoot him if he didn't shut up. Andie Furlong was also in charge of a squad that night.[34] There were eighteen men and they came to divide into six groups of three; and they were to guide these escaping men. I never discovered why Collins called it off, for everything was right. We were to overpower a couple of warders in the wings, get the keys of the external gates and get to the boundary wall, throw a stone over and there we had a ladder.

This rope ladder was later used for Paddy Fleming's escape in the 'Joy.[35]

FRANK AIKEN

(UCDA P17b/93, pp. 1–14, Sept. 1948)

Francis 'Frank' Thomas Aiken (1898–1983) was born on 13 February 1898 into a sturdy nationalist Catholic farming family at Carrickbracken, Camlough, Co. Armagh. He was the youngest of James and Mary Aiken's seven children and was orphaned at the age of fifteen. Along with his sister Nano, Aiken became involved in the Camlough branch of the Gaelic League and was elected secretary in 1914. In the same year, Aiken was also elected secretary of the newly formed Camlough Volunteers.

In the aftermath of the Easter Rising, Aiken became further involved in the republican cause and got his first taste for politics when he canvassed for Éamon de Valera in the 1917 East-Clare by-election. Over the following years, Aiken moved up the local ranks of the IRA and became Commandant of the Camlough Company IRA in 1919 and Vice Commandant of the Newry Brigade in 1920. In March 1921, he was appointed O/C of the 4th ND, which spanned across South and West Down, all of Armagh and

North Louth, and was one of the more active and organised divisions in the North.

After the Anglo-Irish Treaty, Aiken adopted a unique stance of neutrality and tried to avert Civil War. He sided with the republicans after being arrested and imprisoned in Dundalk by members of the pro-Treaty 5th ND in July 1922. His division played no significant part in the Civil War. He was appointed IRA Chief of Staff after Liam Lynch's death in April 1923 and shortly afterwards gave the order to 'dump arms'.

Aiken was elected a Sinn Féin abstentionist candidate in the Louth constituency in 1923 and held this seat for over fifty years. He has the distinction of being one of the longest serving members of Dáil Éireann, and acted as Minister for Defence (1939–45), Minister for Finance (1945–8), and Minister for External Affairs (1951–4, 1965–9). Aiken's period as Minister for External Affairs is often regarded as a 'golden age' of Irish foreign policy due to the bipartisan stance his delegation adopted at the United Nations, the promotion of decolonisation, and his support for a vote on the admission of China to the UN. Aiken's interest in disarmament led to the 1968 Nuclear Non-Proliferation Treaty, of which Aiken was the first signatory.

Aiken was reticent to speak about the revolutionary period for fear that it would only 'bring the whole thing up again'.[1] This interview is composed of a number of documents and letters copied by O'Malley.

[1L] (Notes of Frank Aiken, O/C 4th Northern [Division])

[Fourth] ND formed end of March 1921 [comprised:] County Armagh, South and West Down, North Louth, South West Antrim small area, Moy in Tyrone.

July 11th [1921]: about 1,200 men and 35 rifles.

End of July: [Richard] Mulcahy Chief of Staff and [Eoin] O'Duffy Deputy Chief of Staff inspected the area.[2] At a divisional council, he asked us to work hard and be prepared for a renewal of hostilities.

Beginning [of] August: [Michael] Collins, TD for Co. Armagh, attended a meeting in Armagh. O'Duffy threatened 'to use the lead'.[3]

[Eoin] O'Duffy, at end of September, told a few of us that GHQ had asked the President [Éamon de Valera] to keep the negotiations going until the winter (which is the most favourable season for the weaker side in guerrilla war).

After two or three months, both officers and men, in units which were not well-disciplined, were inclined to have a good time and do no work. In our [4th Northern] Division we had to dismiss two officers for getting drunk in the late autumn. There is no doubt the months of September, October and November would have demoralised the army [IRA] were it not for the fact that practically all the senior officers commanding their units were very sober and in earnest about training their units.

At the end of October [1921], I was instructed to go to GHQ. On the night on which I was instructed to report Mulcahy, then Chief of Staff, accompanied, as far as I remember by the Adjutant General. Gearóid O'Sullivan[4] met seven or eight divisional commandants including myself at Vaughan's Hotel [Dublin]. It was a peculiar meeting; none of us knew what we were there for until Mulcahy put [it to] each of **[2R]** us in turn: 'what would be your attitude if the British offered us something less than a Republic'[?] Each of us replied in turn that it was for a Republic and the complete freedom of Ireland that we had fought and that only we were asked to fight and work for complete and absolute freedom we would not have joined the army at all. Our answers drew no comment or remark from Mulcahy … when he had all answered the questions, we knew as little as when it commenced about the negotiations or Mulcahy's opinions of them.

I do not believe Mulcahy had anything like the Treaty in his mind that night … I think he must have been thinking of some settlement on the lines of Document No. 2,[5] because I remember John Quinn [his QM][6] telling me that he was with Mulcahy when he (Dick Mulcahy) first saw the terms of the Treaty and heard him say about it 'This will never do'.

Sometime afterwards I got a circular which Cathal Brugha,[7] Minister of Defence, sent to all senior officers asking them to accept new commissions, which he intended to issue to all officers so that the army would be on the same footing as all other national armies.[8] It was thought that (in the event of further hostilities) at the time that by thus regularising the position of the army, the British would not execute captured volunteers. This circular was the first we ever received from the Ministry of Defence and it was accompanied or quickly followed by a note from HQ saying simply that it was authentic and might be signed.

I was speaking to O'Duffy some days later and when **[3L]** I asked him to explain the idea of the new commissions, he said I might not bother about them (I had signed it) and gave me to understand by some remark that GHQ Staff did not think a whole lot of Cathal Brugha. This was the first I heard of that sort of thing at GHQ.

[Treaty] 6th Dec[ember]: at a class the daily paper arrives. I called the class to order. I told them that whatever the outcome of the treaty in the South, whether there would be peace or war in the twenty-six counties, there was bound to be fighting in the North; and that it was our duty to be prepared for it.

Evening of 6th: a volunteer concert and céilidhe in Clones to which all the principal officers in the North and Midlands had been invited. [Eoin] O'Duffy, Joe McKelvey,[9] Seán Mac Eoin[10] and several other important officers were present. O'Duffy assured us with great vehemence that the signing of the Treaty was only a trick; that he would never take that oath and that no one would (be) asked to take it. He told us that it had been signed with the approval of GHQ in order to get arms to continue the fight. … but we felt that if it (the Treaty) were allowed to come into operation, it would be, because of the type of men who would work it, an obstacle instead of an aid to independence. I told O'Duffy what I felt about it, and he again assured us that he would never dream of taking the oath to the British king or asking anyone to take it and that the sole object of signing the Treaty was to get arms.

[4R] Those deputies did not vote for the Treaty on its merits; they all declared it repugnant to them and all maintained, some publicly and some privately, that they would not have voted for it only on understanding that the oath clause vote was not compulsory and that, on the formation of the Boundary [Commission] clause, all the nationalist constituencies in the six counties would be taken from the northern parliament, thereby making it impossible for the remaining unionist three and half counties to keep up a Parliament independent of an all-Ireland Parliament. O'Duffy, at the concert in Clones, started the campaign for the Treaty. 'There are people,' he said 'who are now calling Mick Collins a traitor, who were under the bed when there was fighting to be done.' From that night to the attack on the Four Courts,[11] he worked like a fiend for the success of the Pro-Treaty party … without him and Mulcahy and McNeill [Eoin MacNeill],[12] the Civil War, I believe, would not have occurred.

Debates on the Treaty. I have always considered it a great mistake, that the President's [de Valera] alternative to the Treaty was not pressed vigorously by the members who voted against the Treaty. Had this been done and Document No. 2 been pressed as a practical immediate alternative to the acceptance of the Treaty, I have no doubt the discussion in the Dáil and in the country would have had much more reason and a lot less bitterness in it.

[5L] On the night the vote was taken on the Treaty, all the volunteers were ordered to stand to arms and Lloyd George shook his fist at the TDs by ordering the Auxiliaries to parade the streets of Dublin in armoured cars and in full war kit.

Sometime in the Autumn of 1921, every Division got from our GHQ a copy of a circular which the British had sent on to their police and military: in it, it was said that British HQ had information that nearly every young man of military age in the South and West was in the IRA and that this would simplify matters greatly in the event of a renewal of hostilities as they would know that 'no mistakes could be made'.

[Judge O'Connor[13] in [a] letter to the *Daily Mail* … 1925 about [Alfred] Cope [Dublin Castle][14] and Mick Collins, pointed out that Alfred Cope was always at Mick's elbow during the negotiations in London informing him confidentially what dreadful things would happen if a breakdown came and how frightfully determined the British were.

Jan[uary] 10 1922: [Arthur] Griffith elected President; Mulcahy M. D. [Minister of Defence]. Griffith said, 'I will keep the Republic in being until the Free State is established'. Mulcahy [said] 'The Army will remain the Army of the Republic'. Later that evening, in response to a summons from GHQ, nearly all officers of the GHQ Staff and officers commanding Divisions and Independent Brigades met in the Mansion House. Mulcahy arrived later, and a few minutes afterwards called us to attention as Mr de Valera entered the room. Notable absentees were: Cathal Brugha, Liam Mellows, Rory O'Connor and Ernie O'Malley. I think it was Mr de Valera **[6R]** who began the meeting: he sat at the head of the table. He made a short appeal to us to keep the army intact, and alluding to a matter that happened in Clare, he appealed to Mulcahy to make sure that arms were not removed from any unit nor anything else done which might cause uneasiness amongst Volunteers.

Dick Mulcahy repeated the assurance which he had given the Dáil earlier that day, that the Army would remain the Army of the Republic. Mick Brennan [was] afraid the arms in County Clare might be used in land disputes.[15]

Liam Lynch.[16] He was very deeply moved and broke down. He declared that the Treaty was not what he fought for. He alluded to the great sacrifices that had been made in his own Division. He concluded by saying that he could not take any orders from GHQ.

The meeting ended by Mulcahy asking Liam and other officers who had spoken bitterly against the approval of the Treaty to wait after the meeting concluded so that he might have a chat with them.

I did not speak out at this meeting at all. It is rather difficult to describe my attitude. I was against the Treaty but so much reliance did I put on the promises then being made about the Irish interpretation of the treaty and the elimination of the Oath and Partition, and so greatly did I appreciate the difficulties of the situation that I remember saying to a comrade just after the Treaty was approved of by an Dáil, in answer to a tirade of his against the actions of the majority, that I thought it possible that I might have voted for the Treaty if I had been a member. I would have done my utmost to get the president's alternative to the Treaty [**7R**] adopted. I felt that the united influence of those who voted against the Treaty and of those who voted for it, on the understanding that the oath and Partition would not come into operation, should be expected to see that those promises were kept when the constitution was being framed, so that the TDs and army could honourably avail themselves of the powers ceded by England under the Treaty to develop and strengthen the nation and especially to abolish partition. I did my very best to keep these elements together in the Army, when I saw they were going to split. On 10 January 1922, I held my peace because the meeting was over before I realised that there was a danger of a split. I did not think Liam Lynch meant what he said when he told Mulcahy that he would not take any further orders from him.

[8L] [Notes from IRA Army Executives]

	1st Convention 26 March [1922][17]	9th April	28th June
1.	Liam Lynch		–
2.	Liam Mellows		–
3.	Rory O'Connor	–	
4.	Joe McKelvey		–

5.	Ernie O'Malley	–	
6.	Seán Moylan[18]		–
7.	Frank Barrett[19]	–	
8.	Michael Gallagher[20]	Michael Kilroy[21]	
9.	Peadar O'Donnell[22]	–	
10.	Frank Carty[23]	Liam Deasy[24]	
11.	Seamus Robinson[25]	P. J. Ruttledge[26]	
12.	Joe O'Connor[27]	Séamus Robinson	
13.	Oscar Traynor[28]	Seán O'Hegarty[29] (resigned)	Tom Barry[30]
14.	Liam Pilkington[31]	Florrie O'Donoghue[32] (resigned)	Pax Whelan[33]
15.	John Barry[34]	Tom Hales[35] (resigned)	Tom Derrig[36]
16.	Tom Maguire[37]	Joe O'Connor	

Army Council
Liam Mellows[38]
Liam Lynch
Seán Moylan
Rory O'Connor
Tom Barry

[8R] Published 9 April 1923, *Independent*[39]

	16–17 October [1922]	Substitute	24/28th March [1923]
1.	Liam Lynch	Liam Pilkington	Liam Lynch
2.	Liam Deasy	Mick O'Brien	Seán Hyde (Sub)[40]
3.	Tom Derrig	Mick Cremin[41]	Tom Derrig[42]
4.	E. O'Malley	Austin Stack[43]*	Austin Stack
5.	Tom Barry	Paddy O'Brien[44]	Tom Barry
6.	M. Kilroy	Tom Ruane[45]	[TR] absent (delayed)
7.	Frank Barrett[46]	Tom Maguire	[FB] absent (delayed)
8.	P. J. Ruthledge	F. J. McDonnell	[PJR] absent (sick)

9.	Pax Whelan[47]	Humphrey Murphy[48]	Humphrey Murphy
10.	Seán Moylan	Tom Crofts[49]	Tom Crofts
11.	[Séamus] Robinson	Seán Fitzpatrick[50]	[SR] absent sick (Jimmy O'Meara Sub)[51]
12.	Joe O'Connor	Seán Russell[52]	Seán Dowling[53] Rory O'Connor
13.	Con Moloney[54]	Seán Hyde	Bill Quirke Sub.[55] Liam Mellows
14.	Seán MacSwiney[56]	Dan Donovan[57]	Seán MacSwiney Joe McKelvey
15.	Frank Aiken	Paddy Quinn[58]	Frank Aiken Peadar O'Donnell
16.	Tom Johnson[59]	Thomas O'Sullivan[60]	[TOS] Custody

*Joe O'Connor [Austin] Stack's substitute resigned the IRA.

5 April 1923. On 20 April [1923] Captain '...' [was] appointed, but would not accept. M. Carolan appointed a substitute of Manning on 11 July.[61]

[9L]	20th April 1923	11/12 July [1923]	27/28 January 1924	Sub[stitute]
1	Liam Pilkington		Frank O'Brien	Tom Kearney O/C 5th Brigade
2	Seán Hyde		Absent	
3	Bill Quirke			
4	Mick Cremin absent			Liam Doherty[62]
5	Austin Stack captured	Michael Carolan		Moss Twomey[63]
6	Seán Dowling		absent	

7	Frank Aiken			Tom Rogers[64]
8	*Tom Barry		Paddy O'Brien	S. Noonan O/C Cork[65]
9	Tom Ruane			Seán Barrett
10	Frank Barrett captured	(B. Ryan killed, Tom Maguire appointed 11th July)	Tom Maguire	Mullins[66]
11	Thomas O'Sullivan			Tomás O'Connell, O/C Carlow
12	Humphrey Murphy absent sick	J. J. Rice	Humphrey Murphy	J. J. Rice
13	Seán MacSwiney		Dan Donovan	Mick Murphy[68]
14	Tom Crofts			M. Donegan[69]
15	P.J. Rutledge			
16	Jack O'Meara[70]	Seamus Robinson absent	Seamus Robinson	Ned Reilly[71]

*Resigned

[9R] [Letter from Tom Barry to the Army Executive]

11 July 1923

To the Chairman, Army Executive Council IRA

1. Accept my resignation from the Army Executive Council, Army Council and as an officer of the I.R.A.
2. Lest my resignation be interpreted as a result of my wanting to compromise, I wish to make it clear in this as in former communications, that any policy I suggested was suggested

only if the majority of the Executive decided that such policy did not (a) compromise any National Principle, (b) Deny the right of any future party to prevent by force of arms if necessary the functioning of any Government not based on the complete independence of Ireland.

3. I also wish to state that the rumours propagated in some cases by Republicans as to my negotiating for peace with the Free State are absolutely false. Lies, suspicions and distrust are broadcasted and I have no option but to remove myself from a position in wherein I can be suspected of compromising the position. I have never entered into negotiations for peace or compromise with the Free State.[72]
4. I cannot withdraw my responsibility in sending you the signed communication with the then Division O/Cs. I believed then and now that we are bound to arrange further safety of our men by every means in our powers, once A/B of paragraph 2 was not infringed on. I admit a technical breach of discipline, but I do not withdraw my act.
5. When arms are taken up again in a fight for the complete independence of Ireland, I will again be available for service. Should it be decided at any future date that the Executive should have to bear any responsibility for any acts of our Army committed in the war, I should like to be included.

(Signed) Tom Barry (Commandant General)

[10L] [Letter from Frank Aiken to Anti-Treaty IRA]

(Ref no: Special army orders)

Department of the Chief of Staff
General Headquarters
Dublin
April 27th, 1923

To O/C's Commanders and Independent Brigades

<u>Suspension of Offensive</u>

1. I order to give effect to the decision of the government and Army Council embodied in attached Proclamation of this date. You will arrange the suspension of all offensive operations in your area as from now, Monday April 30th.
2. You will ensure that while remaining on the offensive all units take adequate measures to protect themselves and their munitions.

Chief of Staff.

[10R] [Letter from Frank Aiken] To the Director of Publicity

1. Eoin O'Duffy as Mulcahy's Chief of Staff at time of attack on Four Courts must have signed an order to Ennis to carry out the attack, he signed one to me to attack the volunteers in Dundalk who were directly under the Executive and he had naturally to supervise Ennis' plan of attack.
2. From the 28 June until he was transferred to the Civic Guard he certainly took an active part in the war. I was in Limerick the week of the Lynch/Brennan/O'Hannigan[73] truce (12th July week) O'Duffy was personally in charge of a relief column, bringing more troops, arms and armoured cars to Brennan. The day he arrived in Ennis both the Free State and Republican forces in Limerick had been withdrawn to their peace time posts. O'Duffy sent for Brennan and O'Hannigan and after consultation with them (Brennan told me he reprimanded them for the truce) sent Seamus Hogan (the professor)[74] to surrender both of them and take charge of operations in their areas. The next morning the Free State forces, without giving the promised notice to Liam Lynch, broke the truce and re-occupied the posts they held during the fighting that took place during the first week of July 1922. I was with Liam in the New Barracks when I heard of this dishonourable action of Brennan and immediately went to his headquarters. In reply to my appeal to him to withdraw his forces and keep his word of honour he said 'I can't – Hogan is now in charge.' I told him he could if he liked; that Hogan's appointment

was merely a blind to cover up a breach of the truce, and that his (Brennan's) conduct was most dishonourable.

[11L] While I was remonstrating with Brennan, Liam reoccupied his fighting posts also – as, of course, he had every right to do – and fighting recommenced. I forgot to say that Brennan said that the posts were only being re-occupied by the Free State forces as precautionary (measures) methods and that they would not recommence the fighting. I told him that this was damn nonsense; and that it was merely a matter of time until fighting commenced between the two opposing forces in a position of readiness for battle and a matter of hours in this particular instance. It was only two hours before it commenced and I was stuck because of the heavy fire in Brennan's headquarters until next morning when I left without seeing him or Hannigan.

Brennan and Hannigan, of course, were immediately responsible but only for O'Duffy they would not have started. As Brennan said, 'I don't see how serious fighting can take place here, our men have nothing against the other lads.' Mr (Churchill) could never have worked his will only for the bitterness [of] O'Duffy, bred and nurtured wherever it was possible, and for the influence of Mac Neill who again miscalculated Irish spirit, or Mulcahy.

When Mulcahy became Chief of Staff, Collins' Commander in Chief, O'Duffy was appointed Free State O/C Southern Command. He was in charge of the advance by land on the 1st Southern Division, W. R. E. Murphy was his adjutant and it is said the real general. From a military point of view, the strategy of the whole Free State campaign was good, but their commanders in the field did not handle men in action as well as ours. O'Duffy's junior officer (Paddy Daly)[75] afterwards said a thing to Humphrey Murphy which gives a good idea of how they reached Cork and shows that they relied on sheer weight of lead rather than O'Duffy's (EOM: N.B. Free State had no prestige to maintain as defeat did not matter) **[11R]** or WRE Murphy's tactic to carry to Cork.[76] He said, 'you put barriers of mud to stop us and we knocked them down with human divisions. What did we care about them?'

After our men evacuated all the towns and took to guerrilla warfare, O'Duffy was ambushed a few times and once at least was in a serious engagement with our friend Fionán Lynch.[77] Fionán, as you know, left the fight and found safety under a table in a farm house. Our men say O'Duffy left his men, commanded Fionán to the safe place and stayed there until the fight was over. Shortly after this O'Duffy was transferred to the Civic Guard and it was believed by some of our men who did not know his capabilities, that this meant he was fired from the army. I believe he was appointed commissioner because he was the best man the Staters had for the job.

O'Duffy told you a lie when he said he had a man shot for saying that Terry MacSwiney was committing suicide.[78] There was a Volunteer shot in Monaghan as a traitor, but he was shot in the spring of 1921 for giving away about twenty men of his own company to the Peelers. The traitor was arrested by the Auxiliaries and after a threatening he gave away all he knew. On release he confessed all he had done and asked to be shot, I believe.

April 29th, 1924.

[12L] Synopsis of [the] History [of] the Executive 20th March [1922]–Jan 28 1924

1. 1922: 26 March: Convention held. Decision to form an Army Executive to govern army, and appointment of temporary executive to frame constitution.
2. 9 April: Convention held. Election of Executive and adoption of constitution. Three members: Tom Hales, Florrie O'Donoghue, and Seán Hegarty resigned shortly after convention. Tom Derrig, Tom Barry and Pat Whelan were co-opted to fill their places.
3. Fighting in Kilkenny, etc. Truce 3 May. Negotiations with Beggars Bush. Joint Army Council formed. Proposals known as 'Beggars Bush Proposals' rejected by a majority of the Executive.[79] Extraordinary convention summoned to consider them. Breach of Declaration of war with England and number of delegates withdrew. 28 June. Attack on Four courts. Joint statement issued signed by all members of the Executive.
4. Executive meeting held October 1922. Co-options to replace four casualties. Proclamation calling on president to form a

government. Allegiance given to government. Arranged that all future vacancies be filled by co-option of substitutes nominated by the members who became casualties.

5. 1923: Executive meeting held March 23 to 26. Peace Resolution defeated by one vote. Adjournment to 19 April in order that the reports of Western Divisions and results of attempts to secure artillery might be available.
6. 10–20 April: Chief of Staff (Liam Lynch) killed and three members captured. Remainder dispersed.
7. Executive Meeting held 20 April. Election of Chief of Staff Frank Aiken. Proposal to offer peace to enemy on condition of their openly accepting the principles of the sovereignty and the unity of the nation. The powers of peace and war given to the government and army council. Appointment of Special Army Council of three. **[12R]**
8. Meeting of a government and Army Committee 26/27 April. Decision to issue 'Suspension of Offensive' order and president's proclamation of 27 April.
9. 13-14 May. Meeting of government and army. President reported failure to make peace with the Free State 'government' on terms consistent with the sovereignty and honour of the nation. Submitted all documents relative to the negotiations which he had carried out. Decision to issue 'cease fire-dump arms' order.
10. 30 June 1923. Meeting of government and army council. Rejection of proposal to destroy arms of the army. Discussion on Tom Barry's letter to the Chief of Staff. Instruction to Chief of Staff to provide assistance for men on the run, wounded men, dependents of men killed, and employment for unemployed Volunteers. Decision to summon Executive meeting.
11. Executive meeting held 11/12 July 1923. Adoption of minutes of government and army council. Decision regarding strengthening of organisation and discipline of army. Reorganisation of Sinn Féin, forbidding emigration. President requested to co-opt on cabinet. Resignation of special army council.
12. 1924: Executive meeting held 27/28 June. Adoption of GHQ report on hungerstrike. Decision to forbid secret societies, regarding enemy Constitution, regarding in keeping in force of

order No. 8 forbidding signing of forms if undertaking to secure release from enemy custody.

8 August 1924. Chief of Staff.

[13L] [Letter from Frank Aiken to all members of IRA][80]

HQ 4th Northern [Division]
17 July 1922

To all Officers and Men,
Position of the 4th N[orthern] D[ivision] from January 1922 to 17 July 1922.
(Jan 1922)

As a result of a letter of Commandant General Rory O'Connor and Commandant General Liam Lynch and other officers to the Minister of Defence demanding an immediate Convention of the IRA, a meeting of divisional commandants and HQ staff was held. At this meeting I proposed that, at that time, if a convention was held a split was inevitable. The convention should not be held until after the publication of the constitution and then we should be able to see if we have to split and with whom we had to split. The meeting ended with Commandant General Rory O'Connor and Minister of Defence agreeing that the convention should be held in March.

The convention in March was proclaimed by the President of Dáil Éireann [Arthur Griffith] with the advice of the Minister of Defence, Commandant General O'Connor and Commandant General Lynch and other officers called on all delegates to attend. No representative of the 4th Northern attended, and the night before I wrote asking Commandant General O'Connor to postpone it until after the constitution was published.

The convention was held and the Executive formed. Only one brigade staff and two battalions of this brigade went over to the Executive. The divisional staff and the rest of the division decided to remain under the Dáil Ministry of Defence until the publication of the constitution, unless they were asked to do something that they could not honourably do.

On 6 July I wrote the Minister of Defence [Dick Mulcahy] to ask him to call a truce so that the Dáil might get at the constitution and call a convention of the army. He said he could not see his way to advise the government to do so. I told him then that, if ordered, I would not attack the Executive forces, but on the other hand, I thought the Executive should quit and if I had to leave his army I should not fight him, because the fight would only ruin the country without gaining any grounds for the Republic. When [**13R**] leaving him, I said I would try to get Commandant General Lynch to quit. On leaving the Minister of Defence I went south to see Commandant General Lynch. I saw him on 8 July and put to him that he could do more for the Republic by propaganda than by fighting men of the old army, most of whom thought they were doing their best for the Republic, and who would never countenance the king as in the constitution, and also that although he had the moral right to fight, it was bad tactics, since he could only fight for a few months or years without any chance of a successful revolution. I failed in my mission and returned to my division.[81]

When I reached my division's headquarters I found there orders to attack the Executive forces in my area, and also an order for myself, divisional staff and brigadiers to report at GHQ on Saturday, 15 July.

On Friday, 14 July I met all (including Executive) brigade and battalion commandants and divisional staff. We agreed that if the Provincial Government did not give the Anti-Treaty parties, civil and military, a constitutional way of carrying on for the Republic, such as withdrawing the oath for admission to parliament, we would give them no support, moral or material. On that day, 14 July, I ordered all arms and war material in the division to be concealed and that if we broke with GHQ all military posts and camps were to be evacuated, the division's organisation to be kept intact along volunteer lines until an ordered state of government, obtaining in the South, we could attack the North, with a chance of getting an united Ireland, which was always the immediate job for us northerners.

I reported as ordered to the Minister of Defence and laid our news before him. He told us his situation and the government's [**14L**] and advised me to give more detailed plans as to when I thought the position could be fixed up and also write a memo to the members of the government on the subject. I returned to our barracks to do so.

I wrote the memo that night, 15–16 July, and at 5.30 in the morning of the 16th I awoke with two Thompson [machine guns] at my nose.

An officer who had been reduced for inefficiency, some men who were under arrest for drunkenness, opened the gates and so – Brilliant Victory of the National Army! Three hundred Irregulars arrested! Not a shot fired![82]

I got parole that evening and went to the Minister of Defence and demanded my own release and that of my officers and men and that the full truth be published, so that it could be said that three hundred of the IRA meant to fight, and were such military fools or such cowards as to be arrested without firing a shot.

The M[inister] [of] D[efence] assured me and I believed him – he did not know our barracks was to be attacked on that particular morning.[83] He told me also that GHQ had information that some of my officers had arranged at a meeting to attack government troops. I told him that they had got an untrue account – from an officer who had been reduced – of that meeting, which simply decided that they would not take any part in the fighting and would protect their area and keep law and order in it. I told him also that however Dick Mulcahy might dislike it – that if the M[inister] [of] D[efence] attempted to govern without the consent of the best people, he would be driven to use rotten men and means.

He asked me to get my arrested officers to sign an assurance that, if released, they would not attack the government or destroy life or property. I told him **[14R]** that, although I could assure him they would not do so.

I was sure they would not sign any guarantee unless the government withdrew the oath of allegiance to the British king from the constitution, that there would never be peace in the country while it (the oath) was in it. Before I left he sent an order to the officer in charge of his troops in the Dundalk Barracks that my officers were to be treated as officers confined to quarters and that I was to get parole to fix up the mess that had been made of the situation.

Today, Monday 17 July, I applied to officer in charge for parole to visit my men outside. He refused. I asked by what authority. He said not of O/C 5th ND but of the officer over him. I asked him to press that officer for my parole and to inform the Minister of Defence I guaranteed to him in writing that if I got parole I would accept absolute responsibility for all that would occur in my divisional area three hours afterwards.

At three o'clock he came and told me that my request for parole had been refused and that my officers that had been arrested were to be sent to prison. I asked him was the Minister of Defence aware of that. He said not. I said then that washed my hands of the whole business and declared if anyone was killed in this area, on one side of the other, that the officer over the O/C 5th ND was guilty of murder. Finally, I besought him (the officer in charge) not to attack our men further without the sanction of the M[inister] [of] D[efence].

Now there must be no ill-wills borne to the men who attacked this barracks. They did not know the circumstances and from a military point of view, it was a nice well-organised piece of work.[84]

[15L] [Report from 4th ND to Richard Mulcahy on 14 July 1922]

(Copy)

Decision reached by Senior Officers 4th ND on the Friday before Dundalk Barracks was taken by Staters and which was reported to Mulcahy on the Saturday.

We are agreed:

1. That the Provision Government must provide a constitutional way for the republican parties and carry on towards the Republic such as withdrawing the oath for admittance to the parliament and unifying the IRA under an elective army council with liaison between council [and] government.
2. That if this is not done we will not give any support, moral or material.
3. That the present is an occasion, probably the last, to say to England that the opposition to the whole Treaty cannot be suppressed unless Ireland is allowed to frame her own Constitution.

Reported to Mulcahy by F[rank] Aiken, P[ádraig] Quinn, M[ichael] Fearon[85] in Portobello Barrack.

Notes

MICHAEL O'HANLON

1 Sarah O'Hanlon, Military Service Application, MSP34REF59647.

2 Spelled 'Bourke' by EOM, Thomas 'Squint' Burke of Portumna, Galway was also a medical student at UCD. He later served as O/C of No. 2 Offaly Brigade.

3 Spelled 'Flannigan' by EOM, Flanagan was Captain and later Commandant of the Dublin Brigade and was the oldest member of the Squad. See his interview with O'Malley, UCDA P17b/115.

4 See interview with Frank Aiken in this collection.

5 Andrew Cooney hailed from Nenagh, Co. Tipperary and studied medicine at UCD. After the Truce, he was appointed O/C of No. 1 Kerry Brigade, IRA. He was imprisoned in Mountjoy Gaol during the Civil War. In 1925, he succeeded Frank Aiken as Chief of Staff of the IRA. Cooney was also interviewed by O'Malley, P17b/107, p. 116.

6 Seán Dunne was later resident superintendent at Grangegorman Hospital.

7 Paddy Quinn, or later Pádraig Ó Cuinn, was born in Liverpool and raised in Newry. He was also a medical student in UCD. He was later Adjutant of the 4th Northern Division in 1923. His brothers, Malachy and Seán, were also very active IRA officers.

8 Jack Egan studied medicine at UCD.

9 Gerald Davis was involved in Volunteer activity in Kilrooskey, Co. Roscommon. In 1917, he moved to Dublin to study medicine at UCD and joined C Company, 3rd Battalion. He later served as army pathologist at St Bricín's Military Hospital. He was also interviewed by O'Malley (UCDA P17b/90, pp. 106, 117, 118, 137).

10 The Sack of Balbriggan took place on 20 September 1920. Black and Tans based at Gormanston's military camp looted and burnt the town of Balbriggan, destroying fifty-four houses.

11 Donagh Healy's store on Usher Quay.

12 Mick White and his brother George were both in C Company of the 3rd Battalion.

13 Originally from Cranny, Co. Clare, Peadar Clancy served with the Irish Volunteers in the Four Courts during the Easter Rising. He was V/C of the Dublin Brigade during the War of Independence. He was arrested, along with Dick McKee and Conor Clune, on the eve of Bloody Sunday and taken to the Detective Office in Exchange Court. All three lost their lives on the morning of 21 November 1920 under controversial circumstances; official reports claim they were shot after throwing grenades at their officers. However, it is suspected that they may have been killed in retaliation for the murder of the Cairo Gang, the group of British Intelligence agents who were killed on Bloody Sunday.

14 Thirty-one people lost their lives on 21 November 1920, surrounding the events of Bloody Sunday. Fourteen British agents were shot by the Squad in the early morning. In the afternoon, fourteen civilians were shot at Croke Park and three Irish republican prisoners (Dick McKee, Conor Clune, and Peadar Clancy) were shot the following morning.

15 This may refer to Dick Sweetman, a member of the Dublin Brigade, who later joined the Guards and was a member of the Broy Harriers, named after Garda Commissioner Ned Broy, who challenged the Blue shirts and left republicans alike in the 1930s after Fianna Fáil gained political power.
16 Joe Carroll was a member of Dublin IRA ASU, Section 3.
17 The *Daily Sketch* was a British tabloid newspaper.
18 The man in question is Captain Brian Keenlyside, who was residing at 28 Upper Pembroke Street. His wife, Mrs Keenlyside, is noted to have 'most gallantly struggled with the murderers and thereby frustrated their purpose'. According to evidence given by Keenlyside, he was shot four times, in the arms and in the jaw.
19 The men killed at 28 Upper Pembroke Street were Captain L. Price, Major G. M. C. Dowling, and Lieutenant-Colonel Hugh Ferguson Montgomery (who died later from his injuries). Captain Keenlyside, Colonel Woodcock, and Colonel Montgomery were also shot. Emmet Dalton had courted a maid in the house in order to gather information about where the men slept.
20 The porter at 28 Upper Pembroke Street was James Greene and he was given a ten-year sentence for opening the door on Bloody Sunday.
21 O'Malley escaped from Kilmainham Gaol on 14 February 1921 along with Frank Teeling and Simon Donnelly. Donnelly's interview with O'Malley can be found at UCDAP17b/92.
22 See interview with Peadar O'Donnell in this collection.
23 Jeremiah Joseph, or 'Ginger', O'Connell hailed from Ballina, Co. Mayo. He succeeded Dick McKee as director of training in November 1920. He was a supporter of the Treaty and became deputy Chief of Staff of the Free State army in 1922.
24 Charles McAllister was a volunteer in Glenariff, Co. Antrim. He was shot by British forces in May 1922.
25 Emmet Dalton was IRA Director of Intelligence and was involved in the Squad along with his brother Charlie. He was a Major General in the Free State army during the Civil War. He later worked as a film producer.
26 Leo Duffy was involved in Squad activities on Pembroke Street on Bloody Sunday, and was also a witness to the shootings at Croke Park that afternoon.
27 Oscar Traynor was a volunteer during the Easter Rising and was O/C of the reorganised Dublin Brigade during the War of Independence. He succeeded Dick McKee as Commandant of the Dublin Brigade after McKee was shot in November 1920. Traynor was elected to the Dáil in 1925 and served as a Fianna Fáil TD until 1961. See his interview with O'Malley (UCDA/P17b/096,097, p. 101).
28 The Lewis machine gun was widely used by the British army during the First World War.
29 Frank Carney was appointed Commanding Officer of the 1st Northern Division of the IRA in 1920. He served as a Fianna Fáil TD from 1927 until his death in 1932.
30 Rory O'Connor was IRA Director of Engineering from 1918. He earned the nickname 'director of jail deliveries' after successfully organising a number of prison escapes in both Ireland and England, including the daylight escape of Piaras Béaslaí and Austin Stack from Strangeways in Manchester. O'Connor was one of the leaders of the anti-

Treaty garrison which occupied the Four Courts in April 1922. He was arrested after the storming of the Four Courts and was executed by the Free State in an extra-judicial reprisal on 8 December 1922 with Liam Mellows, Joe McKelvey, and Dick Barrett.

31 The six men executed were Frank Flood, Patrick Moran, Thomas Whelan, Patrick Doyle, Bernard Ryan, and Thomas Bryan.

32 Tom Lawless was a student at the Royal College of Surgeons.

33 See interview with Charlie Daly in this collection.

34 Spelled 'McCormack' by EOM, Michael McCormick was O/C of the 3rd Southern Division from 1921. During the Civil War, he authorised a number of strong measures against anti-Treaty soldiers.

35 Joseph J. O'Connor was a member of the Squad and served as Commandant of the 3rd Battalion of the Dublin Brigade. He was later elected as a Cumann na nGaedheal senator and served until 1936.

36 Pádraic O'Connor was part of the Dublin IRA Active Service Unit. He later joined the Free State Dublin Guard.

37 Patrick 'Paddy' Smith (1901–82) hailed from Bailieborough, Co. Cavan. He joined the Volunteers in 1917 and by 1919 was the youngest serving IRA commandant in the country. He was court-martialled and sentenced to death in 1921, but was saved by the announcement of the Truce. He was a founder of Fianna Fáil and has the distinction of being the longest-serving member of Dáil Éireann (1923–77).

38 Seán Boylan was Commandant of the Meath Brigade, 1919–20 and O/C of the Eastern Division in 1921.

39 Diarmuid O'Hegarty was V/C of No. 1 Dublin Brigade following the Easter Rising. He became director of Organisation of the IRA in 1920 and was one of the three assistant secretaries to Erskine Childers during the Treaty negotiations.

40 Benny Lynch was a member of C Company, 1st Battalion, Dublin Brigade.

41 Peter 'Peeney' Smith had a pub on Upper Street in Cavan town which served as a rendezvous for Volunteers.

42 Eoin O'Duffy and Joe McKelvey: see biographical sketches.

43 Tom Rogers served as Battalion Quartermaster of the Dundalk Battalion. He was injured during the attack on Dundalk on 14 August 1922. He emigrated to the USA, *circa* 1927, against the advice of the IRA.

44 Crossley Tenders were small lorries used by the British army during the War of Independence.

45 See interview with Woods in this collection.

46 Felix McCorley was a prominent member of the Belfast Battalion. See interview with his brother, Roger McCorley, in this collection.

47 Rory McNicholl was part of an ASU belonging to D Company, 1st Battalion, Belfast Brigade.

48 John Quinn (also known as Seán Quinn) was Quartermaster of the 4th Northern Division. He was shot by Free State soldiers in early 1923 and later died from his injuries. His brothers, Pádraig and Malachy, were also active IRA officers.

49 Misspelled 'McKay' by EOM, see John McCoy interview in this collection.

50 Charlie McGleenan was vice O/C of the Armagh Battalion in 1921. He joined the Anti-Partition League of Ireland (APL) in 1945.

51 Peadar Mac Mahon was active in organising and recruiting Volunteers into the Mid-Limerick Brigade in 1917. He was a Major General in the Free State army and acquired guns from the British to attack the Irregulars in the Four Courts. He was General Officer Commanding in the Curragh, February 1923.

52 Seamus Woods was appointed O/C 3rd Northern Division after Joe McKelvey was dismissed in March 1922.

53 Chuck Byrne was a Belfast anti-Treatyite and was wounded operating in Louth in 1922.

54 Wish Fox was O/C of B Company in Belfast.

55 McConville hailed from Lurgan and was involved in IRA activities in Co. Armagh. He was O/C of the Derrytrasna Company and later Lurgan Battalion O/C.

56 Misspelled 'MacMullen' by EOM, Captain McMurrin was Commandant of the B Specials Constabulary in the South Part of Armagh. He was held as 'a hostage for the good conduct of the Crown Forces in South Armagh'. He was detained in Dundalk Military barracks and was released in July 1922 when the Free State troops took over the barracks.

57 This occurred on 16 July 1922.

58 Dan Hogan: see biographical sketch. It has been speculated he may have acted on his own initiative in capturing Dundalk. Emmet Dalton gave Hogan command of the 4th Northern Division after Aiken's arrest.

59 This operation took place on 27 July 1922, when a mine was detonated at the gaol wall and 105 men escaped.

60 Hanratty and Mallon were both members of the Armagh Company.

61 This section of the narrative jumps back to Aiken's attempts to remain neutral in the Civil War prior to his imprisonment in Dundalk Gaol.

62 This meeting took place on 7 July 1922.

63 Cathal Brugha: see biographical sketch.

64 Jerry Ryan was commandant of the 1st Battalion of the No. 2 (Mid-) Tipperary Brigade during the War of Independence. He was pro-Treaty, and held Thurles against Republican forces.

65 Michael Brennan led the pro-Treaty First Western Division of the IRA, and with support from Donnchadh O'Hannigan's 4th Southern Division took control of Limerick city on 20 July 1922. See biographical sketch.

66 Liam Lynch: see biographical sketch.

67 Peter Hughes was a pro-Treaty TD. His home and business premises were targeted by IRA bomb attacks in early 1923 in retaliation for the shooting of republican prisoners by the Provisional Government.

68 This probably refers to Tom Rogers, battalion quartmaster of Dundalk.

69 Tom Sheridan was vice O/C of the Ballinagh Battalion in 1919. He died in May 1920 after being shot by an RIC sergeant during an IRA ambush.

70 Incorrectly spelled 'Ivor' by EOM, Eiver Monaghan was from Poyntzpass, Co. Armagh, and was an officer in the 4th ND.

71 Owen Meegan was captain of the Inniskeen Company in North Louth in 1916. He commanded a Flying Column in the 5th Battalion of the Monaghan Brigade in 1921.

72 Patrick Baxter hailed from Cavan. He was elected TD for the Farmer's Party in 1923 and was later a Senator for Fine Gael.

73 James Goodfellow was an officer in No. 1 (North Louth) Brigade.

74 Hare Park, in the Curragh.

75 Mick O'Neill hailed from Celbridge and was an officer in the North Kildare Battalion, No. 1 Brigade, Meath.

76 Seamus Maguire was from Glenidan. He was O/C of Castlepollard Battalion in 1919 and served as O/C of the Mullingar Brigade in 1921.

77 Pat Farrelly served as Captain of the Carnaross Company and later as O/C of No. 3 Brigade of the 1st Eastern Division in 1921.

78 John Henry Collins was a solicitor from Newry. He was a Nationalist MP at Stormont for South Armagh from 1925 to 1929 and for South Down from 1929 until 1933. He took a leading part in the Sinn Féin movement from 1918 onward and supported the election campaigns of several Sinn Féin candidates, including Éamon de Valera and Michael Collins.

79 Henry O'Hanrahan was a brother of Michael O'Hanrahan, who was executed for his involvement in the 1916 Rising.

80 Dr John Loftus was Medical Officer 6th Battalion, Dublin Brigade, South County Dublin in 1920. See his interview with O'Malley: UCDAP17b/86.

81 Rory O'Connor, Joe McKelvey, Liam Mellows, and Dick Barrett were executed in Mountjoy Gaol on 8 December 1922.

82 This may refer to Thomas Maguire, the 2nd Lieutenant of A Company (Castlepollard), No. 5 (Mullingar) Brigade, 1st Eastern Division.

83 Paddy Hegarty was O/C of an ASU in North Mayo and Sligo. See his interview with O'Malley, P17b/137.

84 Dr Francis Ferran was originally from Co. Fermanagh but worked as a doctor in Foxford, Co. Mayo. He was O/C of the 4th Battalion, North Mayo Brigade. He was elected Sinn Féin TD for East Mayo–Sligo in 1921 and again in 1922. Dr Ferran died in the Curragh in 1923.

85 Michael Kilroy was O/C of the 4th Western Division in 1921. He opposed the Treaty and led the Western Command in 1922. He was imprisoned in November 1923 and during his imprisonment was elected Sinn Féin TD for South Mayo. He was elected for Fianna Fáil in 1927 and served as a TD until 1937. See interview in *The Men Will Talk to Me: Mayo Interviews*, pp. 35–72.

86 Willie Malone was O/C of the Westport Battalion in 1922.

87 Tom Scanlon was from Ballina and was a ranking officer in the Sligo Brigade. See O'Malley interview with Scanlon (UCDA P17b/133, 136).

88 This may refer to Jimmy Donnelly of the 4th Dublin Battalion, who was also interviewed by O'Malley. See UCDAP17b/115.

89 Seán Gormley from Dundalk was adjutant of the North Louth Brigade in 1920 and Divisional Adjutant to the 4th ND.

90 Thomas 'Squint' Burke of Portumna, Galway was a medical student in Dublin and was O/C No. 2 Offaly Brigade.

91 Billy Byrne, was 1st Lieutenant of E Company, 2nd Battalion, No. 1 Dublin Brigade in 1917, and subsequently O/C until the Truce.

92 Owen O'Brien was 1st Lieutenant of the Ahane Company in 1917, and later Brigade vice O/C Limerick in 1921.

93 Jim Boyle was O/C of the Foxford Battalion.

94 Annie Cardwell's death is listed as having occurred on 17 December 1922. She was eighteen years old and a first cousin of Frank Aiken. She died of 'shock and haemorrhage due to gunshot wound accidentally inflicted by Patrick Brady'. *Deaths Registered in the Union Of Celbridge (3417310).* A 'Miss Cardwell' is noted as being a member of the Leixlip branch of Cumann na mBan in 1921, although this may be one of Annie's sisters, Stella or Eva.

95 Paddy Mulally led the Meath/Kildare Flying Column during the War of Independence. See his interview with O'Malley (UCDA P17b/106, p. 110).

96 Paddy Cahill was anti-Treaty and defended Tralee from the Free State army. He also commanded the Dingle column. He was elected Sinn Féin TD in 1921 and 1923.

97 Humphrey Murphy was a Major General in the Free State army and O/C of No. 1 (Kerry) Brigade.

MICHAEL DONNELLY

1 Micheal Donnelly, *World War I Draft Registration Cards*, New York City, No. 146, Form 4517, No. 113.

2 *Irish Press*, 10 March 1944, p. 3.

3 Seán MacEntee was born in Belfast, and lived and worked in Dundalk from 1914. See biographical sketch.

4 Conradh na Gaeilge (the Gaelic League) worked to promote and preserve the Irish language. The Dundalk branch of the Gaelic League, established 1899 and located in Seatown Place, famously hosted the 1915 Oireachtas and Ardfheis at which Douglas Hyde resigned as president due to the increasing politicisation of the organisation.

5 MacNeill's order was distributed across the country during Easter Saturday night, cancelling Volunteer mobilisation. It was also published in the *Sunday Independent* on Easter Sunday.

6 A Dundalk native, McHugh was an active member of Sinn Féin from a young age and was a lieutenant in the Irish Volunteers in Dundalk in 1916.

7 Joe Boyle was a volunteer from Dundalk.

8 Patrick Hughes was the President of Sinn Féin in Dundalk and the officer commanding the town's Irish Volunteers after its establishment in 1915. He served as Consul of Ireland in San Francisco in the 1950s.

9 Spelled 'Hannigan' by EOM, Donald O'Hannigan (also known as Dónal or Dan) was sent to Dundalk from the Dublin branch of the Volunteers at the beginning of April 1916, apparently by Pádraig Pearse at the request of Paddy Hughes.

10 Wakefield Gaol is located in West Yorkshire, England.

11 James Hanratty was a member of the Dundalk Battalion, A Company, which mobilised on Easter Sunday 1916. After his release from Frongoch, he was elected to Dundalk Town Council with Sinn Féin. He opposed the Treaty and was interned in Newbridge. The Tempest Press is a family printing press founded in Dundalk in 1859. It was later known as the Dundalgan Press.

12 Spelled 'McSweeney' by EOM, Terence MacSwiney. See biographical sketch.

13 Spelled 'Dobbin' by EOM. From Belfast, Dobbyn was later a member of the IRB Supreme Council, 1917–21. He shared a cell with Éamon de Valera in Lincoln Gaol and helped coordinate the escape in 1919.

14 In Merionethshire, Wales.

15 Denis McCullough: see biographical sketch.

16 The father of Séamus Dobbyn, Henry Dobbyn was prominent in the IRB in Belfast since the 1880s. Due to his age, Dobbyn was not permitted to mobilise on Easter Sunday 1916 and his sons were ordered not to inform him of their plans. Despite this, Dobbyn mobilised at Coalisland, Co. Tyrone, with the other Belfast Volunteers on Easter Sunday. Both Séamus and Henry served two years hard labour in Mountjoy and were released shortly after the Treaty.

17 Seán (also John) O'Mahony (1864–1934) was nicknamed 'Comrades'. Later elected Sinn Féin MP for Fermanagh–Tyrone and member of the First and Second Dáil; he opposed the Treaty.

18 Neil Kerr was a native of Charlemont, Armagh. He was member of the IRB Head Centre for Liverpool and an agent for Collins in England.

19 The *Gaelic American* was published by John Devoy (1842–1928) in New York from 1903 to 1927 to promote the work of Clan na Gael. Born in Kilkenny, Devoy was exiled to the USA in 1871, where he dominated Irish republican politics for much of the remainder of his life. After a dispute with de Valera in 1920, Devoy supported the Treaty.

20 Liam Mellows: see biographical sketch.

21 Two companies were formed in Dundalk: B Company was originally recruited from members and supporters of the O'Rahilly Gaelic Football Club.

22 See interview with Frank Aiken in this collection.

23 The incident took place in April 1920.

24 Seán Gormley was adjutant of the North Louth Brigade in 1920.

25 The ambush took place on 6 June 1920. Two men were killed: RIC sergeant Tim Holland and civilian Peter McCreesh.

26 Also known as Flying Columns.

27 'Stuff' is an IRA term for arms/ammunition.

28 Richard Walsh (1888–1957) was a Brigade Adjutant in Mayo, 1918–20. He was later a Fianna Fáil TD for Mayo South.

29 A native of Monaghan, Patrick McKenna was sent from Dublin in 1920 to act as local IRA commandant. He was accidently blown up by his own men on 14 August 1922 during an attack on the Military Barracks.

30 Brother of the prominent Sinn Féin businessman, James McGuill, O/C Volunteers Dundalk 1918 and IRB centre for Louth, 1919–20.

31 Carrolls' cigarette factory.

32 The attack on Newtownhamilton took place on the night of 12–13 May 1920.

33 Spelled 'McKay' by EOM. See interview with John McCoy in this collection.

34 County Inspector George Craig hailed from Naas. He was injured in Cork on 17 July 1920 when Gerard Bryce Ferguson Smyth was shot by Dan 'Sandow' O'Donovan's No. 1 Cork Brigade on 17 July 1920.

35 Emmet Dalton was the IRA liaison officer in Dublin, with headquarters in the Gresham Hotel post-Truce July 1921. Bernard McAllister (BMH WS 0147) was a member of the 5th Battalion (Fingal) Dublin Brigade.

36 This meeting, early in 1919, initiated the reorganisation of the Irish Volunteers.

37 Also known as Séamas Kennedy.

38 The banned IRA General Army Convention was held at the Mansion House, Dublin, on 26 March 1922. It was agreed that the army would no longer be under the authority of Richard Mulcahy, Minister of Defence.

39 Richard Mulcahy, then Minister of Defence of the Free State government. See biographical sketch.

40 Eoin O'Duffy, then Free State Chief of Staff. See biographical sketch.

41 Aiken was maintaining a neutral stance at this time.

42 Donnelly may be referring to the swapping of arms during the joint Northern offensive in order to disguise the provisional government's complicity.

43 Eamon Rooney was Captain of the Lusk Company.

44 This attack took place on 27 July 1922 and resulted in the freeing of Aiken and his men from Dundalk Gaol.

45 Joe Bergin was a Free State Military Policeman at Tintown. He was brutally killed in December 1923 after being intercepted carrying messages for Republican prisoners.

46 Sheehy was the nephew of a farmer, Parkinson, prepared to shelter escapees.

JOHN MCCOY

1 See the Appendix for a discussion of the discrepancies between McCoy's witness statement and his O'Malley interview, as well as a comment on O'Malley's notes on McCoy's interview.

2 Beggars Bush barracks was a former British army installation on Haddington Road in South Dublin, which operated as headquarters of the pro-Treaty IRA GHQ after January 1922. On 28 March, the Executive, which represented the anti-Treaty majority within the IRA, repudiated the authority of GHQ and the Minister of Defence. Richard Mulcahy.

3 On 6 August 1920, Seán MacEntee, TD for South Monaghan, petitioned the Dáil on behalf of his fellow Belfast citizens to boycott goods produced in Belfast and withdraw savings from Belfast-owned banks. This led to a widespread campaign across the country, which lasted until March 1922.

4 There were two Craig–Collins agreements, between the Chairman of the Provisional Government, Michael Collins, and the northern Prime Minister, James Craig. The first in January, the second, referenced in the interview, was signed in March and failed like its predecessor.

5 Liam Lynch's 1st Southern Division arranged an arms transfer with the pro-Treaty GHQ at Beggars Bush as part of the proposed joint-IRA northern offensive in spring 1922. Lynch exchanged IRA guns for rifles with the serial numbers chiselled off which Beggars Bush received from the British.

6 On 14 April 1922, 200 anti-Treaty IRA, led by Rory O'Connor, occupied the Four Courts.

7 The 4th ND did not act in what was in fact the second offensive of the joint IRA campaign. The 2nd ND (Tyrone and South Derry) launched their attack on 2–3 May, killing six crown forces. The 3rd ND (Belfast, Antrim and East Down) went out on 18–19 May.

8 Spelled 'McKoy' by EOM.

9 Poyntzpass (population in 1910: 500) is a predominantly unionist village on the Armagh–Down border just under ten miles north of Newry.

10 John Quinn (also known as Seán Quinn) was Quartermaster of the 4th Northern Division. He was shot by Free State soldiers in early 1923 and later died from his injuries.

11 Blackwatertown is a small nationalist village on the border between Armagh and Tyrone. The IRB were traditionally strong in the area.

12 As he notes in his BMH statement, McCoy was shot during a police raid on his father's house in Mullaghbawn on 24 April 1921. He states, 'The bullet entered on the back of my neck alongside the spinal column and came out on the right side of my face, fracturing my lower jaw.' (BMH WS 0492, p. 92).

13 Hugo Mac Neill (1900–63) O/C 1st Battalion Fianna (South Dublin) 1919–20; Director of Organisation and Training, Fianna, 1920–21, accepted the Treaty and rose to prominence in the Free State army. Ballykinlar was an internment camp outside a small village eight miles southwest of Downpatrick.

14 St Mary's Hall was the location of Eoin O'Duffy's office as Liaison Officer for Belfast.

15 McCoy is highly critical of the sectarian nature of constitutional nationalism, or Hibernianism, in his BMH statement. He described the AOH as 'definitely sectarian and anti-Protestant and in its policy it has no doubt played a most sinister part in all northern counties' [116/1R], as it 'caused unionists [Protestants] who had liberal or nationalist tendencies to get suspicious or alarmed'.

16 Patrick McDonnell of Nenagh, North Tipperary was listed as O/C No. 1 Tipperary Brigade, 3rd Southern Division in July 1922. Misspelled 'Mac Donald' by EOM in the original. See his interview with O'Malley (UCDA P17b/114, pp. 125, 130).

17 Thomas Burke of Portumna, Galway, was a medical student in Dublin. He was appointed GHQ organiser for the No. 2 Offaly Brigade in the spring of 1921 and became Brigade O/C after the internment of Seán Mahon.

18 This would appear to be Patrick Mulcahy of Engineer's Battalion, the Dublin Brigade, who was a second lieutenant in the Free State army.

19 Three Free State soldiers, including two commandants, Seán 'Jack' Collison and Austin McCurtain, were killed in a republican mine and gun attack on a troop lorry in Co. Tipperary on 4 August 1922.

20 This section of the interview refers again to the 1921–2 period.

21 Charles McAllister was a volunteer in Glenariff, Co. Antrim. He was shot by British forces in May 1922.

22 Hilltown is a small nationalist village in the parish of Clonduff, ten miles north of Newry. A constable Waring was seriously wounded in the shoulder in an ambush in Newry in April 1922.

23 Frank Carney: see biographical sketch.

24 Seamus Monaghan was the first O/C of the 3rd Battalion, No. 2 (Newry) Brigade, 4th ND.

25 Warrenpoint (population in 1910: 1,817) is a seaside resort on the Co. Down side of Carlingford Lough.

26 Born in Middletown on the Armagh–Monaghan border, Éamon Donnelly (1877–1944) was a leading republican figure in Ulster. He led the Sinn Féin majority on Armagh City Council in 1921. A critic of the Treaty and partition, he was twice elected to the northern parliament as an abstentionist republican.

27 'Mick O'Hanlon Athlone Commdt' written at top of page.

28 Misspelled 'Jerry Tippen' by EOM in the original, Gerard Tipping of Edward Street, Lurgan, is listed as a volunteer in B Company (Lurgan), 3rd Battalion (Lurgan), No. 3 Brigade (Armagh), 4th ND. He was listed as Divisional signalling officer, 1921–2.

29 A native of Monaghan, Patrick McKenna was sent from Dublin in 1920 to act as local IRA commandant. He was accidently blown up by his own men on 14 August 1922 during an attack on the Military Barracks.

30 Seán Gormley from Dundalk was Divisional Adjutant to the 4th ND.

31 Castleblayney (population in 1910: 1,576) is a market town in North Monaghan close to the Armagh border.

32 Dan Hogan: see biographical sketch.

33 Hope Castle, also referred to as Blayney Castle, is an eighteenth-century house built in the town.

34 This is probably a reference to Redmond O'Hanlon.

35 Patrick Creggan and Thomas Crawley were abducted from their homes in Derrymore and Whitecross. Their bodies were left on the road where mines had been placed by the 4th ND during a previous ambush.

36 Castleshane is a small village on the outskirts of Monaghan town; the Castle Shane Estate lies in the same area.

37 Spelled 'McKeown' by EOM, Seán Mac Eoin. See biographical sketch.

38 Head Constable Eugene Igoe was born in Attyma, near Ballina. Bunnyconnellan was the name of his birthplace. He led an RIC secret team who fought against Collins' Squad in Dublin after the assassination of the Cairo gang on 21 November 1920.

39 An enfilade is a volley of gunfire directed along a line from end to end.

40 Gerald Davis was a volunteer in C Company, 3rd Battalion Dublin Brigade and was posted in Atlone during the War of Independence.

41 On 31 March 1922, six Special Constables were ambushed in Hill Street, Newry, opposite Hyde Market. Constable Allen was killed and Constable Waring seriously wounded.

42 On 3 June 1922, two Newry Volunteers, Eddie O'Hare and Edward Fullerton, shot dead James Woulfe Flanagan, a Resident Magistrate.

43 On 26 May 1922, a thirty-hour gun battle started between the IRA and USC when the USC raided Paul Gallagher's Public House at Flurry Bridge, Jonesborough.

44 This many refer to the ambush led by Aiken at Dromintee on 17 June 1922 as a reprisal for the mistreatment of Mrs James McGuill by the USC. This ambush occurred on the same night as the attack on Altanaveigh in which five Unionists were killed. Although not detailed here, McCoy mentions this in his witness statement.

45 'Johnny Grant had a column also' written at top of page.

46 Captain McMurrin was Commandant of the B Specials Constabulary in the South Part of Armagh. He was held in early June 1922 as 'a hostage for the good conduct of the Crown Forces in South Armagh'. He was detained in Dundalk Military Barracks and was released in July 1922 when the Free State troops took over the barracks.

47 Tom McNally: see biographical sketch.

48 Rory McNicholl was part of an ASU with Thomas Flynn, Captain D Company, 1st Battalion, No. 1 (Belfast) Brigade, 3rd Northern Division.

49 Pádraig Quinn was listed as 5th Northern Division Quartermaster in the summer of 1922. He succeeded Tom Rogers and was replaced by Ned Fitzpatrick. His brother, Seán, was divisional commandant in 1923.

50 Spelled 'Raneleagh' by EOM in original.

51 Frank Mallon, Ogle Street, Armagh was Adjutant, No. 3 (Armagh) Brigade, 4th ND.

52 Under the Special Powers Act, the unionist government interned 700 republicans between May 1922 and December 1924. They were housed in Larne Workhouse, Derry Gaol, and most notoriously on board the *Argenta*, a prison ship moored off the coast at Larne. Woods was interned on 14 November 1923 as a Free State Commandant. He was the last prisoner to be released on 17 April 1924.

53 Seamus Woods: see biographical sketch.

54 Dan McKenna: see biographical sketch.

55 Tom Morris: see biographical sketch.

56 Seán Corr from Carrickmore was an active republican before the formation of the Irish Volunteers. A member of the IRB, he was Brigade Quartermaster for No. 1 (East Tyrone) Brigade, 2nd Northern Division.

57 Joe McKelvey: see biographical sketch.

58 Charlie Daly: see biographical sketch.

59 See interview with Donnelly in this collection.

60 This may refer to Eamon Rooney, who was Captain of the Lusk Company. Donnelly details this incident in his interview in this collection.

61 Kevin O'Higgins: see biographical sketch.

62 Eddie O'Hare was a Newry Volunteer involved in the shooting of James Woulfe Flanagan, a Resident Magistrate, on 3 June 1922.

63 Edward the Bruce (1280–1318), brother of Robert, King of Scotland, was proclaimed High King of Ireland in 1315, but was killed at the Battle of Faughart. His body was not buried in the vicinity.

64 Frank Aiken and many of his men were arrested on their return to Dundalk on 15 July and were at this stage held at Dundalk Gaol.

65 'War flour' and 'cheddar' are names for explosives manufactured and used by the IRA.

66 Greenore is a fishing village with a deep dock on Carlingford Lough.

67 On 23 April 1923, seventy-one republican prisoners escaped from the recently built Tintown No. 1 at the Curragh.

68 On 1 July 1923, the Free State held 11,316 republican prisoners. In 1922, Republican prisoners were held at Hare Park, the Glasshouse, and in Keane Barracks. Tintown No. 1 Camp opened in early 1923. Tintown No. 2 and No. 3 were located on the right and left of No. 1 Camp.

69 Commandant Patrick Geraghty (1890–1923), O/C 3rd Battalion (Tyrellspass) No. 1 North Offaly Brigade was arrested in possession of arms on 10 November 1922. Geraghty and another Volunteer, Joesph Byrne from Daingean, Co. Offaly, were executed by Free State firing squad in Portlaoise Gaol on 27 January 1923.

70 Liam Deasy: see biographical sketch. Deasy was also interviewed by O'Malley (UCDAP17b/86).

71 Twomey, a former member of the Dublin IRA, was Free State governor of Portlaoise.

72 This appears to be Joe Griffin, the Intelligence Officer of F Company, 1st Battalion, Dublin Brigade and close associate of Harry Boland. He was ATIRA Director of Intelligence. For Griffin's interview with O'Malley, see UCDA P17b/87.

73 On 29 August 1922, five republican inmates were injured when 200 cells were burnt as part of an escape attempt from Portlaoise Gaol. John Hickey died after being wounded in the thigh.

74 Dr Francis Ferran from Foxford was Medical Officer for the Mayo IRA and a TD for Sligo–East Mayo. He died on 10 June 1923, while interned in the Curragh.

75 In his prison memoir, *The Gates Flew Open*, Peadar O'Donnell identified Tom Mullins and Paddy Cannon, both Mayo Volunteers, as the originators of the tunnel.

76 'T. M. for a while lives in Howth' written at bottom of page.

77 'Dublin' written underneath.

78 Jimmy Grace was a Dubliner and had formed part of the garrison at Clanwilliam House during Easter Week 1916.

79 Patrick Brennan was O/C of the Kilcullen Company, before becoming vice O/C of 6th Battalion, No. 7 Brigade, 1st Eastern Division. He was O/C of Executive forces in Kildare and was arrested in September 1922 in an attack on the Free State Intelligence Department at Oriel House, Dublin.

80 See Mick O'Hanlon interview in this collection.

81 The Hill of Allen is a volcanic mound in West Kildare. Athgravan is a village beside the Curragh.

82 Kilcullen Bridge is a small town on the River Liffey in Co. Kildare, five miles east of the Curragh.

83 Matthew Malone of Rinawade Upper, Celbridge, Co. Kildare, was listed as a farm labourer in the 1911 census.

84 Leonard Cardwell and Susan Cardwell were the aunt and uncle of Frank Aiken. They were originally from Armagh and lived in Beatty Park in Celbridge. Six escapees were recaptured in this raid.

85 Kill is a village and parish on the western side of the Kildare–Dublin border.

86 Jim Rush was O/C ATIRA, West Mayo Brigade.

87 Tom Scanlon was a leading IRA man in Sligo town and had served as prisoners' O/C in Longford Military Barracks before being moved to Tintown.

88 McGee owned a shop in Ardee, but no Louis McGee appears in the 1911 census.

89 In October 1923, and in sympathy with a hunger strike in Mountjoy Gaol. In total, 3,390 men in Tintown and 100 men in Hare Park joined the mass hunger strike. Commandant Denis Barry died on 11 November 1923, Andy O'Sullivan on 22 November, and Joe Lacey on 24 December. There had been earlier hunger strikes in the Curragh which had also led to deaths – Daniel Downey, from Dundalk, died from the effects of a hunger strike on 10 June 1923, while Joseph Whitty (19), from Wexford, died on hunger strike on 2 September 1923.

90 Thomas Derrig: see biographical sketch.

91 A military policeman who carried messages in and out of Tintown No. 3, the body of Corporal Joseph Bergin was found in the canal at Milltown on 15 December 1923. He had been tortured and shot six times in the head. During his torture, Free State soldiers tied Bergin to the rear of a car and dragged him behind it at speed. They then delivered his bloodstained cap to his girlfriend, Peg Daly, in Kildare town. Captain James Murray was found guilty and sentenced to death, though his sentence was later commuted to life imprisonment.

92 John Costello of the 5th Battalion, Sligo Brigade, was wounded and captured in Ballytogher in December 1922. He was then interned at Newbridge Camp until March 1924.

93 Born in Meedin, Tyrrellspass, Co. Westmeath, Thomas Malone reorganised the Irish Volunteers in Counties Tipperary, Offaly, and Westmeath in 1917, and in early 1918 was appointed Irish Volunteer Brigade Adjutant for Offaly. In March 1919, Malone travelled to Co. Limerick under the name of Seán Forde and was appointed Brigade vice O/C for East Limerick. He escaped from Spike Island on 30 April 1921. Malone served as IRA Director of Operations in the 2nd Southern Division area and was captured by Free State forces on 7 August 1922. He took part in the burning of Portlaoise Gaol and escaped from Tintown No. 3 in July 1923.

94 Dr Andrew Francis Cooney was attached to the North Tipperary Brigade. He then joined GHQ and was sent as GHQ organiser to Kerry. He was with the Four Courts

Garrison and was interned in Newbridge, Arbour Hill, Kilmainham, and Harepark before being released in May 1924.

95 Lady O'Donoghue was the wife of Sir James O'Donoghue, chair of the Urban District Council, Galway city.

96 Mossy Donegan was an officer in the Bantry Battalion and later in Cork No. 3 Brigade. See his interview with O'Malley in *The Men Will Talk to Me: West Cork Interviews*, pp. 96–118.

97 Spelled 'Fahey' by EOM, Francis Patrick 'Frank' Fahy (1880–1953) was the TD for Galway and served for nearly thirty-five years for Sinn Féin and then Fianna Fáil, before serving as *Ceann Comhairle* for nineteen years.

98 Charles George Wickham (1879–1971) was a British army officer and commander of the RUC (1922–45). He also helped secure the right-wing dictatorship in Greece after the Second World War.

99 Henry Wilson: see biographical sketch.

100 Major General Eamon 'Bob' Price was IRA Director of Organisations before the Truce and a Free State general stationed in Portobello barracks.

101 The Sinn Féin Hall was burnt on 19 December 1920.

102 The Ancient Order of Hibernians was an exclusively Catholic and nationalist fraternal society. In the first decade of the twentieth century, a faction of the AOH (the Board of Erin) was effectively taken over by the nationalist MP for West Belfast, Joe Devlin. This grouping evolved from a marginal, plebeian political network in southwest Ulster to become a major force within the ranks of the IPP, with membership soaring from 5,000 in 1900 to 64,000 in 1909.

103 Patrick Donnelly (1878–1947), a solicitor from Newry, was the IPP MP for South Armagh from February 1918 until 1922, when the seat was abolished.

104 The post-war British general election in which Sinn Féin won 73 out of 105 Irish seats. In Ulster, Sinn Féin won ten seats, while the IPP won six as a result of the Logue Pact. Ulster Unionists won twenty-three seats in Ulster.

105 Cardinal Michael Logue (1840–1924) was an ultramontane conservative Catholic bishop, appointed cardinal in 1887. A staunch opponent of popular nationalism of any character, he was vocal in his criticism of Sinn Féin. He supported the Treaty.

106 Although Joe Devlin won handsomely against Éamon de Valera in West Belfast, the pact gained seats for the IPP in areas where Sinn Féin appeared to enjoy the majority of nationalist support, i.e. South Armagh, South Down, Tyrone Northeast, and East Donegal.

107 Patrick Rankin joined the IRB in 1907. He cycled from Newry to Dublin to participate in the 1916 Rising. He later served as O/C of the Newry Brigade during the War of Independence.

108 Founded in September 1920, the full-time A Specials were disbanded in 1925 and the C Special reserves never remobilised after 1922, leaving the part-time B Specials only. The force was firmly based on the UVF and had a reputation for highly partisan treatment and occasional brutality against the Catholic community in Ulster.

MICHAEL MURNEY

1 *Irish Press*, 21 October 1943, p. 2.
2 This incident occurred on 8 December 1920, as described by Seán McConville (BMH WS 0495).
3 The Ulster Special Constabulary, or B men, are commonly believed to have been founded on 22 October 1920.
4 This is probably a reference to raids on mail trucks.
5 Oswald Swanzy was shot in Lisburn on 22 August 1920. See biographical sketch.
6 This is a reference to William Barrows, governor of the Crumlin Road Gaol, whose son, Major W. R. Barrows, served as governor of Portlaoise Gaol until 1945.
7 See interview with McLogan in this collection.
8 Peadar McMahon was active in the Easter Rising. After his release from Frongoch, he organised the volunteers in Limerick, Leitrim, Mayo, Kilkenny, and Cavan. He later became a Major General in the Free State army and was General Officer Commanding in the Curragh, February 1923.
9 Rory O'Connor was jokingly referred to as 'director of jail deliveries' during the War of Independence. He escaped from the Curragh by disguising himself as a workman and walking out through the camp gates. See biographical sketch.
10 Tom Glennon was a Belfast Volunteer and was appointed full-time IRA organiser for Antrim in November 1920. After his escape from the Curragh internment camp in 1921, he became Adjutant of the 1st Northern Division. He supported the Treaty and generated a certain antipathy among republicans due to his role during the Civil War in Donegal.
11 Joseph Lawless (BMH WS 1043) was a Lieutenant of the Sword company of Volunteers up until 1916. He was involved in the Howth Gun Running operation and took part in the Battle of Ashbourne during the Rising. He ran a business on Parnell Street which also operated as a bomb factory. He was arrested in December 1920 and was prisoners' V/C at the Rath Camp. He was an avid photographer and took a number of photos of Camp life before his escape, which are held at the National Museum of Ireland. After the Treaty he became a Colonel in the Irish Army in the Free State.
12 Glennon and Lawless did indeed escape in September 1921 by hiding in a refuse cart.
13 Dave Gibbons was a native of Armagh and joined the IRA in 1917. His obituary claims he successfully escaped from Belfast Gaol, the Curragh Camp, and Kilkenny Gaol.
14 Frederick Hubert Vinden served in the British army during the Battle of the Somme and the Battle of Arras. He was stationed at the Curragh from 1920 and tried to deter escapes by enacting the mock shooting of a British guard dressed as an internee.
15 John Boland was appointed deputy governor of Mountjoy in 1906. He managed the suffragette hunger strike in Tullamore in 1913 and was publicy condemned due to his association with the forced feeding of Thomas Ashe. He was forced to retire after the mass escape of forty-nine prisoners from Kilkenny Gaol in November 1921.

16 Fr Patrick H. Delahunty was an influential young parish priest based in Callan, Co. Kilkenny. He established a local Sinn Féin club and re-established a company of Irish Volunteers in 1917. Fr Delahunty went on to become President of the Southern Kilkenny Executive of Sinn Féin.

17 Ned Punch was Captain of F Company, 2nd Battalion of the Mid-Limerick Brigade.

18 Seamus Monaghan was a native of Banbridge, Co. Down. He was arrested, along with his father and brother, for defending their house against an attack from the UVF and RIC in July 1920. After his release from prison, he served as adjutant of the 4th ND. He ran as a Fianna Fáil candidate in the 1927 election.

19 According to newspaper reports, Patrick Murry received such a beating that he had to see a doctor in custody. See *Irish Independent*, 16 February 1922, p. 5.

PATRICK 'PADDY' LOGAN

1 See interview with Roger McCorley in this collection.

2 Martinstown barracks was an RUC installation in Glenravill, Co. Antrim.

3 Eoin O'Duffy: see biographical sketch.

4 Séamus Woods: see biographical sketch.

5 Gearóid O'Sullivan, Michael Collins, Richard Mulcahy: see biographical sketches.

6 Tom Morris: see biographical sketch.

7 Seán Larkin: see biographical sketch.

8 Diarmuid O'Hegarty was secretary to the Free State government in 1922. After Collins' death he served as Director of Intelligence and Commandant General of the Free State army until May 1923.

9 Charlie Daly: see biographical sketch.

10 Moneyglass (from the Irish, Muine Glas) is a small village and townland in Co. Antrim near Toome Bridge.

11 Séamus Dobbyn was present at the foundation of the Irish Volunteers in Belfast in 1913. Dobbyn was later a member of the IRB Supreme Council, 1917–21. He shared a cell with Éamon de Valera in Lincoln Gaol and helped coordinate the escape in 1919.

12 Terence MacSwiney: see biographical sketch.

13 Walton Gaol was a large prison built in Liverpool between 1848 and 1855. It was later attacked by the IRA as part of the S-Plan bombing campaign in 1939.

14 On 28 June 1920, at Jullundur in the Punjab, a company of the Connaught Rangers, led by James Daly, refused to perform their military duties as a protest against the activities of the British army in Ireland.

15 Major General Eamon 'Bob' Price was IRA Director of Organisations before the Truce and a Free State general stationed in Portobello Barracks.

16 McLogan was appointed one of the IRA's 'Evacuation Officers' to oversee the transfer of barracks from the British in early 1922.

17 Emmet Dalton was IRA Director of Intelligence and was involved in the Squad along

with his brother Charlie. He was a Major General in the Free State army during the Civil War. He later worked as a film producer.

18 Hugo MacNeill (1900–63) O/C 1st Battalion Fianna (South Dublin), 1919–20; Director of Organisation and Training, Fianna, 1920–1, accepted the Treaty and rose to prominence in the Free State army.

19 The Freemasons' Hall is on 17 Molesworth Street, Dublin 2. It was occupied by the British military during the War of Independence; Sir John Keane (1873–1956) was an Irish barrister and politician who served in the Irish Seanad and was connected to the Shannon electrification scheme.

20 Charles McAllister was a volunteer in Glenariff, Co. Antrim. He was shot by British forces in May 1922.

21 For all commandants mentioned consult biographies or biographical sketches.

22 Seán Mac Eoin: see biographical sketch.

23 This refers to the raid on Musgrave Street Barracks in Belfast on 18 May 1922, which resulted in the fatal shooting of Constable John Collins, who happened to be a Catholic.

24 Shane's Castle is a ruined castle near Randalstown, Co. Antrim.

25 Part of the Curragh military compound, Hare Park Camp had initially been built to billet large numbers of troops during the First World War but was converted for sorting and holding prisoners during the Easter Rising, before housing Northern neutral IRA and then Republican prisoners during the Civil War.

26 Keane Barracks (now Pearse Barracks), the Curragh.

27 Peadar McMahon was active in organising and recruiting Volunteers to the Mid-Limerick Brigade in 1917. He was a Major General in the Free State army and acquired guns from the British to attack the Irregulars in the Four Courts. He was General Officer Commanding in the Curragh, February 1923.

28 Dan McKenna, see biographical sketch.

29 Felix McCorley was a prominent member of the Belfast Battalion. See interview with his brother, Roger McCorley, in this collection.

30 Over 180 files were seized during this raid. Joe McKelvey: see biographical sketch.

31 The Specials raided St Mary's Hall on 18 March 1922.

32 St Malachi's College is a Catholic Boys' grammar school on Belfast's Antrim Road; Austin Stack was elected to the First Dáil for Kerry West and was Minister of Home Affairs in 1921. He opposed the Treaty.

33 Winifred Carney (1887–1943), a native of Down, was a member of the ITGWU and was the only woman present when the GPO was occupied during the 1916 Rising. In 1917, she was appointed President of the Belfast Branch of Cumann na mBan. From 1920 to 1922, Winnie was Belfast secretary of the Irish Republican Prisoners' Dependents Fund.

34 Andie Furlong was a Wexford man and was active in Belfast.

35 Piaras Béaslaí, J. J. Walsh TD and Fleming were among twenty republican prisoners who escaped in broad daylight, when a rope ladder was thrown over the Mountjoy wall into the exercise yard on 29 March 1919.

FRANK AIKEN

1 'Preface by Frank Aiken Jnr', in Bryce Evans and Stephen Kelly (eds), *Frank Aiken: Nationalist and Internationalist* (Dublin: Irish Academic Press, 2014), p. xvi.

2 Eoin O'Duffy and Richard Mulcahy: see biographical sketches.

3 Michael Collins: see biographical sketch.

4 Gearóid O'Sullivan: see biographical sketch.

5 De Valera's proposed alternative, Document No. 2, recognised partition but rejected the oath of allegiance to the King and the role of a Governor General.

6 John Quinn (also known as Seán Quinn) was Quartermaster of the Newry Brigade and later of the 4th ND. He was shot by Free State forces in early 1923 and died from his injuries shortly afterwards.

7 Cathal Brugha: see biographical sketch.

8 This memorandum was circulated in mid-November 1921.

9 Joseph McKelvey: see biographical sketch.

10 Seán Mac Eoin: see biographical sketch.

11 Anti-Treaty forces under Rory O'Connor occupied the Four Courts from April 1922. They were attacked by the Free State army on 27 June 1922. This marked the beginning of the Civil War.

12 Eoin MacNeill: see biographical sketch.

13 Sir James O'Connor (1872–1931), a Dublin-based lawyer who was appointed Attorney-General in 1917. During the peace negotiations, he acted as a conduit between the government in London and the Irish and facilitated meetings between Fr Michael O'Flanagan and Sir Edward Carson. He controversially won his case to be readmitted as a solicitor in Ireland in 1929 after practising in England.

14 Sir Alfred Cope (1877–1954) was Assistant Under-Secretary in Ireland, 1920–2, and was committed to achieving a negotiated peace settlement. He established strong relationships with Collins, Griffith, and Éamon Duggan and is believed to have influenced the plenipotentiaries in their acceptance of the Treaty.

15 Michael Brennan: see biographical sketch.

16 Liam Lynch: see biographical sketch.

17 The first anti-Treaty convention was held on 26 March 1922 in the Mansion House in Dublin. A vote was taken to repudiate the Treaty.

18 Seán Moylan led the Newmarket Battalion and was O/C of No. 2 Cork Brigade during the War of Independence.

19 Frank Barrett was commandant of the Mid-Clare Brigade, 1918–21. He was later O/C of the 1st Western Division and a member of the anti-Treaty Executive.

20 Michael Gallagher served as O/C of the No. 2 (West Tyrone) Brigade.

21 Michael Kilroy was appointed Commandant-general of the 4th Western Division of the IRA in 1921. He was anti-treaty and was elected as a Republican TD for South Mayo in August 1923 while still in prison. See his interview with O'Malley in *The Men Will Talk to Me: Mayo Interviews*, pp. 35–72.

22 See interview with Peadar O'Donnell in this collection.

23 Frank Carty: see biographical sketch. See his interview with O'Malley (UCDA P17b/128).

24 Liam Deasy: see biographical sketch.

25 Séamus Robinson commanded the South Tipperary Brigade. He was elected Sinn Féin TD for Waterford–Tipperary East in 1921. He later served as a Senator for Fianna Fáil. He too was interviewed by O'Malley (UCDA P17b/65, 99, 101).

26 P. J. Ruttledge qualified as a solicitor in 1918. He served as Intelligence Officer of the North Mayo Brigade and 4th Western Division. He was elected as a Sinn Féin TD for Mayo North and West in 1921, while imprisoned in Galway Gaol. See his interview with O'Malley in *The Men Will Talk to Me: Mayo Interviews*, pp. 264–81.

27 Joseph J. O'Connor was a member of the Squad and was Commandant of the 3rd Battalion of the Dublin Brigade. He was later elected as a Cumann na nGaedheal senator and served until 1936.

28 Oscar Traynor was Commandant of the Dublin Brigade from November 1921. He was later elected to the Dáil, in 1925, and served as a Fianna Fáil TD until 1961.

29 Seán O'Hegarty: see biographical sketch.

30 Tom Barry was Deputy Commandant and Training Officer of the 1st Southern Division in 1921, before transferring and leading the No. 3 Cork Brigade. His memoir, *Guerilla Days in Ireland* (Cork: Mercier Press, 2013), details his exploits during the War of Independence.

31 Liam Pilkington served as Commander of the 3rd Western Division. He was appointed to the anti-Treaty Executive Council in April 1923.

32 Florence O'Donoghue: see biographical sketch.

33 Pax Whelan was O/C of No. 1 Cork Brigade, and later a signatory of the Treaty.

34 John Barry was vice O/C of the 5th Cork Battalion.

35 Tom Hales was commander of No. 3 Cork Brigade. He was arrested by the British army in Cork in July 1920 and was permanently disfigured after being interrogated and tortured. He opposed the Treaty. His brother Seán was elected as pro-Treaty Sinn Féin TD in 1921 and was later shot by anti-Treaty IRA.

36 Thomas Derrig: see biographical sketch.

37 Tom Maguire became Commandant of the South Mayo Brigade in 1920. He was elected TD for Mayo South and Roscommon South in 1922. See his interview with O'Malley in *The Men Will Talk to Me: Mayo Interviews*, pp. 208–27.

38 Liam Mellows: see biographical sketch.

39 The *Irish Independent* does not seem to contain this list of Executive members on this date.

40 Seán Hyde was an Executive Member. He initially supported Eoin O'Duffy after the Treaty split, but subsequently joined the anti-Treaty side.

41 Mick Cremin was involved in gun running from Germany in 1921. He was sent to London by the Army Executive in early 1922 to recruit volunteers for the anti-Treaty side. He served as Director of Publicity from 1922.

42 Thomas Derrig: see biographical sketch.

43 Austin Stack was elected to the First Dáil for Kerry West and was Minister of Home Affairs in 1921. He opposed the Treaty.

44 Possibly Patrick O'Brien, who commanded No. 4 Cork Brigade from 1921. He opposed the Treaty.

45 Tom Ruane of Ballina was O/C of the North Mayo Brigade in 1921. He was anti-Treaty.

46 Frank Barrett was O/C of the 1st Western Division. He was anti-Treaty.

47 Pax Whelan, or Pax Ó Faoláin, was O/C of the Waterford Brigade. He was anti-Treaty and spent six weeks on hunger strike when imprisoned in Mountjoy during the Civil War. He was interviewed by O'Malley: see UCDA P17b/095/103/117/118/130.

48 Humphrey Murphy was O/C of IRA Kerry No.1 Brigade and supported the Treaty.

49 Tom Crofts was Commander General of No. 3 Cork Brigade. He commanded the 1st Southern Division after the death of Liam Lynch in April 1922.

50 Seán Fitzpatrick was Commandant Adjutant of the 3rd Southern Division. He was anti-Treaty.

51 This may be Séamus (James) O'Meara, O/C Athlone Brigade.

52 Seán Russell was Director of Munitions. He was imprisoned by the Free State but escaped from Mountjoy Gaol in November 1925. He died in 1940 aboard a Kriegsmarine U-boat on his return from Germany, where he was trying to collaborate with the Nazis.

53 Seán Dowling was an IRA Executive member and Director of Organisation. He was O/C of No. 4 Dublin Brigade and Director of Operations and Organization. He was anti-Treaty.

54 Con Moloney was Adjutant of the 2nd Southern Division and a member of the Army Executive in 1922. He was Adjutant General of the IRA from 1923.

55 Bill Quirke was a member of the Army Executive and O/C of the 2nd Southern Command. He emigrated to the USA for some years before returning and serving as a Fianna Fáil senator.

56 Spelled 'MacSweeney' by EOM, Seán MacSwiney was Quartermaster of No. 1 Cork Brigade. He was anti-Treaty.

57 Dan 'Sandow' O'Donovan was vice O/C of No. 1 Cork Brigade. He opposed the Treaty. See his interview with O'Malley, UCDA, P17b/95.

58 Paddy Quinn, or later Pádraig Ó Cuinn, was born in Liverpool and raised in Newry. He was divisional adjutant of the 4th Northern in 1923. His brother, Seán, was divisional commandant in 1923.

59 Thomas Johnson was leader of the Labour Party, and thus Leader of the Opposition, 1922–7. He organised a general worker's strike in April 1922 to protest against the rise of militarism since the signing of the Treaty.

60 Thomas O'Sullivan led the South Wexford Brigade of the IRA and later was O/C of the 3rd Eastern Division. He opposed the Treaty.

61 Michael Carolan was Director of Intelligence of the Executive. During the War of Independence, he was imprisoned in Mountjoy Gaol and participated in the mass hunger strike in August 1920 which led to the death of Terence McSwiney.

62 Liam O'Doherty was an IRA Officer in 1920. See his interview with O'Malley (UCDA/P17b/91).

63 Spelled 'Tuomey' by EOM in the original text, Maurice (Moss) Twomey was a General Staff Officer. He was subsequently IRA Chief of Staff, 1926–36. Twomey was also interviewed by O'Malley: see UCDA/P17b/096, p. 107.

64 Tom Rogers served as Battalion Quartermaster of the Dundalk Battalion. He was injured during the attack on Dundalk on 14 August 1922. He emigrated to the USA, *circa* 1927, against the advice of the IRA.

65 Seán Noonan (1888–1937) of Liscarroll, Mallow was listed as O/C No. 4 Cork Brigade during the Civil War.

66 This may be Billy Mullins, Quartermaster of No. 1 Kerry Brigade.

67 John Joe Rice was O/C of the No. 2 Kerry Brigade in 1922. He opposed the Treaty and was elected as an abstentionist TD for Sinn Féin in 1957. See his interview with O'Malley in *The Men Will Talk to Me: Kerry Interviews*, pp. 280–316.

68 Mick Murphy was Battalion O/C No. 2 Longford Brigade. See his interview with O'Malley (UCDA/P17b/131).

69 Mossy Donegan was an officer in the Bantry Battalion and later in No. 3 Cork Brigade. For his interview with O'Malley, see *The Men Will Talk to Me: West Cork Interviews*, pp. 96–118.

70 Jack O'Meara was active in the South Tipperary Brigade.

71 Ned O'Reilly was V/C of No. 3 South Tipperary Brigade. See his interview with O'Malley (UCDA/P17b/125, 126, 127).

72 Barry is believed to have approached the IRB in an attempt to end the Civil War. This led to a falling out with other members of the Army Council.

73 Donnchadh O'Hannigan was O/C of the East Limerick Brigade Column. He is thought to have been a reluctant supporter of the Treaty. He commanded the 4th Southern pro-Treaty Division and supported Michael Brennan's 1st Western Division in occupying key locations of Limerick city in the lead-up to the Civil War, while the anti-Treatyites, under Liam Lynch, occupied four military barracks and most of the town.

74 Seamus (also James) Hogan was a Professor of History at University College Cork and served in the East Clare column during the War of Independence. He took leave from UCC in 1922 and served as Assistant Adjutant-General in the Free State army.

75 Paddy Daly: see biographical sketch.

76 General W. R. E. Murphy was a high-ranking officer in the British army during the First World War. In 1922, he became a general in the Free State army and was to become second-in-command to Eoin O'Duffy. He imitated the tactics of the British military by trying to encircle the anti-Treaty IRA columns in West Cork and South Kerry, although this tactic had little success.

77 Fionán Lynch was a Gaelic Leaguer and was in the Four Courts during the 1916 Rising. He was elected to the First Dáil in 1918 as a Sinn Féin abstentionist TD for South Kerry. He was a member of the Treaty delegation in 1921. He was Minister for Education, April–August 1922, and was also promoted to the rank of Brigadier-General in the Free State army during the Civil War.

78 Spelled 'McSwiney' by EOM in the original text, Terry MacSwiney was appointed as Lord Mayor of Cork in 1920. He was also Commander of No. 1 Cork Brigade and was arrested and sentenced to two years' imprisonment in August 1920. He died after a seventy-four-day hunger strike, and his death garnered media attention both at home and abroad.

79 The Beggars Bush Proposals recommended the establishment of a unified Army Council.

80 This letter was written while Aiken was imprisoned in Dundalk Gaol. A copy of this letter is in NLI MS 17143.

81 At this time, Lynch's anti-Treaty forces occupied most of Limerick's military barracks and had a considerable advantage over the provisional government's forces under Michael Brennan and Donnchadh O'Hannigan. The anti-Treaty forces were later forced to evacuate Limerick after Free State reinforcements arrived from Dublin.

82 Aiken is referring to the fact that Dan Hogan's 5th Northern Division entered Dundalk on the morning of 16 July and easily took hold of the town.

83 It has been speculated that Dan Hogan acted on his own accord in capturing Dundalk. However, while Aiken was in Limerick, Mulcahy sent Emmet Dalton to Dundalk to consider the situation and following this Dalton assigned Hogan with the command of the area of the 4th ND. See Mathew Lewis, *Frank Aiken's War: The Irish Revolution 1916–1923* (Dublin: University College Dublin Press, 2014), pp. 179–80.

84 Here, Aiken is referring to the fact that on 27 July, 105 men, including Aiken, escaped from Dundalk Gaol after a number of Fourth Northern Division officers detonated a mine at the gaol wall while the prisoners were doing their morning exercises.

85 Michael Fearon was O/C of the Camlough Battalion.

SHORT BIOGRAPHICAL SKETCHES OF INDIVIDUALS REFERENCED IN THE ENDNOTES

Béaslaí, Piaras (1881–1965): Born in Liverpool to Irish parents, Béaslaí was a prominent member of the IRB. He helped the organisation seize effective control of the Gaelic League in 1915 and fought in Dublin in 1916, serving three-years penal servitude in Portland and Lewes prisons. Editor of *An tÓglach*, he served as TD in the First and Second Dáil. He supported the Treaty and acted as publicity director for the Free State army and Free State censor.

Bergin, Joseph (1900–1923): A military policeman who carried messages in and out of Tintown No. 3, Bergin's body was found in the canal at Milltown, Co. Kildare on 15 December 1923. He had been tortured and shot six times in the head. During his torture, Free State soldiers tied Bergin to the rear of a car and dragged him behind at speed. They then delivered his bloodstained cap to his girlfriend, Peg Daly, in Kildare town. Captain James Murray was found guilty and sentenced to death, though his sentence was later commuted to life imprisonment.

Brennan, Michael (1896–1986): Joined Na Fianna in his native Clare in 1911. A member of the IRB, he became a central figure in the East Clare Brigade in 1916. He was arrested and interned in Frongoch. He was also interned during the German Plot arrests but escaped, returning to Ireland to rejoin his brigade. He was O/C of the East Clare Brigade and also O/C of the Clare Brigade Flying Column. He supported the Treaty and became a Free State general.

Brugha, Cathal (1874–1922): Born Charles Burgess, Brugha took part in the South Dublin Union battle during the 1916 Rising and was badly injured. He was elected Sinn Féin MP for Waterford in 1918 and was the first Ceann Comhairle of Dáil Éireann in 1919. He was also Minister of Defence in the First Dáil and had an uneasy relationship with IRA GHQ under Michael Collins and Richard Mulcahy. This tension increased when Brugha opposed the Treaty. On 5 July 1922, he was wounded during the O'Connell Street battle, dying of his injuries on 7 July. The letter in the Charlie Daly collection was part of an apparent move to assert authority over the IRA at the expense of Collins, Mulcahy, and GHQ.

Carney, Frank (1896–1932): From Enniskillen, Co. Fermanagh, and ex-British Army, Carney was O/C Fermanagh Brigade in June 1918. He was subsequently appointed O/C 1st ND (Donegal). Carney was at the centre of a dispute with Peadar O'Donnell. He was arrested at the Dungloe home of Joe Sweeney in May 1921 and subsequently interned at Ballykinlar until December of that year.

Carty, Frank (1897–1942): Commandant No. 4 Sligo Brigade, Carty was twice imprisoned and twice rescued. In June 1920, a group led by Billy Pilkington sprang Carty from Sligo gaol and in February 1921 he was rescued from Derry gaol by a group led by Charlie McGuinness. He was arrested a third time and transported to Scotland, where a third attempt was made to rescue him. But this attempt failed resulting in the death of one police escort and the injury of another.

Clancy, Peadar (1888–1920): Born in Clare, Clancy joined the Irish Volunteers in Dublin, where in 1916 he was part of the Four Courts garrison. A member of Michael Collins' Dublin Squad, he was captured with Dick McKee on 21 November 1920, the eve of Bloody Sunday. In reprisal for the Cairo Gang killings, Clancy, McKee, and Conor Clune, from Clare, were tortured and murdered by the Auxiliary Division in Dublin Castle on 22 November 1920.

Daly, Paddy (1888–1957): One of the original twelve apostles in Michael Collins' squad, as Commandant of Free State forces in Kerry, Daly gave the order which led to atrocities against republicans. In March 1923, twenty-three republican prisoners were murdered in the field and five executed in four weeks. At Ballyseedy on 6–7 March, nine republican prisoners were tied to a landmine, which was then detonated, Stephen Fuller miraculously survived. Two similar incidents subsequently took place at Countess Bridge and Cathair Saidhbhín.

de Valera, Éamon (1882–1975): The only surviving commandant from Easter Week, de Valera was elected president of Sinn Féin and the Irish Volunteers in October 1917 and was president of the First Dáil. He rejected the Treaty and proposed his own Document No. 2 instead. Sidelined during the Civil War, he formed Fianna Fáil in 1926 and emerged as the dominant figure in Irish politics.

Deasy, Liam (1898–1974): V/C of the 1st Southern Division, Deasy was second to Liam Lynch. See his interview with O'Malley in *The Men Will Talk to Me: West Cork Interviews*, pp. 178–201. A member of No. 3 Cork Brigade (West Cork) flying column under Tom Barry, Deasy also led the republican forces at the Battle for Limerick in July 1922. He was arrested in January 1923, when he ordered his men to lay down their weapons, an action which provoked a great deal of controversy and recrimination against him.

Derrig, Thomas (1897–1956): Arrested after the 1916 Rising, Derrig was arrested again and interned in the Curragh, and subsequently elected to the 2nd Dáil for Mayo North and West. He was interned during the Civil War and lost an eye when he was shot while under arrest. He was Minister of Education in the first Fianna Fáil government.

Healy, Timothy 'Tim', KC (1855–1931): A conservative Irish nationalist politician and barrister, Healy played a leading role in the downfall of Charles Stewart Parnell. Closely associated with William Martin Murphy and the Catholic Church, he formed a splinter party from the IPP named the All-for-Ireland League. He was the first Governor-General of the Irish Free State.

Hogan, Dan (1894-?): Born in Tipperary, his brother, Michael, was killed at Croke Park on Bloody Sunday. Dan Hogan served as O/C 5th ND (Monaghan). He was arrested on 14 January 1922 in Dromore, Co. Tyrone, apparently on the way to watch a GAA match in Derry. The Dromore footballers were travelling to Derry Gaol to rescue fellow Volunteers, Thomas McShea and Patrick 'Poppy' Johnston, who were under sentence of death. He joined the Free State army and was Major General of the Eastern Command, leading the attack on Dundalk Barracks against Aiken's 4th ND in August 1922. He later served as Chief of Staff 1927–9 before emigrating to America. Hogan reportedly abandoned his wife and there is no official record of his whereabouts after 1941.

Larkin, Seán (1897–1923): Born in Loup, Co. Derry, Larkin led the IRB in South Derry and the Bellagharty Company, mobilised in 1916. He was Commandant of Cookstown Battalion, No. 3 Brigade (South Derry), 2nd ND. During the Civil War, he joined forces with the IRA in Donegal where he remained until his arrest in November 1922 by Free State troops. On 14 March 1923, Larkin was executed by firing squad alongside three Kerrymen: Charlie Daly, Timothy O'Sullivan, and Dan Enright in retaliation for the killing of Lieutenant Bernard Cannon.

Lynch, Liam, aka Liam Ó Loingsigh (1893–1923): Born in Barnagurraha, Anglesboro, Co. Limerick, Lynch moved to Mitchelstown and then to Fermoy, Co. Cork to work as an apprentice in a hardware store. He was the O/C of No. 3 Cork Brigade and led the Flying Column. In August 1920, he was arrested at Cork City Hall with Terence MacSwiney, Seán Hegarty, Joe O'Connor, Dan O'Donovan, and Mick Leahy. All except Terence MacSwiney were released. Lynch was appointed IRA Chief of Staff during the Civil War and co-operated with pro-Treaty forces in the northern offensive (March–May 1922). He was killed by Free State forces on 11 April 1923.

McCullough, Denis (1883–1968): A prominent member of Sinn Féin in Belfast and President of the IRB during Easter 1916. McCullough had taken over the IRB in Belfast in 1905, with his associate, Bulmer Hobson, and founded the Dungannon Clubs, which were later absorbed into Sinn Féin. He founded the Irish Volunteers in the city and called off the mobilisation of the Belfast Volunteers at Coalisland, Co. Tyrone, on Easter Sunday. He was elected to the first and second Dáil and subsequently supported the Treaty.

MacEntee, Seán (1889–1984): Born in Belfast, MacEntee lived and worked in Dundalk from 1914. He was sentenced to death for his involvement in the 1916 Rising, during which an RIC officer (Charles Magee) was shot dead at Castlebellingham. This sentence was commuted to life imprisonment and he was released in 1917 as part of a general amnesty. As TD for Monaghan

South, he gave the most forcefully anti-partitionist speech during the Dáil debates on the Treaty. He later became a founding member of Fianna Fáil, a government minister, and was Tánaiste from 1959 to 1965.

Mac Eoin, Seán (1893–1973): Born John Joseph McKeon on 30 September 1893, at Ballinlough, Granard, Co. Longford, Mac Eoin was the son of a blacksmith. He went on to become O/C of the 1st Battalion, Longford Brigade and was elected TD for Longford–Westmeath in the May 1921 elections while imprisoned for killing an RIC inspector. He was released after the Truce and voted in support of the Treaty, before joining the Free State army. He was involved in the kidnapping of border unionists in early 1922 as part of the joint-IRA northern offensive.

McKelvey, Joseph (*c.*1885–1922): Born in Stewartstown, Co. Tyrone, McKelvey led the 3rd ND until the Treaty split. He was part of the republican garrison which took the Four Courts in April 1922. McKelvey was executed along with Liam Mellows, Rory O'Connor, and Dick Barrett on 8 December 1922 in reprisal for the shooting of pro-Treaty TD Seán Hales.

McKenna, Daniel (1892–1975): An Irish Volunteer from Maghera in South Derry, McKenna joined the IRB in 1913. He was promoted to the position of V/C 2nd ND after Eoin O'Duffy replaced Charlie Daly with Tom Morris as O/C in March 1922 in order to secure the division's support for the Treaty. He went to Keane Barracks in the Curragh with the pro-GHQ element of the 2nd ND, though did not formally join the Free State army until September 1922. He retired in January 1949, having spent nine years as army Chief of Staff.

MacNeill, Eoin (1867–1945): Born John MacNeill in Glenarm, Co. Antrim, MacNeill was a university lecturer and president of the Irish Volunteers, who countermanded the orders for mobilisation on Easter Sunday 1916. He later assumed a prominent role in Sinn Féin and was elected to the First Dáil in two constituencies, Derry City and the National University. He supported the Treaty, acting as Minister for Education in the Free State government, and strongly supported the policy of reprisal. He acted as the Free State representative on the Boundary Commission, which ended in failure in November 1925, due in no small part to MacNeill's own ineptitude.

MacSwiney, Terence (1879–1920): Appointed Lord Mayor of Cork in 1920, MacSwiney was also Commander of No. 1 Cork Brigade and was arrested and sentenced to two years' imprisonment in August 1920. He died on 20 October 1920, after a seventy-four-day hunger strike, and his death garnered media attention both at home and abroad.

Mellows, Liam (1892–1922): Born in Manchester, England, Mellows was a prominent republican-socialist who led the Irish Volunteers in Galway during Easter Week. After the Rising, he went on the run and escaped from Liverpool to New York. In October 1917, when attempting to return to Ireland with false papers, he was arrested along with Dr Pat McCartan on charges of conspiring to impersonate an American seaman. He was elected to the First Dáil for Galway East and Meath in 1918. He returned to Ireland at the end of 1920 and joined GHQ as Director of Purchases, with responsibility for procuring arms and equipment. He was returned to the Dáil for Galway in May 1921 and was fiercely opposed to the Treaty. After the storming of the Four Courts in 1922, Mellows was imprisoned in Mountjoy Gaol and executed on 8 December 1922 by the Free State alongside Rory O'Connor, Joe McKelvey and Dick Barrett in an extra-judicial reprisal killing.

Morris, Tom (1897–1979): Born on the Tyrone–Derry border outside Cookstown. He served as a major in the British army before joining the Irish Volunteers in 1919. Arrested in September 1920, on his release in early 1922 he accepted the Treaty and replaced Charlie Daly as O/C 2nd ND. He then moved to Donegal as a supposedly neutral commander, but effectively co-operated with the Free State. He later held command of men at Lifford, Co. Donegal and then in mid-1922 took his men from the 2nd ND to the Curragh, Co. Kildare to train, where the men of the 2nd ND who refused to join the Free State army were effectively interned.

Mulcahy, Richard 'Dick' (1886–1971): Fought alongside Tomás Ághas in Meath during Easter Week 1916. He was Chief of Staff of the IRA GHQ prior to the Treaty and then Minister of Defence in the Free State. A strong supporter of Michael Collins, he assumed responsibility for the Civil War after the latter's death and effectively disbanded the pro-Treaty northern IRA.

Nixon, John (1880–1949): A Cavan-born RIC District Inspector and said to be head of the Cromwell Club, a group of loyalist extremists within the security forces responsible for several sectarian atrocities. The Free State government alleged that Nixon and County Inspector Richard Harrison colluded with a police murder gang operating out of Brown Square Barracks in the Shankill area. Nixon received an MBE in 1923 and later sat in the Stormont parliament.

O'Connor, Rory (1883–1922): Director of Engineering at IRA GHQ. O'Connor opposed the Treaty and acted as spokesman at a famous press conference on 22 March 1922. He was arrested after the storming of the Four Courts and was executed by the Free State in an extra-judicial reprisal on 8 December 1922 with Liam Mellows, Joe McKelvey, and Dick Barrett.

O'Donoghue, Florence (1895–1967): Intelligence Officer of No. 1 Cork Brigade, Adjutant and Intelligence Officer of the 1st Southern Division during the War of Independence and later Adjutant-General of the anti-treaty IRA. O'Donoghue opposed the Treaty, but remained neutral during the Civil War. In May 1922, he was in talks with Dick Mulcahy in an attempt to overt a conflict and in July 1922 resigned from the Army. After the Civil War he served in the Irish army and later convinced Éamon de Valera to establish the Bureau of Military History, which would record personal accounts from the Civil War.

O'Duffy, Eoin (1892–1944): Joined the Irish Volunteers in 1917 and was O/C 5th ND (Monaghan). O'Duffy was briefly appointed O/C 2nd ND (Tyrone) in March 1921. He was pro-Treaty and served as Chief of Staff in the Free State army. He also served as TD for Monaghan in the second and third Dáil.

O'Hegarty, Seán (1881–1963): A major figure in the Cork IRA, serving as vice O/C of No. 1 Cork Brigade, and, following the murder of Tomás Mac Curtain, appointed O/C in 1920. O'Hegarty is noted for leading the Coolnacaheragh ambush in February 1921 and succeeded Terence McSwiney as Commander of No. 1 Cork Brigade in 1921. Although he was opposed to the Treaty, he adopted an auxiliary, non-combatant role during the Civil War.

O'Higgins, Kevin (1892–1927): A member of the Irish Volunteers and also Sinn Féin. While in an English prison O'Higgins was elected to the First Dáil as TD for his native Laois. As Minister of Justice, in 1922–3 he sanctioned the execution of seventy-seven republican prisoners, including Rory O'Connor, the best man at his wedding a year earlier. He was recognised as a dominant figure in the Free State government up until his assassination on 10 July 1927 by anti-Treaty members of the IRA, in revenge for the executions of the IRA prisoners during the Civil War.

O'Sullivan, Gearóid (1891–1948): Soldier and politician, O'Sullivan was born on 28 January 1891 at Coolnagrane, Skibbereen, Co. Cork. He fought in the GPO in 1916 and was interned in Frongoch. He served as Adjutant-General of the IRA during the War of Independence, and later as Adjutant-General of the Free State army. He also served as a pro-Treaty TD until 1923.

Swanzy, Oswald (1881–1920): Born into a unionist family in Castleblayney, Co. Monaghan, Swanzy moved north for his own safety because of his connection with the murder of the Lord Mayor of Cork, Tomás Mac Curtain, on 20 March 1920. Swanzy was assassinated by an IRA ASU on 22 August 1920 in Lisburn. His death sparked a mass pogrom against the nationalist population of Lisburn and then Belfast.

Tobin, Liam (1895–1963): A member of Michael Collins' squad and later Deputy-Director of Intelligence for the Free State, in March 1924, Tobin led the Army Mutiny with Colonel Charles Dalton. The Mutiny was organised by a group of disgruntled Free State officers in the wake of troop reductions and was a consequence of apparent dissatisfaction with the Free State government's perceived inactivity on partition.

Wilson, Henry (1864–1922): Born in Cavan, Wilson was involved in the Curragh Mutiny in March 1914, when he encouraged senior officers to resign rather than move against the Ulster Volunteers (UVF). He was Chief of the Imperial General Staff by the end of the war and was bitterly opposed to any type of Treaty. He was allegedly assassinated on the orders of Michael Collins, but his death actually led the British to pressure Collins into attacking the republican garrison in the Four Courts on 28 June 1922.

THE ERNIE O'MALLEY INTERVIEWS: METHODOLOGY, CHRONOLOGY, INTERVIEWEES

From the late 1930s up to 1953, Ernie O'Malley conducted more than 660 individual interviews with almost 450 separatist nationalist veterans of the Irish independence struggle (1916–23). These interviews complement Bureau of Military History (BMH) witness statements and Military Service Pension (MSP) records and are the third wing of a trio of attempts between the 1930s and the 1950s to document (retrospectively and for varying purposes) the independence struggle.[1] Each of the three collections embodies its own distinctive combinations of oral history, personal testimony, public memoir and folklore. All record both the experiences and the mentalité of Ireland's revolutionary generation. At their best, O'Malley's interviews are uniquely gritty, atmospheric, occasionally profane, punctuated with graphic descriptions of political violence and, in terms of their Civil War (1922–3) content, unrivalled. Though long recognised as an essential source for the anti-Treaty perspective on the Civil War, O'Malley's notoriously illegible handwriting has made it difficult for all but the most diligent to make effective use of them, and virtually impossible to construct an accurate overall assessment of his aims and methodology.[2]

The vast majority of O'Malley's 122 'combatant' interviews notebooks were bequeathed to University College Dublin Archives (UCDA) in 1974 by his son Cormac. In theory, these divide neatly into two series: one (the 'first series') containing his original interview notes, and the other (the 'second series') containing his re-transcribed and re-organised interviews. In practice, it is not so straightforward. His interview notes are interspersed with transcribed I.R.A. and Irish Army communications, extracts from newspapers, sketches of ambush sites, lyrics of local ballads, transcribed B.M.H. witness statements and M.S.P. correspondence. O'Malley's notes, and gaps in the numbering system he used to organise the notebooks, also suggest that an indeterminate number are missing. So far, one September 1949 notebook (which he misplaced mid-transcription) was handed in to the Military Archives of Ireland by an anonymous donor, and a few others turned up in the Archive of Irish America's (AIA) collection of O'Malley papers in New York University. That said, it can be safely assumed that most of the notebooks have survived. The majority of interviews can be dated by cross-referencing the first and second series and checking them against his diaries, address books and indexes.[3] Approached chronologically, the course and evolution of O'Malley's initiative comes into much sharper focus.

His combatant interviews were the most extensive and fully realised of a number of interviewing initiatives. O'Malley also collected songs and lore in Clew Bay, County Mayo, in the 1940s. He interviewed artists involved in the first Irish Exhibition of Living Art in 1943 and joined the Folklore of Ireland Society that year. He also met with Séamus Ó Duilearga, Director of the Irish Folklore Commission, who was at that time lobbying for the government to establish a committee to 'gather information from those who took part in the political & cultural movements of the past 50 years'.[4] O'Malley began making notes during informal conversations with former comrades and friends in the 1930s as part of his research for the still unpublished Civil War section of his memoir, *On Another Man's Wound*. Around the same time, during semi-clandestine visits to Dublin Castle and the Irish Army's archives in Griffith Barracks facilitated by Thomas Markham and Ginger O'Connell (respectively), he transcribed their commentary and the documents as they went through the material.[5] By 1945 his project had coalesced into a planned history of the Civil War period for which he was actively seeking interviewees and information.[6] Dating his earliest interviews can be tricky, but by the end of 1947 O'Malley had conducted around 50 interviews, mostly to do with the Civil War. Many of these interview notes were never re-transcribed, although some of them were amalgamated into later interviews with the same individuals.

From the summer of 1948 the pace of O'Malley's interviewing increased substantially. By late 1949 he had conducted over 200 interviews, more than half with individuals based in Dublin. From this period onwards, his interviews were also much more likely to cover the War of Independence (1919–21) as well as the Civil War (he never showed much interest in events before 1918). These interview notes often lack the polish and attention to detail that characterise his later efforts. An added complication is that less than 50 per cent of his original notes for these two years survive. They might simply have been mislaid, or perhaps he did yet see the value in keeping them.

His interviewing skills improved as time went on, gradually transitioning from private notes for personal research to more formal interviews. By the end of 1949, the style and substance of O'Malley's notes had improved dramatically, and he embarked on his first extended trips to different parts of the country for the express purpose of interviewing. He made several more over the next two years, often in the last quarter from September to mid-December when his youngest son Cormac was away at boarding school. He travelled to Cork, Tipperary, Mayo, Kerry, Limerick, Waterford, Roscommon, Leitrim, Offaly, Sligo, Donegal and Kilkenny. There are no interviews from Cavan, Monaghan, Westmeath or Meath, nor did he carry out field work in Northern Ireland. Most of his interviewees from the Northern IRA divisions or Britain were based in Dublin.[7] He conducted at least 340 interviews in 1950 and 1951 and his notes (now systematically dated in a series of clearly numbered notebooks) captured the speech patterns and modes of expression of his interviewees with far more precision than before.

O'Malley regularly mined his interviews when writing about the War of Independence, but it is not entirely clear why he decided to concentrate on interviewing rather than writing a Civil War history himself (or even finishing his memoir).[8] His personal correspondence suggests that the physical, mental and emotional toll of years on the run or in prison was a factor. In a letter written in 1953 to his friend Paul Strand he remarked: 'When I was too disturbed I thought it better to collect the information, because in Ireland the men will tell me the truth about themselves. I take notes at speed as fast as they can talk, but again that had to be re-written into notebooks. It is a long piece of work.'[9] O'Malley continued to research and re-transcribe his interviews up to his death in 1957 despite his deteriorating health. He was clearly winding down after 1951. The number of interviews dropped to under forty the following year. He conducted what were to be his final seven in January 1953. Two months later he suffered a heart attack from which he never fully recovered.

Interviewees

Almost 80 per cent of veterans interviewed by O'Malley had been active in Munster and Leinster. He drew largely on the cohort of former IRA officers from (or based in) independent Ireland who, by the late 1940s, had effectively become the new establishment in Irish political life. Made up primarily of anti-Treatyites now reconciled to the state through joining Fianna Fáil, and smaller numbers of neutral and pro-Treaty veterans who had made their peace with former opponents, many of his interviewees were, like O'Malley, successful MSP applicants. Over 160 of O'Malley's interviewees also spoke to the BMH, although they frequently discussed different events. One factor setting O'Malley's interviews apart is the access he had to hardcore anti-Treaty republicans who either remained active in the IRA, Cumann na mBan and/or Sinn Féin after 1926 or, if no longer actively involved in politics, remained very much on the radical end of the republican spectrum. They included Peadar O'Donnell, Paddy McLogan, George Gilmore, Sighle Humphries, Moss Twomey, Brian O'Higgins, Seamus O'Donovan, Kathy Barry Moloney, Jim Moloney, Pax Whelan, Tom Maguire, Billy Aherne, George Plunkett and Tommy Merrigan. These individuals were much less likely to cooperate with the BMH or to apply for a pension. For them, Fianna Fáil were the new 'Free Staters', and de Valera was a hate figure, particularly after the coercion and execution of republicans in the wake of the IRA's 1939 bombing campaign and its clashes with the state during the Emergency (1939–45).

O'Malley described his Mayo fieldwork and his combatant interviews alike as 'folklore'.[10] He never made what would today be an important distinction between interviews documenting individual experience (oral history) and those that record received tradition (folklore). Nonetheless, although he did not use the terminology, O'Malley was an oral historian by instinct and inclination. He was also a formidable researcher, one very attuned to the necessity of using retrospective personal testimony in combination with contemporary source material and archival research. No other veteran attempted to collect accounts with such sophistication and ambition. His interviews provide a unique and indispensable lens through which to view the life and afterlife of the Irish Revolution.

Eve Morrison

Endnotes

1 Eve Morrison, 'Witnessing the Republic: the Ernie O'Malley Notebooks and the Bureau of Military History Compared' in *Modern Ireland and Revolution Compared: Ernie O'Malley in Context* (Newbridge: Irish Academic Press, 2016), pp. 124–40.

2 This account of O'Malley's interviewing project is based on research into the notebooks I conducted as an Irish Research Council postdoctoral fellow in University College Dublin from 2013-2015. In the course of this research, I cross-referenced and dated (as far as was possible) the two UCDA series plus those notebooks located elsewhere and identified almost all of the interviewees.

3 About 60 per cent of the interviews are fully dated, and all but a few of the remainder can at the very least be assigned to a year, and usually, month and year.

4 Diary Entries 26 Jan. 18 Feb. 1943 (UCD Folklore Archive, Séamus Ó Duilearga Diaries, uncatalogued).

5 Thomas Markham (death 1939) (UCDA, Ernie O'Malley notebooks [EOM nbks]), P17b/101) pp. 91–100; Ginger O'Connell (death 1944) (UCDA, EOM nbks, P17b/134), pp. 1–21; Ginger O'Connell ((Tamiment Library [TL], New York University, Ernie O'Malley papers [EOMP], AIA.060/14/2A and AIA.060/16/5C)

6 Andy Doyle to O'Malley, 6 Feb. 1945 (TL, EOMP, AIA.060/3-52); Florrie O'Donoghue to O'Malley, 16 October 1945 (UCDA, Ernie O'Malley papers, P17b/181).

7 Three interviews with veterans of 1st Battalion, 4th (South Donegal) Brigade, 1st Northern Division were not discovered in time to include in this volume. Although the interviewees discuss northern events, due to this battalion having been attached to the North Sligo Brigade at one point, O'Malley included them with other Sligo interviews. See Thomas MacShea, Nov.1951 (UCDA, EOM nbks, P17b/69, pp. 76–90; P17b/136, pp. 18–22); John and Joseph Sheeran/Sheehan (joint interview) 4 Nov. 1951 (UCDA, EOM nbks, P17b/69, pp. 91–96; P17b/136, pp. 23–6)

8 See Cormac K.H. O'Malley (ed), *Rising Out: Seán Connolly of Longford* (Dublin: UCD Press, 2015); Ernie O'Malley, *Raids and Rallies* (Cork: Mercier Press, 2011); Ernie O'Malley, 'Bloody Sunday' (Cork: Mercier Press, 2009, 1st ed. 1948), pp. 283–94.

9 O'Malley to Paul Strand, 9 December 1953, in Cormac O'Malley and Nicholas Allen (eds), *Broken Landscapes: Selected Letters of Ernie O'Malley, 1924–1957* (Dublin: The Lilliput Press, 2011), p. 313.

10 O'Malley to John Kelleher, 30 January and 15 February 1950, *Broken Landscapes*, p. 275.

IMAGE CREDITS

Peadar O'Donnell, Courtesy of Mercier Press; Joseph 'Joe' Sweeney, Donegal Annual (1966); Patrick McCartan, kindly reproduced with permission from the National Library of Ireland; Charlie Daly, kindly reproduced with permission from Dónal Casey; Seamus Woods, courtesy of Jim McDermott; Roger McCorley, courtesy of Tom and Rory Fitzpatrick; Tom McNally, courtesy of Jim McDermott; Jack 'Seán' Leonard, courtesy of Loretta Leonard and Pearse Leonard; Michael O'Hanlon, courtesy of Dr Rory O'Hanlon; Michael Donnelly, courtesy of Louise Donnelly; John McCoy, courtesy of Art and Aisling McCoy, The Photo Album of Ireland; Michael Murney, *Irish Press*, National Library of Ireland; Patrick 'Paddy' McLogan, courtesy of Len Costello; Frank Aiken, courtesy of the Aiken family and UCD Archive.

INDEX

Note: Page locators in bold refer to pictures.

Aherne, Billy, 247
Aiken, Frank, 13, 14, 40 n. 11, 91, 119 n. 41, 128, 133, 159, 163, 168–9, 173, 180, **196**, 196–213, 214 n. 5, 217 n. 58, 217 n. 61, 219 n. 94, 221 n. 41, 221 n. 44, 224 n. 44, 225 n. 64, 226 n. 84; actions during the Truce, 134, 152, 162, 164–5, 174; and the Civil War, 6, 93, 102, 106, 109, 136–8, 170, 238–9; and Dundalk Gaol, 92, 135–6, 148; and the Northern Offensive, 33, 165–6, 191; peace missions for cessation of hostilities, 92, 167–8; and the Treaty, 155, 197–201; and the War of Independence, 30, 132, 149–50, 177
Aiken, Nano, 17, 20 n. 64, 196
An Phoblacht (newspaper), 22
Anglo-Irish Treaty, the, xii, 6, 29, 32, 48, 91, 97, 100, 159–60, 167, 236, 238, 240; and Dáil debates and vote on, 1, 12, 29, 49–50, 199–201; impact on the northern IRA, 10, 12–13, 155–7
AOH (Ancient Order of Hibernians), the, 2–4, 25, 108, 178
Archer, Liam, 30–1, 40 n. 17
Argenta (prison ship), 94, 166, 182, 187
arms dumps, 23, 34, 111, 136, 156
arms exchanges for attacks in Northern Ireland, 156–7
arms supplies, 24, 33, 71, 98, 102, 106–7, 109–10, 111, 133–4, 136, 150, 152, 192
Ashe, Thomas, 184, 188, 228 n. 15
Auxiliaries, the, 36, 88, 96–7, 129, 160, 184, 200, 208, 237
B Specials, the, 91, 98, 138, 161, 182, 183, 186–7
Ballyseedy massacre, the, 97, 112 n. 35
Barrett, Frank, 31–2, 41 n. 31, 202, 204, 231 n. 19, 233 n. 46
Barrett, Richard, 23, 37 n. 6, 39 n. 34, 240
Barry, John, 202, 232 n. 34
Barry, Kevin, 115, 125 n. 23
Barry, Tom, 26, 202, 204–6, 208–9, 232 n. 30
Barry Moloney, Kathy, 247
Baxter, Paddy, 138, 218 n. 72
Béaslaí, Piaras, 32–3, 49, 93, 215 n. 30, 230 n. 35, 236
Beatty, Willie, 95
Beggars Bush Proposals, the, 208
Belfast boycott, the, 68, 106, 156, 176
Belfast pogroms, the, 7, 8, 87, 90, 91, 97–9, 100–1, 156
Belfast Telegraph, The (newspaper), 91
Bell, The (newspaper), 22
Bergin, Joseph, 153, 173, 236, 221 n. 45, 226 n. 91
Best, Richard, 95
Birches Barracks, Portadown, 181, 182
Bloody Sunday, 100–1, 116, 128, 129–30, 237
Blythe, Ernest, 37, 45 n. 85
BMH (Bureau of Military History), the, 242, 244, 247
Boland, Harry, 49, 50, 78 n. 32, 154, 225 n. 72
Boland, John, 184, 228 n. 15
Boundary Commission, the, 12, 240

Boylan, Seán, 132, 216 n. 38
Boyle, Con, 31, 40 n. 18
Boyle, Jim, 145–6, 172, 219 n. 93
Boyle, Joe, 148, 219 n. 7
Breen, Dan, 32, 41 n. 32, 79 n. 38
Brennan, Michael, 31–2, 137, 200, 206–7, 236
Brennan, Paddy, 171, 172, 225 n. 79
Breslin, Paddy, 32, 41 n. 33
Brick, Nora, 74
British interests in Ulster, 11
Brugha, Cathal, 23, 31, 49, 50, 54–6, 91, 106, 136, 137, 198, 199, 200, 236–7
Burke, Tom, 128, 131, 160, 223 n. 17
Burke, Chuck, 134, 217 n. 53
Byrne, Ben, 51
Byrne, Billy, 144, 219 n. 91
Byrne, John Henry, 134

Camlough RIC Barracks attack, the, 155, 176, 177
Cannon, Lt. Bernard, 35, 43 n. 63, 54, 239
Capuchin Annual, 89
Cardinal Logue Pact, the, 4
Cardwell family (of Celbridge), 145, 172, 226 n. 84; Annie Cardwell, 291 n. 94
Carney, Frank, 22, 23, 30, 131, 161, 174, 237
Carney, Winifred, 17, 195
Carolan, Micky, 90, 194, 195, 203, 233 n. 61
Carroll, Joe, 129
Carson, Edward, 7–8
Carter-Campbell, Gen., 158
Carty, Frank, 31, 173, 202, 237
Casement, Sir Roger, 47
Casey, Patrick, 103, 122 n. 33
Chicherin, Georgy Vasilyevich, 49, 78 n. 29
chronology of events, xvi–xxii
Churchill, Winston, 9, 16, 166, 175, 207
Citizens' Army, the, 21
Civil War, the, 1, 22, 25–6, 34–6, 54, 91, 101–4, 134–42, 152–3, 166–74, 189–95, 206–7, 242; and the Ballyseedy Massacre, 97, 237; and execution of anti-Treaty prisoners, 26–7, 29, 35, 51, 54, 139, 239, 240, 241, 243; and Frank Aiken, 6, 93, 102, 106, 109, 136–8, 168–9, 170, 238–9; and the Free State Army, 69, 72; impact of the Treaty on operations in the North, 155–7; and Michael Collins, 33, 37; and split in the IRA, xii, 134
Clan na nGael, 23, 46, 49
Clancy, Peadar, 23, 31, 129, 154, 237
Clann na Poblachta, 47
Clarke, Martin, 151
Clarke, Tom, 3, 33, 47
Cohalan, Daniel, 47
Collins, John Henry, 140; and pact with Sir James Craig, 156, 166, 176
Collins, Michael, 13, 28, 30, 31, 34, 50, 52, 91, 103, 131, 151, 159–60, 167, 169, 195, 197, 200; and the Civil War, 33, 37, 190; and the Northern offensive, 12, 192, 193; and the northern pro-Treaty IRA, 86, 192, 193; and a republican constitution, 13–14, 16; and the Treaty, 12, 29, 48, 109, 199
Collins/Craig Pact, the, 156, 176
commissions to officers in the IRA, 55–6
Conlan, Dr Peter, 183
Connelly, Seán, 129
Connolly, Ina, 7
Connor, Paddy, 142
Cooney, Andie, 128, 132, 141, 174, 214 n. 5
Cope, Alfred, 200, 231 n. 14
Corr, Seán, 166, 176, 224 n. 56
Coyle, Eithne, 17
Craig, Sir James, 8–9, 10, 16, 87, 156, 166, 176
Crany, Tom, 187
Crawford, Fred, 8, 9, 10
Cromwell Club, the, 242
Crossgar RIC barracks attack, 87, 96, 105
Crowley, Tadhg, 116, 126 n. 26
Crumlin Road Prison, Belfast, 183, 195–6
Crummey, Frank, 36, 44 n. 70, 108

Culhane, Seán, 96, 113
Cullen, Tom, 30, 51, 93
Cullyhanna RIC barracks attack, 150
Cumann na mBan, 74, 80 n. 45, 128, 182, 186, 219 n. 94, 230 n. 33, 247
'cunning of history,' the, 1
Curragh Army Mutiny, the, 36, 86, 93–4, 243
Curtis, Lionel, 13
Cusack, Seán, 98, 120 n. 4, 195
Customs House burning, the, 85, 86–7, 96

Dáil Treaty debates and vote, the, 1, 12, 29, 49–50, 199–200
Dálaigh, May, 53
Dalton, Charles, 243
Dalton, Emmet, 130, 132, 151, 191, 215 n. 19, 215 n. 25, 217 n. 58, 229 n. 17
Daly, Charlie, 2, 5, 10, 14, 15, 23, 28, 29, 31, 35, 43 n. 59, 43 n. 62; 53–7, **53,** 68–76, 131, 167, 175, 190, 191, 237, 239, 240, 241; removal as O/C of 2nd ND, 5, 57–68
Daly, Paddy, 94, 207, 237
Daly, Phil, 177
Daly, Tom, 56, 65, 70, 80 n. 1
Davis, Jerry, 128, 130, 131, 132, 164, 214 n. 9
Dawe, Felix, 151
de Blácam, Aodh, 181
de Valera, Eamon, 3–4, 12, 31, 32, 48, 49, 50, 51, 56, 182, 196, 199, 200, 238, 242, 247
Deasy, Liam, 91, 170, 202, 238
Delahunty, Fr., 184, 185, 229 n. 16
Derrig, Thomas, 173, 238
Derry Gaol escape, 31, 237, 238
Devlin, Felix, 110, 124 n. 27
Devlin, Joe, 2–3
Devoy, John, 47, 50, 149, 220 n. 19
Diamond, Patrick, 66, 81 n. 16
Dillon, John, 12
Disability Pensions Board, the, 155, 182
Dobbyn, Henry, 149, 220 n. 16
Dobbyn, Séamus, 100, 121 n. 17, 149, 189
Document No. 2, 24, 32, 50–1, 200, 238
Doherty, Dominic, 169
Doherty, Joe, 30, 32, 40 n. 10
Doherty, Patrick 'Hun,' 33, 42 n. 51
Dolan, Joe, 26, 39 n. 27
Donegan, Ben, 108, 110, 123 n. 18
Donegan, Mossy, 83 n. 42, 175, 204, 227 n. 96, 234 n. 69
Donnelly, Barney, 115
Donnelly, Éamon, 162, 223 n. 26
Donnelly, Michael, 147–53, **147,** 167, 177
Donnelly, Patrick, 178, 227 n. 103
Doyle, Andie, 25, 26, 38 n. 20
Drumboe executions of IRA volunteers, 4, 5
Drysdale, A.D., 94–5
Duffin, Pat & Dan, 88, 89, 118 n. 10
Duffy, Leo, 130, 215 n. 26
Duggan, Lt-Col. J., 158
Dundalk Gaol, 128, 135–6, 138, 148, 151, 155, 170
Dungannon Clubs, the, 47, 239
Dunne, Seán 128, 214 n. 6
Dunne, John, 195

Easter Rising, the, 3, 148–9
Egan, Jack, 130, 214 n. 8
Ennis, Tom, 93, 120 n. 48
Enright, Daniel, 29, 80 n. 5, 239
executions of anti-Treatyite IRA, 26–7, 29, 35, 51, 54, 139, 239, 240, 241, 243

Facts and Figures of the Belfast Pogroms (book), 101
Fagan, Brian, 145
Farrelly, Pat, 139, 141, 218 n. 77
Fearon, Michael, 213, 235 n. 85
Fenianism in Ulster, 3, 4
Ferris, D.I., 44 n. 69, 88, 97, 118 n. 10, 118 n. 15
Finn, Mary, 114
Fitzgerald, Desmond, 188
Fitzpatrick, Ned, 224 n. 49

Fitzpatrick, Seán, 203, 233 n. 50
Fitzpatrick, Thomas, 103
Flanagan, Paddy, 128, 129, 130, 214 n. 3
Flanagan, Wolfe, 164
Flannigan, Seán, 128, 230 n. 35
Flynn, Malachi, 169
Fleming, Paddy, 195, 230 n. 35
Flynn, Tommy, 110, 123 n. 9, 124 n. 26
Folklore of Ireland Society, the, 25
Fox, Tom, 89, 96, 107, 108, 111, 113, 114, 118 n. 22
Fox, 'Wish,' 134–5, 217 n. 54
Free State, the, 17
Free State army, the, 86, 103, 106, 108, 113, 207
Free State GHQ and the Northern IRA, 11–16, 33, 69–71, 86, 130–1, 156–7; and the removal of Charlie Daly as O/C 2nd Division, 57–68
Frongoch Camp, 28, 149, 188, 236
Fuller, Stephen, 237
Furlong, Andy, 195, 230 n. 34

GAA clubs in Ulster, 178
Gaelic American (newspaper), 47, 49, 149
Gaelic League, the, 189, 196, 236
Gallagher, Daniel, 34
Gallagher, Seán, 123 n. 16
Gallagher, J.H., 32, 42 n. 39
Gallagher, Michael, 81 n. 16, 82 n. 35, 231 n. 20
Gallagher, Paddy, 117, 126 n. 35
Gallagher, Seán, 123 n. 16
Garda Special Branch, 189
Gaugin, Seamus, 130
Gavan Duffy, George, 47, 49, 76 n. 2
Gavronsky, Dmitry, 48
general election (Dec 1918), 179, 188
Gibbons, Dave, 183, 228 n. 13
Gilling, Tommy, 107
Gilmore, George, 247
Ginnell, Laurence, 48, 77 n. 14
Glennon, Kieran, 7, 10
Glennon, Tom, 34, 43 n. 60, 69, 81 n. 22, 82 n. 27, 84–5 n. 50, 183, 228 n. 10, 228 n. 12
Glenties RIC barracks attack, 30
Glover, John, 97
Goodfellow, Jimmy, 138, 218 n. 73
Gordon, Dawson, 7
Gormley, Seán, 144, 150, 151, 162–3, 168, 176, 219 n. 89, 220 n. 24, 223 n. 30
Gough, Tom, 153
Graham, Seán, 183
Grey, Michael, 88, 118 n. 12
Griffin, Joe, 153, 170–1, 173, 225 n. 72
Griffith, Arthur, 12, 49, 78 n. 33, 91, 200, 210
Gunn, Jimmy, 145

Hales, Seán, 27, 39 n. 34, 240
Hales, Tom, 202, 208, 232 n. 35
Hanratty, James, 149, 220 n. 11
Hanratty, John, 136, 217 n. 60
Harland and Wolff, 9
Harrison, George, 189
Harrison, Richard (County Inspector), 97, 114, 115, 118 n. 11, 119 n. 29
Hart, Peter, 17
Haskin, Robert 'Rory,' 7
Haughey, Seán (John), 6, 33, 36, 42 n. 49, 62, 66, 81 n. 16
Healy, Tim, 32, 113, 116, 114, 115, 125 n. 14, 238
Healy, Donagh (shop), 129, 213 n. 11
Hegarty, Paddy, 141, 143, 218 n. 83
Herron, Archie, 7
Herron, Samuel, 7
Hobson, Bulmer, 239
Hogan, Dan, 14, 26, 36, 37, 92, 93, 109, 135, 137, 138, 148, 163, 167, 169–70, 191, 235 n. 83
Hogan, Séamus (also Jimmy), 34, 43 n. 56, 111, 124 n. 33, 206, 234 n. 74
Home Rule and Ulster, 2
hostility of civilian Ulster population to the IRA, 2

Hughes, Paddy, 148, 217 n. 67, 219 n. 8, 220 n. 9
Hughes, Peter, 138, 217 n. 67
Humphries, Síghle, 37 n. 1, 247
hunger strikes, 172–3, 188, 241
Hyland, Tom, 183, 187

Industrial Workers of the World, 21
internment, 106
IPP (Irish Parliamentary Party), the, 3, 4, 178–9, 238
IRA (Irish Republican Army), the, xii, xv, 2, 8, 179–80, 189, 247; 1st Midland Div, 191; 1st Southern Div, 14, 71, 109, 207, 238, 242; and Army Executive notes, 201–6, 208–9; and the Civil War split, 29, 136, 197, 211–13
IRA Convention (March 1922), 194, 210
IRB (Irish Republican Brotherhood), the, 3, 4, 12, 14, 32–3, 37, 47, 151, 159, 179–80, 188, 236
Irish Exhibition of Living Art, 245
Irish Folklore Commission, the, 245
Irish Press, The (newspaper), 47
Irish Red Cross Society, the, 29
Irish Volunteers, the, 3, 108, 240

Johnston, Patrick 'Poppy,' 238
Johnston, Tom, 22
Joyce, John, 34, 43 n. 57

Keane, Charles, 191
Keane, Sir John, 191, 230 n. 19
Kelly, Bill, 176
Kennedy, Jim, 151, 221 n. 37
Kerr, Neil, 149
Kerry Flying Column, the, 53
kidnap attempt of commissioner of Armagh City Council, 161–2
Kiely, Rory, 172
Kilkenny Gaol prison escape, 181–2, 184–6, 187
Kilmainham Gaol, 139–40
Kilroy, Michael, 142, 145, 202, 218 n. 85, 231 n. 21
King, Seán, 93
Kyle, Sam, 7

Larkin, Seán, 23, 29, 31, 35, 66, 71, 81 n. 16, 239
Leahy, Mick, 239
Lehane, Seán, 14, 34, 54, 68, 70, 72
Leonard, Jack 'Seán,' 89, 107, 112–17, **112**, 125 n. 10, 125 n. 14
Lloyd George, David, 9, 10, 12, 13, 16, 99, 103, 200
Logue Pact, the, 179
Lynch, Benny, 132, 216 n. 40
Lynch, Diarmuid, 48, 77 n. 17
Lynch, Fionán, 207–8, 234 n. 77
Lynch, Liam, 14, 16, 25, 33, 51, 56, 91, 92, 106, 137, 167, 197, 201, 206, 207, 239
Lynn, Liam, 193

Mac Curtain, Tomás, 44 n. 69, 118 n. 16, 242, 243
Mac Diarmada, Seán, 3, 47
Mac Eoin, Seán, 6, 36, 151, 163, 191, 199, 240
MacAllister, Johnny, 139
MacBride, Seán, 32, 41 n. 37
MacCurtain, Thomas Óg, 189
MacEntee, Seán, 49, 86, 147–8, 219 n. 3, 222 n. 2, 239–40
MacMahon, Seán, 37, 45 n. 87, 107, 106, 176
MacNeill, Eoin, 48, 148, 240
MacNeill, Hugo, 26, 36, 39 n. 33, 158, 191, 222 n. 13, 230 n. 18
MacNelis, Donncha, 29–30, 34, 40 n. 9
MacNicholl, Rory, 107, 134, 137, 139, 175
MacSwiney, Mary, 51
MacSwiney, Terence, 149, 190, 195, 208, 239, 241
MacSwiney, Seán, 203, 204, 233 n. 56

Magan, Tony, 189
Magee, Charles, 239
Magennis, Fr. Peter, 48, 51, 76 n. 8
Maguire, Seamus, 139, 218 n. 76
Maguire, Titch, 141
Maguire, Tom, 202, 204, 232 n. 37, 247
Maisky, Ivan, 48, 77 n. 12
Mallon, Frank, 136, 166, 224 n. 51
Malone, Michael, 226 n. 83
Malone, Peadar, 25, 38 n. 19
Malone, Thomas, 173, 226 n. 93
Malone, Willie, 142, 218 n. 86
Maloney, P. J., 49
Maloney, Dr. William J., 51, 79–80 n. 42
Markham, Thomas, 245
Maryborough Gaol, 170, 173
McAllister, Bernard, 151, 221 n. 35
McAllister, Charlie, 130, 160, 191, 215 n. 24, 223 n. 21
McBrearty, Eddie, 36, 44 n. 76
McBrearty, Hugh, 34, 42 n. 55
McCann, Bernard, 181
McCarrick, Tommy, 183
McCartan, Dr. Pat, 14, 23, **46,** 46–52, 128, 241
McCarthy, Matt, 36, 44 n. 73, 99, 108, 113, 121 n. 12, 124 n. 8
McCole, Patrick, 29
McCorley, Felix, 96, 134, 193, 194, 216 n. 46
McCorley, Roger, 4, 9, 10, 13, 36, 87, 89, 91, 92, 96–104, **96,** 107, 109, 110, 113, 134, 189, 190, 192, 194
McCormack, Pat, 193
McCormick, Michael, 131, 216 n. 34
McCoy, John, 2, 4, 110, 134, 135, 136, 144, 145, 146, 150, 153, **154,** 154–80
McCracken, John, xxi, 69, 82 n. 30
McCullough, Denis, xvii, 47, 90, 116, 149, 239
McCullough, Sir Crawford, 91
McDevitt, Danny, 87, 117 n. 4
McDevitt, John, 114
McDevitt, John (Seán), 114, 125 n. 13
McDonnell, F. J., 202
McDonnell, Paddy, 160, 222 n. 16
McGarrity, Joseph, 46, 47, 48, 49, 50, 76 n. 4
McGee, Louis, 145, 146, 172, 226 n. 88
McGleenan, Charlie, 135, 217 n. 50
McGonigle, John James, 117, 126 n. 33
McGoran, Seamus, 93, 108, 110, 119 n. 44, 123 n. 16
McGowan, Martin Bernard, 117, 126 n. 30
McGuigan, Nellie, 90
McGuill, James (Mrs), 224 n. 44
McGuill, John, 150, 152, 221 n. 30
McGuinne, Joe, 90, 119 n. 27
McGuinness, Charlie, 31, 41 n. 24, 237
McGuinness, David, 99, 121 n. 13
McGurk, Joe, 37 n. 4, 55, 58, 60, 62, 81 n. 7, 81 n. 24
McGurran, Henry, 6
McGurran, Seamus, 177
McHugh, Paddy, 148, 219 n. 6
McKay, Frank, 24, 38 n. 17
McKee, Dick, 151, 214 n. 13, 237
McKelvey, Joseph, xxiii, 6, 14, 25, 26, 33, 85, 86, 100, 107–8, 109, 132, 134, 167, 194–5, 199, 201, 203, 240
McKenna, Dan, 31, 35, 36, 102, 166, 193, 194, 240
McKenna, Paddy, 150, 152, 158, 162, 167
McKenna, Seamus, 111, 124 n. 30
McLogan, Paddy, 183, 188–95, **188,** 247
McMahon, Peadar, 36, 134, 183, 193, 228 n. 8, 230 n. 27
McMurrin, (Captain), 135, 165, 168, 175, 217 n. 56, 224 n. 46
McMurrin, Kevin, 166
McNally, Joe, 111, 124 n. 31
McNally, Peadar, 37, 44 n. 81
McNally, Tom, 7, 36, 100, 101, 105–11, 165, 166
McShane, Hugh, 181
McShea, Thomas, xi, xii, 238

McWhinney, Winston Charles, 24, 38 n. 13
Meegan, Owen, 138, 218 n. 71
Meenbanad train ambush, the, 22, 29
Mellows, Liam, xxiii, 12, 14, 23, 25, 26–7, 49, 50–1, 91, 149, 200, 240, 241
Merrigan, Tommy, 247
Military Service Pension Act (1934), the, 155
Moloney, Con, 203, 233 n. 54
Moloney, Jim, 247
Monaghan, Eiver, 138, 169, 218 n. 70
Monaghan, Seamus, 161, 174, 182, 186, 187, 229 n. 18
Morris, Joe, 191
Morris, Tom, 5, 14, 58, 59, 62, 102, 166, 190, 240, 241
Mountjoy Gaol, 26, 141, 148
Moville raid, the, 30
MSP (Military Service Pension) Records, 244
Mulcahy, Gen. Richard, 36, 37, 48, 51–2, 54, 56, 64, 75, 86, 91, 92, 135, 140, 152, 178, 190, 200–1, 207, 211, 212, 213, 241; and Frank Aiken, 135–6, 137, 167–8, 197, 198; and policy towards the northern IRA, 13, 86, 102–3, 130–1; and the removal of Charlie Daly as O/C 2nd Northern Div, 65, 66
Mulcahy, Paddy, 160
Mullen, Johnny, 141
Mullins, Billy, 234 n. 66
Mullins, Paddy, 172
Mullins, Tom, 142, 145, 171, 172, 173, 225 n. 75
Murney, Annie (née Duignan), 182
Murney, Michael, 181–7, **181**
Murney, Peadar, 181
Murphy, Barney, 49
Murphy, Dick, 96, 104, 113
Murphy, Humphrey, 203, 204, 207, 219 n. 97, 233 n. 48
Murphy, John (Archdeacon), 50, 79 n. 38
Murphy, WRE, 104, 122 n. 36, 207
Murray, Barber, 33, 42 n. 52
Murray, Edward, xxi, 82 n. 28
Murray, Hugh J., 102, 122 n. 30
Murray, James (Captain), 226 n. 91, 236
Murray, Joe, 36, 44 n. 69, 104, 111, 124 n. 29, 124 n. 30
Murray, John, 182
Murray, Patrick, 186–7

Na Fianna, 96, 236
National Aid Association, the, 50
National Volunteers, the, 3, 98
nationalist support in Ulster, 4
neutralisation of partition, the, 14
Newtownhamiton RIC barracks attack, 150–1
Nixon, D.I. John, 89, 90, 94, 100, 118 n. 18, 119 n. 29, 242
non-sectarianism of Irish republicanism, 178–9
Northern offensive plans, the, 12, 16, 33, 54, 101–4, 165–6, 175–6, 180, 189, 191–2, 239, 240
northern republicanism in historical accounts, 1
Nuorteva, Santeri 'Santtu,' 49, 78 n. 30

Ó Duilearga, Séamus, 245
Ó Murthuile, Seán, 37, 45 n. 88, 50, 79 n. 39, 151
oath of allegiance, the, 212
O'Brien, Owen, 144, 219 n. 92
O'Connell, Ginger, 130, 131, 132, 215 n. 23, 216, 245
O'Connor, Art, 145
O'Connor, Col. Paddy, 25
O'Connor, Joe, 202, 203, 216 n. 35
O'Connor, Pádraic, 131, 216 n. 36
O'Connor, Rory, 14, 25, 26, 57, 131, 141, 143, 183, 200, 201, 210, 215 n. 30, 240, 242, 243
O'Connor, Seán, 26
O'Doherty, Liam, 203, 233 n. 62

O'Doherty, Kitty, 50, 79 n. 38
O'Doherty, Seamus, 48, 50, 76 n. 11
O'Donel, Lile, 22
O'Donnell, Barney, 30
O'Donnell, Frank, 25, 34, 35, 38 n. 18, 43 n. 61
O'Donnell, Peadar, 15, **21**, 21–7, 30–1, 35, 40 n. 20, 41 n. 33, 130, 131, 141–2, 146, 171, 202, 203, 225 n. 75, 237, 247
O'Donoghue, Florence, 69, 71, 242
O'Donovan, Dan 'Sandow', 107, 123 n. 13, 203, 204, 233 n. 57, 239
O'Donovan, Seamus, 247
O'Donovan Rossa GAA club, 105
O'Duffy, Eoin, 4, 12, 14, 35, 54, 86, 102, 106, 132, 152, 159, 166, 168, 190, 197, 206, 207, 208, 242; and new commissions for IRA commandants, 55–6, 198–9; and the raid on Dundalk Barracks, 92, 93; and the removal of Charlie Day as O/C 2nd Northern Div, 5, 57–64, 65, 66, 67; and the Treaty, 13, 29, 51, 167
O'Flaherty, Sam, 24, 32, 38 n. 14, 41 n. 34
O'Hanlon, Michael, 127–46, **127**, 171, 172
O'Hanlon, Sarah, 128
O'Hanlon, Redmond, 163, 223 n. 34
O'Hannigan, Donald, 148, 220 n. 9
O'Hannigan, Donnchadh, 206, 207, 217 n. 65, 234 n. 73, 235 n. 81
O'Hanrahan, Henry, 140, 218 n. 79
O'Hare, Eddie, 169, 224 n. 42, 225 n. 62
O'Hegarty, Diarmuid, 26, 39 n. 30, 102, 122 n. 32, 132, 151, 190, 216 n. 39, 229 n. 8
O'Hegarty, P.S., 48, 50, 79 n. 36, 151
O'Hegarty, Seán, 37, 71, 202, 239, 242
O'Higgins, Brian, 247
O'Higgins, Kevin, 37, 94, 111, 167, 243
O'Kane, George, 94, 95, 120 n. 56
O'Kelly, J. J. (Sceilg), 49, 78 n. 26
O'Keefe, Mick, 173
O'Keefe, Paudeen, 26, 32 n. 39
O'Kelly, Seán, 183
O'Mahoney, Batt, 54
O'Mahoney, Dan, 53
O'Malley, Ernie, xii–xv, 24, 30, 31, 32–3, 35, 52, 177–8, 200, 244–7
On Another Man's Wound (book), xiii, 245
O'Neill, Mick, 139, 140, 218 n. 75
O'Neill, Seán, 86, 89, 100, 117 n. 2, 121 n. 16
O'Reilly, Ned, 204, 234 n. 71
Orange Order, the, 11, 178
O'Sullivan, Andy, 226 n. 89
O'Sullivan, Gearóid, 35, 36, 37, 48, 51, 93, 94, 102, 151, 190, 198, 243
O'Sullivan, Timothy, 29, 203, 204, 233 n. 60, 239

partition, 1–2, 11, 12, 14, 15
peace moves between pro and anti-Treatyites, 51; efforts for cessation of hostilities by Frank Aiken, 92, 167–8
Pearse (Mac Piarais), Pádraig, 28, 37
Pettigo and Belleek battles, the, 33–4, 113, 116–17
Pilkington, Liam, 202, 203, 232 n. 31, 237
Plunkett, George, 247
Price, Éamon (Bob), 81 n. 14, 93, 120 n. 46, 176, 227 n. 100, 229 n. 15
prison escape from Kilkenny Gaol, 181–2
prisoners as hostages, 166–7, 168, 175
Protestant republicans, 7–8
Protestants and Home Rule, 2
Punch, Ned, 185, 229 n. 17

Quinn, Malachy, 161, 166, 175, 214 n. 7
Quinn, Paddy, 128, 133, 134, 135, 165, 168, 175, 203, 213, 214 n. 7, 224 n. 49, 233 n. 58
Quinn, Seán (John), 138, 159, 161, 169, 174, 177, 198, 216 n. 48, 222 n. 10, 231 n. 6

Rankin, Paddy, 159, 179, 227 n. 107
Rath Camp, the Curragh, 183–4

Redmond, John, 2, 3
Reilly, Andy, 138
removal of Charlie Daly as O/C 2nd Northern Division, 5, 57–68
Republican Congress, the, 22
republican police and courts, 180
Republican Prisoners' Release Association, 189
RIC (Royal Irish Constabulary), the, 30, 47, 86, 108, 160
Ricardo, General, 9, 10, 11
Rising Out: Sean Connolly of Longford, 1890–1921 (book), xiii
Robinson, Séamas, 51, 79 n. 40, 202, 203, 204, 232 n. 25
Rogers, Tom, 133, 136, 174, 204, 216 n. 43, 217 n. 68, 224 n. 49, 234 n. 64
Rogers, John (Monsignor), 51, 80 n. 47
Rooney, Eamon, 152, 167, 177, 221 n. 43, 225 n. 60
Rooney, Joe, 34
RUC, the, 178
Rush, Jim, 141, 145, 172, 226 n. 86
Russian visit by Dr. Pat McCartan, 48–9
Ryan, Dr. Arthur, 90, 118 n. 26
Ryan, Dr. Jim, 51, 80 n. 43
Ryan, Robert, 116, 126 n. 26

Scanlon, Tom, 142, 145, 172, 218 n. 87, 226 n. 87
Scottish Farm Servants' Union, the, 21
sectarianism in Ulster, 7, 8–11, 17, 87, 90, 91, 97–9, 100–1, 156
Sheehy, Mick, 153, 170, 221 n. 46
Sheridan, Tom, 138, 217 n. 69
Shields, Paddy, 23, 24, 37 n. 4
signal training, 178
Singing Flame, The (book), xiii
Sinn Féin, 4, 8, 160, 197, 239
Smyth, Col. G.F., xviii, 8, 221 n. 34
Smyth, D.I. Gerald, 99
socialism and republicanism, 8
Solly-Flood, Gen. Arthur, 90–1, 119 n. 30
South Armagh by-election (January 1918), 178
southern recruits to the IRA Northern Divisions, 70, 71, 72, 96
Spanish Civil War, the, 22
Specials, the (*see* USC (Ulster Special Cnstabulary), the)
Stack, Austin, 195, 202, 203, 215 n. 30, 230 n. 32, 232 n. 43
Stapleton, Bill, 26, 39 n. 29
Stapleton, John, 119 n. 31
Stapleton, Jerry, 186
stepping stone strategy to a republic, the, 13–14
Stevens, John Joe, 117, 126 n. 34
Stronge, Frank, 55, 58, 60, 61, 81 n. 6
Sturgis, Mark, 13
Sunday Press, The (newspaper), xiii
Swanzy, D.I. Oswald, 8, 85, 88, 89, 96, 99, 107–8, 112–14, 118 n. 16, 118 n. 22, 125 n. 10, 183, 243
Sweeney, Barney, 36
Sweeney, Joe, xviii, 4, 5, 14, 15, 22, 23, 24, 28–37, **28,** 40 n. 22, 41 n. 32, 42 n. 41, 54, 68, 69, 72, 73, 101, 103, 191, 192, 237
Sweetman, Dick, 129, 215 n. 15

Tallents, Stephen, 10–11
Tan War, the, xii, xvi–xxii, 2, 6–7, 15, 22, 23–5, 28–34, 54, 85–92, 96–7, 105, 107–17, 128–35, 148, 149–50, 154–5, 157–8, 177, 181–7, 237, 242
Thornberry, Paddy, 87, 117 n. 7
Thornton, Frank, 151
Thunder, Frank, 116, 126 n. 27
Timoney, Phil, 117, 126 n. 35
Timoney, Seamus, 92, 101, 119 n. 38, 122 n. 25
Tintown 2, 170
Tintown (Curragh Camp) escapes, 141–6, 153, 155, 171, 172–3, 236
Tipping, Gerard, 162, 223 n. 28

Tobin, Liam, 48, 51, 52, 93, 151, 243
tÓglach, An (newspaper), 236
Tone, Wolfe, 17
Traynor, Oscar, 130, 131, 202, 215 n. 27, 232 n. 28
Treacy, Seán, 23, 38 n. 10
Trodden, Ned, 88, 89
Truce, the, 10, 54, 99, 100, 151–2, 160–5, 174–7, 182, 194
Tudor, General Henry, 9
Twaddell, William, xxii, 86, 92, 120 n. 54
Twomey, Jack, 170, 171, 225 n. 71
Twomey, Moss, 203, 247

Ulster Council, the, 14
Ulster IRA, the, 4, 10, 11; 1st Midland Div, 6; 1st ND (Northern Division), 4–5, 16, 22, 191; Derry City Bn, 4, 22, 24; No. 1 Bde, 22, 28–9; No. 2 Bde, 24; No. 3 Bde, 24, 30; No. 4 Bde, 24; 2nd ND, 5, 14–15, 16, 33, 54, 55, 57–64, 70, 102, 103, 110, 165, 166, 191, 192, 193, 239, 240, 241; No. 3 Bde, 66, 71; No. 4 Bde, 62, 67; 3rd ND, 5–6, 14, 16, 86, 99–100, 103, 106–7, 134, 157, 165, 191, 193, 194; Belfast Bde, 105; 4th ND, 6, 17, 102, 110, 128, 133, 134, 155, 165, 174, 181, 182, 191, 196–8; Armagh Bn, 6, 182; Banbridge Bn, 133; No. 1 Bde, 151, 162–3, 167; No. 2 Bde, 152; No. 3 Bde, 158, 163; 5th ND, 5, 128, 132, 134, 135, 148, 191, 197, 212
USC (Ulster Special Constabulary), the, 9, 10–11, 15, 17, 68, 69, 90, 97, 98–9, 133, 155, 180
UVF (Ulster Volunteer Force), the, 2, 10, 17, 183

Victoria Barracks prison, Belfast, 113, 115, 158, 183, 190, 191

Wade, Micky, 145
Walsh, Mutt, 35, 43 n. 66
War of Independence, the (*see* Tan War, the)
Ward, Joe, 24, 30, 38 n. 15
Whelan, Pax, 202, 203, 232 n. 33, 233 n. 47, 247
White, Mick, 129, 130, 214 n. 12
Wilson, Gen. Sir Henry, xxii, 33, 42 n. 43, 48, 52, 90–1, 103, 243
Wilson, Joe, 194
women's roles in the IRA, 16–17
Woods, Séamus, 4, 36, 85–95, **85,** 100, 103, 106, 107, 109, 110, 111, 165, 166, 192, 224 n. 52